KOVACSLAND

A
BIOGRAPHY
OF

ERNIE KOVACS

BY

DIANA RICO

HARCOURT
BRACE
JOVANOVICH

SAN DIEGO
NEW YORK
LONDON

Library of Congress Cataloging-in-Publication Data
Rico, Diana.
Kovacsland: a biography of Ernie Kovacs/by Diana Rico.
p.   cm.
Includes bibliographical references.
ISBN 0-15-147294-7
1. Kovacs, Ernie, 1919–1962.   2. Comedians—United States—Biography.
3. Television personalities—United States—Biography.   I. Title.
PN2287.K7R5   1990
791.45'028'092—dc20
[B]   89-24506

Design by Camilla Filancia
Printed in the United States of America

First edition   A B C D E

Photograph credit for title page: CBS
Photograph credits for part-title pages:
Part One: Courtesy of Kippie Kovacs
Part Two: New York Daily News
Part Three: Andrew C. McKay Collection
Part Four: NBC/Courtesy of the Museum of Broadcasting
Part Five: NBC/Courtesy of the Museum of Broadcasting

To my mother,
GEORGINA CARLO RICO,
who taught me
to love show business,

And to the memory
of my grandmother,
AMELIA BALLESTER,
a woman of visionary spirit.

CONTENTS

Two eight-page sections of photographs follow pages 144 and 240.

I first encountered the work of Ernie Kovacs in 1981, when I was working as an editor and writer for the Academy of Television Arts & Sciences' (ATAS) *Emmy* magazine and was assigned to write an article on Kovacs' pioneering television shows of the 1950s and early '60s. (Kovacs was five years into the TV industry when I was born, but my family preferred the more straightforward slapstick of Lucille Ball and Red Skelton and the verbal comedy of Jack Benny and Phil Silvers over the surreal oddities of Ernie Kovacs.) I was completely taken by what I saw when I screened videos at the ATAS/UCLA Television Archives and at the home of Edie Adams, the comedian's widow. This was a fearlessly iconoclastic and bizarre variety of comedy, nearer in structure and in spirit to absurdist theater and dadaist and surrealist art than to the sitcoms and stand-up routines that have defined most of television comedy since the earliest days. Kovacs was one of the first—and to this day remains one of the relative few—to comprehend that television was not merely radio with pictures added or theater captured on film, but a totally different medium with distinctive traits that could be exploited in unique ways.

A Kovacs drollery might be as simple as a shot of his own head cropped onto an animal's body or as complicated as the contents of an office come to life in sync to a tango melody. It might be gentle and tightly controlled, as in the famous 1957 special starring his silent alter ego Eugene, which became the only U.S. television show presented at the 1958 World's Fair. Or it might be freewheeling and assaultive, as when, in his earliest shows out of Philadelphia, he hurled eggs and pies at the camera and thus, it appeared, at the viewers at home. Via the magic of the television cameras, Kovacs could vacuum the ceiling, fence with himself, make a beard disappear with one touch of a razor, or read poetry from the surface of an egg (made up as his lisping poet laureate, Percy Dovetonsils).

Whether visual, verbal, or a combination of sight and sound, a Kovacs joke always subverted expectation. As his character Mr. Question Man, Ernie was once asked, "I have heard that the earth is not flat, but round like a ball. If this is so, how come people don't fall off it?" "You have stated a common misconception," he replied. "As a matter of fact, people are falling off all the time." He liked to say that he viewed the world at an eighteen-degree angle. His was a deeply personal vision, brought forth within the context of purely commercial entertainment but rooted in cutting-edge artistic experimentation.

Ernie Kovacs' life was cut short by a car accident in 1962, just a week before his forty-third birthday. The offbeat nature of his comedy, combined with his fierce refusal to compromise, had won him a loyal following (including many television critics of his day) but had also prevented him from achieving the mainstream network success of a Gleason or a Caesar or a Berle. However, his legacy grows in importance with each passing year. His experimental work has influenced, directly or indirectly, an astonishing number of video practitioners. The music videos on MTV and other channels, the TV-show and movie spoofs of *Saturday Night Live* and *Second City TV*, the blackouts, teasers, and funny credit sequences of *Laugh-In, Monty Python's Flying Circus*, and *The Benny Hill Show*, the casual revelations and deliberately cheap effects of *Late Night with David Letterman* and *It's Garry Shandling's Show* all owe a formal or spiritual debt to Kovacs' pioneering work. Nor has his influence been limited to commercial television. Video artists as divergent as Wolf Vostell, Nam June Paik, Teddy Dibble, Mitchell Kriegman, and Bruce and Norman Yonemato have all explored ground first broken by Kovacs.

In the course of working on the *Emmy* piece, I discovered that twenty years after his death there were still Kovacs fans, people of many different ages and walks of life—not only painters and performance artists, writers and musicians, photographers and animators, but also a switchboard operator, a sales executive, a Xerox clerk, a radio disc jockey. The pattern of my encounters was always the same: Ernie Kovacs' name would come up in passing, and the fan (whose fanhood I had previously not suspected) would instantly recount, without prompting and with a good deal of excitement, his or her favorite memory of Kovacs' comedy. The depth of their delight convinced me that interest in Kovacs had not waned; it had merely gone underground.

The more I learned about him, the more I felt that there was a need for a serious, in-depth biography. (David Walley's 1975 *Nothing in Moderation*, later reprinted as *The Ernie Kovacs Phile*, laid out the groundwork but contained many factual errors and passed over some areas of his life that I consider important.) Ernie's story is partly that of the wild, adventuresome days of early TV, when anything went because there weren't yet any rules; it is the story of a fascinating and powerful industry in the process of creating itself. It encompasses as well the worlds of theater, radio, newspapers, fiction, and films—all media in which Kovacs labored at different times. His personal history is equally compelling, filled with dramatic highs and devastating lows.

This book is based on primary sources; at its core are personal interviews with nearly a hundred individuals who knew Ernie Kovacs, representing every stage and facet of his life. A number of these people had never spoken about him for the public record, and they illuminated many heretofore unexplored aspects of his history, personality, and art. Edie Adams, Ernie's second wife, and a few friends, such as Jack Lemmon, chose not to participate in this project, and I have relied on previously published or broadcast interviews for their comments on Kovacs. However, I received the full cooperation and support of Elisabeth and Kippie Kovacs, Ernie's daughters by his first marriage, and I found many others who were eager to share their reminiscences: classmates, neighbors, and teachers from his childhood years in Trenton; intimates from his days in Long Island summer stock and New York theater school; close friends who watched him enter adulthood in Trenton during World War II and witnessed the progress of his postwar marriage to Bette Lee Wilcox; colleagues from the Trenton radio station where he did his first work in an electronic medium; crew members, writers, performers, producers, and executives who worked with him in television in Philadelphia, New York, and Hollywood; members of the film industry who worked with him in the movies; and personal friends who followed his life to the end. Over and over again I heard the word *aura* used—people remember his ethos, a special combination of quiet gentleness, unfettered imagination, and vivid enjoyment. There was another word I heard over and over. "I hope I have let you understand that I *loved* this man!" one crew member in his sixties exclaimed at the conclusion of our interview. Many people loved Kovacs deeply and still do. They all let me understand that.

The interviews were augmented by my extensive screenings of Kovacs' video work, not just his own television shows but his appearances on many other programs of his day, ranging from chat shows like Edward R. Murrow's *Person to Person* to dramatic anthologies such as *Alcoa/Goodyear Theater*. I also viewed and researched the ten feature films in which Kovacs appeared and which have been given short shrift in previous discussions of his work; I was surprised to discover that he was a good and meticulous actor, working hard to create interesting characterizations even when his roles were secondary (as they often were). I spent many months poring over scripts, production notes, correspondence, and other documents pertaining to his television and movie work; examining the daily columns he wrote for the *Trentonian* in the 1940s; tracing facts in church, school, court, and other public records; and reading through hundreds of newspaper, trade paper, and magazine articles written about Kovacs both during his lifetime and up until the present day. (Some of the print material was exceedingly rare: the late Minerva Davenport, for example, provided me with radio scripts she had written for Ernie in the 1940s, the only written material I have ever been able to find pertaining to his early radio work in Trenton; and Laurel Spira of the New Jersey Network passed on to me a trove of reviews and programs she had uncovered relating to the summer stock studio where Ernie worked just after leaving high school.) In only one area was I frustrated: the Philadelphia court files covering Kovacs' early 1950s divorce and custody fight turned up empty. Elisabeth and Kippie Kovacs, to whose lives these papers directly relate, have never seen them and could only speculate as to how they might have disappeared. TV writer April Smith was under the impression that she was working from original court documents, yellowed and crumbling with age, when she wrote the script for the 1984 ABC TV movie *Between the Laughter*, based on this period in Kovacs' life; she says she was loaned them by Edie Adams. Adams, however, says that she has no knowledge of any such files that are part of the public record, so the disposition of these papers remains a mystery.

During my research I visited many places in Trenton, Philadelphia, New York, and Los Angeles where Ernie Kovacs spent his time. Having grown up bicultural (a Puerto Rican transplanted to Los Angeles as a child), I was particularly interested in tracing the Hungarian immigrant community and family influences that had shaped his youth. It had always seemed to me that his humor was deeply rooted in these influences, not only the gallery of goofy ethnic characters he created but in the sense one gets, watching his sketches, that one is traveling through a world where the logic is foreign and bizarre. The bilingual Kovacs also delighted in playing with language and accents, and he understood the inherent funniness in the sounds of different languages, quite apart from the meanings of the words.

Two elements of this book require brief explanation. First, the title is taken from the name of one of Kovacs' Philadelphia shows, *Ernie in Kovacsland*. Second, I have reconstructed Ernie's comedy bits from my own screenings, colleagues' descriptions, reviews of the time, and similar sources; to convey the spirit in which they were created and performed, I have written them in the style of Ernie's early scripts.

Finally, I would like to note that although countless books have been written about the seminal talents who shaped the American film industry—Chaplin and Keaton, Hitchcock and Hawks, Lubitsch and Lang, Capra and Ford—our television history is still woefully under-explored. Ernie Kovacs was as significant to TV as these filmmakers were to movies. Ultimately, I believe that he may have been more significant to our current culture—to our everyday lives—because his was the medium that has dominated our consciousness since the 1950s, when the American movie studio system began to crumble and cinematic outings were replaced by evenings in front of the tube. Kovacs well understood the power of which television was capable. "This TV medium has never been fully explored," he once said. "It's completely different from movies and the stage. It has to be developed on its own." Perpetually fighting against the industry's self-imposed limitations, he violated barriers, overturned expectations, and exuberantly celebrated the silliness of life. His courage is to be respected, and his magical wit—the products of which still carry the power to astonish, still seem fresh and funny and smart—is to be cherished.

PART
ONE

BEGINNINGS
1919 – 1941

On a steep, winding street off Coldwater Canyon in Beverly Hills, a rambling house hides behind a high, thick hedge and a wrought-iron gate. Made of brick with a black slate roof, the structure is set on a rise above the street, fronted by a modest lawn and flower beds. Nothing distinguishes it from the other houses in this quiet neighborhood— at least nothing that is immediately visible.

Back in the early 1960s, however, the accoutrements that had been added to make life comfortable in this house were far beyond those of the typical upscale Coldwater Canyon home. The house featured an enormous mechanized turntable in the driveway so that friends who dropped by at odd hours could easily turn around their Jaguars and Rolls-Royces and Mercedes-Benzes. The two older girls in the family could frolic in the backyard pool, which was next to a Japanese garden; the youngest girl, a baby, had her own nursery in a new two-story wing. An intricate system of television sets and hi-fi's piped entertainment indoors and out. A sixteenth-century antique harpsichord and a pet donkey named Piccolo were among the more unusual inhabitants. Callers who phoned when the owners were not home were greeted by an answering machine message with an impeccable English accent—this at a time when answering machines were virtually unknown.

A graceful brick archway over the driveway divided the main house from a smaller structure, a garage that had been transformed into a den. For its owner, Ernie Kovacs, this comfortably cluttered, wood-paneled, leather-furnished den was the pulsing heart of the house, the material and symbolic manifestation of the comedian's lifetime motto, "Nothing in moderation." Once a poor Trenton boy from an immigrant Hungarian family, now a rich television and movie star, Ernie had outfitted his den with most of what was significant to him in life.

Dominating the uppermost level of the three-story space was a green-felt card table for his favorite (some said dangerously so) pastime, poker; here he would hold marathon card parties with such close friends as Jack Lemmon, Tony Curtis, Dean Martin, and Billy Wilder, quite often losing but never wanting to stop. A library was filled not just with books but with a beautiful collection of valuable military artifacts: "a brace of French dueling pistols," as one visitor observed, "helmets (Spanish, Roman, Saracen), an old Persian shield, Spanish breastplates, a Chinese cannon, an ivory-inlaid blunderbuss, medieval shields and suits of armor." The library also contained an oversized desk built especially to accommodate Ernie's six-foot-two, 215-pound frame. This held a panel of electronic controls from which he could communicate with his household via an intercom network, manipulate the gadgets inside the house and out, and experiment with the video and sound effects that he loved. Decorations included a stuffed rhinoceros head, an indoor waterfall, and an enormous polar-bearskin rug, onto which his collection of 14,000 records often overflowed. In the original bath he had enlarged the shower and added a steam-bathing room, and several times a day (or night) he might repair to the latter for a lengthy steam bath. Beneath the main space was a wine cellar stocked with the finest wines and champagnes, which his special-effects men sprayed with rubber cobwebs and fuller's earth to lend a properly aged look. Most important of all was the electric sign just outside the den's entrance. Like a home-style version of an ON AIR sign, it read NOT NOW, and nobody—colleagues, family, friends, servants—was allowed to enter when it was lit. Often he'd spend all night there, for he worked best at night, and his daughters or his second wife, singer-actress Edie Adams, would wake to find the sign still on and wonder whether he had slept at all.

This was an extraordinary level of escape to have achieved, an extraordinary amount of control to have over one's environment. But why did he need to escape; why did he crave the control? By 1961—in only a decade—Kovacs had made a unique mark upon the young medium of TV. Behind his signature black mustache and ever-present Havana cigar, Ernie Kovacs possessed the most bizarre, anarchic comedic mind ever to have hit the tube. He instinctively understood the special, intimate qualities and vast electronic potential of the small screen, and he was adventuresome and imaginative and funny enough to exploit them:

ERNIE DRAWS A STICK OF DYNAMITE . . . IT EXPLODES

ERNIE SAWS THROUGH THE TREE BRANCH HE'S SITTING ON . . . THE TRUNK FALLS

ERNIE DRIVES A GOLFBALL INTO THE CAMERA LENS . . . THE
GLASS SHATTERS

ERNIE PAINTS OUR TV SCREEN BLACK

The comedy that Ernie was creating was truly visionary. It could not exist on the vaudeville or nightclub stage, would not work in the oversized scale of the motion picture screen. It took view of the fact that the audience was sitting around at home watching a magical box that hadn't been there a decade or two earlier. Ernie's special gift to his viewers was to enter their living rooms and pull as many delightful visions out of his head as he could, like rabbits out of a hat.

Ernie Kovacs was a man of vast extremes, an ambitious and supremely gifted workaholic, a compulsive and self-destructive gambler, a generous and sometimes frustrating lover, father, and friend. He deliberately lived his life at a fever pitch, and by 1961 he had experienced much joy, but he had also trapped himself within many situations from which he yearned to escape.

Always the high roller, the biggest of the big spenders, at the peak of his professional stature he had driven his finances into the ground. He was deeply in debt from gambling, from excessive high living, from overspending on production budgets, and from having neglected to pay his income taxes. He was working for superhuman stretches of up to forty hours with little or no sleep and pouring whatever energy he had left into frantic efforts to hide the monetary problems from his wife, whom he felt it was his duty to protect. There were other difficulties— disappointment over his failure to do auteur-level work in the movies, for example, and frustration with his inability to make progress on various literary projects. Cracks were beginning to show in his marriage and family life; strain was beginning to show in his darkly handsome face.

"I like to be onstage," Ernie once confided to his writer Rex Lardner, "because nobody can bother me there. Lawyers, process servers, insurance salesmen—anyone." On a sound stage, behind the shielding glass of the television screen, Ernie Kovacs felt safe and in control, and these were the conditions he attempted to reproduce in his extravagant Beverly Hills den made-to-order. Performing on TV or locked up inside his den, protected by electric signs warning people away, Ernie could shut out the rest of the world, with its never-ending money worries and personal conflicts and professional frustrations. He could take control and let his imagination run wild and create glorious illusions to bring pleasure to his audiences and to himself. He could live in a dream, his own private Kovacsland.

The archetypal start for a life of high drama is to be born into humble surroundings. This Ernest Edward Kovacs was, in Trenton, New Jersey, on January 23, 1919. His father was Andrew John Kovacs, a tall, big-boned, kindly man with bushy black eyebrows, thick hair, and an equally thick foreign accent. He had emigrated from the town of Pálháza, Hungary, in his teens, had learned to speak English, and had recently obtained a job as a foot patrolman in the first and second precincts of Trenton. Ernie's mother, born Mary M. Chebonick to Hungarian parents who had also immigrated to Trenton, was a devout Catholic who nevertheless swore gustily in both Hungarian and English (a trait she would pass on to her only son). Ernest was baptized on February 3 at St. Stephen's Catholic Church, in the heart of Trenton's Hungarian community, and Mary would raise him as a Catholic. Although he stopped attending church regularly as an adult, his daughters would later remember him kneeling by his bed every night to pray before removing the St. Christopher medal he always wore and placing it on the night table next to him.

Andrew Kovacs was part of the great wave of Hungarian immigrants who made the arduous and uncertain journey to America between 1880 and 1914. Like the vast numbers of Irish, Italians, Germans, Slavs, Swedes, Greeks, Chinese, and others who also went through the port of entry at Ellis Island, the Hungarians were motivated almost exclusively by economic considerations. Largely young men of peasant stock, they were "the people who had been displaced from their traditional agricultural pursuits," according to historian Steven Bela Vardy. "Having been made superfluous in their native village, and finding no meaningful employment opportunities in the country's industrial centers, they were forced to seek their fortunes abroad, particularly in the United States."

Of the 1.7 million Hungarians who transplanted themselves to the United States during this period, the largest number came in 1907: 185,000, nearly 1 percent of Hungary's entire population. From Ellis Island the arriving immigrant had to make his or her way to a job, waiting family members, a community of others from the same homeland. Many were attracted to nearby New Jersey, whose burgeoning industrial and commercial cities provided a wealth of job opportunities. The capital, Trenton, was a particularly strong magnet, with its potteries and foundries, rubber manufacturers and cigar factories. The main highway bridge over the Delaware River into Trenton announced the city's manufacturing prowess with a gigantic sign: TRENTON MAKES— THE WORLD TAKES.

András János Kovács had immigrated in 1906, at the age of sixteen. He chose to settle in Trenton, and there is a record of his having obtained a job as a diemaker at a wire-rope factory in Trenton—probably the enormous John A. Roebling's Sons Company, which was started by the civil engineer who had built the Brooklyn Bridge. Like most immigrants, he found room and board with a family from his homeland, Joseph and Elizabeth Homa.

As of the 1910 census, when he was living at the Homas' house only a few blocks from Roebling's, Andrew had not filed for U.S. citizenship. He married shortly thereafter, and in 1912 his wife bore a son, Thomas. The marriage ended in divorce within a few years. Andrew took on the responsibility of raising Tommy, who would grow up to look like a tall, thin version of his father, although without the thick head of hair.

It is not known how and when Andrew met Mary Chebonick, but a Trenton directory of the period shows them living very near one another—Andrew having moved by 1917 to South Clinton Avenue, in Trenton's Hungarian neighborhood, and Mary living with her family on Genesee Street, just a block south of Clinton. Andrew's status as a divorced man apparently didn't bother the Catholic Mary, who was wedded to him on January 13, 1918, at St. Stephen's Church; he was twenty-seven and she, twenty-one. The union would be a mixture of happiness and conflict. Their common ethnic heritage was a significant bond, and both loved to throw parties. But they also shared a tendency toward volatility, and they would fight when Mary's fierce ambitions ran up against Andrew's more relaxed attitude toward their fortunes.

Maria M. Csebenyák was born on December 5, 1896, most likely at her family's home (her birth certificate shows her birthplace as Genesee Street). Both her parents had emigrated from Hungary. Mary's father, John Chebonick, found work in a Trenton factory, and when he was in his early twenties he suffered an industrial accident so severe that he had to have both legs amputated. (Violent maiming and death were common in the industrial workplaces where many Hungarian immigrants took jobs.) John developed gangrene and died, leaving his wife, Susanna Torony Chebonick, with a houseful of children to raise. Mary was eight years old. "She had no idea of what death was at eight, so she just went on," says Kippie Kovacs, one of Mary's granddaughters. "She would tell me, with tears running down her face, 'I just went out to play. I didn't understand anything about death.' "

If life had been difficult for the Chebonicks before John died, the loss of the family's primary breadwinner made things even tougher. Susanna took in wash in order to earn money, but it wasn't enough, so when Mary turned eleven, she started working in a local cigar factory, lying about her age to get the job. "She worked feverishly from morning until night," describes Kippie, "and she wasn't allowed to be a child, to play and have fun. Because of this, in later years she wanted everything for her son. She wanted the best, and he got the best—too much of the best."

Though extremely intelligent, Mary was also uneducated—a frustrating combination of circumstances. She was strong and could be overbearing, especially when compared to sweet, friendly Andrew. "She was extremely powerful," her granddaughter Elisabeth Kovacs remembers, "a force of life." From the moment her only son was born until the day he died, she would pour her vast, loving energy into making his life everything that hers had not been.

By 1920, the year after Ernie was born, Trenton had experienced the greatest population swell in its entire history. In 1880, at the start of the great migration, its population had been a modest 29,910; by 1920, when the United States tightened its immigration quotas and put an end to the immigration wave, Trenton's citizenry had quadrupled, to 119,289. Fully one-fourth of its residents were foreigners, and numerous others were children born to them in Trenton. These immigrants would cluster in neighborhoods with people from their own country and run their own churches, markets, and shops, maintaining the traditions that had sustained them back in Europe. Their first-generation American children almost always grew up to be bilingual; at home and in their communities they would speak their parents' native tongue, and in school or outside their neighborhoods they would be exposed to English. Sometimes their parents, the immigrants, would find that they didn't need to learn English at all, because everybody they encountered in daily life— the produce vendor, the letter carrier, the tavern keeper, the foreman— had emigrated too.

In the Hungarian community of which the Kovacses were a part, social life centered around the churches. St. Stephen's, where Ernie was baptized, was more than just a place of worship; it ran a parochial school and a night school, and the parish owned picnic grounds where summer outings were held. St. Stephen's pastor, Father John Szabo, had immigrated in 1921; he was described at the time as "an aggressive worker on behalf of his flock." (Toward the end of his life Ernie was working on a historical novel that he titled *Mildred Szabo*, possibly remembering his childhood priest.)

Beyond the walls of the church, community ties were kept strong by many means. Workplaces such as Roebling's employed large numbers of Hungarian immigrants, who thus were able to interact on a daily basis. (John A. Roebling himself had been an immigrant, from Prussia.) The news was carried in three Magyar-language newspapers published in Trenton in the 1920s, the *Independence*, the *Jersey Hirado*, and the *Cross*. Partly because of the high numbers of factory accidents, partly to provide a means to fraternize, Hungarian immigrants throughout the United States had established a tradition of beneficial societies to aid their compatriots, and Trenton was home to many such orders. The city also had numerous Hungarian clubs; some were social, like the American-Hungarian Political and Social Club, and others were cultural, like the Trenton Hungarian Reformed Church Singing Society. At the corner of Genesee and Hudson was the brand-new Magyar Home, which represented "the genuine desire for enjoyment of the best community life, and their wish to give their children every educational advantage," as one publication reported shortly after the opening of this important gathering place. "It encourages members to keep their homes clean and looking their best and as a result many Hungarians have a high standard of living."

Mary K. Toth, who was a little girl living a few doors down from the Kovacses when Ernie was a baby, recalls that the Hungarians in Trenton were "very active. They were always having big to-dos to stick together. It was fun. They had the Hungarian hall on Genesee Street at that time, and that was the meeting place. They had dances and plays; actors and actresses would come through New York from Europe." Ernie's parents were often involved in these functions, and Mary Kovacs, who was tall and dark-haired and liked to dress up, stood out. "She was well known," says Toth. "Nobody liked her because she thought she was better than everybody else. She dressed beautifully: We were all poor people working, and she would wear fur coats, scarves. She didn't belong down there, in that neighborhood."

"That neighborhood" in Ernie's earliest years was an ethnic working-class area on Union Street. A few blocks away was the city's well-known farmers' market, with the Delaware River and wharves for a backdrop. Andrew was running a saloon on Union, his job as a policeman having lasted no more than a couple of years. Indeed, although as an adult Ernie would describe his father only as a former policeman, in truth Andrew's career was far more checkered than that suggests. His pattern was generally to try his hand at something for two or three years before moving on to another business. This tendency must have frustrated Mary, both because her husband never seemed to be getting anywhere and because his lack of ambition made it difficult for her to provide her son with the sort of life she envisioned for him.

Mary's whole life was centered on her baby boy. She would dress him up like a beautiful little doll and take him with her on errands. "We'd laugh: 'She's nuts. He's a little boy. What's she dressing him up like that for?' " says Toth. When he was old enough, Ernie was given a pony, which was kept in the backyard of the saloon. Nobody else on Union had a pony. In the morning, on their way to school, the neighborhood kids would climb up on the fence to look at this rare pet. Then they would repeat the action coming home in the afternoon, as if they couldn't believe their eyes.

As well as Mary treated her own son, there were whispers in the neighborhood that she cared little for her stepson. It was Tommy who seemed to be most often put to work; he would be seen mowing the lawn or helping out in the saloon, whereas Ernie was busy going to school, getting the education that his parents never had. Of course, at seven years Ernie's senior, Tommy could probably help out more than his little brother. But Ernie himself said that he was encouraged to be helpless: "Even as a kid when I started to do something my father would say, 'Here, let me do it.' I couldn't even mow a lawn properly."

Like Tommy, dark-haired Ernie resembled their father, but Ernie was a chubby child—Mary never denied him anything, especially food—and he would have to struggle to keep his weight down all of his life. Despite the difference in the way the boys might have been treated by Mary and Andrew, early on there was a special feeling of closeness between seven-year-old Tommy and his baby half brother, a closeness that was protective and intuitive. One day, while Ernie was learning to walk, Tommy stood him up against the wall of the kitchen. Although there were other people in the room, Ernie took his first faltering unassisted steps directly to his big brother, a choice so meaningful to the older boy that Tom recounted it to an interviewer, with sweetness, some fifty years later.

Soon after learning to walk, little Ernie got lost, and he was in potential danger because of Union Street's proximity to the river. Tommy's sixth sense about his baby brother helped save his life. "I could almost sense where he was," he said. He found Ernie "on the edge of the river—he was only one or two—and we got him before he went in." In adulthood, those who knew Ernie best, including some family members, did not perceive his relationship with his half brother as being particularly close; perhaps they grew apart as the gulf between their ways of life widened. But when he was young, Ernie looked up to Tommy and "hero-worshipped him," says August P. Ciell, who became friends with Ernie in the seventh grade. "Ernie really thought a great deal of Tommy, and Tommy certainly did of Ernie," says Helen Wilson, who befriended Ernie around the same time. "I always felt that Tommy might have gotten a little more attention than he did in the family. But I don't think Ernie ever neglected him."

For all the differences between Andrew and Mary, their household seems to have been a cheerful one. Their lively discussions were heavily peppered with Hungarian, and Tommy and Ernie grew up bilingual. There was always music around the house, especially folk songs from the old country, which Mary performed lustily on the piano. She was also a born storyteller, and she loved to spend time with children. "She was very nice to us and often sat around the kitchen table with us kids playing cards," says Ciell. "Usually poker. We used pennies supplied by Mrs. Kovacs. She was very hoarse, and looking back now, I think she probably had polyps on her vocal cords." She tended to remain aloof from her neighbors and was therefore perceived by some as a snob. But those whom she let close remember her as essentially kind. "I thought she was a very sweet person," says Ernie's school friend Virginia Wales, "very polite and good-natured. The only thing that bothered us was that she spoiled Ernie so much. But that was because he was her baby."

Unlike his wife, Andrew socialized a great deal with his neighbors. He was down-to-earth, as accessible as Mary seemed snobbish, and "he did love to drink," says his granddaughter Kippie Kovacs, who also remembers him as "warm, sweet, generous." Everybody called him Andy, and with his bighearted, gregarious spirit, he was well liked. Ciell remembers him as "a very big, florid individual, very hearty and friendly." His idea of fun was to hire an organ-grinder to play on the police chief's lawn in the middle of the night. With Ernie he was warm and loving, and Ernie would treat his father with the utmost respect all of his life.

In school Ernie "was very enthusiastic. He wanted to learn," recalled one of his schoolteachers, Mary Walker. "He was never a bad boy, but you might say he'd been spoiled a little." Partly because he was accustomed to doing whatever he wished, partly because anything that made you laugh was valued in the Kovacs family, Ernie displayed a strong streak of brattiness that sometimes drove his schoolmates up the wall. Once, on April Fools' Day, he passed out candy and gum to all of the children in his class. "The chewing gum was in Chiclets boxes, but it was Feen-a-mint, which is a laxative," remembers Virginia Wales. "It wasn't too long before the whole class had a problem. And the candy he passed around had soap on it." Girls in particular were perfect targets for torment. "He was the biggest kid in the class and I was the smallest," says Wales, "so I got the brunt of his teasing. I had worn a brand-new dress one day to school, and he sat in front of me, and he turned around and took the ink bottle and turned it upside down on my lap. And he was always hitting me with his big, fat hands. Just generally a brat. But he wasn't a bad kid, he just wanted attention."

He did not limit his pranks to school. At home he would draw footprints along the floor of his bedroom, up the wall, over the ceiling, and out the window—to freedom. One day "I pretended I was frying the cat in the oven," Ernie said. He ran into the living room yelling, "Cheddar is on fire! He's in the oven!" His parents raced into the kitchen and flung open the oven door. There Ernie had rigged up "a cardboard cutout of a cat, with a little sign around its neck, saying, 'Phew, that was a close one!' "

When he wasn't playing pranks, he was reading a great deal or fooling around on the piano, which he had learned to play by ear. At one point Mary bought him a new piano, and "he was so excited that he could hardly stand it," says Chuck Muscatine, a schoolmate who saw the instrument being delivered. "The men took the piano off the back of the truck, and they started to carry it up the drive toward the house, and he started to play the piano while they were carrying it—he couldn't wait for it to get in the house." Another friend remembers Ernie composing a piece that he titled "Damp Grass and Frogs."

Ernie's first ten years were probably the most stable of his life. Suddenly, at the peak of Prohibition, Andrew found the only major business success he would ever have, as a bootlegger. In January 1929 he moved the family out of the less prosperous south side of Trenton and into a large Dutch colonial house at 1104 Parkway Avenue in Ewing Township. Located in a neighborhood of stately brick homes set on wide, treelined streets, the house cost the then-substantial sum of $9,000. Later that year the stock market crashed, but Andrew's business flourished so much that before the close of 1929 he was able to buy a second property, in the old ethnic neighborhood on Genesee Street.

Ernie was enrolled in the sixth grade at the Parkway School that fall, when he was ten. Andrew's profession was listed in school records as "trucking," but his bootlegging activities were no secret. Ernie sometimes delivered his father's product to his customers, who evidently included some of Trenton's most prominent citizens. To protect their identity, he was instructed never to address the client by name. In later years he would have terrible trouble remembering names—a problem he attributed to this childhood practice—and would sometimes panic when he had to introduce people.

With Andrew's sudden fortune, the Kovacses went wild with spending. The new two-story house was organized around a central hall flanked by a living room with a fireplace on one side and a formal dining room on the other; it also had a large sun porch and a music room, into which a baby grand piano was installed. Before they moved in, Andrew and Mary hired a decorator to design custom furniture and redo the interiors.

Much of the new money was lavished on Ernie. In the spacious backyard they had a large playhouse built especially for him, "like a small bungalow almost," describes Warren Ermeling, one of Ernie's school chums. "It had a pool table in it and a Ping-Pong table. We used to play a little cards in there, but it wasn't poker—maybe pinochle, some of the more innocent card games." He kept a pony at the Parkway property and acquired a buggy to go along with it. He also developed quite a gun collection. "Ernie loved guns, and he had a great many air guns, slug guns, et cetera. I went hunting with him on several occasions," says August P. Ciell. George Riker, who married Mary Kovacs' sister Susan, remembered that "every birthday Ernie used to ask for a gun. When he lived on Parkway Avenue he used to take a little BB gun and shoot all the ornaments off the Christmas tree."

Some of the gifts he got were less destructive. According to Bob Fell, Virginia Wales's brother, "his father bought him a brand-new Iver Johnson bicycle every Christmas," and he also had a spiffy little rowboat that he kept behind their house in Birks Pond. Fell and some other boys built themselves a raft, Huck Finn style, and used it to go fishing in the summer. "Ernie's boat went adrift every once in a while, and we had the raft," he says. "Mr. Kovacs would come over and say, 'Would you boys go out and get Ernie's boat for me?' And he would give us fifty cents."

Despite their change in fortune, the Kovacses maintained a connection with their old way of life. Familial ties were important, and on Sundays they would return to the old Hungarian neighborhood to spend the day with Mary's sister, Susan Riker, who lived on Genesee Street with her husband and her two children, Margaret and Colin. Helen Wilson, who was two years younger than Ernie and lived next door to the Kovacses on Parkway, was often invited to these Sunday outings. They would have vast Hungarian feasts, "things that I'd never heard of. The Hungarians were great for Sunday brunches and that sort of thing."

Andrew was generous by nature, and now that he had lots of money, he enjoyed spending it on others, including his son's friends. When Ernie's eighth-grade class held its annual picnic at Washington Crossing, Andrew paid for all the food and soda pop—an extravagant gesture that few of the other parents, if any, would have been able to afford. For one of Ernie's birthdays, his whole class was invited to the house for an elaborate sit-down supper party, complete with hired help. When the kids' fathers showed up around 10:30 to pick them up, Mary and Andrew invited them in, and they all disappeared in the kitchen for a few drinks. "As twelve-year-olds we weren't supposed to stay up so late," recalls Warren Ermeling. "The next thing we knew, it was close to midnight. When we got home I really caught it, but my father caught it more than I did."

His parents' ostentatious spending habits—and the fact that much of the money was lavished specifically on him—put Ernie in a difficult relationship to his peers. Their new neighborhood was "moderately well-to-do," according to Ermeling, but this was the Depression, and many in the neighborhood were struggling just to get by. Ernie's parents were much better off than any other family there, and they were not shy about showing off their wealth. Ernie was perceived, correctly, as spoiled and somewhat of a mama's boy. Some of the kids were jealous that he was given anything he wanted at a time when people had very little, and they picked on him and made fun of him. "Kids are cruel," says Helen Wilson. "You might be jealous because you don't have a horse and buggy, so you laugh at somebody who does. It must have hurt."

If it did hurt, Ernie never let on. Around school or playing with other kids at home, he was always jovial and high-spirited, and he was quick to share what he had. "I never could quite understand why other kids didn't take to Ernie, but I'm sure it's because they were jealous more than anything," says Ermeling. "He was full of fun and little practical jokes. He was very outgoing and fun-loving. Happy. Always had a smile on his face."

Ernie was sensitive to what his family's money meant in the eyes of his peers. He had attended an expensive private school, the Bowen School, for a year, but he hid that fact from all his friends at the public Parkway School. And Helen Wilson remembers that her friend's big, expensive birthday party was "a little sad because Mary was, unfortunately, very pretentious. The birthday party wasn't like when we kids had birthday parties, and I always had the feeling that Ernie was a little embarrassed."

In the seventh grade, during his second year at Parkway, Ernie was chosen to play the male lead role of Old King Cole in an operetta about Mother Goose. In a photograph of him in the part, he looks younger but also bigger than his schoolmates, most of whom are outfitted in the beak-headed costumes of Mother Goose's goslings. Chubby, with a wide face and eyes set in a regal stare, Ernie is splendidly arrayed in a royal cloak of velvet trimmed in fur, a big crown on his head and a jeweled scepter in hand. He followed this performance with a portrayal of King Ferdinand of Spain in a play about Columbus, and for both kingly parts his mother traveled to a costume rental house in Philadelphia and returned with outfits so splendid that "we had to work hard with our cheesecloth to make the queens' costumes worthy of them!" said teacher Mary Walker.

The scuttlebutt around the school was that Ernie was picked to play Old King Cole specifically because his parents could afford to rent the expensive costumes. There may have been some truth to this. "You'd have to know Parkway School," says Helen Wilson. "I was the tallest person in the eighth-grade class, so—much to my chagrin—I had to play Abe Lincoln. It wasn't that your talent was great; it was that what you had to choose from was very small." But these roles made an impression on Ernie. They marked the beginning of his enthusiasm for costumes—for dressing up and making believe, for transforming his identity through the power of dress. In slightly later pictures, slimmed down from tennis and football, he mugs happily for the camera in somebody's backyard; in one snapshot he wears a fake animal-skin toga and wields an oversized club, while in another he strikes a ballet pose in a pair of tights.

Ernie's ability to escape into fantasy was about to stand him in good stead. In 1933, a year after he graduated from the Parkway School, Prohibition was repealed. And suddenly, as quickly as he had acquired it, Andrew's bootlegging fortune was gone.

2

Ironically, the decline in his family's fortunes may have helped Ernie's standing among the neighborhood kids. He was intensely private about family troubles, a trait he would carry into his adulthood, but all his friends knew what had happened. "You could tell," says Warren Ermeling. "He became more or less like the rest of us."

It wouldn't have been hard to tell. Andrew had been open about his bootlegging activities, and the end of Prohibition could only mean death to his business. Also, the pony was gone. So was the family's run of the big Parkway house: "They made the second floor of their home into an apartment," says August P. Ciell, "and the chief of the FBI in Trenton rented it."

Soon after falling on hard times, Andrew and Mary opened a fancy restaurant called the Silver Palms on the south side of Trenton. Whatever money they had left was now poured into the restaurant. Like the interior-decorated house and the birthday party with the sit-down supper, the Silver Palms in the midst of the Depression "was just a little bit too much," says Helen Wilson. "Trenton, even as a state capital, was not a big, glamorous town. And then of course Mary would be the hostess in the evening gown. The people would come, I think, out of deference to Mr. Kovacs rather than out of liking Mrs. Kovacs."

Ernie treated the Silver Palms as another place to entertain his friends. "As you entered, there was an enormous soda fountain on the left-hand side, and the restaurant was further back," remembers Ciell. "Every Saturday, Ernie would get behind the soda fountain and invite all of us kids in. Then he would entertain us with jokes and witty stories and make all kinds of concoctions—ice cream sodas, banana splits, everything. When we left we'd all have tummy aches."

But beneath the jokes and the witty stories, Ernie was beginning to have some problems. When he graduated from the Parkway School in June 1932, his report cards for the previous three years showed consistently good marks. At Junior Three, the ninth-grade intermediary school that he attended before entering Trenton Central High, he maintained A's in all areas having to do with personal character, such as cooperation, initiative, physical vigor, and reliability. But his academic level dropped. With the exception of music classes, which he apparently loved, his grades were peppered with D's; French he failed completely.

The A's in character traits showed that Ernie was capable of achievement when he wanted to be. Moreover, he had ambitions to go to college—or at least so he claimed; a school survey from this period indicates that he wanted to graduate from high school, go to college, and become a physician. This may have been a real intention, but more likely it was said in order to please his parents, who were eager for him to attend college and make something of himself. Certainly he was sending them a double message, speaking of plans for higher education and then earning grades just one step above total failure.

Ernie may have been bored by his classes, as intelligent children sometimes are. He may have been sabotaging his parents' college plans for him, even as he paid lip service to their desires. He may even have been living up to the image of total helplessness that they sometimes seemed to expect him to fulfill. But the fact that his academic performance plunged at exactly the time that his father lost his business suggests one thing more: that Ernie was more troubled by his family's problems than he was letting on to his friends. Indeed, at home the financial pressures were mounting, and the unhappiness between his parents was growing. He loved both of his parents, and although their marriage had never been ecstatic, it must have been painful for him to watch it deteriorate before his eyes.

Ernie maintained this same academic pattern all the way through Trenton Central High School. He would get B's in the subject he liked, which in high school was English literature and composition, but do poorly in all his other classes. It wasn't because he couldn't do well; in the eleventh grade, for example, he initially achieved a B in Latin, but by the end of the year he had failed it. When he repeated Latin in the twelfth grade, he started out with an A but once again failed it by the end of the year.

Ernie was due to graduate from high school in 1936. In 1936, the Silver Palms failed; creditors took over the building, the kitchen equipment, the furniture, everything. Andrew and Mary seem to have separated then as well (although they did not divorce until 1943); school records show the residence of the parent or guardian as 1104 Parkway, but the pupil's residence is listed as 116 North Broad Street. According to Helen Wilson, "It was very soon after they went out of business that I remember hearing they had separated. I think there was little money left at that stage, because they had put a lot of money into this restaurant, and when they lost it, they lost a great deal. His mother got a little apartment. It was quite a comedown."

In 1936, the year the troubles at home peaked, Ernie's school attendance suddenly plunged; he missed twenty-seven days out of his first semester and nearly as many his second. In the one class he had previously enjoyed, English, he ended the year with a D. D was the lowest passing grade, but among his other courses he did not even manage to scrape together enough D's to be able to graduate. And so, at seventeen—an age by which his father had already left his homeland and his family, crossed an ocean, and forged a whole new life for himself—Ernie flunked out and had to postpone his graduation a full year, to make up the grades.

His picture in the 1936 yearbook reveals a handsome face with full lips, thick dark hair combed carefully back, suit and tie as neat as a pin; he looks serious and purposeful, hardly capable of failure. But the seriousness actually masked an inner sense of helplessness. "I was thoroughly frightened when I left high school. I had no particular ability, and I had no way of making a living," Ernie would later tell Edward R. Murrow over national TV. Having to repeat his senior year—whether Ernie caused it deliberately or unconsciously—allowed him to escape taking on adult responsibilities, at least for another year. It also suggests an adolescent boy giving in to an urge toward self-destructiveness. He would do battle with that urge many times and in many different areas of his life as he grew older.

Despite his fears and his trouble with grades, however, Ernie's years at Trenton Central High were not just one long, lazy fling. In 1934, his sophomore year, he sang in the boys' glee club, participated in the annual spring musicale, and worked the hall patrol, acting as a disciplinary presence between classes. The next year he dropped the hall patrol—it probably wasn't fun enough—but he continued to perform in the glee club and the spring musicale every year; and in 1936, when so much else was going wrong, he added the school yearbook to his extracurricular activities.

As the city's main high school, Trenton Central was a large establishment with an ethnically and racially mixed population of nearly four thousand students. Even in this huge group, Ernest Edward Kovacs stood out. He was physically large, with a commanding presence; having inherited his father's build, he towered over many of the other students. (At Junior Three he had weighed 159 pounds and measured five feet eight, and he had only just begun his adolescent growth.) He also loved doing things to get attention and was forever showing off. "You couldn't help knowing that Ernie was in the school," says Sarah Christie, who was the assistant drama teacher. "He was always in the fore. You always looked at him." A reference to him in the yearbook suggests the way he was regarded by his fellow students: "October 10, 11, 12—Ernie Kovacs terrorizes Washington with deadly Zap Gun. J. Edgar Hoover names him Jr. G-Man No. 2.75." (It resembles some of the goofy fake news items he would later invent for TV. For that matter, even the title of the yearbook, *The Bobashela*, sounds wackily Kovacsian.)

Actually there was another, more positive reason why Ernie might have wanted to stay in school for one more year. In 1936 he was practicing in the chorus for the spring musicale, which was Gilbert and Sullivan's *HMS Pinafore*. The head drama teacher, Harold Van Kirk, was busy conducting the principals on the school's main stage when a student director who had been working with the chorus interrupted him.

"He said that this young man was giving him so much trouble, he couldn't control the others. Would I come please and do something about it?" recalled Van Kirk. The distinguished drama teacher leaped off the stage and strode to the back, where the young troublemaker was pointed out to him: "Tall, good looking, with mischievous twinkling eyes—in short, a character," said Van Kirk, who promptly walked up to the "character," pulled him forward by the top button of his coat, and inquired menacingly, "Do you like being in this show?"

"Yes, yes, I do," the boy responded.

"Are you *sure* you like being in this show?"

"Yes, yes, I'm sure."

Then Van Kirk issued a warning in his deepest, most stentorian tones: "Remember: *One more mistake like this, and you're OUT.*" With that he turned on his heels, and the choral work resumed without further interruption. "And that," said Van Kirk, "was my introduction to Ernie Kovacs."

It was the beginning of a long and glorious relationship, one of the most significant Ernie would ever have. Harold Van Kirk was the Mr. Chips of Trenton Central High. "Any student who ever had him loved him and swore by him. Whatever he did was what each one of them wanted to do," says Sarah Christie, who was originally hired to take on the overflow of drama students clamoring to study with Van Kirk. If Ernie was commanding, Van Kirk, who possessed the added distinction of age, was even more so: very tall and lean, with a shock of white hair and a sonorous, classically trained voice. Adding to his attractions was his bohemian style of dressing: he wore casual tweed sports coats and slacks rather than the three-piece suits that were de rigueur teacher's attire in the 1930s, and sometimes he even donned sandals. "But he was always a gentlemanly bohemian," says Christie, "never sloppily arty. He was a very fine, striking figure of a gentleman."

Nathaniel Doughty, who was in Van Kirk's drama program with Ernie, describes the teacher as "very masculine and strong, but a tremendously aesthetic guy, extremely arty. I remember his playing a record of a German classical playwright, in German, and tearing up, crying visibly. Oh, he was heavy." He was also a good director, says Doughty. "He knew his stuff, and I'd say he was a hell of a good, strong influence on everybody who worked with him. He pointed out our weaknesses and gave us every incentive to do better. No ham bone, no excuses for silly stuff. Do it right."

Van Kirk sensed that underneath Ernie's "ham bone" lay some raw talent, and he proceeded to take the boy under his wing. Staying in school for an extra year meant that Ernie could work with Van Kirk, a prospect that must have thrilled the otherwise directionless teenager. Ernie was accustomed to being treated as an inept child, but the disciplined, highly professional Harold Van Kirk, the beloved head of the drama department, was exhibiting an interest in him and willing to give him a chance. If this teacher, with his worldly demeanor and exacting standards, was going to take him seriously, then he would work as hard as he could to live up to his mentor's expectations.

For a somewhat bucolic Depression-era community, Trenton boasted a fairly intense high school drama program. Around 1930 Van Kirk had worked closely with the principal on plans for the school that included a new stage the size of an average professional stage, complete with spacious dressing rooms. Van Kirk also had built a little theater where productions written, performed, and directed by his students could be put on at noontime—a different show every week. For all his dignity, Van Kirk had a streak of the pixie in him: "We did the necessary homework for the college board examinations in the first six weeks of a semester," he once confessed with glee, "and then we were free to go ahead and do what we pleased." In essence, Van Kirk was providing his students with an experience close to that of professional summer stock. It was a form with which he was amply familiar, for the teacher spent his summers directing stock company productions at the John Drew Memorial Theater in East Hampton, Long Island. These Trenton High teenagers were learning to pull together productions in a circumscribed amount of time, try a variety of roles as the productions rotated, project their characters to an audience from a professional-scale stage—they even got to use real dressing rooms.

In 1937, the drama department decided to mount another Gilbert and Sullivan production, *The Pirates of Penzance*, for the annual spring musicale. Always having been in the chorus before, now Ernie was about to be handed a grand opportunity. Van Kirk called him into his office and said, "Ernie, do you sing?" "Ohhh, no," Ernie replied, embarrassed, "I don't sing. I sing in the bathroom I guess, but that's all." But Van Kirk would have none of it. "As of now," he declared, "you sing!" And he cast Ernie in the role of the swaggering Pirate King.

Gilbert and Sullivan's Pirate King was precisely the sort of part in which attention-loving Ernie could shine. Tom Durand, two or three years behind Ernie in high school, recalled watching a rehearsal, and Ernie was noticeable right away. "He was in costume, doing a solo. There were big columns on either side of the stage, and he was leaning against one of them and holding a note forever and eternity. Here was this big guy in his big pirate's costume, singing in his big voice. He was larger than life."

Ernie was about to learn that talent can have some reward. He did so well as the Pirate King that Van Kirk invited him, along with just three other Trenton High students, to accompany him on his regular summer sojourn to East Hampton. The invitation was generally recognized as an honor and an extraordinary opportunity. Because he was a chosen one, his fellow drama students "stood in awe of him," said Tom Durand.

Van Kirk met with Mary Kovacs and convinced her to entrust him with her most precious boy for the summer. Indeed, Van Kirk quickly developed enormous respect for Ernie's mother, for he saw that she had her son's best interests at heart and felt that she exerted a beneficial influence. Now there was only one hitch: A family with creditors at its heels in the middle of the Depression was in no position to pay the tuition asked by the dramatics program into which Ernie was being invited. It was here that Van Kirk's support really became critical. He was able to help Ernie obtain a scholarship from the program's scholarship fund for needy students, and as suddenly as that, Ernie had a purpose and a place to fit in after leaving Trenton Central High. Ex-

cited about the adventure before him, he completed his studies, graduated from high school, and was off to Long Island with his mentor.

The program into which Ernie was admitted was the Rollins Studio
of Acting. Founded by Leighton Rollins as a theatrical laboratory for
training promising students in every aspect of professional theater, the
studio produced a full season of eight plays every summer. These were
the plays Harold Van Kirk had been helping to direct, with the members of East Hampton society, the local artists' colony, and sojourners
from Manhattan and other East Coast cities forming an interested and
supportive audience.

Leighton Rollins had come to East Hampton from the Bar Harbor
Playhouse, a summer theater that he managed in the early 1930s. According to Martin Manulis, his young assistant director who would go
on to produce television's pioneering *Playhouse 90*, at Bar Harbor there
was "a professional company with an apprentice group attached to it."
Students played the bit parts—as well as building sets, working the
lights, and so forth—while the professionals performed the leading roles.
When Rollins established the studio at East Hampton, however, he did
away with the professional actors and made it "altogether a student
company," says Manulis. "He felt, I think, that it was one thing for
the students to do all the apprentice jobs, but they should also have the
advantage of doing the good parts as well as the bits in the plays."

Jane Vosper Hess, a student at the studio who became very close to
Ernie, recalls Rollins as "a very educated man, bitterly disappointed
that he wasn't born an Englishman. He loved reading poetry to us;
Gerard Manley Hopkins was one of his favorite poets. Looking back
now, I believe that he was homosexual, although in those days nobody
knew. But he was an entrepreneur. He loved the theater, and he also
had the ability to interest wealthy, elderly ladies in helping with either
cash or real estate." Possibly he worked his magic on Mrs. Lorenzo E.
Woodhouse, a widowed philanthropist who was prominent in East
Hampton, for some of the facilities at the studio complex seem to have
been donated or loaned by her.

The Rollins Studio productions were directed by professionals, such
as Rollins, Van Kirk, and Frances Esmond Pole. The staff also included
assistant director Martin Manulis, a choreographer named Ingeborg
Torrup, with dramatically arched eyebrows and red bee-sting lips, and
an assistant director named Henry Levin, a Van Kirk protégé from
Trenton who would eventually direct dozens of Hollywood films. Aside

from directing, the students did just about everything in this laboratory setting. Starting in July and running through September, they mounted eight full-length plays and various smaller productions—a scholarship-fund-raising night of vaudevillian skits, for example—as well as working on scenes from different plays within their classes. They would try out for roles, memorize their parts, attend classes and rehearsals, paint flats for the sets; they would learn how to light a stage, how to manage a crew, how to move the body and project the voice, how to create and sustain a character. In sunny weather their lectures were held on the lawn. Sometimes groups of them would take off for the nearby beach, enjoying a quick swim before flinging themselves onto the sand dunes, scripts in hand, to practice. Other times they would dress up for garden parties or dinner dances given for such visiting luminaries as Queena Mario of the Metropolitan Opera, film star Ramon Novarro, or Broadway actress Josephine Hull, who held a chair on the professional interests committee of the Rollins Studio.

In the late 1930s East Hampton was a tiny village with a strong sense of local history and a support for the arts that dated back to an art movement begun in the 1870s. "In the summer the so-called rich came, and they had their summer houses. They were called 'cottages,' but they weren't," laughs Martin Manulis. "Mostly they came from the East, a good many from Manhattan. But they were quiet people and they were not looking for notoriety of any kind. It did not have the kind of reputation it has today."

The Rollins student group was based at Graycroft, a roomy, many-winged structure with a facade resembling a barn. Some blocks away was a larger complex called Guild Hall, which held three picture galleries and spaces for public meetings and social functions as well as the elegant and well-appointed John Drew Memorial Theater, where the major Rollins productions were presented. "The theater was beautiful," says Jane Hess. "It was considered really new and had everything that a theater was supposed to have. I remember the chandelier; it was like a giant cluster of great balls that looked like colored balloons, and the paint was a soft mauve. It was a lovely feeling walking in there." Rollins provided an entirely professional environment in which to learn theater; the plays were even regularly reviewed in the press, which meant that the students had to confront their own vulnerability at the hands of professional critics.

To a boy on the brink of becoming a man, a boy as restless and unfocused and insecure as Ernie was that summer of 1937, an intense and responsibility-inducing program such as that of the Rollins Studio held a clear-cut appeal. And what teenage boy—particularly one with a penchant for fantasy—wouldn't want to escape a recently broken home to work in an elegant theater under the auspices of a supportive male mentor? During his first summer away from home, Ernie constructed and painted sets for Dodie Smith's play *Call It a Day*, portrayed one of the "Cowboys and Farmers" in Lynn Riggs's tale of the Oklahoma Territory, *Green Grow the Lilacs* (the basis for Rodgers and Hammerstein's *Oklahoma!*), and was exposed to classical theater in the studio's season-end production of Aristophanes' *The Birds*, in which he played two small roles, Kinesias and Heracles. He also earned himself his first professional notice. In early August the Rollins Studio mounted "Stunt Night," a special program of pieces written and performed by the students for the Guild Hall season subscribers. Presented before a packed audience "with standees outside the doors," according to a local critic, "the entire program was amusing and greatly enjoyed; but a few numbers were so outstanding that they might have been the work of professionals in the theatre. Isabella Gardner, as the toothless old Irish woman, was priceless; Pauline Kissell, singing 'Parlez Moi d'Amour' in French, was extremely appealing; and Ernest Kovacs, doing the Jersey family and the tramp, brought down the house." Ernie was always a sharp observer of types, and—as he would later demonstrate on TV—he could do a quick, twisted satirical turn that cut right to the heart of a character.

As he had in high school, Ernie stood out among the mixture of rich kids and needier scholarship students that made up the Rollins Studio group. "One can never know what's going to happen to anybody in the future, but he really did seem an enormous talent," says Martin Manulis. "He was this very young kid, but with a big body. And he had a really infectious personality." Jane Hess remembers him "horsing around a lot backstage. I loved him, but a lot of the people thought that he was disruptive. He was always getting in trouble with Leighton Rollins."

Sometimes he would have moments of melancholy, but he kept them very private. That summer George Gershwin died, and Ernie, who had memorized "Rhapsody in Blue," cried for an entire night. Then, one day, Jane Hess was walking near the rehearsal barn and heard the sound of music. "I looked in, and Ernie was playing 'Rhapsody in Blue.' It was so sad. When he finished, he just sort of went"—she slumps her head down—"and sat like that. A little depressed. I had been standing by the door, and I went up to him and put my arm around him and said, 'Oh, Ernie, I love the way that . . .' And then he cheered up and said, 'Well, wait till you hear this!' " Whatever sadness he experienced when he was alone was always covered up quickly around others, even his closest friends. "It was, I think, his defense. You know, get in there first. You make the joke, and then there's no way anyone can find you," says Hess.

Ernie did well enough to be invited to return, again on scholarship, for the summer of 1938. In the opening production of that season— Julian Thompson's satirical tale of Amazon warriors, *The Warrior's Husband*—his fellow student Betty Comden, who would later achieve fame as a writer of Broadway and Hollywood musicals teamed with Adolph Green, was among those singled out for praise by a critic who always signed himself "The Observer." In the role of the half-witted Hercules, The Observer added, "Ernest Kovacs [is] now ready to claim the spotlight in our best of musical comedies."

Sometimes Ernie's portrayals were far off the mark—too broadly played, or not deeply considered. Of the Rollins Studio's production of George Bernard Shaw's *Arms and the Man*, one critic wrote: "Obviously, the director miscast the [role of] Major Petkoff played by Ernest Kovacs. . . . As the father [he] was a vaudevillian rather than a legitimate actor." And in Edna Ferber and George S. Kaufman's *Stage Door*, Ernie in the small role of Adolph Gretzl earned this admonishment: "The Observer issues demerits, gentlemen first, to Mr. Kovacs, for an unrealized portrait of the noxious Hollywood producer in the final scene, a role well within his power. . . ." (Ernie also helped construct and paint the play's sets, which were not commented upon.)

Van Kirk, who recalled that Ernie was discouraged by the negative review of his acting in *Arms and the Man*, felt that Ernie's personality was so forceful he would inadvertently dwarf his fellow performers and then be criticized by reviewers for playing too broadly. "That review would have hurt him," says Jane Hess. But she believes that "there were some bad reviews about Ernie because he horsed around. He got embarrassed because he was afraid that he wasn't going to be a good actor, so his escape was to kind of make fun of his part in the play." Although Ernie was comfortable performing his own creations (the Jersey family and the tramp on "Stunt Night") or roles that hewed very closely to his own personality (the Pirate King), he had to work very hard to take on characters that did not come naturally. "There was a line in a James Barrie play that we did," says Hess. "The female character said something like, 'I am a woman.' And Ernie said, 'A woman? That is just what you are not!' And for some reason he couldn't get that line right. You'd hear him practicing, 'A woman? That is just what *you* are not!' 'A woman? *That is just what you are not!*' He just couldn't lose himself in the part, like most actors. Ernie was always Ernie."

Despite these less-than-apt performances, Ernie was acting often enough that The Observer could chart his progress and gain a sense of his strengths, weaknesses, and capabilities, a valuable and unusual level of feedback for a performer not yet twenty. And he was acquiring a significant depth and range of experience. That same summer he stage-managed Lennox Robinson's Irish tale *The Far-Off Hills;* he played the lead role of Cornelius Van Tassell in *The Headless Horseman,* a new operetta by composer Douglas Moore and librettist Stephen Vincent Benét (author of "The Devil and Daniel Webster"), and in the Hungarian playwright Ferenc Molnár's *Liliom* (on which Rodgers and Hammerstein based *Carousel),* Ernie redeemed himself with The Observer, who wrote, "Among the 'character actors' of the troupe, those who brought theatre values to their roles most successfully [included] Ernest Kovacs as the heavenly Magistrate."

As he left behind the role of the helpless, spoiled child that his parents had encouraged him to play, Ernie was beginning to see possibilities for his future. He was fully aware that he owed this to Harold Van Kirk, and in later years he gave credit to his old mentor for his having gone into show business. "Van Kirk was a fascinating man. He had very piercing eyes, and when he talked with you, he was just absolutely glued and in total contact with you," remembers Martin Manulis. The teacher struck everyone as "very Svengali-like. He had a mesmerizing stance. Ernie had enormous admiration for him. Young people then were much more apt to respect authority." Van Kirk would surprise everybody when he ran off with one of the East Hampton students, Isabella Stewart Gardner, who came from a wealthy Boston family. The elopement caused a bit of a scandal because of the difference in their ages and because of the clear-cut hierarchy that existed between students and teachers at the time.

Van Kirk was not the only person who affected Ernie's life at East Hampton. He fell in love there for the first time, with a girl he met during the summer of 1938. Suzanne Ludey, like Isabella Gardner and many other girls at Rollins, came from a rich family (hers from West Virginia). She was very tall, almost as tall as Ernie, and model-thin, with high cheekbones and brunette hair parted down the middle, giving her an elegant look. Ernie had many female buddies, both at East Hampton and back in Trenton, and to all of them he confided his new romance. Ernie found a good deal of comfort in his platonic friendships with women, and he would maintain strong ties with many women throughout his life. But around a girl who was something more—who was an object of romantic love!—the young, inexperienced Ernie turned "shy and tended to be unrealistic," says Jane Hess. "He would put them on a pedestal right away. That was his approach." With Suzanne, there was no hiding his feelings; he wore his heart on his sleeve. Around her he was "very soft, sort of like a St. Bernard puppy," remembers Hess. He was sensitive, too, to the vast difference in their family backgrounds. "There was so much difference in background that it was unbelievable," says Ernie's East Hampton roommate, Jim Miller. "But this was happening all along at East Hampton. Everybody had somebody they were in love with."

If with Suzanne Ludey he was vulnerable and adoring, among his other fellow students Ernie continued to cast himself as the jester. Jim Miller recalls that he would get in his car and "it wouldn't go anywhere, because Ernie would have jacked the rear end up on my own jack." He also loved to play with language, and he made up a multipurpose joke word, *foo*, which he would invoke in speech and in writing. Once he sent Jane Hess a series of tiny photographs he had taken; three snapshots of a water garden were labeled "Water Foo," "Water Foo," and "More Water Foo"; a tenor who got all the plum roles was identified as "Foo Peterson"; and an overexposed picture of him with Suzanne Ludey was a "Foo Print." (A picture of Harold Van Kirk, however, was respectfully marked "Mr. V. Kirk.") "He'd come onstage," says his Trenton friend Eddie Hatrak, "and start talking to his leading lady with some innocuous line like, 'Tennis anyone, today?' And he would blink his eyelid, and across his eyelid he would have the word *FOO*. Then when the leading lady would get all choked up and try to camouflage it, he would say, 'You shouldn't get all choked up over a little thing like playing tennis. You get all emotional.' "

Indeed, breaking people up onstage was one of Ernie's favorite anarchic amusements. In *The Warrior's Husband*, Hercules (played by Ernie) and his partner Theseus are brought before the throne of the Queen of the Amazons (played by Jane Hess). "I'm supposed to say something fairly stern because they encroached on Amazon territory," describes Hess. "Ernie had all this crepe-paper hair on his chest, which was part of the makeup. And when he came on he had the lion skin and all this hair falling out, and he had his hand like this"—she cups her hand over her chest. "When he got in front of the throne and was facing me, with his back to the audience, he just silently opened up his hand and let a moth out. I cracked up! It was just terrible. I had to say something; the plot demanded that something be said. He just stood there. Never cracked a smile."

It was all pure silliness, an enjoyable antidote to the increasingly serious events taking place in Europe, where many of Ernie's Trenton friends (and possibly Ernie himself) still had family members living. In March 1938, Hitler had annexed Austria, and now he was gearing up to occupy Czechoslovakia. In Spain, a bloody civil war was being fought with the fascist Franco, who was being given support by Mussolini and especially by Hitler. Although the United States was officially staying out of these strifes, there was much popular sympathy with the Spanish Republicans who opposed Franco, and young American men were making their way to Europe to help (illegally) in the fight. Against this background, Leighton Rollins staged the highlight of the 1938 summer season at Graycroft, an ambitious production titled *Disasters of War*. Ernie was nineteen, at an age and at a point in history when a young man would certainly be thinking of what it would mean to fight in a war.

Rollins, cosupervising the production with Martin Manulis, based the play on Goya's damning series of etchings of the same title. Comprising thirteen scenes framed by an introduction and a conclusion, *Disasters* consisted of tableaux vivants composed by Ingeborg Torrup and backed by a Greek-chorus-style commentary written by Rollins. Ernie performed in three of the tableaux, and their titles give the flavor of the whole work: "They Don't Know the Way; Desolate, Disillusioned, Lost"; "And There Is No Remedy; Man Has Come to This"; and "Nor Do These; Madre, Madre, Madre / Cried the Child." He also participated, along with the rest of the studio members, in a singing chorus at the conclusion.

Considered experimental theater at the time, *Disasters of War* was presented on four consecutive evenings in early August and was widely attended and praised. "Something revolutionary in dramatic art came into being last week," wrote the *Southampton Press* critic. "*Disasters of War* [is] a searing spectacle, to frighten and freeze forever the impulse in human beings to resort to the stupid violence of self annihilation, which is war."

Unforeseen by many Americans in 1938, within three years the United States would be entering a war that had grown to worldwide proportions. Ernie would not fight in this conflict—but not for reasons of conscience or of politics.

At 119 West 57th Street in Manhattan, a producer-director named Elizabeth B. Grimball operated the New York School of the Theater. Grimball's rigorous two-year program emphasized the fundamentals of theatrical work, covering both its technical aspects, such as pantomime, improvisation, speech, and stage makeup, and its cultural side, such as theater history and dramatic analysis. A catalog of the time boasts that the establishment "is the most modern school of the theatre in the East" and advises the potential student that he or she stands before "a far greater opportunity than ever before in the history of theatrical endeavor":

> Not only is dramatic art stimulated by violent changes in the structure of our civilization, but through the mechanical inventions of this age, the media for interpreting life and art have increased greatly. . . . With the establishment of the Talking-picture, Radio, and Television, the technical requirements for the student who plans to enter the theatrical world have become more exacting and varied. . . . Success in any art requires talent. But talent is not enough.

It was to the New York School of the Theater that Ernie repaired upon finishing the 1938 summer stock season at the Rollins Studio of Acting. Carnegie Hall and the Art Students League were also on West 57th Street, and Ernie had only to walk to the nearest corner and look straight down Seventh Avenue to see the brightly lit marquees of Broadway and the pulsating crowds of Times Square. There in the very center of Manhattan, studying for the only career that had ever presented itself to him, Ernie was truly on his own for the first time.

In a portrait shot taken that year—wearing a tweed sports coat, a black snap-brim hat tilted rakishly over one eye—Ernie looks as grown up as can be. He is clenching a pipe between his teeth, as if attempting to seem more adult and cultivated, and over his lip can be detected a slender new mustache, the first appearance of the appendage that would later become so famous. He looks happier than he did in high school, lighter somehow, as if a great weight has been lifted.

Students who applied to the New York School of the Theater had to audition before the faculty, provide good references, and explain their theatrical aims in writing, as well as come up with the hefty annual tuition of $500 and provide their own costumes, wigs, makeup, and room and board. It was thrilling to have been accepted into the program; it promised individual attention on a daily basis, performances before the public, field trips to rehearsals of Broadway plays, and introductions to agents, directors, and producers after completion of the two-year course.

Naturally, Ernie could not hope to come up with the tuition, and once again Harold Van Kirk helped him to obtain a scholarship. Then his mentor was off to Cambridge University to work for a year. Ernie, whose parents had no money to speak of, was about to experience grinding poverty for the first time.

He found a walk-up room in a brownstone on a dirty little side street in midtown Manhattan. "It was so dark inside," remembers his Trenton chum Helen Wilson, "you had to have the lights on all the time." Jane Hess had introduced Ernie to her friend Dwight Dickinson, who was studying at Harvard, and Dickinson would come down to New York and stay overnight with Ernie. "He had one narrow room, probably twenty feet long and about five feet wide," says Dickinson. "I think somebody had taken a larger room and cut it into this shape. As I remember, it had no bathroom. I don't want to say it was cell-like, but it was pretty dreary. A door at one end and a window at the other. Just a long, narrow room with a small bed in it."

In his room, Ernie would fix little packets of Nestlé's instant chocolate for himself. When Dickinson came to visit, the two young men would dine "at spaghetti joints around Times Square. Ernie lived on huge plates of spaghetti with tomato sauce," says Dickinson. "I think they cost twenty-five cents, and you could fill up and feel fine. There were people who would just come in and eat the sauce from the dirty plates and get out again. Really, it was that bad. I remember seeing a drunk man sitting near us with spaghetti over his ears and down his front. Tramps would come in, sit down, and eat whatever was on the table—eat tomato ketchup or whatever."

Despite the hardship, Ernie was "always great, even under the worst of conditions," says Dwight Dickinson. "He was a scream. He couldn't say anything without being funny." Andrew and Mary visited him regularly—separately, of course—and they seemed cheerful too. In truth both were having a hard time of it back in Trenton. Mary was so poor that she had to borrow the bus fare to New York, but she always made a point of dressing as elegantly as she could, and so did Andrew. And if Mary railed against Andrew for having failed at the family's business, or if Andrew resented Mary for having talked him into something he hadn't wanted to do in the first place, Ernie would have none of it. "He was caught between the two, but I never heard him say an unkind word to his mother about his father and vice versa," says Helen Wilson, a close lifelong friend. "Nor would he allow anyone else to say anything. If his mother had something to say about his dad, he spoke up for his father."

Ernie's tuition was covered by the scholarship, but in order to earn the ten or fifteen dollars a month he needed for rent, plus money for the spaghetti dinners and the professional equipment at school, Ernie worked as an usher in a movie theater for a time. He also obtained work in the theater department at Finch Junior College, an Upper East Side finishing school where Frances Esmond Pole, one of the directors from the Rollins Studio, headed the drama department. "I think Frances Pole kind of subsidized Ernie," says Jane Hess, who was attending Finch that year. "She was very fond of him, and the theater department at Finch was quite active. Mostly we put on plays that used a whole lot of female characters. But there always has to be a man, maybe a father or the brother or the caller. He would play those sorts of roles, maybe paint some scenery. Frances Pole liked Ernie very much, and it may be that she made up jobs for him so at least he'd have some income."

For Jane Hess, whose mother had pulled her out of Radcliffe and enrolled her in straitlaced Finch because "she didn't like the way I was behaving," the presence of her antic friend from East Hampton was a great comfort. "A finishing school had a real connotation," she says. "It was a school for young ladies who were taught to be ladies and to be cultured and to have manners, and it just drove me up the wall." She was seeing a young man behind her mother's back, and Ernie would help her get out to meet him. "If you lived there, you could only go out with someone who had been identified and approved by your parents. And Ernie was an approved person. My mother adored Ernie because he was warm and gentle and bumbly and funny—and also, I wasn't romantically interested in him. So Ernie would come to pick me up. And two or three blocks away was the guy I really wanted to see, and Ernie would take off."

Ernie had another reason for hanging around Finch Junior College:

Suzanne Ludey. Like Jane Hess, Suzanne was enrolled at the $1,800-a-year finishing school that year and was active in Pole's drama department. In pictures of some productions at Finch, she wears makeup for the first time, and she looks more svelte, hollow-cheeked, and elegant than ever. "He was very much in love with her," remembers Hess—so much in love that after many months he finally worked up his courage and asked Suzanne Ludey to marry him. Suzanne told Jane about the proposal, taking the attitude that "it's always very flattering. But she was from a family that was pretty snobbish. She had been at Finch finishing school and of course Ernie was not suitable," so she turned him down. Ernie had never professed his love to a girl before, and Suzanne's rejection pained him so deeply that he didn't even bother to hide it. Nor was he oblivious to the reasons behind it, and he was "sort of furious at her," says Hess, "because it hurt his feelings. He was young, vulnerable. It was bad to cut him like that. And it was a two-fold cut. It was a social-snobbery kind of thing."

But there was nothing to be done about it. Ernie continued to attend his daily classes at the New York School of the Theater, which had a strict attendance policy: students who missed more than 15 percent of class time would not be included in public performances. That spring he was general stage manager for some of the school's public productions, including J. B. Priestley's *Dangerous Corner* and Noel Coward's *Hay Fever*. In the latter he also performed the part of Sandy Tyrell, attired in a Cowardesque tuxedo.

During the summers Elizabeth B. Grimball ran a six-week apprenticeship program in affiliation with a professional company at The Playhouse in Brattleboro, Vermont. Ernie was accepted into the program for the summer of 1939 and was again granted a scholarship to cover the $230 tuition and boarding fee. The Playhouse was located on the grounds of an old estate in the center of the colonial town, and Grimball's students lived with the professional company in a historic brick mansion on the same grounds.

Ernie threw himself into the apprenticeship program. He painted backdrops and built sets and stage-managed productions. He learned and rehearsed and performed bit parts alongside the professional players, who took the leads. He attended classes in body work and acting technique and diction. And backstage, long after the audience had gone home, he played poker with the other actors and stagehands, sometimes staying up all night.

Ernie's health had always been vigorous, but a year of living on spaghetti dinners, combined with the intense routine at Brattleboro, was wearing him down. Finally, he fell ill. "It had been beautiful summer weather, and he'd gone out and gotten himself totally sunburned," says his friend Dwight Dickinson, who was working at the New York World's Fair that summer. "And he had gone to bed unable to put any clothing on or even to get under the covers. As it does in New England, it got cool, but he was uncovered and hot and didn't realize that he was lying in cold air." Ernie came down with two serious lung diseases, pleurisy and pneumonia. Because he had no money, he was sent as a charity patient to Welfare Island, across the East River from Manhattan.

Stuck in a desolate, roach-infested ward with several dozen other sick and penniless patients, "I used to sit in bed looking out the window," Ernie later recalled. "A big guy was digging a hole in the street and I'd have given anything to be able to take a shovel and dig. Or a guy drove past in a convertible with a girl and I lay there realizing I might never get out of bed. . . . I saw so many people die; outside my window they built the $2.00 coffins and sooner or later the cart would come through and they'd roll the body on." It had to have been a sobering sight for a twenty-year-old boy who had only recently begun to take anything in life seriously.

In 1939 on Welfare Island, an undernourished, worn-out, very sick young man who was being exposed to other people's diseases in an open ward faced at best a tough road to recovery. But then something happened to make Ernie's situation even worse. One day a nurse came by and said, "We need to have another sputum test." He asked, "What's that?" And she said, "That's where you spit into the little dish." "I never did that," he said. "And then it turned out," says Jane Hess, "that a man had died just as Ernie was being admitted, and his records went in under Ernie's name. And they had collapsed Ernie's lung on the basis of that misinformation! The treatment for tuberculosis used to be that they would collapse a lung, and it heals over a period of time, and then they reinflate the lung. Primitive." Because of the mix-up in records, Ernie was put into the tuberculosis ward, "where of course he contracted tuberculosis because he was weak and having the lung collapsed was very debilitating."

Sometimes Jane Hess and Dwight Dickinson visited Ernie on Welfare Island. "Gurneys would roll past with people on them but with a sheet over their head," describes Hess. "And I had to wear one of those gauze masks." Dickinson remembers that Ernie would be "in hospital pajamas, and he was able to sit up. He did seem thin; previously he'd seemed quite sturdy. But he was cheerful even in the hospital—funny, cracking jokes."

Ernie and Harold Van Kirk had written one another while Van Kirk was in Cambridge, but as both became busier, the letters dwindled. Consequently Van Kirk knew nothing of Ernie's confinement at Welfare Island until he returned to the United States in late 1939 and was told the story by Henry Levin, his assistant director at East Hampton, who had remained friends with Ernie. Van Kirk bitterly blamed himself for having lost contact with his young protégé; many years later he said he was never able to forgive himself.

Martin Manulis remembers that "we were all approached to raise money for Ernie's medical expenses. Van or Henry promoted it." Levin and Van Kirk raised enough to get Ernie transferred to Deborah Sanitarium in Browns Mills, New Jersey, the area's well-known tuberculosis sanitarium at that time. It was closer to Trenton, and friends like August P. Ciell and Helen Wilson came to visit him. Mary took advantage of the shorter distance to hitchhike rides out to Browns Mills. Andrew, who was running a service station, would drive to the sanitarium after working until eleven o'clock at night and tap on the window of Ernie's groundfloor room.

At Deborah, Ernie literally had a captive audience, and he used his talents to keep his fellow inmates entertained. Van Kirk and Isabella Gardner, his newlywed wife, found him surrounded by "these badly afflicted people, and here was this young man who didn't bear any stigma about him at all, and to see him cheer these people, see their faces lighten—I think that was one of Ernie's really great shows," remembered the drama teacher. To while away the hours, he would run poker games in the men's lavatory or read stacks of books or listen to classical music on a radio brought to him by Van Kirk and Levin (who had also managed to provide a small allowance for him—secretly, for Ernie would never have accepted it had he known). There was no end to the practical jokes he could play in a sanitarium; he especially enjoyed disrupting his fluoroscopy sessions by taping messages in tinfoil to his chest, which then showed up when the doctors turned on the fluoroscope.

Sometimes—particularly to close male buddies, to whom his squishy fears could perhaps not be comfortably confessed—he would portray the whole experience as a sort of comedy. Later he told his Trenton friend Eddie Hatrak that he had been given only three months to live and that he recuperated because "his mother smuggled in cigars and beefsteaks and also . . . that he used to sneak out at times, go on the town, make merry and—I don't know if her name was Mary—and then sleep all day." But in truth, Ernie's long illness affected him very deeply. It forced on him an awareness of the fragility of life, and it cemented his determination to savor every precious minute. In interviews many years later, after he became famous, he would always cite this experience as the turning point of his life.

Eighteen months of bed rest and relative isolation were about all the ever-restless Ernie could bear. "I know he was frustrated," says Helen Wilson. "He didn't feel he was sick enough, I guess." So one day early in 1941 he got up without permission, sneaked out of the sanitarium, and went home to his mother in Trenton. Mary nursed him back to health "with home cooking," as Ernie would later say. "Even then, she had the joy of living. She [would spend] her last money on dinner for me— charlotte russe and steak."

"Home" was a tiny apartment that Mary had rented over a penny-candy store. They had very little money, and the steak and charlotte russe came rarely; more often "they would have one meal a day," says Kippie Kovacs. "They would go out, and they would split a spaghetti dinner, and that was it." In the little apartment, remembers Edna Vine, who befriended Ernie in this period, "there was an outer room and a bedroom. And over the bed—I've always loved this—there were two swords, crisscrossed."

To bring in much-needed money, Ernie obtained a job at the Switlik Parachute and Equipment Plant, his first and last venture into the industrial work prevalent in his hometown. He was assigned one of the preferred jobs, hand sewing hardware onto the parachute harnesses, in a department where he was surrounded by Hungarians from his neighborhood. But Ernie's heart was not in manual labor. One day, "my uncle, who was the production manager, came up alongside of him, and there instead of needle and thread, Ernie had a script he was studying," remembers Richard Switlik. "My uncle was friendly to him. He said, 'Ernie, you don't want to work, do you?' He said, 'No, not really.' So at the end of that week Ernie terminated his employment."

If the routine of manually rigging parachutes bored Ernie, the theater excited him to his very soul. It wasn't long before he would have an opportunity to return to the stage—and for money. In the summer of 1941 "a man came into Trenton with his wife, in a very big yellow Cadillac, and said he was starting a road company," says Edna Vine. "He had apparently taken names at random, and he got Ernie's name and mine and a few others." The people he contacted were mostly kids around Ernie's age who were enthusiastic about the theater. For the premiere production, *Dark Victory*, the promoter "hired a telephone staff and sold maybe three thousand tickets," says Vine. "Everybody was to be paid on percentages. He gave Ernie the biggest percentage because Ernie was made the director. We were very young and naïve and just figured that it was wonderful."

Ernie's cut was supposed to be about $100, a healthy sum in those days, but the percentages never materialized. "Four days before the show was to open," Ernie later described, the promoter "drove up to my house in his Cadillac convertible and explained that [his] partner had opened the safe and stolen all the money. He said he'd shoot him on sight if he found him. Then he drove off, and I never saw him again."

Of course, the flashy promoter turned out to be "a con artist," says Edna Vine, "and as soon as he sold the tickets and got the money, he left." He allegedly absconded with between $3,000 and $5,000, and according to Vine the police were after him at one point. Meanwhile, hundreds of ticket buyers were expecting to see *Dark Victory*, and the swindled youngsters had no means of refunding their money, "so we had to give the play," she remembers. "However, all the expenses were now on us, because he provided nothing. We hired a women's club called the Contemporary, a very elegant place like a New York brownstone that had a theater on the side. And we made do. Ernie got together props and things. We provided our own costumes. But I remember we didn't pay royalties, and that made for some trouble with the publisher."

To Ernie, who would do whatever he wanted to do and was by now accustomed to living on the edge financially, it didn't matter too much that there was no money for his salary. In the summer of 1941 he threw himself into the productions at the Contemporary Club, directing *Dark Victory* and *Our Town* and both staging and acting the lead role in *Dr. Jekyll and Mr. Hyde*. He painted and built sets, oversaw props, sold tickets, and even swept the floors. It was like a return to the heady days of summer stock, a place where he could accomplish something tangible after eighteen months of enforced inactivity.

Sometimes his creative judgment was off, a problem that would dog him later in his television work. In *Our Town*, which is commonly staged with virtually no scenery or props, he decided to use a real coffin for the burial scene. "He thought it was just great to get an undertaker to give us a coffin. He loved shock," says Vine. "But it was horrible." Harold Van Kirk saw the play on opening night and explained to Ernie that the coffin came as too gruesome a blow to the audience, so he removed it the next night. Overall, however, "he was a very, very good director," says Vine. "His sense of timing was fabulous, for one thing. He could pace. He could get out of people what he wanted, without dictating. He knew what he wanted in a play." He also found a way to incorporate his love of classical music into the productions. "We couldn't afford live music," remembers Vine, who used to swap classical records with him, "but he had incidental music, and it was done with records, which was very innovative at that time. It wasn't constant; he would pick scenes and then he would pick music to set the moods."

As a result of these productions, Ernie had a brainstorm: the group should become a traveling players' company! "His mother had a boyfriend named Mr. Leach, and he provided a truck with a speaker," says Vine. "We went around trying to advertise these plays throughout the city. And we were going to take it traveling—to Burlington, Bordentown, surrounding areas." But the traveling company was not to be. Instead, when the summer was over, the group disbanded, and Ernie accepted an offer to direct plays for the Young Men's Hebrew Association. For a brief time he staged YMHA productions in Trenton's Cadwalader Park. Later he joined the Prospect Players, who performed on a little stage in the auditorium of the Prospect Street Presbyterian Church.

But he still needed to make a living, and he took a job as a drugstore clerk in Princeton, a reasonable commute north of Trenton through great stretches of fields and woods. For $14 a week Ernie trudged to and fro in this "very long store," as he described it, filling orders and taking back merchandise whenever customers changed their minds. "You'd go get the thirty-nine-cent toothpaste and then they'd decide to buy the fifty-nine-cent kind," he complained. "You'd bring that, and they'd decide they had to have a toothbrush, too." Soon he managed to find a position much more to his liking: working behind the cigar counter at Trenton's United Perfumery Company, a cut-rate drugstore on the corner of State Street and Broad, within walking distance of the apartment he shared with his mother. Here at the center of downtown Trenton, he got to show off and trade jokes with a somewhat captive audience. In front of customers, "he always tried to play the clown," remembers Marion Shapiro, who worked with him at the drugstore. But in private, "when the store was empty, he would do little scenes from Shakespeare." The new job paid a couple of dollars a week more than the previous one. It also enabled him to indulge in smoking cigars, a habit he had picked up from his father.

Cigars were not the only addictive pleasure that Ernie relished. By now he was an ardent poker fan, and while working at the parachute factory he and some fellow workers had started holding poker games on Friday nights, frequently at Ernie and Mary's apartment. After taking the drugstore job, he continued to play cards with his ex-factory cohorts, bluffing wildly and keeping everyone amused with a stream of jokes. He could never sit still; the minute a hand was over he'd leap up to light another cigar or grab a beer.

For a while, he evidently continued to carry a torch for Suzanne Ludey. To Edna Vine, who was three years his junior, he confided that he had fallen in love with a girl at East Hampton, but she had wanted him to leave the theater and go into business with her father and that didn't interest him. "He had her picture at home, and he was very impressed with her affluence," says Vine. "It's not that he wanted it. Money never meant anything to Ernie. But she used to buy him silk shirts with monograms. He thought that was fantastic."

Before long he was falling in love again. "He fell in love all the time," says Vine, who admits that she herself was attracted to him. "But I wasn't mature enough or strong enough to compete with his constant 'in love' business. He did make advances, and we'd laugh about them, and then he'd find a girlfriend. The ones who I knew he had were fluffs. I don't think he thought about their intellect; he would pick something that he liked, maybe physical attraction or some little trait. And then he'd be without a girlfriend, and he would make advances. But nothing ever came of it, because it was just a relationship we couldn't change." Edna spent a lot of time at Ernie's apartment rehearsing their productions and listening to classical records. One night he plied her with wine. "Mr. Leach was there, and we were reading scripts. I ended up sick, so he had to take me home, and that was the end of it. Probably the most romantic night we had."

At one point Ernie began dating a divorcée who had two little children. "His mother was having a fit," recalls Vine, "because he decided he was going to marry her. Oh, he was always going to marry everybody. He was madly in love with this girl, but that didn't last long. I'm sure his mother was delighted." She probably was. Fiercely possessive of Ernie and convinced that no woman could possibly be good enough for him, Mary was often jealous of any woman in whom Ernie took an interest. The relationship didn't have to be more than platonic for Mary to feel slighted. Ernie's friend Marion Shapiro, who was promoted to buyer at the drugstore and subsequently gave Mary Kovacs a job there, remembers that "one time, on my birthday, he brought me a bunch of violets—that's all he could afford. But he bought his mother a bunch too. He knew just how to handle her."

Mary's obsessive concern for the welfare of her only son led her to take bizarre steps at times. According to one of Ernie's female buddies, "One fateful night, in between girlfriends, she took me aside and said, 'You know, Ernie has to have sex.' I was eighteen or nineteen at the time, and this hit me like a ton of bricks. I didn't say anything to her, but she couldn't imagine what was wrong with me. She really was so totally possessive of him that even encouraging somebody to have sex with him was a very meaningless thing. It was just something that Ernie needed, like, 'Now it's dinnertime.'"

As a result of her single-minded devotion to her son, Mary's own relationships with men suffered. Occasionally she would invite a man home for dinner, but if Ernie was there she always gave him the biggest portions "because my grandmother cared more about my father," says Kippie Kovacs. "Naturally the men would be insulted and angry. Then after a while the dates stopped, because her gentlemen callers got sick and tired of getting small pieces of steak when my dad was getting big ones." In 1942 Mary filed for divorce from Andrew, and it was granted in 1943. Andrew would marry one more time, but Mary never did.

By the end of Ernie's first year back in Trenton, the United States had entered World War II. Because of the condition of his lungs, Ernie was rejected for military duty. "He took an awful lot of abuse in the store because of it," says Marion Shapiro. Suddenly all the young men in town were off to the war, including his older half brother, Tom. But here was "this big, strapping, six-foot-two man and not in the service. I think it bothered him a lot. He couldn't pass the physical, and he was working in the drugstore behind a cigar counter, in view of the public, because they really needed the money. Ernie was really the sole support of his mother at that time." But in the face of censure, his pride— or his anger—kept him from revealing the legitimate reasons for his remaining behind. "He just took the flak and developed these pat answers for it," says Shapiro, "which didn't endear him to people either."

Because of the war, however, within another year Ernie would be presented with an opportunity that would forever alter the course of his somewhat aimless life. That opportunity would come, not in the theater, but in radio, the most pervasive and popular medium of the time.

PART
TWO

RADIO WAVES

1941–1950

Radio had begun to capture the imaginations of Americans the year after Ernie was born. In 1920 the Westinghouse Electric and Manufacturing Company had founded station KDKA at its home base in Pittsburgh; that November, KDKA went on the air with what is generally considered the world's first scheduled radio broadcast, the election returns from the Harding-Cox presidential race. Within a year Westinghouse was marketing the first affordable radio receivers for the home, and by the end of the decade some 13 million Americans were tuning in to *Fleischmann Hour* "air concerts" by Rudy Vallee and his Connecticut Yankees, the antics of Amos 'n' Andy and King Fish and Madame Queen, writer-producer-actress Gertrude Berg dispensing motherly advice on *The Rise of the Goldbergs*, and such history in the making as the Washington, D.C., welcoming ceremonies for Charles Lindbergh's return from his flight across the Atlantic.

In the 1930s, with the shortages and financial difficulties brought on by the Depression, the habit of seeking entertainment at home became well entrenched. A family could sit enthralled before a huge mahogany cabinet with a fabric-covered speaker, and the whole world would be brought right to them at the flick of a dial. "In people's homes it was tremendously important," says Steve Allen, who would make a name for himself in radio in the 1940s before moving on to TV. Allen remembers strolling down a Chicago street one summer night in the late 1930s and listening to a radio broadcast of a Joe Louis fight emanating from every open window. "I had to go someplace, but I simply heard the fight as I was walking down the street. They had nothing else on. That's typical of how important radio was." Radio altered the very substance and form of American culture, bringing "the same entertainment to rural dwellers as to their city cousins, reaching deep into 'pockets of culture' almost unchanged since the early nineteenth century," according to broadcast historian Irving Settel. "New expressions were popularized, new names became nationally famous, and new modes of eating, dressing, and thinking were almost hypnotically suggested by the voices from the box in the living room."

Today American radio programming is dominated by music and talk; it has dwindled to a dull sameness that would have been unthinkable in the 1930s, when the national networks and local stations offered the tear-wrenching trials of such daily soap operas as *Stella Dallas, One Man's Family*, and *Portia Faces Life;* the elegant movie adaptations of *The Lux Radio Theater*, performed by Hollywood's biggest stars and introduced by Cecil B. de Mille; the show-biz gossip of Walter Winchell, who addressed his rapid-fire broadcasts to "Mr. and Mrs. America"; the verbal sparring of George Burns and Gracie Allen, Goodman and Jane Ace, Edgar Bergen and Charlie McCarthy, and Fibber McGee and Molly; and the danger-laced adventures of *I Love a Mystery, Suspense*, and *The Shadow*. Shows like *The Mercury Theater on the Air* offered original dramas and literary adaptations, while the popular *National Barn Dance* and *Kay Kyser's Kollege of Musical Knowledge* provided musical variety. The serious-minded could listen to religious shows *(National Radio Pulpit)* and public affairs broadcasts *(American Town Meeting of the Air)*. Radio was especially thrilling for children, who could not only follow the cliff-hanging adventures of their favorite heroes but also protect themselves with a Buck Rogers Solar Scout space helmet, drink their Ovaltine out of a Little Orphan Annie shake-up mug, learn lariat tricks from a Tom Mix secret manual, and break down enemy codes with a Captain Midnight decoder badge.

Radio possessed the special ability to keep listeners in instant touch with the hard, everyday facts of current world events. Consequently the medium took on a crucial importance as war escalated in Europe and Asia and, finally, drew the United States in. Letters from the front were highly censored, and newspapers and movie newsreels, although they provided important information, could not match the terrifying immediacy of Edward R. Murrow's radio reports from London in the Blitz or the strengthening solace of President Roosevelt's "fireside chats."

In Trenton, the long-established radio station, WTNJ, had recently been challenged by an upstart. The new outfit, WTTM, had its studio in the center of town on State Street, right between the city's two large hotels, the Stacy-Trent and the Hildebrecht. (Popular performers such as Paul Whiteman and his orchestra played the Hildebrecht's Mirror Room.) WTTM offered a variety of fare: local news reports, talk shows hosted by the prominent Trentonian ladies Mrs. Davenport and Mrs. Wolf, broadcasts of Trenton Symphony concerts, a program of Polish dance music announced by "polka king" Bernie Cosnowski, live Hungarian and Italian music programs, and a Puerto Rican show that featured Maltese station engineer Michael Fonde announcing in the stereotypical nasal "Spanish" voice of the time (think of Bill Dana as José Jiménez in the 1960s) and playing the records of Xavier Cugat and other Latin—not necessarily Puerto Rican—bands.

Because of the war, WTTM was short of personnel. "At the station most of the help had been drafted, and I worked from 6:00 A.M. till 1:00 A.M. every day with no help in sight," remembers Fonde, whose function as a radio engineer was deemed so critical to the war effort that when he tried to volunteer for the army he was turned away and told "that my job at the station was just as important as going overseas." Edna Vine was working across the street from WTTM, and through a connection she lined up a job interview at the station. (During this period WTTM hired its first female announcers.) But at the last minute, Vine decided that Ernie should go in her place. "He looked like he thought that was foolish," she says. "And I said, 'Please, Ernie, go. You can always change your mind. But I've already got the appointment. So instead of my going, you go.'"

The interview turned out to be an audition for a staff announcer's job. Since the program director had recently left, job candidates were being auditioned by an ad hoc "program committee" of three young men: piano player Eddie Hatrak; WTTM's first announcer, Tom Durand; and another announcer named Russ Andrews. "I'll never forget that first audition," says Eddie Hatrak. "Ernie took some piece of copy that he'd just picked up, some commercial, and at first he read it straight. And then he started to go off. He had us all in hysterics. He just had that knack of being funny on the spur of the moment if he wanted to be. He could talk about the weather and make it funny."

Ernie was assigned to work on a nightly music show that involved his playing about twenty records interspersed with commercials and station announcements. "When Ernie got onto it," says Hatrak, "gradually the records disappeared." Hatrak was producing some amateur contests, and Ernie began asking Eddie to bring some of the contest talent onto his program. He also started reading comics such as "Dick Tracy" on the air, while Eddie Hatrak taking the part of Eighty-eight Keys and Ernie performing the rest of the roles. The commercials got "pushed all the way to the end of the program," says Hatrak. "There were certain things that had to be done—not only for sponsors, but some FCC things you have to do. He bunched them all in five minutes and did them all 'Rrrrrat-ti-ti-tat!' Rapid fire." Hatrak had first met

Ernie in 1937 at Trenton High (Ernie had shaken his hand with a palm buzzer), and at WTTM they formed a close and enduring friendship. After a while, "wherever you saw Ernie you saw Eddie," says George Quinty, Sr., a Trenton-based big-band sax player who used to visit Ernie at the drugstore.

Because he and Mary needed the money, Ernie continued to work behind the United Perfumery cigar counter during the day while manning the WTTM microphones at night. "Ernie was always playing it pretty close to the vest," says Hatrak. "The radio station didn't pay very much." His friends and family, who visited him frequently at the drugstore, would now find him immersed in writing up ideas for the radio. If anybody wanted to buy cigars, he would tell them to help themselves and leave the money on top of the cash register.

Although Ernie was initially hired only for the short announcing shift, he was soon taking on more and more duties—and more and more airtime. He ran quiz programs for which Edna Vine recruited panelists on the spur of the moment. "One was a puzzle," she recalls. "He would make up the questions in poetry form, and you had to figure that out. They were subtle, so he needed good panels." Another one was called *The Kudra College of Knowledge*, which he created as an advertising vehicle for his friend George Kudra's House of Kudra Furs. Modeled after the college quiz shows that were then popular in radio, the program offered three winners $3.33 each; the total represented the address of Kudra Furs at 999 South Broad Street.

Ernie also performed in radio plays, for which, again, he would enlist Edna Vine's aid. Vine remembers bringing a woman to WTTM to act in *The Little Foxes* because "she wanted very much to do it. So I told him she was good, and he didn't audition her. On the air she would miss a line and say, 'Oh, I'm sorry,' and then go on. I'll never forget Ernie's face. He expected you to be good if you were doing something." At one point he even convinced Minerva Davenport, a writer and actress who hosted a daily women's talk show, to devise a running dramatic series for him. "He wanted a script where he could play two people, do a voice change and a character change," explains Davenport. She created *The Last Time I Saw Paris*, a half-hour series in which Ernie took the lead role of Paris Greene, a roguish private detective, and the secondary part of Harvard Herrigan, Greene's occasional henchman.

"Paris was a Frenchman, an admirer of women," describes Davenport. "The other character was his friend, a tough fellow of the streets. So he had to use two dialects. And I played Arabella Donahue, an old

maiden lady who loved him as a son. He'd always take her along because he felt that she had a woman's intuition." Actually, a good deal
of flirtation went on between the feisty Arabella and the suave Paris in
these light and charming tales. Each episode opened and closed the
same way: over a man's voice whistling "The Last Time I Saw Paris,"
one would hear a woman pleading, "Kiss me again, Paris. Please kiss
me again!" then a second woman vowing, "I love you, Paris. Now I
know I love you!" These were followed by screams, gunshots, and
Arabella's voice reminiscing: "Music . . . romance . . . adventure. That
to me means . . . Paris!"

Among his other regular programs was *Coffee with Kovacs*, a weekday morning show in which he played popular music of the day, talked
about what was happening around Trenton, and occasionally interviewed guests. Eventually Ernie took on the 6:00 A.M. announcing shift
as well. Fonde recalls that Ernie was forever late, driving fast over State
Street, dashing into the station, colliding with the postman, and then
complaining to his listeners about the terrible pothole on State Street
that jostled his car. (So vociferously did he complain that a cop finally
staked him out and caught him speeding.) "He never knew how to
drive slowly," says Fonde. "He used to come from West State Street—
ooh, flying!"

Between the radio shows and the cigar-counter job, Ernie was becoming quite a fixture in Trenton. "He wanted to be recognized," says
Joe Butera, a musician whose combos often free-lanced at WTTM. "If
there was a customer he thought he recognized, he'd run from the station and go over and sell the guy a cigar. Or if not, he'd smoke a big
cigar on the corner." Even at private affairs, he enjoyed commanding
attention. Ernie's old Parkway Avenue neighbor Helen Wilson, who
dated him off and on during the war, remembers escorting him to a
party and "him jumping into the room and saying, 'Here I am, you
lucky people!' Everybody said, 'Wow! Who's this?' And then he would
proceed to be the life of the party."

Though Ernie had deeply loyal friends in Trenton, some people
"viewed him as an unworthwhile eccentric, I'm afraid," says Edna Vine.
"The people who were so totally sober here thought him a screwball.
He never would fit into the norm—never. This is what I found very
exciting, but other people didn't. And then, from what I understand,
he owed some money. He would get things and maybe not be able to
meet the payments, and the people he owed the money to didn't think
kindly of him." In fact, he was becoming known for spending money
promiscuously, even while he was obviously struggling hard to make

ends meet. "If Ernie had it in his pocket, he had to spend it. I think he got it from his father," says Marion Shapiro. (The management of finances did seem as much of a mystery to Andrew Kovacs as to his son. In 1943, while working as a police guard for Westinghouse, Andrew finally filed for bankruptcy; he owed bills going back to the 1930s, for products and services ranging from tobacco, coal, gasoline, and groceries to clothes, furniture, car parts, and surgery.)

But even while owing money, Ernie loved to lavish it on others. One friend remembers Ernie taking him downtown and saying, "Will you go in the store with me and try on some clothes? I want to buy someone some Christmas presents, and he's just about your size." They picked out a complete outfit—jacket, shirt, shoes, everything. When Christmas rolled around, Ernie presented the friend with an enormous box containing the outfit they had chosen. But when Ernie was put in the position of receiving from somebody, he became embarrassed. Michael Fonde says that once he loaned Ernie $40, and Ernie, who had taken up photography as a hobby, gave him his camera as collateral. Fonde later tried to return the camera, "but he would never take it back." Donald Mattern, who joined WTTM as an announcer after the war, remembers Ernie covering for him on three shows while he went on vacation. "When I came back, I said, 'Ernie, I owe you some money for doing the shows.' He put out his big ham of a hand and said, 'All right. Lay it in there.'" After Mattern had counted the money into his hand, Ernie said, "Put your hand out" and gave the money back. "I said, 'Ernie, I owe you this.' He said, 'No, you don't.' He really didn't like to take things from people."

Nevertheless, Ernie always seemed in need of money. "Anytime there was a paying announcer's job, he wanted in," recalls Joe Butera. "We opened the Diamond Casino up in Burlington. 'I've got to have that job, Joey, I've got to have that job!'" For a while Kovacs and Johnny Thompson, a singer at WTTM, worked part-time at a plant nursery owned by their agent. "They didn't know the difference between poison ivy and an oak tree," says Mattern. Customers came in and spouted off their requests in Latin, and Ernie would engage them in conversation while Johnny ran to the back to look up the plant in a book. "Then he would stand in the next aisle of trees and shrubs and read from the book, and Ernie would very pompously announce it as newfound knowledge," says Mattern.

But his favorite jobs were the radio jobs, and eventually he phased out his other odd jobs and worked at WTTM more than full-time. It helped that Ernie had joined the station at an auspicious time in its history. "WTNJ had bigger coverage than WTTM had at the time," says Joe Butera, who played music for both stations, "but WTTM had better salesmen, and they went network." In fact, the young WTTM became an affiliate of the NBC Radio network quickly, at the end of World War II. "The network affiliation made a big difference, because then we had all the major names—the Bob Hopes, the daily soap operas," Donald Mattern says. Chunks of local programming were interspersed with the major national shows throughout the day, and sometimes programs originating from WTTM were broadcast nationally over NBC. "For example," recalls Mattern, "Paul Whiteman came down from his farm above Lambertville and did a daily record show from our station, but then they would feed it to the network from Trenton." The network affiliation made WTTM an excellent training ground for anybody serious about radio. "You had to do everything— your own production, your own announcing, even your own selling whenever possible," says Mattern. "We were a very energetic bunch and very ambitious."

One of the things that Ernie did was to form a team with engineer Michael Fonde to produce "remotes," as coverage outside the studio is called. Together they would drive around to report on events in Trenton and outlying areas. In those days there were no live feeds except from the studio, so remotes were recorded in the field and then brought back to the studio to be replayed on the air. The equipment was primitive: wire recorders, weighty and cumbersome machines on which spools of wire took a magnetic impression of sound. They were hard to use because the wire "would get knotted and twisted and break," says Tom Durand, who was working as an announcer, newsman, and program director at WTTM; if the wire broke, an entire story might be lost. A little later they began to use the earliest sorts of recording tape, actually paper tape coated with copper oxide, to capture, again, magnetic impressions of sound—a "sound mirror," as Fonde describes them. "The machine was almost as big as a coffee table and really heavy," Durand says. As for WTTM's remote "mobile unit, so-called, it was nothing but a big delivery truck with a desk in it, and on the desktop were the tape recorder and a converter to convert power to AC, which was needed to run the machine."

Though crude by today's standards, in the 1940s this was state-of-the-art technology. And the technology of the medium was one of its true fascinations then, not just for the people working in radio but for the listeners, too. "What gripped radio's first audiences was the medium, not the message," Norman Corwin, a distinguished radio writer, director, and producer who now teaches at the University of Southern California, has pointed out. "Content mattered less than the distance over which a program was heard. Fans in the East would stay up until 3:00 A.M. to try to pull in Chicago, and if they succeeded they bragged about it the next day." People would buy "Radioplause Cards" (twenty-four cards for twenty-five cents, remembered Corwin), log things they heard from a great distance, mail their cards to the originating stations, and receive verifications that the station "had indeed broadcast this or that at the time noted; and these cards," according to Corwin, "like the foreign hotel stickers that once illuminated the luggage of travelers, became showoff items, trophies to be displayed on a wall."

If the technology fascinated listeners, it absolutely captivated Ernie. He loved doing remotes, which allowed him to seem to be everywhere at once, and they greatly expanded on the limited possibilities of the studio. "We were always out," says Fonde. "They used to say, whenever anything was happening in Trenton, 'Oh, there's Ernie and Mike. I guess we'll be hearing about it on the radio.'" They would get the word that a story was breaking, grab the keys to the remote truck, and rush to the site, where Ernie reported on the events in progress while Fonde manned the recording equipment.

The remotes became such an integral part of Ernie's work at WTTM that Eddie Hatrak, who left Trenton for a couple of years to tour with Belle Baker's band, was surprised when he returned to find that Ernie had become the station's "director of special events." Many times Kovacs and Fonde's remotes covered everyday people or occurrences. Ernie's cousin Colin Riker remembered dropping in on his remotes at the Famous Restaurant. "He'd ask people questions and give them a dollar if they won. Usually it was something like, Who was the first president of the United States?" He would also do interviews at the Lincoln Theater, a downtown movie palace with a fancy organ that rose out of the floor. During intermissions, organist Bolton Holmes would play, "and they used to flash words on the screen and people would sing along," remembers Trenton resident Elaine Vulgaris. "Ernie would go down the aisles with a microphone, and put it in front of people so their voices would carry, stop and ask questions, things like that."

But at other times the remotes brought real news to WTTM listeners. When the national commander of the American Legion came to town, "Ernie followed him all day in the wagon from the radio station, recording what he had to say, what other people had to say," recalls Francis J. Lucas, a frequent advertiser on WTTM. Eddie Hatrak remembers Ernie interviewing the governor of New Jersey during this period. In the late 1940s, on a show called *Talk of the Town*, he would cover such events as the opening of Canal House 16, an art-movie theater in New Hope, Pennsylvania, and interview such celebrities as author Budd Schulberg and television how-to artist Jon Gnagy (whom Ernie would later spoof on TV). And in 1949, when an army veteran in Camden went berserk and shot sixteen people, Ernie got there fast enough to interview witnesses to the massacre. "He was like Johnny-on-the-spot on that one," says Hatrak. Kovacs' news reporting eventually earned him an H. P. Davis broadcast journalism award (named after one of Westinghouse's early and visionary vice-presidents).

Sometimes Ernie's remotes tilted toward the imaginative and wacky. Once, to cover a Christmas parade in Trenton, Fonde strapped Ernie to the front of the vehicle, and he drove in the parade as Ernie reported. After they finished their report, they followed Santa Claus through the packed streets, playing the recording back like mischievous elves. When Kovacs decided to treat his listeners to the experience of learning how to fly, he "cooked up a deal with flying lessons" at the Morrisville airport, says Tom Durand. To record each lesson, he had to attach a big battery to a converter that was in turn attached to the heavy wire recorder and strap all this equipment down in the plane. "He took all this up for every lesson, and the interest on the part of the listeners was building, week by week," says Durand. "Then finally it came time for Ernie to solo, and he panicked! He was up there trying to figure out how to pilot the plane, too terrified to speak. On the wire he brought back, there were big pauses where all you heard was the motor."

Ernie was forever "cooking up deals" such as this one for the flying lessons, which were presumably gotten for free. In 1949, as a promotional stunt for WTTM, it was decided that Ernie would do a live broadcast nonstop for a week from the New Jersey State Fair, which was held every September. A temporary broadcast booth was set up on a platform on the fairground midway, and billboard signs went up promising that WTTM's Ernie Kovacs would not sleep for one week. A newspaper report described the marathon in grueling detail: "His daily round includes interviews with visitors at the fair at 12:15 P.M., a half-hour of commentary, news, and interviews at 1:00 P.M., the commercials and station identification at fifteen- or thirty-minute intervals the rest of the day, from midnight until 9:00 A.M. each morning a disc jockey session with intervals of reading the news, [and from] 9:00 A.M. to 12:15 P.M. more commercials and station identifications." But the report neglected to mention Ernie's favorite part of the schedule. He had cleverly invited chefs from Trenton's finer restaurants—the ones whose cuisine he particularly wanted to enjoy—to promote their establishments on the air; they accomplished this goal by preparing and serving Ernie his dinner at the fairground each evening during the broadcast, on a table covered with white linen and set with china.

Fortified by his gourmet meals, Ernie did finish the sleepless weeklong marathon, but most people never found out that he had not remained at the fairground the entire time. "At times," explains Michael Fonde, "I recorded him so he could go home and take a shower and change his clothes." Tom Durand confirms this story. What audiences heard was, at least part of the time, an illusion created by the technology of radio. Both men, however, insist that Ernie really did not sleep during that week, even when he sneaked home.

The stunt of staying awake for a week, an enormously difficult (if not impossible) feat for most people, was actually based on Ernie's minimal need for sleep. "I could never understand how he got along with the amount of sleep he got," says Eddie Hatrak. "It seemed to me that he was constantly getting two or three hours of sleep a night. Because I would be with him. I would know what time he got to bed." Many people tell similar stories, and the fact has become a part of the mythology surrounding Ernie Kovacs.

Two other WTTM remotes have become part of the Kovacs legend. They apparently never occurred, but people believe the stories because they fit the image they have of Ernie. Once, it is said, Ernie wanted to let his listeners know what it felt like to be a rabbit during hunting season, so he took his microphone into a trench in a field and recorded the sound of bullets whistling overhead. Another time, the tale goes, in order to report on what it feels like to be run over by a train, Ernie lay down on the tracks in the Trenton trainyard. Faced by an oncoming locomotive, he suddenly lost his nerve, and audiences heard the train pulverizing the mike he had left behind. These anecdotes have been printed and reprinted and passed on; the train-track stunt even serves as the opening sequence of the 1984 ABC Television movie *Ernie Kovacs: Between the Laughter*. But Michael Fonde, who engineered virtually all of Ernie's remotes, has no recollection that these incidents ever occurred, nor do other former WTTM staff members. Indeed, these daring remotes strike Fonde as sounding "too dangerous even for Ernie."

When he wasn't doing remotes, he was back in the WTTM studio, where he seemed to be in a perpetual state of motion. He'd dash in just as the NBC chimes were sounding, grab a microphone, deliver a thirty-second commercial, and then dash out again. Or he'd be on the phone wheeling and dealing, lining up freebies or sponsors or devising new ideas for commercials or shows. "He used to wear a wraparound camel's hair coat. But the belt was always dragging behind him, and the coat was always open and flapping in the breeze," Donald Mattern says. "So he comes in like that one day and says, 'I just heard a story.' Everybody stops to listen. 'It's the story of a man who went hunting for bear. He saw the bear, and he held his gun. He motioned with his index finger for the bear to come. The bear started after him, and the man lifted the gun to shoot, but the trigger wouldn't work. So the bear rushed up, grabbed the gun, rushed back ten feet, and motioned with his index finger to come.' And that was it. He was gone. He'd make an appearance, tell a story, and then leave."

But telling stories was a relatively sedate activity for Ernie to engage in; more often, he preferred to invent and carry out practical jokes. (In a group portrait shot around this time, Ernie, very neat in a nicely cut pinstripe suit, takes his place among his WTTM colleagues. Every other person is looking seriously at the camera. Ernie is glancing sideways, just on the verge of breaking up, as if an invisible spirit is whispering a wonderful joke in his ear.) Anyone might become a target of his assault at any moment: colleagues, superiors, sponsors, guests. Anarchy was the rule, and illusions—visual, aural, or technological—were often the means to this highly entertaining end. Once he lowered a rubber spider in front of a singer as she was performing. "She started screaming on the air," says Fonde. Another time he taped down the receiver buttons on all the phones, then threw the switchboard switches to make them all ring at once. Mattern remembers being on the air as Ernie crawled into the studio, disappeared underneath Mattern's table, and brought up his oversized hand waving the microphone plug, as if he had disconnected it. Durand tells of Ernie fooling "an extremely jumpy chief engineer" into thinking that he, Ernie, had broken an expensive plate glass window while practicing golf indoors; Ernie had created this illusion by taping a split Ping-Pong ball onto the window and decorating the glass with grease-pencil shatter marks.

Ernie was constantly stepping outside the established bounds in this way. "There was one announcer who was very serious and pompous," says Billie Durand, an actress and writer who free-lanced for WTTM and was married to Tom Durand. "Ernie would set his script on fire." Indeed, sometimes it seemed that Ernie was on a self-appointed mission to keep all around him off balance. "Breaking them up and not letting them be self-contained—it was almost as though he were competing with them," says Mattern. "He would not let people be themselves. But the time he finished breaking them up, they were laughing so hard that they didn't care anyway. And if you did get mad, he would turn it right around on you, make another joke out of it."

One group of people probably did get mad at him. Ernie could become verbally abusive, says Tom Durand, and his anger "would be directed mostly toward management and sales personnel. Sales he considered to be cheap, aggrandizing people who'd never give announcers an even break." A salaried announcer who performed a commercial for a sponsor was eligible for an extra "talent fee," paid by the sponsor. "Ernie hated the salesmen because they were reluctant to ask for the talent fee," says Durand. "If the talent fee was the breaking point for selling a show, the salespeople would not take it. That sort of thing made Ernie very angry."

Consequently, Ernie would bypass the sales staff and negotiate his own deals. "He would sell himself and set his own fees," remembers Mattern, who says this procedure was unusual. Mattern, however, felt that Ernie bypassed the salespeople because he did not want them to boss him around on behalf of their clients. "He was completely undisciplined. He wanted to do it strictly his own way and not be badgered or have a salesman say, 'Look, the client is complaining about you. He didn't like the way you read his commercial. He didn't like this. He didn't like that.' That's why he didn't like the salesmen—they would create problems for him."

Even though he was perpetually in need of money, Ernie also refused to compete against the other staff announcers for jobs that would earn him the extra talent fees. "He would have a show, sell it on his own, or have a friend develop a show for him and put it on himself," Mattern says. "But if a sponsor came in and said, 'I want to hear some auditions,' Ernie did not get involved in that. He would not compete. 'Take me as I am.' He didn't like to subject himself to the possibility of losing an audition, and he could not stand criticism."

Ernie's attitude was often one of outrage against any form of authority. His was a deeply rebellious nature, and the older he became and the more he confronted and thought about the world, the more recalcitrant and irreverent he grew. Ernie's rebelliousness—his feeling that integrity lay within *him* and that society imposed strictures upon him primarily as a way to thwart what he wanted to do—was a double-edged sword. It would become the source both of some of his best work and of some of his deepest difficulties in the years ahead.

Bruce L. Rhoads, a high school buddy of Ernie's, remembers that at this time Ernie was known for loving fancy cars, cigars, and "gals." Once Rhoads was riding with him in one of those extravagant cars, which, he said, Ernie kept "like the back of a dump truck. It was literally littered with everything imaginable, and on the front seat of the car as I got in to sit down alongside of Ernie were several empty Coke bottles." As they drove along Ernie "was looking on both sides of the street— he had a very definite eye for pretty girls. And as he spotted one on the right hand side of the street, he gaily waved to her and shouted." As he was doing so, a bus stopped in front of them. Ernie applied his brakes, but a Coke bottle had gotten jammed underneath the pedal. "Of course, our speed continued the same as ever, and we went into the back of the bus at thirty miles an hour. If you can visualize what happened after that— smoke, steam, hot water; and I can still remember Ernie as we were towed down the street by the wrecker, still waving at the girls on both sides of the street."

Publicly, Ernie acted rakish, the lively boulevardier with a penchant for pretty women. The mischief that he exhibited among his radio colleagues extended to his relationships with women as well. Helen Wilson remembers that one time Ernie was late to pick her up for a movie. "We were walking along downtown to go to the Lincoln, and of course I was giving him a bad time that we were going to miss the first part of the movie. So he went over to this man walking down the street and said, 'I don't know if you know this or not, but it's very important. You're probably missing the first part of the movie at the Lincoln.' Well, I had to laugh." After the movies they would go to Child's for scones and tea, and if Wilson complained about the slow service, "Ernie would turn to the waitress and say, 'All right, Helen, now tell the waitress what you just told me about her.'"

Underneath the mischief, Ernie possessed a special ability to make the person he was with feel as

CHAPTER

5

though he or she were the most important person in the world at that moment. "You could sit and talk to Ernie by the hour," says Wilson. "You could talk to him about everything and anything." He also retained an old-fashioned sense of gallantry toward the opposite sex. Michael Fonde recalls traveling with Ernie to New York to interview the ambassador from South Korea for WTTM. Out of respect, says Fonde, "before we recorded, Ernie told her that he wouldn't ask her age on the air." (She responded, however, "Oh, please do. In Korea we always *add* age.") Louis ("Deke") Heyward, a staff writer for Ernie's television and radio shows in the mid-1950s, perceived Ernie as "a frightened gallant. He would put his arms around a woman, I don't think because he wanted to, but because the guy before him had done the same thing, and this made him more one of the boys. I think he treated them—and the word *gallant* I think is proper for him—he was cavalier. He respected women, and to me he did not take advantage of them, and putting your arms around a woman uninvited I think he felt was wrong. He would just as soon have kissed their hand or made a gesture toward that. He was a little out of sync with his time that way."

In the 1940s, when the Hotel Hildebrecht was in its prime, Trentonians used to get dressed up and step out to the hotel's Mirror Room ("Trenton's only supper club," as a newspaper ad of the time boasted); there they would dance and drink and enjoy the floor shows. The WTTM studios were close by, and one night in 1945, while the war was still going on, Ernie dropped in at the Hildebrecht just as a show was starting. His friend Sydney Leavitt asked him to join his party, and during the performance Ernie kept looking at one of the dancers. Leavitt was acquainted with the troupe, so he arranged an introduction for Ernie after the show. The dancer's name was Bette Lee Wilcox, and Ernie wound up marrying her.

Bette Lee Wilcox was born September 3, 1923, in Daytona Beach, Florida. The daughter of Warren and Isabella ("Sally") Watkins Wilcox, she was still making her home in Daytona Beach at the time she met Ernie. (According to Ernie's friend George Kudra, she used the stage name Lolita and "would do these Spanish dances." Sydney Leavitt, however, believes that it was the head of the dance troupe, not Bette, who called herself Lola.) With her petite dancer's body, beautiful pale complexion, liquid brown eyes, and long dark hair framing an oval face, Bette was "very pretty in an exotic way," says Billie Durand. "She was good-natured and likable, and because she was a dancer, she moved beautifully." Her daughter Elisabeth Kovacs remembers going to a school dance to which parents were invited, and "it seemed as though the men were dropping like flies in her presence. She was very sultry. She was just a very attractive woman."

"He fell in love instantly. That was that," remembers Edna Vine. "He was very much in love with Bette." Apparently it didn't take Bette long to return the sentiment, for their courtship was brief. On July 18, in the final days of the war, they applied for a marriage license. On August 11 Japan surrendered, and World War II at last came to an end. Two days later, on a hot and humid Monday, Ernie Kovacs and Bette Wilcox were married at noon by the Reverend Elmer Walker at a quaint Presbyterian church in Ewing Township. It was the first marriage for both of them. He was twenty-six; she, twenty-one.

"They were very much in love," remembers Marion Shapiro, who served as matron of honor and who "liked Bette tremendously. I think there was some Indian blood in her. She was very, very pretty, bubbly and sweet and a lot of fun." Tom Kovacs, having returned safely from the war, was his half brother's best man. The marriage came a little quickly, but "it wasn't so sudden that they didn't have time to arrange a nice church wedding with a small reception afterwards," explains Shapiro. "All of his friends were there, about forty or fifty people. It was a very nice reception for that day, because at that time elaborate receptions weren't the rule. We had champagne. And knowing Ernie, you had to have caviar, of course. That was Ernie. He had everything or nothing."

Bette stopped dancing professionally and settled into the postwar role of "F.W." or "Favorite Wife," as Ernie affectionately referred to her in public. She would accompany her new husband on his WTTM remotes with Michael Fonde. "Every time we went out on remote he used to bring her. He loved that girl and always called her the F.W.," says Fonde. She also kept him company at the wrestling matches at the Trenton Armory, which he announced once a week. "He used to get so excited: 'Boy, did you see this guy with blood on his head?'" remembers Fonde, who says Ernie was upset when he learned that the blood was fake and that the wrestlers were the best of friends.

There was, however, a major problem with the marriage right from the start, and that problem was Mary Kovacs. Ernie was living with his mother on Brunswick Avenue when he married Bette. Although by mid-September he and Bette had moved to Warner Village, it is possible that Mary moved with them, for there was an acute shortage of housing following the war, and in addition it was common practice in Hungarian families for several generations to live together under one roof. In any case, Mary took an immediate dislike to her new daughter-in-law. "She was a volatile woman—screamed and yelled very quickly, flew off the handle. She wanted to keep Ernie for herself. She was furious when he was going to get married," says Marion Shapiro. "One day in the drugstore she was ranting about him marrying Bette. She said, 'Why couldn't he marry a girl like you?' I said, 'If it was me, you'd feel the same way.' 'Oh, no,' she said. I said, 'Oh, don't tell me. It's not Bette, it's any girl Ernie might marry.'"

The WTTM staff became accustomed to seeing Bette with Ernie on remotes or Mary with Ernie at the station, but they rarely if ever saw all three together. "Mary did not travel with Bette at all," says Donald Mattern. There was a common perception that Mary was upset because Ernie had been her meal ticket and now that he was married he would have less money to spend on her. Michael Fonde felt that Ernie "was afraid of her. To me she was too dominating, too selfish. Give her this"—he rubs his fingers together to signify money—"and she's okay."

Money did in fact become the focus of some of the conflicts. Several friends recollect that whatever Ernie bought for his new wife, he had to buy in duplicate for his mother. But money wasn't really what Mary cared about; it was her son's love and attention that concerned her, and this she always had from him. "Ernie got along with her beautifully," says Edna Vine. "Maybe when he got married and there were really important fights, maybe he fought. But I never saw him get angry with her. He definitely was in control of it with her. They understood each other; they had this intrinsic bond, and it wasn't just mother and son. He just understood her personality and what she needed." (It is possible too that Bette may have had her own problems with jealousy. Vine says that after Ernie was married, "he told me that she'd better not see us together, that Bette was very jealous.")

Ernie's solution in the face of conflict on the home front was to escape into work. Even though Bette went with him on the WTTM remotes, these were only a small portion of his radio duties. And around the time of his marriage he added a new job to his schedule, in a different medium. On June 15, 1945, a local media man named Sam Jacobs had begun publishing a small weekly newspaper called the *Trentonian*, working at first out of a photography studio run by Michael Fonde. Jacobs was a flamboyant Trenton character who loved good food, cigars, and talk; he was near Ernie's age, and they had been friends for some years. "It was a one-man newspaper," says Eunice Jacobs, his widow. "My husband wrote, picked up the ads, delivered the paper. Since Ernie was naturally humorous, Sam thought he'd be able to write a good column. I mean, if you spent an evening with Ernie, you'd die laughing."

Jacobs hired Kovacs to write a column for the fledgling paper, to be called "Kovacs Unlimited." Basically, Ernie started out writing up plugs of Trenton restaurants, in exchange for which he would receive free meals, often not only for himself but for friends he brought along. Soon he was "reviewing" restaurants farther afield, in places like Seaside Park and Atlantic City. But the column changed into something much more interesting and personal when the *Trentonian* was acquired by the International Typographical Union as the result of a labor strike.

The ITU's Trenton Local 71 had been in conflict with the *Trenton Times*, the city's wealthy and powerful monopoly daily newspaper, since 1943, when ITU workers refused to cross a Teamsters' picket line at the *Times* and the paper was forced to shut down its plant for a month. Relations steadily worsened, and in the winter of 1945–46 the union went on strike. To provide the striking typographers with jobs, the union acquired the *Trentonian* in April 1946. By August the new publishers had moved the paper out of Sam Jacobs' old headquarters and increased its publication to twice weekly, then to three times weekly, then, fairly quickly, to daily. The *Trentonian* is one of the few strike-born papers in the United States to have survived to this day (although a new publisher took it over from the ITU in 1949).

Ernie was taking an active part in unions throughout this period. In September 1945 he had joined Local B-1343 of the International Brotherhood of Electrical Workers, the radio employees' union. (To the question "How long have you been in the business?" on his application form, Ernie answered, "Nine years," which refers back to his *Pirates of Penzance* performance in high school.) He succeeded Michael Fonde as president of their IBEW local in 1949, and in 1950 he was reelected to the post. Among other duties, the presidency required Ernie to negotiate the local's annual contracts with WTTM and national IBEW representatives, to line up potential job candidates if any positions opened up at WTTM, and—in a chilling sign of the times—to submit an affidavit that he was not a Communist. He was also involved peripherally in the typographers' union, as the announcer for the ITU's weekly broadcasts on WTTM. So when the ITU took over the *Trentonian*, he was invited to continue his column for the new publishers.

For his friend Sam Jacobs, he had written the column as a lark and in trade for meals—no pay; now he was offered the princely sum of twenty-five cents per inch of text. Ernie's column was renamed "Kovacs" and topped with a new logo, a drawing he made of a cow with stick legs and a stick torso and stick grass in its mouth. The cow's eyes were dollar signs, as was the grass growing beneath her feet, waiting to be eaten. "Kovacs" ran every day, usually directly opposite the paper's Broadway column, both flanking the funnies that were displayed across the middle of a two-page spread. Chatty and thoroughly unpious, "Kovacs" rambled through personal escapades, local gossip, plugs (no longer limited to restaurants, Ernie now plugged everything from the newest Spike Jones record to the hottest Broadway show), philosophical pronouncements by funny invented characters, and criticism of popular performers such as Perry Como and Rudy Vallee. (These generated angry letters, which Ernie typed up and submitted as text for his column, charging his usual rate per inch.)

In the tradition of cracker-barrel columnists, Ernie wrote his daily piece as if it were a hometown letter to an old friend—or, more accurately, to a large group of friends. Always referring to himself as *we* and addressing his readers as *ridders*, he drew his newspaper audience into his intimate inner circle by creating a special language to share with them, sprinkling his printed prose with the kinds of misspellings typically made by children learning to write. The column was the *kolimm*, an erratum became an *omittum*, weeks were transformed into *wikks*, anything local was rendered as *lokkil*, orchestras were abbreviated to *orks*, all examples were prefaced by *f'r'n'st'nce*, and the police officers to whom he often addressed kudos, complaints, and advice were respectfully called *Ahficcah*. The silliness of Ernie's secret language was made doubly pleasurable because it was surrounded by straightforward journalistic prose.

In the column Ernie let his mind roam to any subject that happened to catch his fancy. He would inform readers that the "F.W." was searching high and low for a corduroy jacket, let them know that Charlie (the Lincoln Pharmacy pharmacist) had just returned from visiting his cousin Henry (a director of Rosalind Russell movies), and advise them that the Bordentown diner's "'personal juke box' at table No. 3 is busted and the music plays continually without putting in any money." Small personal incidents showed up in the paper, transformed into minor Kovacsian causes:

Dear Commissioner [Magee, the commissioner of police]:
 If it is possible to get fined because of poor taillights (which we think is a good idea), why not a fine for drivers who do not turn down high lights for approaching cars.
 The eternal flame of the high light is behind more night acci-

dents than Messrs' Haig and Haig. We have solved it by simply closing our eyes and letting go of the wheel when such a headlight approaches, but there may be other motorists who are not this clever.

Other causes were more serious. "The restaurants skirting Baltimore could form a good basis for a piece of legislation requiring the food and drug law officials to examine an eating place before they could nail 'Restaurant' over any doorway," he wrote after a trip out of state. "We were just maad about the jernt in Maryland that featured a big sign saying 'Whites Only,' with so many flies inside that if the proprietor ever took time out for swatting, he'd have less for racial prejudice."

Indeed, readers of Ernie's daily *Trentonian* column could gain a fair idea of his system of values. He instantly felt and was unashamed to express compassion for people he saw in difficult straits. In one especially touching column he described a visit to a small club where he was shocked to see a five-piece combo headed by trumpeter Del Forrest, who had once had his own big band. Ernie wonders, "How come the five-chunker," and is saddened to discover that Forrest is selling venetian blinds by day to support his family. "Incidentally," Ernie finishes up, trying to restore the musician some of his dignity, "his take-off on [Bunny] Berrigan's 'I Can't Get Started' is nothing short of perfect." At times Ernie even appealed directly to his readers to help somebody in need. In 1947, while housing was still difficult to obtain, he ran a letter from a pregnant woman with polio. She had been warned by the doctor that she would lose her baby if she didn't stop climbing stairs (it had happened once before, the previous summer), but she and her husband couldn't find a first-floor apartment. "Please help us get a place for our coming baby," the letter ended. "I pray there is some way you can help us." Ernie omitted her name (as if, again, to protect her dignity) and implored his readers, "If anyone has a first floor apartment for this couple, please contact us c/o WTTM."

As much as he loved to help people, he also enjoyed grousing about their habits and about incidents that annoyed him. Sometimes the complaints were expressed indirectly, sarcastically, as when he was evidently asked by some higher-up at the newspaper to assuage the feelings of an offended local business owner: "Erratum: The Creston Delicatessen on Nottingham Way is NOT a 'small' delicatessen, as we wrote. We hear it is the largest in the world. (We hear.)" He might even turn on his audience if they irritated him enough. One election day he wrote:

We'll be broadcasting rizzults over WTTM tonight until 2 ayem and three hours of box scores are tuff on the tonsils. Inevitably, on each election night, the first ten calls we get don't like the music we're playing and don't think we're talking slow enuff.

So, we change the music and talk slower. We get ten more calls. "Why did you change the music?" and "Can't you talk any faster than that?" Yezzir, it's here again.

One of Ernie's most frequent subjects of grievance—and a subject about which he wasn't always clear-headed or logical—was money. Money was a source of power and fun, and he needed it to support his family and himself and to live his life at the intense pitch he enjoyed. ("One of Ernie's pet sayings," recalls Joe Butera, "was that he was going to die with diamonds on his vest and owe a million.") But the mature management of money forever eluded him. He could get money, or live as if he had gotten it, but somehow it would mysteriously end up slipping between his fingers. And so he would go away on vacation, describing to readers how he and Bette "put four miles on the car before leaving the neighborhood, chasing around for the mailman (who is a very patient guy with us), to tell him about leaving our mail at some neighbors' home where the sight of isinglass-windows on envelopes wouldn't cause the heart failure we [suffer] at our joint every first-of-the-month." And then, upon return, he would use the column to vent his self-righteous anger when the mortgage came due: "We have never seen more impatient people [the finance company]. Fellas! We just got back from our vacation. We are broke. Busted. Sans moolah. Let us alone, paleese!" His resentment and frustration were most neatly summed up in a pronouncement he put in the mouth of one of his recurring column characters, the ever-cranky Aunt Torchy: "Rich people are only poor people with money."

Besides his monetary grousing, readers were treated to full-blown expositions on the delights of Ernie's trips. A vacation with Bette to Jacksonville in September 1947 became the subject of a series titled "Journey into 'The Soufland.'" The reporting began with the exciting pretrip breakfast at the local diner, where "Mr. Bingeleh Crosby, who very kindly did our last guest shot, was on the juke box singing 'Goodbye, My Lover, Goodbye.' [Whenever Ernie went on vacation, the Trentonian ran guest columns by Bing Crosby, Perry Como, Count Basie, Amos 'n' Andy, or Fibber McGee and Molly.] Though we appreciate the guest column, we thought the vocal send-off was just a trifle maudlin." The tale continued through towns large and small, capturing the dreariness that inevitably accompanies any long car trip: "Somewhere outside Camden [we] ran across a little town Paulsboro—

and you can spell that Paulsbore-o any time you want to." One night, "some 490 miles from the newsstand at State and Broad" in downtown Trenton, Ernie and Bette found themselves in a South Carolina town so small that when he asked to buy a newspaper he was laughed at. "We did the trip down in 1,050 miles, 96 gallons of gas, 110 quarts of oil, and 27 pints of beer and ale," he finally concluded. "We are still seeing 'U.S. Route' signs in our sleep."

Like his work at WTTM, in many ways the newspaper column foreshadowed Ernie's work in the new medium of television. Recurring made-up characters not unlike Aunt Torchy would become a staple on his shows. His casual, irreverent attitude toward everything around him would show up on TV (and much later would directly inspire such television talents as comedian David Letterman). The lampooning of movies, TV shows, commercials, and cultural stereotypes of every sort, which he would bring to full fruition on TV, was showing up in column copy such as this, a "peek into our portable plastic ball" at a radio brocadcast of the future:

> This is WA to Z the Alphabet Soup Network, going on the air. The first hour of broadcasting is sponsored by the Dunka Company . . . Dunka, the only caffeine with coffee completely removed . . . The two hours following the Dunka program are sponsored by Ebony Soap Corporation . . . Ebony, the maker of Zud, the soap powder that does everything . . . cleans teeth, spot welds, tightens leaky faucets, kills ants, roaches, and lice . . . .
>
> And now Zud presents "Texas Dallas." This program seeks the answer to the question on every woman's lips, "Can a Woman of thirty-three find teen-age romance?"

Indeed, one of the smartest aspects of Ernie's television work would be his ability to satirize and deflate the stereotypes and clichés relied upon by the various media, which he felt played down to audiences. He was honing this satirical ability throughout his years at the *Trentonian*. One day he might devote an entire column to tearing apart familiar Hollywood movie clichés. On another he might poke fun at the manufactured marital bliss displayed in a commercial in which a cunning wife assuages her husband's hunger with a can of Campbell's Soup: "Open letter to F.W.: Cookie, if we ever happen to throw open the door with a hungry shout on our moonlike kisses, and should a can of zup be open and ready, ditch it someplace and just say you didn't feel like cooking."

One writer has pointed out that "if you lived in Trenton in the Forties, you lived with Ernie." Actually, you lived with Ernie and Bette, or at least you felt as though you did, because Bette's presence was strong in her husband's *Trentonian* columns. He was always dropping references to her, recounting something they'd done together or, as in his Campbell's Soup commentary, using her as a sort of implied straight man around which he could structure his satirical points. And the frequent newspaper mentions of the "F.W." fit right in with those domesticity-mad times. At the war's end, some 11 million men and women had been released from the American armed forces and come home. With the determined singlemindedness of a people trying to put hard times and painful memories behind them, everybody seemed intent on getting married, buying detached single-family dwellings, and settling down to raise children. Children, especially, suddenly became a national obsession; in 1946 nearly 3.5 million babies were born, representing a 20 percent jump in the birthrate over the previous year.

What the nation was doing, Trenton was doing. "We were all newlyweds at the same time, just starting homes and so forth," says Billie Durand, who had met Tom Durand performing in USO shows on the road; they returned to Trenton in May 1946 and had their first daughter in 1948. Their friend Eddie Hatrak returned from his tour of duty with Belle Baker's band, went back to his job at WTTM, and began writing a music column titled "Back to Boogie" for the *Trentonian*. In September 1947 he devoted a long item to one Sonia Haisonak, featured vocalist with the Polish Falcon Band (she sang some Jerome Kern, Richard Rodgers, and the Russian pretzel song, "Bublitchki," a particular crowd pleaser). Soon afterward they were married—with Ernie serving as best man—and had their own baby, Eddie Jr.

Bette, too, became pregnant, in the fall of 1946. The following April, like many of their friends, the Kovacses bought their first house, a tiny bungalow at 61 Vincent Avenue in Hamilton Township, just off Nottingham Way. It was "a boxes-without-topses, one of those places thrown up after World War II," recalls Tom Durand. According to Billie Durand, "It was a very simple little bungalow; I remember thinking it was bright and cheery." Ernie referred to it as "our ivy-covered rat hole" in his column and thereafter "was always joking about the real estate man," says Michael Fonde. "He would joke about how branches were growing out of the windowsills because the wood of the house was still so green."

Mary Kovacs did not move with her son and daughter-in-law to Vincent Avenue. Nevertheless "she made it miserable for Bette," remembers Marion Shapiro. "She would run in and out of the house a lot. Ernie did manage financially to keep her in her own apartment, but she was constantly calling him: she was sick, she was this, she was that." But at least the move enabled Ernie and Bette to establish a separate life of their own. They decorated their new bungalow in typical 1940s fashion, with floral print drapes, a big chair for the man of the house, and a portable record player on which Bette would play her favorite songs over and over again. Their married friends would drop by "and we'd have a beer, a glass of wine, and sit and talk about kids," says Helen Wilson. "Bette was extremely hospitable. Now, you might go there and you couldn't find your way through the diapers and the toys and everything around, but she'd say, 'Please sit down. Have a cup of coffee.' She loved company."

One thing truly thrilled Ernie in these times: the birth of their first baby, Bette Lee Andrea (as an adult she would go by Elisabeth). During the pregnancy he excitedly attended to his F.W., and *Trentonian* readers received regular reports on the progress of the parents-to-be. Because of his job commitments, when Bette entered the maternity ward of Mercer Hospital, Ernie visited her "after the conventional visiting hours," according Tom Durand. "The security was not tight, and if you knew your way around the hospital, it wasn't any problem at all going through the back door and up to your wife's room to see her. Bette used to have Ernie bring her a hamburger and a milk shake for a little snack." He got away with his late-night visits until she requested onions on her hamburger, "and the nurses smelled the onions and followed it to Bette's room and kicked Ernie out."

On Saturday, May 17, 1947, the day after Bette Lee's birth, workaholic Ernie took a day off from his column, simply running the ecstatic announcement, "It's a Girl!" under the logo of the grass-munching cow. He picked it up again on the following Monday, declaring, "Rizzolved! Never again will we laugh at cartoons about nervous fathers. The cartooned waiting-room pacer has no chance to crinkle these old lips into the same old smile . . . The last-minute dash will be completely bereft of humor . . . And the fact that MY daughter is the cutest baby ever to be born in Mercer Hospital is serious business. Anyway, about as serious as we ever are."

Ernie's column that day exhibits his powers of observation and sense of absurdity as well as his obvious delight over the birth of his baby girl. It also precurses some of his work on television. "Leave me bend your fat ears with this tale of anxiety," he begins, then proceeds to sketch a convincing scenario of frayed male nerves in the early-morning hours. Complaining that there was nothing to read in the maternity ward but a *Trentonian* he had already read, a *Trenton Times* ("ooh, what I wrote!"), and a ten-cent edition of *Western Stories*, he recounts the effect of pulp literature on his already agitated state of mind:

> We stuck another cigar in our spacious mouth without bothering to remove the other two and a half-filled pipe and continued pacing. . . . We tried reading the dam [sic] book, but after 12 "reckons," two "raw steel in his voice," three "whale-bone frames," four "galvanized into action" (which reminded us each time of a garbage pail, well galvanized), and one "she's a peaceful afternoon, I aim she should stay that way," we quit and went back to pacing . . .

A decade later, Ernie would build one of his most incisive series of sketches around a related theme, that of the clichés rampant on TV Westerns.

The next paragraph also foreshadows his television work. It is structured like many of his blackouts, with the payoff having a typically Kovacsian twist: "Two gals who were cleaning gave us some comfort," wrote the jittery father. "The first to enter said our F.W. was resting comfortably and we should expect news in an hour or so and the second came through and said we'd know in a minute or two . . . The third person was the F.W. who came up to sit with us. 'No one to talk to,' she said."

He finishes by indulging in a burst of pride and simultaneously satirizing the indulgence. "Johnny Thompson [a fellow expectant father] and we stood outside the glass window while the very patient nurse again held up our progeny. We told each other how much better off 'you are,' but deep down inside we BOTH knew we each had the best-looking female ever handled by those very swell nurses at Mercer . . . We faithfully promise to never print a single brilliant thing our daughter says. With this kolimm, we end the matter . . . But, now that we mention it, did we tell you . . ."

On January 4, 1949, Bette gave birth to their second daughter, Kip Raleigh. Both girls had thick sable hair and immense brown eyes, but little Bette Lee resembled her mother, with her small build and her love of moving to music; Ernie's pet name for her was Einstein. Kippie took after her father, inheriting his larger, stockier physique and his propensity for clowning around and making people laugh. Ernie was enamored of his little girls; they quickly became the center of his emotional life. "He was a wonderful father. He just idolized the children," says Helen Wilson. He would take them to Cadwalader Park, where there were animal rides and a merry-go-round, and to the annual WTTM family picnics. "He was really great with children, all children. He was always making them laugh," remembers Billie Durand.

With his daughters Ernie was attentive, gentle, and playful; he had the special ability to imagine himself inside a child's mind and heart. Playwright Marc Connelly, who became close to the family in the 1950s, recalled that after Kippie and little Bette had seen the play *Peter Pan*, they asked their father to teach them how to fly. Ernie took them to the New York Athletic Club and put them in the pool and said, "This is very much like flying, except you're doing it in water." "The children were delighted with that consideration, so they flew and enjoyed swimming as they never had before," said Connelly.

Parenthood was less enthralling for Bette, who as the housewife was saddled with many more of the child-rearing responsibilities than her always-working husband. "She was very young, and I think she was beginning to resent being tied down. And Ernie was away from the house a lot," says Marion Shapiro. "I think she was very concerned about her looks, and I think she was sorry that she had married. Maybe she thought she could have gone on to be a great dancer. Everybody has dreams, and I think she felt she'd given up too much."

According to Elisabeth Kovacs, "We always had the feeling that she was very much in her own world, singing in the kitchen while she did dishes." The portable record player in the living room was forever on, and Bette would play songs like "I Love Paris" "over and over and over again, like a teenager would," remembers Elisabeth. "She and I both loved to listen to these 45s. So she'd be in the kitchen singing, and I'd always be dancing in the living room."

The feeling she was left with as a little girl, however, was not that she was sharing something wonderful with her mother but that she was being neglected. "It was happier when my father was there with us," says Elisabeth. "I felt cared for and loved in his presence and not in hers. We were ignored, basically, all day long—put in the backyard or wherever we were out of the way. So if I wanted to play records and dance, I was out of the way." Sometimes, says Elisabeth, Bette would tether them to a tree so that they wouldn't run off, "and the ropes would cut us around the middle."

Marion Shapiro remembers one day "finding little Bette, the older one, running down the street with no clothes on. Mama's in the house, sound asleep. She wasn't a fit mother. She didn't take care of them. The children were dirty. The house was dirty. And Bette would be in bed asleep, and they'd be running around the neighborhood or somebody would bring them home." Helen Wilson suspected that Bette's indifference to the children and the housekeeping was creating strains in her relationship with Ernie. "Wouldn't you be upset if you worked and had to come home and the baby was still taking a nap and the diapers hadn't been washed? I think he wished she'd been a better wife and a mother, and I think he was a little embarrassed that she wasn't a better housekeeper. But he still loved her."

At times the private problems leaked into public view. Helen Wilson's husband, Dean, remembers a dinner at which "they were having a little to-do—I guess what you'd call an argument—and a bottle of guava jelly came flying out the window." Moreover, Bette was growing increasingly unhappy over her mother-in-law's seemingly boundless hostility. She would complain about Mary Kovacs to friends, "and she had every right to," says Marion Shapiro, "because his mother would interfere and would say things to Ernie: 'Bette didn't do this, that, the other thing.' I can understand how Bette felt. But I think he really loved his mother and felt sorry for her. He knew she was wrong in a lot of things, and he knew that she caused a lot of trouble, but it was his mother."

Apparently helpless to smooth over the increasingly jagged edges in the relations between his mother and his wife, Ernie escaped into work or cards. He was putting in an obsessive thirteen hours or so daily at WTTM. At the last possible moment, in order to meet his midnight newspaper deadline, he would dash off his column and run out the door (sometimes in pajamas), calling over his shoulder to Fonde, "Take over, Mike, I have to go deliver my column." "As we'd be sitting there, he'd be doing these *Trentonian* columns," remembers Eddie Hatrak. "He could be having a conversation about anything or watching TV, and he'd be typing away. You'd read the column the next morning, and it would have nothing to do with what we were talking about."

The best escape of all was poker. Donald Mattern remembers playing in a running game every Saturday night at Ernie's house, along with five or six other WTTM people, "in a very tiny dining room, about the size of two or three phone booths put together." They would set an alarm clock for 2:00 or 3:00 in the morning, and when it went off, they would play one last round, dealer's choice. Then Ernie would grandly treat everybody to breakfast. "Everything he had was big," says Mattern. "He had a huge skillet, and he'd cook up scrambled eggs for everyone. Then we'd go out and play golf, maybe thirty-six holes, over in Yardley."

At both poker and golf "he was horrible," Mattern recalls. "He was a plunger, and that made him a poor poker player, because he would always put everything in. He wouldn't conserve anything. And when it came to golf it was the same way. He would just swing wildly and hit the ball maybe fifty yards out, and then the ball would slice and go a hundred and fifty yards this way. But it was fun playing with him because he didn't take himself seriously." During the poker games he kept up a running stream of jokes, and if he lost a lot of money, "it wouldn't mean anything to him. He loved the game. Everything was chancy. Everything was big risk."

The playing cards bewitched him. Sometimes he wrote about them in the *Trentonian*, describing plays in a painstaking detail:

Some weeks ago, we slithered down one of the Shubert Alleys [in New York] until we saw one gent holding a folded magazine out and another gent casually flipping three arched cards back and forth.

We are a live one for this type of carryings-on, so we stopped to bide-a-wee. The gimmick, of course, is to locate the black ace. A fellow appeared in a green homburg and knocked off a five-spot. This interested another chap who threw in five bucks and also won. The gent with the cards said that things were really going against him and how about try again? . . . This time, the fellow won another five and the ante was suggested at ten. . . .

The three-card monte scam is obvious by now, but Ernie continues to spin his "Noo York" encounter into a long-winded, seemingly endless column. So alluring were the cards that they dulled his senses—about what might bore his readers, even about what games might be dangerous to pursue. For a period Ernie was playing in rigged games in the back of a gas station or at the Hotel Hildebrecht, betting against known cheaters. Warned by friends that he was being taken, he would wave them away, saying that he was enjoying himself too much to care. "I think Ernie liked to lose," says Dean Wilson, who used to play cards with him.

Maybe it was willful self-destructiveness that caused him to play so poorly. Certainly, when confronted with the cards, his thinking just became wildly illogical. "Ernie was stubborn," remembers Sydney Leavitt. "One day I had aces wired. So I kicked him. After all, he was my friend. I say, 'Ernie, get out, I got aces wired.' He says, 'I can't get out. I got a pair of deuces.' I say, 'Ernie, I got aces wired!' He says, 'Oh, no, I'm liable to catch another deuce!'" (During his years at WTTM Ernie kept the card games out of the radio station; later, however, even this distinction about what might or might not be appropriate in the workplace would break down.)

Between the poker games and the newspaper writing and the remote work at WTTM, Ernie at twenty-nine was leading a breezy, hectic, highly public life. It was creative and exciting, but hardly a solution designed to save a faltering young marriage. Beneath all that public activity, his relationship with his Favorite Wife was coming apart bit by bit. Sadly, he wouldn't wake up to the problem until it was too late.

Back in 1939, millions of visitors to the New York World's Fair had marveled at a box that issued forth both sounds and moving pictures: a television set. After World War II, manufacturers had begun to market their futuristic product on a wide scale to home audiences. In only a few years television would present a major challenge to the monopolistic hold that radio had enjoyed over Americans for three decades.

The technology of television fascinated early viewers as much as radio's technology had captivated its first listeners. Television sets were displayed in store windows, and crowds gathered to watch this magical new form of entertainment. Bill Freeland, a cameraman who worked with Ernie on television, remembers that in Philadelphia "the first person on any block to get a television set would put it up somewhere so the whole neighborhood could see it, either through a window or out on a porch. And people just lined up." These early sets were "a major investment," costing as much as several weeks' wages. The picture tubes were small—ten inches or so— and the images would be enlarged by a magnifying glass over the screen. Double images and other sorts of interference were more the rule than the exception. "But they would accept any kind of a picture. Even one that now you would turn off and say was unviewable, people then would just say, 'Wow.' Whole neighborhoods would watch it," says Freeland.

In order to seduce consumers into buying this expensive new technology, appliance stores would offer to install TVs into homes for free monthlong tryouts. "Appliance stores were doing anything to get a set into your home, literally to get you hooked on television," says Tom Durand. "And it was at this time, when they were really pushing television, that Ernie worked out a deal with some appliance store somewhere to get a TV into his home."

Ernie became "totally enthralled," Durand says, by the bulky box that combined the immediacy of live theater, the moving photography of motion pictures, and the electronic gadgetry of radio but was something beyond a mere sum of its parts. One didn't get dressed up, go out, and pay money to enjoy television, as one did with theater and movies; one didn't have to imagine the visuals that went with the sounds, as one did with radio. Its pictures appeared on a small screen, a screen of a shape and size that had never existed before, and they were broadcast into the home, so that right from the start audiences' relationship with the medium was intimate, private, and relatively casual.

Ernie asked Michael Fonde whether he thought he should go on TV. "I said to him, 'Ernie, I can't give you advice. If you don't do it and it's a mistake, you'll blame it on me. And if you do do it and it doesn't work out, you'll blame me too. It has to be your decision." But Ernie seemed already to have made his decision.

Sometime in 1949 or early 1950, television station WPTZ in Philadelphia had been looking for a booth announcer—just a voice, not an on-camera presence—to work a weekend shift. "At that time we had two staff announcers," says Preston Stover, who was WPTZ's manager of program operations. "But our broadcast week was getting stretched to the point where those two couldn't cover all the broadcast hours. One of our directors, Elmer Jaspan, knew a young man in Trenton who was a radio announcer and might be available for weekend work." Ernie made an audition recording of one of his ringside wrestling broadcasts and sent it over to WPTZ. There is some doubt, however, as to whether the station management even cracked open the seal. Nobody remembers hearing it, and as Stover points out, "We weren't being too critical. We were looking for a warm body willing to work on Saturdays and Sundays. Voicewise, he was very competent. And he had been trained as an announcer, so he knew how to keep a station log, what to do in case of breakdown, things like that." Being competent enough and willing to work weekends, Ernie was hired for the job.

WPTZ, Channel 3, an affiliate of the NBC Television network, was one of the pioneering stations in TV. It had been started in 1932 under the call letters W3XE as an experimental station by the Philco Corporation, the manufacturer of electronics and appliances. At first it broadcast Philco employee amateur shows, cartoons, and travelogues into the homes of about a hundred Philco workers, mostly engineers, for the purposes of checking the signal and establishing black-and-white telecast standards.

As W3XE, the station was responsible for several TV broadcast firsts, including the first nighttime college football game (in 1939, Temple–Kansas) and the first major coverage of a national political convention (in 1940, the Republican national convention). In 1941 it changed its call letters to WPTZ to signal its new status as a commercial station—the second in the United States and the first in Philadelphia. It continued its pioneering efforts that year with the world's first use of multiple cameras to cover a baseball game.

Wrestling was a popular TV programming item in the late 1940s—hence Ernie's choice of audition material. But his job as the weekend staff announcer was far less exciting than his ringside broadcasts at the Trenton Armory. "He just sat in the booth, did station breaks, and read commercials and any other announcements that were necessary," says Stover. The announcer's booth, an old radio control room converted for television use, contained a TV monitor and buttons that lit up to tell him whether he was on the air.

One day, while Ernie was working the booth at WPTZ, a crew up on the fifth floor in Studio N was counting down to airtime for a new cooking show. "The host had not shown up," says Andy McKay, the stage manager. "We waited till half an hour before airtime, fifteen minutes before airtime. Finally the director called up management and said, 'Where's the host for this show? We don't have anybody.' So they scouted around and said, 'Wait a minute. Maybe Ernie Kovacs could do it. He's downstairs.' "

McKay took the elevator downstairs and told the elevator man to stand by. Ernie wasn't in the announcer's booth, "so I started to go back up, and I saw him down the hall taking a drink of water. I said, 'Ernie, here's your big chance. They need you upstairs. You've got to jump into this new cooking show.' He said, 'Now?' I said, "Yes, now! You've got about five minutes. Come on.' "

They dashed back upstairs, and Ernie was quickly introduced to the show's chef. "He said, 'My name is, what is your name, and where are you from, and what are you cooking,' and in about two minutes flat he was ready to go on the air. And I put my headset on, pointed to him, and said, 'You're on, Ernie.' "

The date was March 20, 1950, and the show was called *Deadline for Dinner*. Local cooking shows were a staple of early TV, and most of them stuck to the same rigid format. But dull formula was anathema to Ernie, who proceeded to turn the genre on its head. "I don't think in the beginning they thought he was going to be that wild," said *Deadline* director Joe Behar, who alternated sometimes with Elmer Jaspan. "They just thought he would be a fairly ordinary host, with a little twist."

The setup was a couple of steps up from Ernie's weeklong stunt at the New Jersey State Fair, with serious chefs from country clubs and well-known restaurants around Philadelphia joining Ernie on a kitchen set that was crammed into a tiny former radio studio along with two RCA Image Orthicon cameras, an enormous Mole-Richardson mike boom, and a minimal crew. "There would be two cameramen, a stage manager, Ernie, and the chef, and you couldn't get anybody else in the studio. It was that small," says cameraman Bill Freeland. Guest chefs would "show their most famous recipes," recalled Behar, who directed the proceedings from a minuscule control room, "and then when he would try to prepare them he would create a mess. He did stay within the framework, however, and [viewers] could, theoretically, copy down what they were doing and make the dishes, so it wasn't a complete burlesque."

No films or tapes of *Deadline for Dinner* exist, but it isn't difficult to imagine Ernie, with his deadpan face and low voice and enormous black cigar, keeping up a half-serious running commentary on his guests' food preparations. Occasionally, the chefs proved uncooperative. Once, according to a magazine account, a cook demonstrated how to make hamburgers in five minutes, leaving Ernie with twenty-five minutes of airtime to fill. Thinking fast, Ernie asked the chef what he suggested serving alongside. "Whatever you like." Ernie pressed for examples. "Everybody likes something different. I wouldn't presume to tell people what to eat with their hamburgers," responded the guest. "Listen," Kovacs finally exploded, "it doesn't take any mental giant to make a hamburger. Now, what do you do to brighten them up?" On another episode, the scheduled chef didn't appear at all. Ernie turned the no-show into an opportunity to demonstrate his own family favorite, "Eggs Scavok" (spell it backwards), actually a mishmash he improvised from ingredients that a panicked assistant had grabbed at random.

Eventually Ernie teamed up with a permanent chef, Albert Mathis, from Philadelphia's fashionable Gulph Mills Country Club. Mathis had a thick European accent and a bubbly, easy manner, but "he was serious about his cooking," says Bill Freeland. "He was more involved with making lunch for the crew than with making dinner for the show, and it was always fancy German sandwiches and things. But he just accepted Ernie. Whatever direction Ernie wanted to lead, Albert would go." Preston Stover remembers that Kovacs and Mathis "worked well together. Mathis wasn't so serious that Kovacs couldn't kid him along. But the show had merit. In other words, the information was of value to housewives interested in cooking."

The half-hour *Deadline for Dinner*, which Ernie soon dubbed *Dead*

Lion for Dinner, ran on Monday and Tuesday afternoons at three o'clock, immediately following Channel 3's daily feature movie. In order to fulfill hosting duties he was commuting between Philadelphia and Trenton; back home, he was still working at WTTM and writing his column for the *Trentonian*. Within a few months, he was presented with the opportunity to add yet another responsibility to his frantic schedule.

WPTZ had in the works a combination quiz and fashion program called *Pick Your Ideal*. The show had been devised by the Philadelphia advertising agency Gresh and Kramer as a sponsorship vehicle for the Ideal Manufacturing Company, a New Jersey women's clothing retailer. Ad man Barney Kramer and WPTZ commercial manager Bink Dannenbaum held auditions for an emcee. "Bink thought he knew everything," remembers Barney Kramer. "Well, maybe he did. But we tried out three emcees for the show: a guy named Tom Moorehead, I think Ed McMahon, and Ernie. The other two guys did it straight, and Ernie came out in a barrel. He rolled up his pants so it looked as if all he had on was a barrel." Ernie proceeded to deliver a withering parody of Vyvyan Donner, the famous newsreel fashion commentator. "Bink and I were in the booth," Kramer says, "and Bink turned to me and said, 'You can take any of those guys, but not the guy with the barrel. He's crazy.' So of course I hired Ernie. And he was just fantastic in it."

Essentially a fifteen-minute commercial for the Ideal Manufacturing Company, *Pick Your Ideal* debuted on Wednesday, August 22, 1950. The local (as opposed to network) weekly afternoon show featured two models wearing nearly identical outfits, one from an expensive fashion source, the other a cut-price knockoff from Ideal. A viewer who sent her name to WPTZ might be telephoned by Ernie on the air and asked to "pick her Ideal." If she guessed which was the Ideal outfit, she won it as a prize. "Network shows aren't the only ones whose call gets the housewife all a-twitter. Women in the know around these parts are just as anxious to get a call from Ernie Kovacs," reported *TV Digest* a year after the show's premiere. The article noted that Ideal's "retail showrooms are housed in quaint Quonset huts on the White Horse Pike, Hammonton, but women have beaten a path to their door, primarily because of the values advertised on TV."

Ernie's attentions were turning more and more to TV. In his daily *Trentonian* column, the references to television and to Philadelphia increased as they became a larger part of his life. He would describe people he'd met on his Trenton–Philadelphia train commute or educate his readers about the state of the industry: "In the total New York area, according to a recent Nielsen report," he informed them in June

1950, "82.6 percent of the TV homes watched the Milton Berle show over a recent four-week period . . . Over the nation, the Texaco Star Theatre was in 77.7 [percent of] homes . . . That's a total of 3,521,000 homes." Other times the television references were directly personal. "Yesterday we started one of the most interestin' jobs we've ever tried," Ernie wrote the day after his fashion show debut. "We have a new TV show [called] 'Pick Your Ideal' and there are *four* (4!) real, live, all female models on the show. . . . All we have to do is sit in the middle and smell different brands of perfume as they collide somewhere in front of us."

Meanwhile, *Deadline for Dinner* was becoming a popular program; it would run for just over two years, a respectable life-span for a local daytime cooking series. "We've had several inquiries as to just what did happen to that food that is cooked on 'Deadline for Dinner' (Channel 3)," Ernie reported in his column several months into the show:

> We've been a little slow in answering but when we received an anonymous note at home saying that it was "sinful to waste that food," we thought p'haps we'd straighten it out a bit.
>
> Not only is all the food cooked on that show eaten but it is a race to see who gets the choicest and the mostest. . . . We made shrimp with Old Bay seafood seasoning last week and by the time the program was over, everyone had sniffed the aroma through the building's air-conditioning system and had seen the stuff on TV sets in offices at the same time. "Wasted Food?" Ha! . . . It was only the quick and the brave that managed to snag a shrimp after the show.

Ernie's job responsibilities and frequent commuting left even less time than he had had before for Bette and their two small girls. He tried to involve Bette in his television shows, as he had in his column. "The F.W. was on our 'Deadline for Dinner' show Tuesday and we were tres proud of her," he announced to his *Trentonian* readers in the spring. But newspaper mentions and television appearances weren't enough to assuage the increasing stresses of the marriage. "I remember arguing," says Elisabeth Kovacs, who was three at the time. "There were words, but I don't remember them."

One day, while Michael Fonde was working with Ernie at the WTTM studio, the phone rang. "He picked up the phone," says Fonde, "and he didn't say anything. He got up and walked right out." He didn't come to work at WTTM for several days, and none of his friends knew what had happened. The Durands, who were on vacation at the shore with their two-year-old daughter, had borrowed a light meter from Ernie and Bette. "When we stopped to return the light meter, we didn't even get out of the car. He saw us drive up and came out of the house and didn't invite us in," says Billie Durand. "He really looked stricken about something, but didn't explain anything. We had never seen him like that. We kind of joked with him, as we always did, and it just wasn't there."

The only person in whom Ernie confided was Eddie Hatrak. Thoroughly agitated, he showed up unexpectedly at Hatrak's door while the musician was giving a piano lesson. "Eddie," he told his friend, "Bette and I have broken up." "He was very distraught," says Hatrak. "Unfortunately, I said, 'Okay, I'll come right over. Just let me finish this lesson.' He really couldn't take that."

Bette Wilcox Kovacs was gone. Several friends assert that she had been having an affair with a married man, a Southerner, and Ernie had found out. The specifics are hazy. One person thinks that she took up with an old boyfriend in Florida and that his wife wrote to Ernie about it. Another believes that the man was a factory owner from Tennessee or the Carolinas and had "promised her the moon." A third says that Ernie discovered the affair when Bette handed him some letters to mail and they turned out to be letters to her lover. None of these remembrances can be confirmed. Indisputably, however, Bette was gone, returned to her native Florida. And, indisputably, Ernie was crushed.

"I'd never seen him the way he was when he left the station. He was a broken man," remembers Michael Fonde. "It was heartbreaking for him, because he was a very happy family man. He really loved his wife," says Billie Durand. "He was gone on his new career after that happened with Bette. He needed something to lose himself in. It just kicked him right out of here."

PART THREE

ERNIE IN
TELEVISIONLAND

1950 – 1952

The split from Bette served as a powerful catalyst for Ernie. He was thirty-one, but until Bette left him, he was as innocently trusting of women as he had been when he fell in love for the first time, with Suzanne Ludey at East Hampton. With a Favorite Wife and two small children snugly ensconced in a bungalow, Ernie seemed to have achieved a stable family center. "I believe he loved her very much," says Kippie Kovacs, "even long after the divorce." But Ernie also had a revengeful streak, and he would never forgive Bette. Her departure was a painful shock; later he said that the experience profoundly disillusioned him about women. But he was supercharged with physical and creative energy, insomniac as ever, and by now deeply accustomed to maintaining a workaholic frenzy. With the new opportunity of television before him, Ernie dove headfirst into his career.

The national habit was still radio. Early television personality Dave Garroway, who developed his famous rambling, intellectual style as the host of a postwar late-night jazz and talk show, *The 11:60 Club*, on NBC Radio station WMAQ in Chicago, told one interviewer that at first television was regarded as "kind of a nuisance. We [he and his writer, Charlie Andrews] thought radio hot stuff." But the bespectacled Garroway allowed himself to be lured to TV in 1949 by the expanding NBC Television network, where he quickly made his mark with a national prime-time variety show, *Garroway at Large*. Ernie, for whom security held little attraction, was perfectly prepared to disembark from the proven medium of radio. By nature a gambler, he had already begun to think that his future lay in television, a virtually unexplored field not much older than his own little girls. The break-up with Bette—and a well-timed offer from WPTZ—impelled him to take the professional plunge.

WPTZ asked Ernie to host a new early-morning wake-up show, to be called *3 to Get Ready* and modeled after the wake-up programs that were then common in radio. It would be a daily ninety-minute slot; Ernie jumped at the chance. The unstructured, fly-by-the-seat-of-your-pants, this-is-your-first-and-only-take ambience of early live TV was perfect for Ernie, who worked best under pressure, loved to take risks, and had a fertile, unfettered enough imagination to be able to use up every second he was given on the air. He quit WTTM and his *Trentonian* column in the fall of 1950. (The newspaper replaced him with Sylvia Porter's practical-minded syndicated column "Your Money's Worth"—an ironic choice, given Ernie's attitude toward money.)

He had his mother, Mary, move into the Mercerville bungalow to take care of Bette, who was just three, and Kippie, still a baby at less than two. To ease his commute, he moved into an apartment in Philadelphia that had recently been vacated by his *Deadline for Dinner* director, Joe Behar. The apartment was situated just a few minutes' walk from the WPTZ studios in midtown Philadelphia, near fashionable Rittenhouse Square. But he would hardly spend any time there—mostly it was an address, a convenient place to hold midnight poker games and catch what little sleep he required. (He may also have rented it in order to establish residency in Pennsylvania, which would make a divorce from Bette relatively easy. "He told me that, according to Pennsylvania law, if your spouse leaves your bed and board for two years, then you can get a divorce without any problem," says his friend from summer stock, Jane Hess.) The bulk of his waking hours would soon be consumed at the station or, on weekends that began as early as he could get out of the city, back in Trenton with his children.

On radio wake-up shows of the period, disc jockeys would read the news, announce the time, forecast the weather, and play records—an easy-to-listen-to mix that people could switch on as they ate breakfast, prepared for work, began their household chores, or dressed for school. Ernie himself had hosted one of those shows for years at WTTM. But it was felt that television, which needed to be watched as well as heard, would be perceived as too much of an interference with the public's early-morning patterns to succeed at this time in the day. As television historian Robert Metz has pointed out, "Morning television was available here and there, but watching it was a taboo in an America dedicated to the work ethic. It was acceptable to listen to morning radio but, like sex and alcohol, television was deemed proper only after sundown. Getting viewers to spend time in front of the set even before leaving for work would take some doing."

WPTZ was one of the stations "here and there" that had experimented with daytime programming. "At one point we said, 'Let's do a movie at six o'clock in the evening.' It was something called *Frontier Playhouse;* it was all Westerns," says WPTZ program operations manager Preston Stover. "Everybody said, 'Nobody's going to watch television at six o'clock; they're all at home eating dinner.' We proved that one very wrong." With that success "under our belts," WPTZ had continued to push back its sign-on time, until by 1950 the station's broadcast day was beginning as early as 11:00 A.M.

Stover remembers that he, WPTZ general manager Rolland Tooke, and Philco vice-president Ernest Loveman "kicked around the idea of going on early in the morning. We said, 'Well, heck, they just might watch television at 7:30 in the morning. Why not provide something for the people who had to work, people who went to school?' I know management talked to NBC about the idea, and as I remember they had no interest in doing that, so we decided to try it ourselves. I think Tooke came up with the title. Three referred to Channel 3—and to 'Three to get ready and four to go,' that old rhyme."

With the decision to program *3 to Get Ready* from 7:30 to 9:00 A.M. daily, WPTZ was truly breaking new ground. Not only was the early-morning time slot a first for the station, *3 to Get Ready* would be the first television wake-up program in the country. The show—which came to be referred to as *TTGR*—made its debut as a local weekday show on November 27, 1950. But at the time WPTZ regarded it as filler, a sort of test to see whether anyone would watch. "They wanted a very inexpensive experiment, so they decided to put us there," remembered Joe Behar, who directed *TTGR*, sharing duties with Calvin Jones. Initially *TTGR* was not much more than a telecast version of a radio wake-up show, with Ernie spinning records, reading weather reports, and ad-libbing to fill ninety minutes while a clock superimposed on the lower left-hand corner of the screen kept viewers apprised of the time. There weren't even any sponsors for the first two weeks; then a local milliner, Stylepark Hats, signed on.

But Ernie had honed his ad-libbing and time-filling abilities well in his years at WTTM radio, and with TV cameras trained on him for ninety-minute chunks, it was inevitable that he would start to exploit visual and aural possibilities. He began straying from the expected by drawing cartoons or twitching his features in sync with the records (or, sometimes, out of sync with them), then by ad-libbing to goofy props that crew members tossed to him from offstage. Very quickly the program blossomed into full-blown (and sometimes dangerous) daffiness, all completely improvised:

ERNIE WITH A LIVE JAGUAR ON HIS BACK BLAHS ON HOW TAME THE ANIMAL IS . . . JAGUAR'S CLAWS EMERGE TO SHRED ERNIE'S BRAND-NEW SPORTS COAT

ERNIE AS HARMON GUGGENFLECKER MAKES CAMPAIGN SPEECH
STANDING ON TOP OF A STATION WAGON ON WALNUT STREET . . .
HE PROMISES ALL CHILDREN OVER EIGHT A CONVERTIBLE AND EACH
VOTER A BARREL OF WHISKEY, TWELVE POUNDS OF PUTTY, THE SE-
CRET OF THE ATOMIC BOMB HANDSOMELY BOUND IN SIMULATED
PLASTIC, AND A PIE ON EVERY TABLE . . . STAGE MANAGER THROWS
PIE IN ERNIE'S FACE

STAGE MANAGER SETS UP LADDER . . . ERNIE CLIMBS UP AND DISAP-
PEARS . . . STAGE MANAGER FOLDS UP LADDER AND TAKES IT AWAY
. . . CAMERA PANS TO DESK WHERE ERNIE IS SEATED

Philadelphia viewers had probably never seen the likes of this on television—much less first thing in the morning—but they quickly responded to the free spirit of the proceedings. They started to write fan letters, and Ernie would read them on the air (a carryover from the days when he would print readers' letters to fill up his daily *Trentonian* column). He also involved viewers by running contests and offering giveaways, to which there were huge responses. The giveaway didn't even have to be valuable: one day he offered free shamrocks, mentioning them only once, and 1,700 viewers wrote in. Another time he ran an ongoing "mystery tune" contest, offering theater tickets as the prize; he had to stop it after ten days because the station was swamped with 3,500 letters.

Contests and giveaways performed an important function in those early days of commercial TV. Because the ratings system was primitive, the mail that a show pulled in provided an important indication of how many people were watching. (For the "mystery tune" contest, Ernie had made his announcement during the first portion of the show, to gauge how many early risers were viewing.) Kovacs' enormous audience response was proof positive that people were indeed watching, and sponsors began clamoring to get on the show. So many potential sponsors requested commercial time on *TTGR* that in September 1951 WPTZ rolled back the start-up time to 7:00 A.M. By December, when it had been on a year, *TTGR* was averaging fifty commercials a week.

Ernie, of course, had had trouble making the early-morning call when he first worked at WTTM, and the intervening years did nothing to improve his punctuality. When *TTGR* began at 7:30, he was sometimes late; when it was pushed back to 7:00, he was just late more often. But if Ernie was going to be casual about his arrival time, so would the director and crew. They began positioning a camera at the end of the corridor leading to Studio S (for "south"), where *TTGR* was shot. While they waited for their belated host to arrive, "we'd be shooting little windup toy monkeys, oscilloscope images, pictures out of magazines," says cameraman Bill Freeland. "We'd shoot whatever we wanted to shoot. We had to fill time. Maybe if he wasn't in before a quarter after, we'd do a commercial and come back. When we heard the elevator coming, we'd have a camera pointed at it, and he'd come off and wave, 'I'm coming.' Then another camera would pick him up and follow him into the studio. And away we went—never, never knowing what was going to happen."

This sort of casual, improvised collaboration took the show in many innovative directions. The remotes that Ernie had milked in radio were not possible at WPTZ—or were they? Studio S was on the fifth floor of WPTZ's Walnut Street facility, and on the same floor was a double-door loading platform with a big iron beam for hoisting unwieldy scenery and equipment; a wire gate prevented people from plunging to an empty lot below. A camera fitted with a seventeen-inch telephoto lens and stationed at these loading doors provided a reasonable "remote" facsimile, picking up Ernie and his coactors pantomiming away in the empty lot or on Sansom Street, which ran behind WPTZ:

ERNIE AND A JUNKMAN HAGGLE OVER SOME JUNK . . . FINALLY PRICE IS SET . . . JUNKMAN THROWS ERNIE OVER HIS SHOULDER AND CARRIES HIM AWAY

ERNIE IN EMPTY LOT HAS A TINY, TINY SHOVEL . . . DIGS A HOLE THE SIZE OF A CELLAR

ANDY MCKAY AS BARBER IN FLOPPY WIG, WIELDS GIANT CARDBOARD SCISSORS AND COMB . . . COAXES ERNIE INTO BARBERSHOP . . . ERNIE EMERGES BALD . . . HE RUNS BACK IN AND COMES OUT WEARING ANDY'S FLOPPY WIG . . . ANDY COMES OUT BALD . . . THEY CHASE ONE ANOTHER

For these "remotes" and for skits inside the studio, sometimes Ernie would have come up with the germ of the idea ahead of time. "I remember him staying up all night preparing the morning show," says Barney Kramer, the advertising man who hired him for *Pick Your Ideal.* "He'd be up all night, scribbling things down, and then he would appear to be ad-libbing everything, which he did, I guess. But he did a lot of homework. He thought about it a lot. He worked hard at it."

Those performances, however, were entirely impromptu. "We never had a script to go by," says Andy McKay, who fulfilled acting, production assistant, and makeup man duties on *TTGR*. "We would talk it over just before we did it. 'You're the barber. We need scissors and a bright comb and a wig. Ernie's going to be the passerby, and you're going to invite him into the barbershop.' They would noodle around in the audio department and do these little musical things while we were down there. Everything was live-action, silent-screen stuff. And if we had any dialogue, we had to hold up big cue cards with giant letters on them."

Within the studio, Ernie broke down the traditional theatrical "fourth wall," the invisible barrier that separates actors from audience and keeps behind-the-scenes machinations hidden. He would walk beyond the bounds of the stage set—absolutely forbidden in those days—and enter the control room, talk to the cameraman, or suddenly take over a camera himself. He would shimmy up a rope or climb a ladder to a twenty-five-foot-high catwalk and pretend to be a monkey or Douglas Fairbanks or the Hunchback of Notre Dame. "When he made these unorthodox forays, the two cameramen had no choice but to follow him with the mike boom and the control room staff in tow," remembers Andy McKay. "The viewers loved watching these off-the-cuff impulses and being permitted to peek into the dark mysteries of studio operation. After all, TV was still new and a novelty to the general public."

It was new and a novelty to Ernie too, and he seemed to love it as much as his viewers. There is a snippet of footage from around this period that seems to sum up his feelings about being in, and on, this marvelously enjoyable new medium. In it Ernie crouches down on a platform that is attached to a TV camera while the cameraman dollies the camera—and Ernie—all over the set. The host looks around avidly, consumed with delight, as he holds onto the camera for dear life. For a fleeting minute he's no longer the star of a Philadelphia TV show; he has become a little boy, being treated to the heady excitement of a merry-go-round ride for the very first time.

The success of *3 to Get Ready*— particularly at the unorthodox early-morning hour— convinced the New York–based NBC Television network, of which WPTZ was an affiliate, to give Ernie a national airing. And so, beginning on May 14, 1951 (with an odd little false start on March 7 through 9), *Time for Ernie* was broadcast nationally from

WPTZ's studios in Philadelphia. This fifteen-minute program (fifteen-minute slots were common then, on both TV and radio) aired Monday through Friday at 3:15 P.M., and it featured Ernie as host—no other actors; music by the Tony deSimone Trio, a local brothers' combo he had hired to replace the records on *TTGR;* and direction by Joe Behar.

Although the show came on with a title card announcing "It's Time for Ernie!," the camera would often catch Ernie casually unprepared, his desk littered with junk. The junk actually provided him with a quick and easy start; he'd pick up a long chain, for instance, and remark, "Left here by a chain smoker" before moving on to various unrehearsed shenanigans. He was resourceful at finding ways to fill up the time. Sometimes the bits he came up with were pure silliness:

> ERNIE TALKS INTO A GIANT TELEPHONE THAT MAKES HIM LOOK LIKE A CHILD . . . "THEY'RE FEEDING ME TO THE NETWORKS? WHAT AM I? HAMBURGER? . . . YOU MEAN THIS SHOW IS NOT JUST IN PHILADELPHIA? IT'S IN TRENTON? BORDENTOWN? HIGHTSTOWN? CHICAGO?!"

> ERNIE TELLS AUDIENCE HE'S GOING TO SHOW THEM A TRICK "FOR ENTERTAINING YOUR FRIENDS AT HOME" . . . ROLLS UP LITTLE PIECE OF PAPER AND WHIPS IT AROUND THE FLOOR WITH A BULL-WHIP

Other times, however, they showed a sophisticated comedic imagination at work:

> SOUND OF BIG BEN CHIME . . . ERNIE LOOKS AT WATCH, PUTS HAT OVER IT TO MAKE IT QUIET . . . KEEPS LIFTING UP HAT AND SOUND SNEAKS OUT . . . SHOOTS IT WITH GUN

> ERNIE HANGS A CONTROL PANEL WITH FOUR KNOBS AROUND HIS NECK AND EXPLAINS, "MOST OF US DON'T TUNE OUR TELEVISION SETS PROPERLY" . . . HIS FACE SQUOOSHES DOWN AS HE TURNS HORIZONTAL HOLD KNOB—"NO, NOT TOO FAR THAT WAY!" . . . HE TURNS KNOB BACK AND CONTORTS FACE THE OTHER WAY . . . THEN DEMONSTRATES VERTICAL HOLD

He understood that a sound (a Big Ben chime) that was incongruous with its visual source (a tiny watch) could be funny—and also that the joke was specifically suited to the smallness, the intimacy of the television screen in a living room; the same joke would lose its power if it were magnified to the larger-than-life scale of the movie screen and presented in a huge darkened room to an audience of hundreds of strangers. He also grasped that the picture on the television screen had certain characteristics unique to the medium. An audience could turn the volume on the radio up or down, but it couldn't really distort the sound of the broadcast; nor could it manipulate the images in a movie— these were fixed in the final form given them by the cinematographer, director, and editor; nor could it have much impact on a live performance in a theater, unless the performers themselves decided to interact with the audience. Ernie's pretending that his face was being distorted by what was being done to the TV set made a particular aspect of television itself the subject of the joke. And the bit was all the more witty for its slightly sadistic edge, its underlying premise that the audience could actually do something violent to a part of his body while he was trapped behind glass in the box.

On May 15, 1951, the day after *Time for Ernie* settled in for its nationwide run, WPTZ put Ernie on another show—this one airing only locally in the Philadelphia area, one afternoon a week. It was a cooking show developed by ad man Barney Kramer for Nat-Gas, a natural gas company. Directed by Elmer Jaspan, *Now You're Cooking* was a mixture of recipes for housewives, which Ernie would demonstrate, and plugs for the gas company. "Ernie couldn't remember any of the commercials, so he would chop up the script and stick it all over the kitchen set," describes Kramer. "He'd walk around and open a door and read the thing from inside the door. He'd move around all over, picking up his script that way. And he would prepare delicious things. He was an excellent cook."

Ernie was still doing *Deadline for Dinner* twice a week, and he was also working hard every morning on *TTGR*, which was growing more and more popular with both audiences and sponsors. WPTZ's *Now You're Cooking* lasted only until June 12 (it would enjoy another brief run from September 18 to October 16 before disappearing entirely), and shortly thereafter NBC ended *Time for Ernie* as well, on June 29. But the network had intended the fifteen-minute afternoon show as a tryout for a much choicer spot. He had performed to their expectations, and they immediately scheduled him into his first nighttime show.

Ernie in Kovacsland was a nationally broadcast summer replacement for the popular puppet series *Kukla, Fran and Ollie*, which had been seen on the NBC network since 1948, and as such it represented an excellent opportunity for exposure. In many ways Ernie was a perfect choice for a summer substitute to NBC's Chicago-based puppet program. In spirit his whimsical world view was compatible with that of *Kukla, Fran and Ollie*, which focused on the antics of Burr Tillstrom's Kuklapolitans—the bald-headed, high-voiced Kukla (from the Russian word for "doll"), the shy one-toothed dragon Ollie (short for Oliver J. Dragon), Colonel Crackie, Madame Ooglepuss, Fletcher Rabbit, and others. His relaxed, gentle persona—like that of Fran Allison, the human hostess of *Kukla, Fran and Ollie* who had been a regular on the radio show *Don McNeill's Breakfast Club*—was beguiling to children (Ernie seemed low-key and unthreatening even when he was violently contorting his face). The puppet program was mostly improvised, as were Ernie's shows at the time. Finally, *Kukla, Fran and Ollie* was notable for its popularity among both children and adults, and Ernie's daytime programs were also enjoyed by children and adults. (Because of the postwar baby boom, children's programming played an important part in the growth of early television. Ernie often made references to the kids in the audience and did bits specifically for them, including capers with hand puppets.) Ernie's ability to appeal to both segments of the home audience had no doubt been a factor in the network's decision.

Ernie in Kovacsland bowed in the 7:00 to 7:30 P.M. time slot on Monday, July 2, 1951. Over the theme song of "Oriental Blues" and after title cards bearing caricatures of Ernie, a voice announced: "Ernie . . . in Kovacsland! A short program, it just seems long." (The song "Oriental Blues" by Jack Newton had originally been arranged for *TTGR* by Tony deSimone, who gave it an up-tempo ragtime piano punctuated by sirens and bells, in the style of Spike Jones. With its promise of slightly skewed fun to come, the arrangement had become linked in viewers' minds with Ernie Kovacs. He would retain it as his theme song for the rest of his life.) The music was provided by the Tony deSimone Trio, who produced a vaguely ethnic sound with their organ, accordion, and guitar. The show was directed by Benny Squires, whose innovative attitude toward his work fit in perfectly with Ernie's. "Benny was a free spirit," remembers Preston Stover, the program operations manager who had helped develop the idea for *TTGR*. "Even though he might be doing cooking shows and Ernie's and other things like that, which can get pretty dull after you've done them a while, his philosophy was, 'I've got to come up with a new thing every day'—a different opening, a little piece of business. Completely irresponsible at times, but a good kid."

With the new addition to his workload, Ernie was allowed to hire

a secretary, a young woman named Angel McGrath, whose organizational abilities served Ernie so well that she would work for him for
several years. In addition, for the first time Ernie was assigned two
writers, Hugh Prince and Ollie Crawford. Ernie read this, perhaps correctly, as an attempt by the network to control the show's content, and
according to Andy McKay he would rewrite the bulk of their material
or just improvise. "When NBC picked him up, they wanted to dictate
everything that happened, and the show fell on its face for a short
time," says Ron Hower, a WPTZ art director who worked on some of
the Kovacs shows. "They wanted to know exactly what was going on,
and they wanted to have their fingers in it. The show went downhill,
and then they pulled their hands out of it and it promptly picked up
again." In substance, form, and spirit, *Ernie in Kovacsland* became basically an evening-time extension of *TTGR*.

Although on his first network show, the fifteen-minute afternoon
Time for Ernie, Ernie had been the lone cast member (with musical
interludes from the Tony deSimone Trio), that was the only program
on which he went solo. On *Deadline for Dinner* he had acquired a
complementary straight man in chef Albert Mathis of the Gulph Mills
Country Club. On *TTGR* he was aided on-screen by Andy McKay; a
tall Scandinavian actor named Trygve ("Trigger") Lund, who had originally been assigned to work as *TTGR*'s stage manager; and WPTZ's
resident newsman, Norman Brooks. (Not surprisingly, Brooks's
straightforward, serious news-delivery style drove Ernie to tortuous
pranks. Once, positioning himself above Brooks on an overhead lighting bridge, Ernie let drops of water fall on the newsman's face, very
slowly, like Chinese water torture on camera. "It was just quietly dripping on his head, running down the end of his nose, running into his
eyes so he'd have to blink to get the water out of them," says cameraman Bill Freeland. "By the time the newscast was over he was soaked.
Never said a word about it." Another time, the hands of the clock on
the wall above Brooks's head—a standard fixture on many news shows
of the period—suddenly started whirling about wackily, as though time
had gone mad. That was Ernie playing with the clock, which could be
controlled from the back of the set.) With *Ernie in Kovacsland* representing an important move into prime time, it was decided to hire some
brand-new talent to assist Ernie on camera: an actor to serve as a straight
man and a "girl singer," for many years a common fixture on TV variety shows.

A young acting hopeful named Joe Earley, newly graduated from
college, stopped by one day at WPTZ, where he had done a Saturday-

night college show called *Stars in Your Eyes*. He was wearing a straw hat with a blue polka-dot band to make him look older, and he was noticed by Trigger Lund, who later called him at home and asked him to audition. When he arrived at the studio, Ernie was present, as well as the Tony deSimone Trio, writer Hugh Prince, and a female singer who had been invited to audition by Ernie's director, Joe Behar. "Oh, a beautiful girl. Blonde hair. A radiant person. I remember seeing her in the hall, carrying her music in her arms," describes Earley, who was subsequently hired for Ernie's show.

Behar had spotted the singer on a recent telecast of *Arthur Godfrey's Talent Scouts*. She had sung Patti Page's pop song "Would I Love You," giving her "luve you-u-u, luve you-u-u, luve you-u-u's" the most liquid vowel sounds she could muster, but she had lost; nevertheless, Behar was impressed enough to ask her to try out for the new program.

"Of course, you have a large repertoire?" Ernie inquired of her at the audition. "Naturally. Anything you'd like me to sing, just mention it," replied the twenty-four-year-old singer—with some nervousness, because she really had memorized only three popular songs, including the Patti Page number. But she sang what she knew, and Ernie listened, and he liked what he heard and hired her to begin in July.

She was billing herself as Edythe Adams, but the last name was borrowed for the stage from her mother's maiden name. She had been born Edith Enke on April 16, 1927, in Kingston, Pennsylvania, the second child and first daughter of Sheldon and Ada Enke. Her mother's side of the family was Welsh; her father's side, generations of Pennsylvania farmers, traced itself back to Hessian soldiers of the Revolutionary War era. Her upbringing was serious, strict, and Presbyterian; decisions were made only after lengthy consideration, and money was for saving, not for fun.

Edith was a model daughter, making good grades in school and saving most of her allowance, except for what she donated to the church. By the time she entered Pennsylvania's Grove City High School in 1942, she was working hard not only at grades but at many extracurricular activities, including singing (which she had begun doing in church) and serving as drum majorette. In the ensuing years her family moved several times, and Edith spent a year at Julia Richman High School in New York City and her last two high school years in New Jersey, at Tenafly High School, joining the dramatics club and singing soprano in the school choir and the girls' glee club. She had a fine enough voice and stage presence to win the roles of Katherine de Vaucelles in the school production of Rudolf Friml's operetta *The Vagabond King* and of Buttercup in Gilbert and Sullivan's *HMS Pinafore*. Tenafly High School's music director, E. Brock Griffith, encouraged her to pursue a singing career after she graduated in 1945.

Intending to become an opera singer, Edith enrolled at the Juilliard School of Music and commuted daily between her family's home in Tenafly and her classes in New York. Her energy was unflagging. On top of studying music at Juilliard, she took drama courses at Columbia University for a year, and she also studied voice privately with the Metropolitan Opera soprano Helen Jepson. During school vacations she found "odd-ball summer jobs," as her parents referred to them; she worked as a camp counselor in drama and music and once taught an exercise and diet class at a hotel in New Hampshire. She also found time to perform in summer stock in Pennsylvania and New Jersey.

In the spring of 1949, an opportunity came that would alter the direction of Edith's life. While performing in a Juilliard student revue called *Lose Your Tempo*, she was spotted by TV scouts, who invited her to appear on a new talent show. Their timing could not have been better. Edith had begun to notice that many of her fellow Juilliard students weren't getting very far in their chosen careers. "They were singing in the Riverside Church, and some of them were in the chorus at Radio City," she later told an interviewer. "That's not what I had in mind. I wanted to be on; I wanted to sing." She had already started singing on the women's club circuit and was particularly popular with clubs in Tenafly and nearby Hackensack. She was also—rather obsessively—entering every amateur contest that she heard about. It was good practice and provided public exposure, although "I never won any money, just toasters and steam irons. For some of the contests, I would have to wear a bathing suit. . . . I guess I won for the bathing suit and not the singing."

Edith won the talent show preliminaries. Although she later lost in the finals, the break led her to enter another contest—one for beauty as well as talent, a sort of Miss Television version of the Miss America Beauty Pageant. This time she won the title of Miss New York Television, which meant she would compete in the finals in Chicago. Fortunately, her parents—who would have disapproved heartily—were out of town. She was staying with her older brother and sister-in-law, and they loaned her money to get to Chicago. "When [mother and daddy] found out, they didn't like the idea of their little girl doing a thing so bold and brazen," she later told a reporter. "Then I won, and suddenly what I'd done was fine. I wasn't a bold, pushy hussy any more."

Winning the title of Miss U.S. Television for 1950, which included an appearance with "Mr. Television," Milton Berle, was just the impetus she needed to switch direction for good. She dropped out of Juilliard and abandoned any idea of becoming an opera singer—or of becoming a music teacher, as her parents had intended. "My mother was a singer and ended up a music teacher and a housewife. She was a frustrated, depressed lady and she didn't have an outlet," Edith said many years later. "I didn't want that." What she did want was to drop her coloratura soprano down two octaves so that she could sing pop songs. A Broadway coach, Bee Walker, encouraged her to move and emote when she sang. "You gotta swim, honey," Walker told Edith, trying to get her to move her arms and hands in time to the music. The Broadway coach also had less respect than Edith for the vocal precision taught at Juilliard. "Honey," she told her student, "it doesn't matter if you sing on key or off key. Just move your mouth around over your face and look sexy."

Miss U.S. Television for 1950 was alerted by a friend that three musicians were looking for a vocalist to join them on a nightclub date in Canada, and she contacted them and was offered the gig. Even though she knew only three popular songs, she reasoned that she could learn more on the way. But more important than songs was an appropriate wardrobe, and she didn't have any money. Once again, luckily, her parents were away on vacation. She went to Lord & Taylor and all the other department stores where they had charge accounts and quickly acquired a $1,000 wardrobe of evening clothes. And so she made her professional debut at the One Two Club and at the Show Bar in Montreal in April and May 1951, earning about $100—and, much more significantly, a review in *Variety*. "Of course, they didn't mention my singing at all," she said. "They just talked about how I looked in all my wonderful gowns. But it was worth it having my name mentioned in *Variety* at last."

The review brought her the attention of Rodgers and Hammerstein's casting director, John Fernley, who asked Edith to audition for an understudy role in *South Pacific*. Though she was not hired, Fernley spent two hours talking to her, and he would later remember her to her advantage at a critical juncture in her career. For now, she kept on entering amateur contests, finally working her way up to the top of the amateur contest heap: *Arthur Godfrey's Talent Scouts*, a well-watched showcase that had originated on radio in 1946 and had been airing on

CBS Television since 1948. She lost to a baritone, but like her unsuccessful audition for *South Pacific,* which would lead to better things, her performance garnered her a handful of job offers—including the one for *Ernie in Kovacsland.*

Although Ernie was beginning to get some attention in New York and was already an established television personality in Philadelphia, Edith had never heard of him. Nor had she ever seen anyone who looked like him. Having grown up strictly among blond-haired, blue-eyed Pennsylvanians, she said she was shocked when she first saw this big, exotic, mustachioed figure. "This poor little Presbyterian girl from Grove City, Pennsylvania, and Juilliard had never seen anything like him," she remembered. "He had this dark moustache, an enormous cigar, and a big, floppy hat. Nobody looked like that in our family. I took one look and I didn't know what it was, but I knew it was for me."

At first, however, Ernie Kovacs paid scant attention to Edith Adams. He was, after all, starting work at 7:30 every morning and not signing off the air until twelve hours later, and his grueling schedule would become even more demanding before his stint at WPTZ ended. More to the point, he was also still married to Bette, as neither had initiated divorce proceedings; in those more traditional times, dating under such circumstances was considered risqué, if not downright sinful. When he managed to carve out a chunk of several free hours, he would always rush to Trenton to spend time with Kippie and Bette. On top of all this were the poker games, which he approached with increasing fervor. Ernie's lack of skill as a card player still didn't stop him from holding weekly card games in his apartment, late at night. If he needed a fourth for gin rummy he'd call up one of his friends and drag him out of bed to play.

But Edith was fascinated with him. This distinctively ethnic older man (he was eight years her senior), with his spontaneous, fearless, irreverent approach to his shows and to life, represented everything that had been forbidden to her throughout her structured, sheltered upbringing in the small towns of Pennsylvania. Nearsighted and not wanting to wear glasses on camera, she would arrive early at the WPTZ studio, her hair still up in pincurls, and memorize the lyrics to the day's songs so she wouldn't have to rely on cue cards. After Ernie arrived she followed him around, although he talked to her only about the show or while they were on the air. Finally one day he asked her out to lunch ("I'm going out to eat. Are you going out to eat?" was his suave invitation). "I tried to ignore Edie Adams," Ernie later explained, "but she was unfailingly pleasant and nice to look at." Then he asked her out to dinner, and soon they were dating regularly. On one early date, he showed up in a brand-new Jaguar he had just bought because, he claimed, he didn't feel like taking taxis. He was making only $125 a week for all three television shows and was supporting two children and his mother; Edith, to whom such unplanned fiscal extravagance seemed as taboo as any of the Seven Deadly Sins, was appropriately awed by the gesture. What she was perhaps too young and inexperienced to realize was that Ernie's high-rolling gestures, all the flash and the dash, really masked a lack of confidence. As Ernie later said, "I couldn't believe that a beautiful, talented girl like Edie found me attractive."

Edith was quickly put to work, not only on *Ernie in Kovacsland* but also, after the prime-time summer replacement show left the air on August 24, 1951, on *TTGR* as well. These early Kovacs television shows, with their extremely low budgets and nonexistent preparation times, could not have been farther removed from the opulent, carefully rehearsed, high-cultural seriousness of the grand opera to which Edith had once aspired. In day dresses from John Wanamaker, Edith would sing hymns on the morning show in front of a flat painted to look like the inside of a church. On the evening show there was another cheap set, a flat painted with a cartoonlike dresser and a funny door; here she would deliver standard renditions of standard songs of the day—"My Funny Valentine," "All the Things You Are"—looking very fresh and young, her blonde shoulder-length hair pulled back in a ponytail or curled under in a June Allyson–style pageboy. Sometimes something more exotic would be tried: on one of the last episodes of *Ernie in Kovacsland* she performs Victor Herbert's "Through the Forest" in a gypsy costume and ribboned headpiece, sitting in a modest forest set.

Like the programs themselves, Edith is still raw and unpolished on these early shows. She is clearly in the process of internalizing the lessons of her old Broadway coach: when she sings her hand movements seem learned and repetitive, not spontaneous, and her voice and face, while lovely, are almost always the same—they don't express the emotion of the song. (Sometimes the incongruity between her expression and the content of the song produces downright surreal results, as when she performs the bittersweet "I'll Be Seeing You" with a Broadway-style let's-wow-'em smile.) But Edith was valiant and full of spunk; she seemed willing to trying anything in the new adventure of live TV. "She wasn't inhibited by Ernie's on-air brashness," says Preston Stover. "She could stand up and hand it back to him. She never looked like she was being put upon." A pie in the face just made her giggle, so she was perfectly fine for the Kovacs cast and crew.

Edith learned many things on these shows. With regard to singing before the cameras, she started to get her sea legs; the same was true of her delivering lines of dialogue—when there were lines to deliver. Often the dialogue and actions were improvised, and under Ernie's tutelage she learned to improvise too. On the Philadelphia shows, her improvisation consisted mostly of providing Ernie with cues—material upon which he could embroider to fill up a few seconds between skits or commercials or station breaks. "Technically I was the singer dash comedienne, but really I was the master of the ten-second fill," she later explained. "If I saw him hanging for what to do next, I'd run to the prop cart, which was one of those old canvas laundry baskets they have in hotels, and I'd go in there digging and hit him with something. Hit him with a chicken—just anything." As important as the ad-libbing and singing experience that she was acquiring, however, was the fact that she was learning how much fun it could be to let herself go and be silly. For straitlaced Edith, working on those early fly-by-the-seat-of-your-pants Kovacs programs—and being around Ernie privately as well—seem to have unlocked some long-sealed psychological door. At twenty-four, she was ready to go right through it.

Edith wasn't the only one who was learning as she went along. Early television was a marvelous training ground for anyone adventuresome enough to be involved in it. Joe Earley had done theater in college and had the TV experience of *Stars in Your Eyes* under his belt, but this was scant preparation for what he was about to plunge into on *Ernie in Kovacsland*. "The cast was just Ernie, Edie Adams, myself, and the Trio, so every other character that he needed a straight man to play against would be me, or in some cases Edie, when she wasn't singing. I would have as many as four costume changes in five minutes," Earley says. "It was the greatest experience in the world, because when you're that age, you're very eager to learn. It was all live, and you never knew what was going to happen. You'd have a script and then he would throw it away on the air, and you'd see whatever he was doing and then go along with it. It made you think quickly." Bits were sketched out the afternoon of the show, and after a scant rehearsal, right before seven o'clock "you'd hear the stage manager say, 'Thirty seconds,' and you'd hear the NBC chimes, and you'd realize that in twenty seconds you were going to be on and everybody across the country was going to see you and you had better not forget what you were going to do. You don't have that today. You have, 'Let's do it again.' You go into a different gear doing things live."

That intrepid spirit was present as well among the crew members. "Most of the people at Channel 3 were young and anything was possible. Nothing had been done previously, so when somebody said, 'Why can't we do thus and so?' we would try to do it—and many times we'd succeed," says Karl Weger, Jr., a technician who was hired at Channel 3 in 1946 as a sound and video operator. Weger was one of the first to bring sophisticated lighting techniques to television. For the very earliest broadcasts, an entire ceiling banked with hot PAR-38 floodlights, each with a footcandle reading of "slightly less than the noonday sun," according to Weger, were turned on to

give as much light as possible. Weger began using spotlights in rehearsals to lessen the washed-out look of the images, to give faces and shapes
some modeling and shadowing. Gradually he persuaded the powers-
that-be that the picture quality would be vastly improved by not turning on all the lights. From lighting work, Weger moved on to special-
effects engineering, where he became involved in working with Ernie.
"Ernie would have a brainstorming session in which he would talk to
the crew: 'I'd like to do thus and so.' Very seldom would you say,
'No, it can't be done.' It would be, 'Well, how about if we did it this
way?'—a variation on what he said. Sometimes he would go along
with the variation, and sometimes he would insist on doing it his way.
He had a smattering of technical understanding, but I would not call
him technically knowledgeable; he was more artistically knowledgeable
in the sense that he knew what he wanted to do and was asking, 'How
can I achieve this?' Then it was our job to come up with the answers.
I can't say that all of the things he wanted to do came about, but many
of them did."

On *Ernie in Kovacsland*, commercials were ritualistically signaled
by this recurring bit: a cast member interrupted the action with cue
cards reading

HOLD IT

DON'T NOBODY MOVE

and everyone froze in place, looking at the camera. The camera would
cut to a commercial, then back to the actors, still locked in position.
No one would move a muscle until somebody said the official magic
word: "Re-e-e-e-e-e-*SUME!*" It was like the children's game of statues, a game made all the more whimsical because adults were playing
it—and in public, on TV. It was also another example of Ernie's imaginative grasp of the comic possibilities inherent in TV's conventions—
the cutaway to a commercial, the return to actors who resume their
activities as if no time had elapsed, or as if they had indeed been frozen
in place. Ernie and his colleagues essentially had no choice but to use
their imagination in this clever way because they had so little materially
with which to work. The phrase "theater of poverty" has been used,
most aptly, to describe these Philadelphia-era Kovacs shows.

On *TTGR*, for example, "we only had $15 a week to cover makeup,
props, and costumes," says Andy McKay, "so we had to scrounge
around. We'd go to thrift stores, the Salvation Army, five-and-tens,
novelty stores—wherever you happened to be at the time. Edie did it,
I did it, Trig did it. We couldn't afford anything new." What truly

made it theater of poverty was that, rather than being covered up, the cheapness was played up, transformed into a deliberate aesthetic. A white bedsheet draped into vaguely Grecian folds would serve fine as a backdrop for a musical number; six-foot-high tubes covered with obviously paper "bark" were deemed adequate for trees—there was never any attempt to make these things appear more expensive or authentic. Moreover, with Brechtian candor, Ernie would freely and frequently comment on his lack of a decent budget. He would complain to viewers about the crummy costumes and ask them to send in their old clothes, or he'd introduce the Tony deSimone Trio with a remark like, "They've all chipped in to come on the program, as I have"; fiscal need became one of the subjects of his shows. (Bill Hofmann, Ernie's sound man, even recorded Ernie saying, "Think of me, folks, I need the money," and he would throw out the line whenever it seemed appropriate.) Sometimes tackiness was celebrated in full-blown skits. One of his favorite opening bits made use of the horse-drawn wagons that still traveled the streets of Philadelphia in the early 1950s collecting garbage. Ernie loved to make a grand entrance atop one of these trash wagons, accompanied by a life-size papier-mâché model of Nipper, the black-and-white RCA Victor dog. Suddenly he'd signal to the driver to stop, hop off the wagon with Nipper under his arm, set his pet down next to a fire hydrant, then pretend to go through all sorts of gyrations while waiting for Nipper to finish what he was doing. He repeated this kitschy "remote" with many variations during the run of *TTGR*.

Theater and its descendants—movies, radio, TV—require an understood contract between creator and audience. The audience is asked to suspend its disbelief in exchange for the creator's promise to convince the audience that what it is seeing or hearing—which is an artifice by definition—is in fact real. Ernie's refusal to fulfill that tacit promise was a form of theatrical anarchy, and it set him far apart from the mainstream of American television's creators then and since. It also indicated his respect for the intelligence of his audience. No thinking person was going to be fooled by two tubes covered with paper "bark"; why insult viewers by bothering to pretend? It was more unexpected— more real, more fun—to acknowledge and even play up the beggarly production values.

There were many ways in which Ernie simply refused to fulfill this tacit promise of illusion. Along with his celebration of cheapness, for example, came an attitude of complete casualness toward being on TV. Ernie saw no mystique about what went on in front of and behind the cameras, and he knew no reason why his audiences should be made to perceive one:

> COSTUMED ERNIE, BATHED IN DRAMATIC MOOD LIGHTING, PER-
> FORMS A LONG, SERIOUS SKIT ON A SET WITH TWO FAKE TREES . . .
> FINISHES, PICKS UP TREES, AND WALKS WITH THEM FROM ONE SET
> TO ANOTHER . . . NONCHALANTLY CHANGES COSTUME ON CAMERA
> AS HE INTRODUCES THE NEXT SKIT

The transitions that existed in reality—walking from one set to the next, changing into and out of costume—were the transitions he showed the audience; why should anything more be needed? Similarly, any-body who watched Ernie's shows during this period and for a few years hence was exposed to all manner of banter between the on-camera host and the off-camera crew (cue cards, hand signals, and other off-camera signs are usually used to hide this communication from the audience):

> ERNIE AS CYRANO DE BERGERAC IN HUGE FAKE NOSE, FOUR-FOOT-
> WIDE HAT AND SWORD . . . "YOU ALL KNOW CYRANO HAD THIS
> TREMENDOUS CAPE" . . . GETS TANGLED UP IN ENORMOUS BLAN-
> KETLIKE CAPE . . . CREW MEMBER OFF-CAMERA: "THIS ISN'T THE
> WAY WE REHEARSED IT!" . . . ERNIE STILL STRUGGLING WITH CAPE:
> "NO, THIS ISN'T THE REHEARSAL METHOD"

Sometimes he exposed the inner workings of the television show infor-mally—for example, as above, by ignoring the rule that says transitions must be concealed. But other times he made a point of his exposés, letting the audience in on backstage secrets as if he was giving them a course in TV production:

> ERNIE SAUNTERS TO EDGE OF A SET . . . "THIS IS WHAT THEY CALL
> SHOOTING OFF THE SET. TWO BITS THEY DON'T FOLLOW ME" . . .
> BUT CAMERAMAN DOES FOLLOW, AND HE LOOKS PLEASED . . . "BE-
> CAUSE THE BIG LAW IS DON'T GO PAST HERE"—POINTS TO EDGE OF
> THE FLAT—"BECAUSE THEN YOU CAN SEE THAT THE WHOLE
> THING"—BANGS ON THE WALL—"IS A FAKE!"

Ernie's attitude and actions were remarkable for their candor about the medium, a candor that is now, after audiences have become jaded from decades of television, both refreshing and shocking to see. His matter-of-fact revelation of what was really going on served another function as well. It was a way of equalizing his relationship with the audience. Never having been very good at dealing with reality on the domestic front, Ernie seemed to be more comfortable working and creating in the studio, and he transformed his shows into clubby, personal affairs, treating his audience like buddies in a secret society. He staged contests just for them, and they responded with outpourings of phone calls and letters. He begged for their donations, and they sent him whatever oddball junk was lying around their homes. He even inaugurated a real club on *TTGR* called the Early Eyeball Fraternal and Marching Society, or EEFMS to insiders. Viewers could join by calling up and requesting an exclusive membership card signed by EEFM (Ernie) or EEFM-1 (whoever else happened to be around). On one side was printed the logo of a half-closed eye, "EEFMS" in medieval script, "WPTZ Channel 3" (as a reminder to watch), and the secret passphrase "It's been real." On the reverse was the Code of the EEFMS (exhibiting Ernie's aversion to waking up early and his irreverent attitude toward money):

1. An EEFM is a male.
   A—Or a female.
   B—Or interested in either political party.
2. An EEFM never sleeps later than 8:03.
   A—Unless he or she is deathly ill.
   B—Unless he or she is deathly . . . er . . . dead, that is.
   C—Unless the EEFM is sleepy.
3. An EEFM makes less than $987,648,001.23 per annum. (Slightly higher in the South and South west.)
4. An EEFM may not raise ostriches or parsley for profit without written permission of EEFM-1.

Below this code was reprinted the secret passphrase "It's been real." A catchphrase that came into vogue after the war, "It's been real" began to be associated with Kovacs as a sign-off on *TTGR*. It would become a Kovacs tradition, one that he carried over to later shows and that is associated with him to this day. The phrase (with its vaguely beatnik sound, although this was the prebeatnik era) possesses a nice double meaning: it is both a direct leave-taking, as in "It's been fun," and a reference to the reality of what has just been presented on TV. At the end of every program "It's been real" would pop up in some unexpected place—beneath a sweeping broom, under a banana peel, across a frost-covered window, on a man's bald spot. In one program of this period, a woman from the audience presents Ernie with a birthday cake that she has baked and decorated with "It's been real" in frosting. Ernie, just turned thirty-three, blushes with pleasure, then happily declares that he will use the cake for the show's closing the next day.

Not everyone within broadcast range of Ernie's WPTZ-originated programs was as much of a fan as the woman with the cake. Ernie's brand of humor and casual attitude were peculiar, and one had to have a taste for the offbeat to enjoy him. "Ernie Kovacs—the most foolish thing and a waste of money. That cigar is disgusting," complained one viewer to Merrill Panitt, then television critic of the *Philadelphia Inquirer*. But Ernie had a strong supporter in Panitt, who went on to become the editor of *TV Guide*. "He made use of the things you could do with television," explains Panitt. "He didn't just take old radio shows and add sight. He saw what television was and saw what could be done with it and didn't hesitate to experiment with it. So you were seeing new aspects of television every time you watched Ernie. He could perform magic with the camera, even in those early days." The *Philadelphia Evening Bulletin*'s television critic, Harry Harris, also supported Ernie's work, although he noted that the shows were often uneven. "When he started, television was pretty drab and humdrum. You know, they just put a camera into a studio, and people just talked into it," remembers Harris, who later worked for *Variety*. "But he did things that were offbeat, and that attracted attention. And a lot of his stuff was pretty bad too. I think he was feeling his way, and some of the material worked well, and others were just fillers and kind of silly. He was always better with the visual values."

With the *Kukla, Fran and Ollie* replacement, Ernie also began to receive press attention beyond the confines of Philadelphia. Critics in New York were looking at his programs, with reactions as mixed as those of viewers. Harriet Van Horne, the TV columnist for the *New York World-Telegram and Sun*, summed up the weaknesses and strengths of Ernie's Philadelphia-based shows when she observed that *Ernie in Kovacsland* was simultaneously "wild and casual, witty and foolish, clever and idiotic. . . . Sometimes his outbursts have the spontaneity we associate with true, moonlit madness. At other times his nonsense is heavy, creaky, and a bore."

In Philadelphia, Ernie's crew was of necessity working with relatively primitive equipment, both because the shows were allotted low budgets and because commercial television was still in its infancy. From the control room, the director could "punch up" such simple special effects as cuts, fades, or dissolves from the image generated by one camera to the image generated by another. The slightly more sophisticated functions, such as superimpositions, reverse polarity (a switch that made positives seem negative), and reverse scanning (which flipped images upside down), were little used because TV generally stuck to realism—most television of the time resembled filmed theater or vaudeville.

Much has been made of the technical wizardry of Ernie's comedy, of the fact that he was ahead of his time in the medium. Enthralled as he was with this new electronic toy's strange and unexplored possibilities, Ernie and his crew freely experienced with techniques that were infrequently used then and have since become commonplace. That was part of Ernie's gambling nature and also part of his special vision. But more interesting than the techniques themselves is what he used them for. "Ernie really saw pictures more than anything else," says Mike Marmer, a writer who would come to work for Ernie within a few years, in New York. "I don't know where they came from, or why— they were just bizarre—but the point is that that's what he saw. He saw the shock of something."

Thus, for example, to Ernie the reverse-scan function was useful because he could invent a bit where he stood in the street, looked at a sign reading FLY MAN WANTED, and then appear to walk into the studio upside down. With the wipe-down capability that electronically obliterated the TV picture, he could, dressed as his lisping poet laureate, Percy Dovetonsils, finish reciting a poem and then sink down in his chair, seeming to be at the mercy of the television as the picture was wiped out from the top to the bottom of the screen. The medium allowed Ernie to play cards or fence with himself, to superimpose a picture of bolts and gears onto his head, or to crop his face (cigar stuck firmly in mouth) onto the body of a dog.

Well-budgeted shows had technical directors who would manipulate the electronic panel in the control room as their directors called out what they wanted done. At WPTZ, however, directors were on their own, working the control panel as well as making the decisions. On Ernie's shows, typically the director sat and watched the performers through a big plate glass window in the control room, trying to anticipate what Ernie was going to do next. (If the director was Benny Squires, however, he'd "direct standing up," remembers Karl Weger, Jr., "because he was so hyper and so wound up that to sit down would have meant he was going to sleep.") While the director pushed and pulled levers in the control room, two or three operators worked the cameras on the studio floor; whenever an operator's camera was turned off, he'd rush to move a piece of scenery or find another prop. The directors and crew who worked with Ernie were adept at improvising visuals and sound effects, sometimes to augment whatever came into Ernie's head to do, sometimes to inspire him to invent something. "The whole crew was in on it," remembers Rene Heckman, the set designer for some of Ernie's shows. "It was just like a bunch of kids in a garage putting on a show. 'What are we going to do?' It was impromptu theater, really. With a show like that we could experiment, and if it failed, it failed. I mean, who cared?" Nobody cared, because everybody knew there would be more hours to fill the next day, the next week—in such an atmosphere, liberal invention was encouraged and rewarded. Ernie reveled in everything they tried, duds as well as the successes. "If something didn't come off, that was a big 'boffo,' " says Bill Hofmann, the audio engineer on Ernie's Philadelphia shows. " 'What a boffo that was!' he would say, and he would laugh. I don't recall him ever getting angry if something didn't have the payoff he thought he could have gotten or was working toward. Everything was just a big joke. He was like the big kid who never grew up."

Many of the more offbeat visions for which Ernie is remembered came about through the free experimentation of this period. Although he often gets sole credit for the style and the substance of his television shows, much of what was being created in Philadelphia sprang not only from his personal (and admittedly idiosyncratic) vision but also from a spirited collaboration among Ernie, his directors, and the crew. Karl Weger, Jr., for example, was always experimenting with various gadgets to invent special effects—things that can be done today by punching a button or two, but in the early days of the medium were "very special," says audio engineer Bill Hofmann, "extremely way far out. Nobody had anything like what Karl was doing."

Something as apparently simple as rotating the image on the TV screen, for example, was virtually impossible with the bulky ninety-pound Image Orthicon camera then in use or, even worse, the enormous Iconoscope camera; the latter weighed so much that two men were needed to lift and place it on a tripod. But Weger cleverly cooked up an image-inverting device consisting of two right-angled mirrors, like those used in periscopes, set inside a tin can. ("I was a great one for fabricating things from cans," he says. "I made some lighting devices for the PAR-38 bulbs out of large-size tomato juice cans. And the optical mechanism we're talking about was done with orange juice or small, individual-serving cans.") When the tin can with mirrors was attached to the front of a camera lens and one mirror was moved in relation to the other, the image magically appeared to revolve—the perfect Scavokian device, as it permitted bodies to be violently contorted, for example.

Weger had developed the image inverter for shows other than Ernie's, but "somewhere along the line Ernie decided he could use it with great humor," he remembers. "Andy McKay generally operated it. Ernie would start to turn his head, and Andy would turn the image inverter at the same time to correct for Ernie's turning his head, so Ernie's head would appear to stay stationary, but the rest of his body would appear to move." With the image inverter, it was easy for Ernie to vacuum the ceiling: McKay simply built a set with all the furniture upside down, including a ceiling light fixture attached upside down to the floor. When Ernie vacuumed this set, the image inverter would tilt the picture so that the room would appear right-side up and Ernie upside down. Another time the device was used to make it look like Ernie was on the sinking *Titanic*. "He'd be sitting at the desk doing something straight," describes Bill Freeland, "and he'd have a monitor nearby so he could see what was going on in the camera. We'd gradually tilt the picture, and he'd go along with it. Anything you did, he'd go along with, no matter how crazy it was." According to McKay, NBC staff members in New York caught sight of the mystifying images on one of the Kovacs' shows and wanted to know how it was done.

One morning Ernie was searching for some new visuals to go with the records he played to fill up time on the wake-up show. Having seen the wonders that could be achieved with a tin can, he taped a kid's kaleidoscope to a small juice can, attached it to a camera lens, and illuminated it from one end with a flashlight. Turning the kaleidoscope in sync to the music, he created abstract moving images—a matching of "sound to sight," as he would later say. (It was extraordinary to be showing purely abstract images on such a mainstream medium as broadcast TV. Even now this bit looks fresh and unusual, so rarely is commercial television used for nonnarrative effects; it's really more like a little piece of early video art.) From this visual trick concocted by Ernie, Weger was inspired to create a similar effect using an oscilloscope display, that straight horizontal line on the fluorescent screen of a cathode-ray tube that vibrates whenever a sound signal is applied to it. Using mirrors set at sixty-degree angles, he could bend and fracture the oscilloscope line into a diamond around the perimeter of the TV screen; when the oscilloscope display vibrated, the diamond blossomed into a circle. This device became known in the industry as a "whirligig."

Weger was also one of the principal technicians who developed television's matting capabilities, which Ernie used to great effect. A matting amplifier allows an image generated by one camera to be cut into an image generated by a second camera; it's what we see when a football game appears behind a sports announcer seated at a desk in a newsroom, for instance, although this is a far more sophisticated example than the early technology was capable of producing. Weger built one of the first matting amplifiers used on television, for a WPTZ show called *Piano Patter*. While pianist Ted Steele played a tune, a canary flew around in reaction to the music, and Steele would in turn respond to the canary—which was actually nowhere near him. "We used a little bird that was light or white," Weger explains. "Then, by taking the peaks of the signal, which were the whites [on camera one, trained on Steele], inverting them to produce a blanking [matting] signal, mixing that with the other one to drive it down into black and cutting it off, clipping it, then adding the second signal portion of the white [from camera two, with the bird] in that hole, you now had a little bird with no bleed-through. And we were able to have the bird appear to fly in and land on top of the piano and so forth."

According to Weger, "Ernie saw this or knew of this because Ted Steele was on around 1948 or '49. It would have been something that had already been achieved and he then wanted to use." At WPTZ, Ernie had himself matted into old movies, dressing up as Cecil B. de Mille and pretending to direct the actors or costuming himself as a cowboy and picking off bad guys with a cap gun. Later, after leaving Philadelphia, his comedy would rely a great deal on matting; it enabled him to create an invisible girlfriend, peer through holes in people's heads, sever bodies in half, and visualize a performer's thoughts (like the "thought balloons" in cartoons).

The sound effects provided by Bill Hofmann were as important an element in Ernie's early television comedy as Weger's visual effects. "Bill would just pull out something like marching feet or a ricocheting bullet," says set designer Rene Heckman. "This sound would come over the air, and Ernie's first reaction, live, was exactly what you'd see." Hofmann, who seems to have been especially sensitive to Ernie, perceived in him a lack of confidence. "I always thought that Ernie, when he first started, felt he needed little crutches along the way—which he totally did not need," says Hofmann. The "crutches" were the props tossed to him by Andy McKay or the sound effects thrown in by Hofmann, devices that gave Ernie something on which to improvise to fill up time. But Hofmann himself downplays the importance of the audio in these shows. A special symbiosis seems to have existed between Ernie and Hofmann, who instinctively understood exactly what sound at what moment would set off Ernie's particular brand of humor. Much of Ernie's later comedy grew directly out of the jokes he and Hofmann spontaneously created in these Philadelphia shows.

Hofmann had free rein to do anything he wanted. In their simplest form, his sound effects helped to carry along some improvised story Ernie was telling; like sound effects in radio, they added texture to a narrative, pushing the audience's imagination a little. "If he were telling a story about this woman he saw walking down the street," says Hofmann, "then maybe I'd bring in a horn, which we would weave right into the story: 'And there was this guy in a big Cadillac, and he just blew the horn.' " Other sound effects weren't tied to a story but were equally realistic. Ernie often had a gun on his desk, "so whenever he picked it up," says Hofmann, "I would go *bang!* with a sound effect. Or if Ernie pointed it somewhere and I brought in the sound of a shot, somebody would drop something at the other end of the studio. And then, of course, he would elaborate on that: 'I just shot a cameraman!' "

But the funniest sounds were the surrealistic ones—the ones that didn't match the visuals or that were wildly improbable within the realistic studio setting. Ernie might beat on a table with a drumstick; Hofmann would bring in a gong. Seeing that Ernie was running out of things to say, Hofmann would throw out an airplane sound and Ernie would duck, or he'd play the sound of a racecar and Ernie would pretend to watch it speed by. Anything violent—as American animators and slapstick comics have long known—held the potential for comedy: "Ernie would walk out a door and then *bang!*, we'd bring in the sound of a person falling down steps. Then Ernie would drag himself back in: 'That last step's a high one,' anything he could think of. We used explosions a lot. He would roll up a piece of paper and throw it towards the camera—and *bam!*, this huge explosion. He always reacted to this stuff. The sound effect wasn't the payoff to the bit; the sound effect *led* to the payoff, which was the great ad lib Ernie came up with."

Working in this improvisational way, particularly on live TV, required enormous concentration and more than a little imagination. The sound effects might have seemed random, but they were in fact the product of Hofmann's disciplined and quick thinking, of his constantly looking ahead and deciding what sound would be funny with what object. "I would watch him. He was a great one for working with props. And I would look to see what was on the table or what Andy McKay was getting ready to throw," he says. "I would try to anticipate what he was going to do and come up with a funny sound. After a while, I almost felt what he was going to go for next." (McKay became adept at sensing the perfect moment to throw Ernie a prop, too. "I had a sense of when he was running dry or overdoing it. The best thing I would throw him was a stuffed fish that had Band-Aids all over it and black eyes. No matter what, he'd find a new angle for the fish.")

Occasionally the sound effects were created live in the studio, but only occasionally—there simply wasn't time. Hofmann could also pull sound effects from WPTZ's record library—a throwback to the days of radio—but, again, that was difficult with time at a premium, particularly for the early-morning *TTGR*. Finally, for expediency, Hofmann and some fellow crew members put together a sixteen-inch record of sound effects that suggested comic possibilities, and it became the primary source of audio effects on Ernie's Philadelphia shows. Some of the sounds were taken from the record library—train whistles, sirens, marching men; others they made themselves—chains dragging across the floor, many kinds of gongs, various slide whistles. There were chimps chattering and dogs barking and a lion roaring ("He would jump on the table and say, 'Get that thing out of here!' I think he even had a name for the lion," says Hofmann). They even stole the *ba-ba-ba-boom* from a famous Ajax cleanser commercial of the time and, from a Warner Bros. cartoon, the voice of Bugs Bunny sneering, "Oh, I wouldn't say that." "We had all these crazy sounds," says Hofmann, "any sound we could think of. Some of them are conventional today, but quite a few years ago these things weren't available as readily." After a while Hofmann became so familiar with the cuts on the record that he could find anything instantly, by sight.

Ernie's interest in remotes, in breaking down the walls of the studio, led him to an interesting experiment in 1951. For the premiere of his first network show, *Time for Ernie*, WPTZ had given him the budget to make a little film. One hot spring day he went with the station's film crew, director Joe Behar, and Andy McKay, who would handle costumes, makeup, and props, out to a high school baseball field; there they shot a four-minute short known only by the bland title *Baseball Film*. But the idea was quite sophisticated, as was its execution: it was the complete story of a baseball game, shot without sound, with Ernie pantomiming every role. He was the tobacco-chewing pitcher on the mound and the umpire who fought him and gave him a black eye; he was the fussy old lady in the bleachers and the screaming child with a lollipop and the beer-guzzling loudmouth and even the fly that landed on a player's arm— this was Ernie's head, cigar in mouth, superimposed onto a drawing of a fly. (The film, which Ernie showed on TV from time to time through the 1950s, may have inspired a 1959 Gillette commercial in which comedian Joe E. Brown performed multiple roles in a baseball game.)

Playing multiple roles wasn't a new trick: Buster Keaton, for example, had done it in the early 1920s in *The Three Ages* and *The Playhouse*. Ernie was quite knowledgeable about film—in one show from this period he dons a German helmet and asks, "Don't I look like Erich von Stroheim?"—and it is possible that he knew of these Keaton movies. In any case, *Baseball Film* was important as the first instance of Ernie's work being given a structure through the editing together of pieces of film (as opposed to being seen exactly as it was played out live, in the rough, within only the loosest of frameworks). It also showed off Ernie's ability to create a character with a few deft strokes—a gesture, a facial expression, a bit of costume, a prop or two. It was an ability for which he had already received attention back in his East Hampton summer stock days, when his portrayal of a New Jersey family and a tramp had brought down the house during a student "Stunt Night."

Ernie eventually became famous for the recurring characters he created for television. The most famous of these was born on a WPTZ show when Andy McKay handed him a pair of goofy joke glasses, the perfect minimal Scavok prop. He put them on and started reading from a book of poetry he happened to have in hand: "How can I leave thee? How can I from thee part?" He named the character Percy Dovetonsils, a moniker he had used on one of his Trenton radio shows several years earlier.

Percy wore a tiger-skin smoking jacket and had a monstrous spit curl decorating his forehead. He lisped his poetic creations from a lace-trimmed volume, punctuating his readings with moues of delight aimed at the camera. (Such a blatantly effeminate caricature would be considered of questionable taste today. Even a decade later, when Ernie was working at ABC, some offended members of studio management pressured him to drop Percy from his repertoire, but he refused.) Percy was a composite of several radio personalities of the time, including Ted Malone (the stage name of Alden Russell), who read sentimental poems on the ABC Radio show *Between the Bookends*; David Ross, who also read poetry on the radio; and theater critic Alexander Woollcott, whose voice on radio's *Town Crier* broadcasts resembled that of Percy.

Not all of the popular characters on Ernie's Philadelphia shows were people. Because the prop budget was so low, Ernie frequently asked viewers to send in their old junk. "We'd take anything that anybody could find or donate—old stuffed animals, whatever they had, an old tire, *any*thing," remembered Edie Adams. "Somebody sent him a seven-foot rag doll named Gertrude, and she was used a lot." Donated on the air by a housewife from Camden, New Jersey, Gertrude resembled Betty Boop with her kidney-shaped head, fluttery painted-on eyes, pouty mouth, and brunette flapper's bob. Viewers soon became familiar with her slender, six-foot form. Sometimes Ernie would treat her nicely, dancing a sultry tango with her or carrying on a deadpan conversation or carefully clipping her nails with gigantic pruning shears. At other times she was subjected to all manner of comedic abuse:

ERNIE IN KOVACSLAND OPENS MINUS HOST . . . "HE'S NOT HERE YET" . . . "I KNOW, LET'S FOLLOW HIM" . . . CAMERA PANS OUTSIDE AND ACROSS SKYLINE OF PHILADELPHIA . . . TRAFFIC NOISE . . . RAGTIME PIANO . . . ERNIE IS SIGHTED STROLLING ALONG THE STREET DRAGGING GERTRUDE AS IF HE HAS ALL THE TIME IN THE WORLD . . . MAN WITH SANDWICH BOX TRIES TO SELL ERNIE SANDWICH . . . ERNIE SHAKES HIM BY THE NECK, PUTS BOX OVER HIS HEAD TO TRAP HIS ARMS, AND HITS HIM REPEATEDLY WITH GERTRUDE . . . ERNIE STOPS AT LUNCHEONETTE, BUYS DRINK, HOLDS GERTRUDE UP, AND LETS HER DRINK FROM GLASS . . . LOOKS AT WATCH, FOLDS GERTRUDE AND PUTS HER DOWN ON SIDEWALK, TAKES OUT CIGAR, AND LIGHTS UP . . . CONTINUES LIGHTING MATCHES AND THROWING THEM INTO OPEN GARBAGE CAN

ERNIE IN STUDIO HAS A FIGHT WITH GERTRUDE . . . THEY BATTLE ALL OVER THE SET . . . MAKE THEIR WAY UP INTO THE CATWALKS . . . CAMERA FOLLOWS THE FIGHT . . . ERNIE FINALLY WINS . . . PLUNGES GERTRUDE DOWN TWENTY FEET BELOW . . . SHE SURVIVES

The violence directed at Gertrude was (and still is) funny in the way the violence-filled American cartoons of the time were funny—although, again, such actions directed at a life-size female form might be viewed as offensive if performed today.

Bill Hofmann's sound-effects record had a couple of cuts especially for Gertrude. One was the sound of a woman screaming, handy when Ernie decided to fling Gertrude off the set. Another was a drastically speeded-up woman's voice, which became solely Gertude's property; so closely was it associated with her that Hofmann had merely to play a moment of it offstage for Ernie to react, "Okay, Gertrude, I'll be right there." Gertrude eventually came apart at the seams—literally. Ernie made an on-the-air appeal: "Would the woman who donated this please come on the air and sew her up, because she's falling apart?" The Camden housewife promptly did so, and Gertrude survived to accompany Ernie to New York.

The nighttime *Ernie in Kovacsland* went off the air on August 24, 1951, when *Kukla, Fran and Ollie* reclaimed its time slot. But soon thereafter, in September, the early-morning *TTGR* was expanded from ninety minutes to two hours to make room for the ever-increasing numbers of sponsors. By this time the show had been refined—insofar as the mostly impromptu ambience could be called refined. (*TTGR* was never scripted as a rule. "There was a rundown to show you when the commercials were coming in, but that was it," said director Joe Behar. "Whatever he wanted to do to fill those two hours was fine with the station.") "There is still enough of the *Hellzapoppin'* type of racket to account partly for its success," reported the trade paper *Variety*. "The emcee has become less uninhibited, but he has compensated for this with finesse and a surer and less forced comedy sense." Over thirty years later, newspaper columnist and CBS commentator Andy Rooney would observe that "having someone who knows how to handle time, with presence, is one secret to the success of a morning show. If the person on-camera takes charge and directs the course the show takes, it can be successful. He or she has to be able to fill casual time in a way that holds an audience." Much of the success of WPTZ's inexpensive wake-up experiment is attributable to Ernie's abilities to meet these criteria. He had a striking and immediately identifiable visual presence, always wearing stylish, immaculately cut suits, his jet-black hair always sleekly combed, his big cigar always in hand or stuck firmly in mouth. With his quiet charm, his good-natured eagerness to try anything (even dangerous things, like putting a jaguar on his back), and his ability "to fill casual time" amusingly and compellingly, he made a good companion for some of the first audiences that enjoyed TV in the early hours.

Audience popularity wasn't the only reason sponsors were clamoring to buy time on *TTGR*. Sponsors' spots normally ran twenty seconds, and the commercial was sometimes supplied on film. But it wasn't uncommon in these early days of television for performers to do a commercial from copy and a fact sheet submitted about a day in advance. Ernie performed many of these on *TTGR*. "I had sold some spots to an antique dealer, Irwin Schaffer, one of the pioneer advertisers on TV," says Robert Jawer, who was working as WPTZ's "one and only account executive" at the time. "I also got Kovacs to do the commercial, and I went with him to meet with Irwin Schaffer and go over some copy. Kovacs would talk to a client about what he had to do; I think when he did commercials he was anxious to please." Sometimes Ernie was asked to write the commercial himself, or he would suggest something in keeping with the shows. As these received a positive response from the viewers, more and more sponsors hired Ernie specifically to create commercials—and they were as wild as can be. Once, taking a pancake batter, he set up a griddle and started making pancakes; each time he finished one he'd throw it somewhere—at an actor, at the booth, at a camera. (Apparently the sponsor didn't mind, for Ernie went on to do many more pancake commercials.) "The clients, having seen him and the way he worked, would give him free rein," explains Harold J. Pannepacker, who ran the station's sales department. "They might buy a minute commercial, but for some commercials we'd go a minute and a half, especially with Ernie. If Ernie liked the client and it was a good product and something he was able to fool around with, he would go on for two or maybe three minutes."

On January 3, 1952, while Ernie continued to do the daily, lengthened *TTGR* as well as the twice-weekly *Deadline for Dinner*, NBC added another show to his schedule. Called *Kovacs on the Corner*, it was a late-morning, nationally broadcast show, thirty minutes daily, modeled after comedian Fred Allen's radio feature "Allen's Alley." On a cartoonlike set with painted building facades and such whimsical touches as a crooked barbershop pole, Ernie strolled and chatted with the inhabitants of Kovacs' Alley—such "type" characters as Pete the Cop (Peter Boyle, Sr.), Al the Dog (a fur-suited actor supposedly invisible to all except children and Ernie), Luigi the Barber (Joe Earley), and "Little" Johnny Merkin, a midget. On one of the first episodes he dressed up as Frankenstein and chatted with Edith Adams, who commented casually upon his entrance, "Hi, Ernie, why are you walking so funny?" The new show originated from Studio B on the second floor of WPTZ's Walnut Street facilities, the only studio available for a permanent street set. It was directed by Joe Behar and written by Marge Greene (who also doubled as an actress on the show), Donald Mattern (who had worked with Ernie at WTTM and was now free-lancing for

WPTZ), and Kovacs. Much about this show, however, was off the cuff:

ERNIE HAS SOAP ALL OVER HIS FACE . . . LUIGI THE BARBER SHAVES HIM . . . LOUD AND HORRENDOUS SCRAPING SOUND

ERNIE DEMONSTRATES HOW TO MAKE TEENY-WEENY HORS D'OEUVRES . . . CUTS BREAD DOWN WITH SCISSORS: "YOU TAKE OUT ALL THE NOURISHING PART" . . . CLOSEUP OF MINUSCULE CIRCLE OF BREAD . . . CUTS AN ALMOST INVISIBLE TRIANGLE OF MEAT AND PUTS ON BREAD . . . "NOW, THERE'S NOBODY WHO CAN COMPLAIN THEY ENJOYED THAT!"

For variety, Edith Adams might sing a popular tune of the day, such as "In a Mountain Greenery," or the Dave Appell Trio, who played Kovacs' Alley's garbage collectors, might perform a polka while wearing their garbagemen costumes. *Kovacs on the Corner* had a live audience and two recurring audience-participation features. In "Kovacs' Knickknack Corner," Ernie, standing behind a counter and wearing a hat several sizes too small, chatted with a "customer" from the audience as he offered bits of junk from his vast knickknack stockpile:

WOMAN FROM AUDIENCE GIVES ERNIE PAPER-WRAPPED PACKAGE . . . IN EXCHANGE HE PULLS OUT LACROSSE STICK BUT DECIDES TO KEEP IT: "THAT'S A LITTLE TOO MUCH" . . . "HERE'S AN OPEN-TOED FOOT FOR AN OPEN-TOED SHOE" . . . HOLDS UP CHAIN "FOR CHAIN SMOKERS—IF YOUR HUSBAND SMOKES CHAINS" . . . PULLS UP A TWO-FACED DOLL'S HEAD HE CALLS A "MOOD CHANGER" . . . BOX OF A THOUSAND RUBBER BANDS . . . FINALLY GIVES HER LONG UNDERWEAR WITH CORSAGE ON IT

The other bit was called "Yoo-Hoo Time!" Picking up on the penchant of studio television audiences to wave to the folks back home, Ernie created a formal time for a selected audience member to perform this broadcasting ritual. The camera took a medium shot of a shack facade; in its window was a lowered shade painted with the words "Yoo-Hoo Time!" Suddenly the shade would zoom up, revealing the lucky audience member waving and smiling and saying "You-hoo!" "That's Sherry Pooner waving hello to her friends in Chicago, Illinois," Ernie would intone.

Unlike Ernie's other WPTZ programs, *Kovacs on the Corner* also featured guests, sometimes famous ones like the dancing Nicholas Brothers, at others times run-of-the-mill vaudeville acts who were making the rounds of television shows—anything from chimps to oddball specialty acts, like a man who tap-danced to George M. Cohan tunes on a strange sort of tap-drum. (After his act, the camera cut to Ernie drumming a tiny drum that was emitting a real—that is, large—drum sound.) In the manner of his *Trentonian* column, where he gabbed informally to and about the locals, Ernie would gently converse with his vaudeville guests or with members of the studio audience. He could find a way to talk to anyone: in one episode he even carries on a straight-faced conversation with an organ grinder's monkey. (He also gives the monkey a donation and asks for change. When the monkey doesn't give it to him, he yells over the organ grinder's music, "Cheapskate!") On other occasions, to fill time, he would simply "blah" about anything that happened to catch his attention. "We always used to say that he looked at the world through rose-colored glasses," remembers sound man Bill Hofmann. "He would say, 'I was coming to work today, walking down Walnut Street . . .' and spin out some terrific funny story. One time he was talking about the perfume that women wore. Just that little bit of perfume would be nothing to anybody else, but to him it was something to make humor out of."

For the most part, however, the format of *Kovacs on the Corner* was too restrictive for Ernie's tastes. He didn't enjoy playing checkers with Al the Dog while Al complained that he couldn't enter dog shows because he was visible only to kids (Ernie informed him of a dog show at P.S. 38 where all the judges were children); it didn't challenge his imagination to play cat's cradle while Tondelaya the Cat told terrible cat jokes ("That should be a howling success!") He regarded the characters and the tone as cloying and flat. Ernie much preferred the freedom of an unformatted show, where he could be freewheeling and inventive and interact with crew members who shared his tastes and interests rather than with character types who had to strive too hard to be cute. (He loved one thing about the show, however. Scenic designer Rene Heckman recalls that before the first broadcast, unbeknownst to Ernie, he had painted a black manhole into the middle of the street on the set. "When he came into the studio he said, 'Rene, I had no idea you were going to do something like this! We're going to go back and rewrite the script. This is fantastic! I love it!' He was very appreciative and immediately saw the possibilities." Ernie did countless bits with the manhole, talking down into it, fishing from it, pretending to fall into it, and the like.)

Part of the problem was that Ernie resented the network's efforts to control what he regarded as *his* creative endeavor. "Ernie did not like interference or what he perceived as interference," explains writer Donald Mattern. Ernie had originally been planning to go on the air and "do the same thing he did on his morning show," according to Mattern. "And the network said, 'We can't go on the air with a show like this Kovacs is going to do.' " Even though Ernie had always produced his own shows, WPTZ assigned B. Calvin Jones to produce *Kovacs on the Corner* because "Cal was very emphatic about everything he did," says Mattern, and therefore could handle Kovacs.

Initially Ernie worked with the writers, director, and producer, but after a while "it became a tug-of-war," says Mattern, so Mattern and Greene were separated from Ernie, and Cal Jones became their liaison. He also resisted Jones's efforts. Jones had directed *TTGR* with little problem, but "this was completely different," explains Mattern. "Suddenly Ernie wasn't controlling the situation." According to Jones, "Ernie's problem was that he couldn't delegate authority, and he was unwilling to work with other creative people. I felt he had to have a creative team around him who knew structures—beginnings, middles, and ends—and knew how to get a payoff, who knew fundamentally what constituted a program. But just to turn the cameras on and let him go, which is what he wanted, was an impossibility. There's no way you can sell anything like that."

But as Ernie was gradually discovering, his true milieu was the television studio space, unencumbered by cute street sets with crooked barbershop poles. In the undecorated studio he could give free rein to the ideas that were springing with increasing frequency to his mind, those surreal mixtures of the commonplace and the unusual which only he could see. Still, he was relatively new at this profession and not yet confident of his capabilities in the medium, nor of his staying power in show business. "I think he had a vision of being able to turn anything into something humorous, but whether that was calculated or just something he had to do to survive, I question at this point," says Karl Weger, Jr. "My opinion is that what he accomplished, he accomplished to survive. The artistic aspects happened to be there and he benefited from them. I don't know that he initially set out with that in mind—he may well have, I wouldn't want to do him an injustice—but I got the impression that many things came from a certain idea he had that would fill a certain amount of time. That might have been more predominant in his thinking than the end result being accepted as an artistic event."

Part of the thinness of *Kovacs on the Corner* can be attributed to Ernie's responsibility for generating some thirteen and a half hours of programming a week. Even with writers, much of Ernie's programming time was used up with improvising or with skits and commercials that he himself wrote. And besides his hosting duties, he is credited as producer on most of these shows. He sometimes complained about the situation. In a 1957 interview with the *Saturday Evening Post*, he recollected his Philadelphia TV days this way:

> Sometimes I used to leave the station at four in the morning and come back at 7 A.M. I was a dead duck and I had a migraine headache for three years straight. Then one day my boss called me and said, "I saw your show this morning. You weren't funny."
>
> "Do you know how many hours I'm on the air each week?" I asked. "As much as some stars are in a whole season. I have no secretary. I run contests. I do my own typing, my own writing. I write out the weather charts and select the music. Do you honestly believe that there's a human being who's not encased in wax in the Smithsonian who can be on thirteen hours a week and still be funny?" . . .
>
> He said, "I'm afraid you'll have to pick up your program, Kovacs. It sags."

But Ernie clearly thrived under the pressure of too much work, and he always created it for himself and would continue to do so until the end of his life. He seemed to need to be inundated with work in order to function happily. One critic described his on-the-air persona thus: "With nervous energy tempered by a cool exterior, Kovacs scurried from one barely rehearsed skit to another, risking at every moment losing control in front of a live audience, very much like a tight-rope walker performing without a net." Ernie never gave himself a net.

The story he told the *Saturday Evening Post* points up another area that drained Ernie's energy: conflicts with people in authority at the station. "As things progressed," says Karl Weger, Jr., "as he got into doing network originations, more and more constraints, if you will, were being placed on him in terms of timing, structure, and so forth, all of which he objected to. Before he left Philadelphia, there was a considerable amount of friction in terms of what needed to be done to satisfy the producers and directors versus what Ernie wanted to do. But he was also under personal pressures, and money became a necessity, so he cooperated in many instances with things he didn't really want to do. He would grumble about it to people near him, but he went ahead and did what he had to do in order to comply with what they wanted."

The personal pressures and the need for money were indeed mounting. For one day, as suddenly as she had left, Bette Wilcox Kovacs dropped back into Ernie's life.

Bette reappeared in 1951, sometime during or after *Ernie in Kovacsland*, which had garnered him a national audience and important critical attention. Ernie told his friend Jane Hess that he thought Bette had seen him on the network show and responded, "This smells like money." Kippie Kovacs, however, thinks her mother may have returned for an additional reason: "I believe that she became lonely." Perhaps there was some truth to this; at the time Ernie implied to his Trenton friend George Kudra that Bette wanted to reconcile with him. "But once you do something to the Hungarians, that's the end," says Kudra. Instead, in September 1951, Ernie filed for divorce in Philadelphia.

Two months later Bette, who was living in Trenton again, sued for custody of their children. But in order to sue him, papers had to be served, and in the case of Ernie, the world-class prankster, this was easier said than done. "He didn't want to be served," remembers Joe Earley, "so the crew would run the subpoena server all over the place. This was constant stuff on these shows." Actually, says cameraman Bill Freeland, the crew members knew that Ernie didn't want "those writs that were going to cost him money" and took it upon themselves to keep his whereabouts hidden: "We were Ernie's friends. Ernie wasn't really a part of it. We did all that stuff on our own."

What they did was deliberately mislead Bette's legal representatives as to Ernie's whereabouts. "Ernie's down on the second floor," or "Ernie's up in the projectionist's room," or "Ernie's just gone to his apartment," they would tell him. "Of course, we were all tied in with headsets," says Freeland, "so we'd tell the projectionist, 'Hey, the writ server's coming up. Send him to the basement.' " According to sound man Bill Hofmann, "After a while we got to know who the process server was, or what an individual who was about to serve papers looked like." The hapless process server would spend the entire day running into dead ends. "Then a couple of times," remembers Hofmann, "we used the crash box. It was maybe three feet wide and about six feet high with junk inside, so if you dropped it, it would make a horrendous noise. One day, while the process server was in the studio, somebody dropped it right next to him, and he almost flew through the ceiling."

For the next year a particularly nasty battle was fought between Bette and Ernie in the Municipal Court of the County of Philadelphia, with accusations hurled not only by the litigants but by Ernie's mother as well. During the trial, Ernie moved Mary and the children and himself into the Rittenhouse Claridge, a beautiful old apartment house right on the square. He did his best to protect his daughters from the strife of the custody trial. "He never was too tired for us; he would take time out," says Elisabeth Kovacs. "In Philadelphia, he got us little nurse's uniforms, and he would let us dress up and take us for a walk in Rittenhouse Square. There was a bronze lion there, and we would climb up on it and play. He also patiently taught us to play chess. He would pretend that we'd won and allow us to feel brilliant." Ernie often mentioned the girls on his shows and occasionally brought them on as guests. Kippie and Bette appear in some home movies that Andy McKay shot on the set of *Kovacs on the Corner* during this period, all dressed up in white gloves, hats, and matching dresses, their flouncy skirts poufed out with the petticoats fashionable at the time. Despite the cast and crew activity around him, Ernie's attention is fixed on his daughters. He puts Groucholike nose glasses on them, lifts them up on chairs so they can reach the boom mike, and sits them down on either side of himself at a piano, where he plays and chats with them. It is clear that he takes them seriously, a sensation children adore. "He was such a fine spirit with children," says Elisabeth. "We loved him to pieces."

When his little girls weren't around, however, Ernie did not bother to conceal his dread. In the 1950s the mother was customarily assumed to be the preferred caretaker of the children, and there was a very real possibility that Ernie might lose his daughters. According to his Trenton friend Helen Wilson, who went to Philadelphia prepared to testify during the trial, "The court clerk said, 'Well, regardless of how bad the mother is, the mother makes a better mother than the father makes a mother.' Ernie was very upset by that."

Throughout the whole ordeal, "he was very emotional," remembers Jane Hess. "No jokes. He didn't think anything was funny. At one point he told me that he had found a place in Brazil. He was going to have his mother go down there, and if the court ruled that the children had to go back with their mother, he was going to fly them out of the country, because there was no extradition treaty in Brazil. He was dead serious, in my opinion, that they were going to get sent off to Brazil if the court behaved as stupidly as Ernie thought it would."

Probably for the protection of the children, the custody hearings were conducted in closed court. Many of Ernie and Bette's old friends from Trenton were called to testify, including Marion Shapiro, Helen Wilson, and Eddie Hatrak. Mostly, it seemed, they sided with Ernie. "We didn't know Bette. Let's be honest," says Wilson. "But we never testified to anything other than things we had seen." Shapiro thinks that "most of his friends came out against her because of the way she handled her house and her children." According to Jane Hess, Ernie also lined up a psychiatrist and a physician who were prepared to testify as to the state of the children, particularly with regard to any abuse they might have suffered in Bette's care.

During all of this, Ernie and Edith Adams continued to see one another, but "they were so careful that there wasn't a breath of scandal," says Shapiro. (The divorce did not become final until February 11, 1954.) Edith naturally sided with Ernie on the custody case, and evidently some rivalry developed between her and Bette. Elisabeth remembers waiting with Kippie outside the courtroom, where they would become "pawns" in this competition. "When my mother was there, she'd have us sing 'Dixie'— 'Oh, I wish I was in the land of cotton . . .'— because she was from the South. And when Edie had us in the hall, she'd have us sing, 'Would you like to swing on a star, and be better off than you are?' But it was inappropriate for her to be there. I think he got in trouble for it once."

The girls "were terrified we'd have to go with our mother," says Elisabeth, who used to pray that she could stay with her father. Both girls were eventually called in to testify. Kippie, who was three, remembers only "sitting on the judge's lap and him asking me personal questions." Five-year-old Elisabeth's day in court was far more dramatic: "I remember begging the judge to give us to our father. There was also a group of people sitting behind a divider rail, and I thought that somehow they were responsible for our fate. I remember running over to where they were sitting and begging them not to give us to our mother. Later I found out that one of them was Sid Shotwell," Bette's stepfather. "I had never seen him."

The custody case was finally decided on October 10, 1952. In a highly unusual move for the court at that time, Ernie was granted custody of his daughters. (His lawyer was the well-known Garfield Levy, whose strong Philadelphia court and political connections probably helped.) Bette was given weekly visitation privileges plus care of her children for two weekends per month. One more stipulation was made: Ernie's custody rights carried the condition that the children be removed from the influence of Mary Kovacs, who was found to be a principal difficulty in the conflicts between the divorcing parents. It may be that Bette agreed to give up custody in exchange for this concession. The order was never actually heeded, however. Mary maintained a relationship with her granddaughters until the day she died.

Unbeknownst to Ernie, just as the disposition of his personal life was being decided in a Philadelphia courtroom, decisions were being made at the network level in New York that would bring his work on Philadelphia television to an end.

Network television had grown directly out of network radio. "Radio not only developed the stars and program formats that were to be adopted by commercial television," broadcast historian Les Brown has pointed out, "but also the entire modus operandi, including the economic system and the affiliate relationships." The United States' oldest radio network, NBC, was also the first to branch into TV, inaugurating the nation's first regular service with its telecast of President Roosevelt opening the New York World's Fair in 1939.

Although the development of television broadcasting slowed during World War II, in the postwar period it shot ahead. CBS, ABC, and the so-called "fourth network," DuMont, were all in place by 1946, and CBS in particular presented tough competition to the top-ranked NBC. In June 1948, NBC again made television history by premiering *The Texaco Star Theater*, a comedy-variety show starring Milton Berle and based on the ex-vaudevillian's radio show of the same name. The series was a phenomenal hit, thereby proving once and for all that television "could (and would) compete effectively with stage and screen as an entertainment medium," according to TV historian Alex McNeil.

The race was on. "Then began the wholesale transfer of shows and stars from radio to TV— everything from *The Voice of Firestone* to the soap operas," writes Les Brown. As network radio declined, CBS, under the shrewd chairmanship of William S. Paley, stole some of NBC's biggest radio stars—George Burns and Gracie Allen, Jack Benny, Amos 'n' Andy, Red Skelton, Edgar Bergen and Charlie McCarthy—and used their talents to boost its ratings on TV. NBC Television soon fell to number two.

Then, as now, this was regarded as an urgent problem; lower ratings meant, among other things, that advertising revenues might be lost and that top talent from screen, stage, and radio might become more difficult to attract. (Then, however, networks tended to seek solutions in fresh rather than formulaic ways—partly because there were no proven ways yet, partly because there was adventure in the air.) Seeking to regain its top position, in 1949 NBC hired a lanky ex-advertising man named Sylvester ("Pat") Weaver, Jr., as vice-president in charge of television. The network gave Weaver carte blanche, and he came up with an idea for a show that, as it turned out, would directly alter the fate of Ernie Kovacs in Philadelphia.

Redheaded and freckle-faced, Weaver was just over a decade older than Ernie. In the early 1930s he had worked as a writer-producer for CBS Radio in California; from there he had moved to New York and joined the ad agency Young & Rubicam, which produced many radio shows for its clients. Y&R assigned Weaver to produce the first full season of Fred Allen's *Town Hall Tonight*; Weaver forever endeared himself to the normally cantankerous Allen when he kicked two strange men out of the studio during airtime, not knowing that they were the presidents of the network and of Bristol-Myers, the show's sponsor.

By the late 1940s, Weaver had accumulated two decades' worth of deep and varied experience in broadcasting and in advertising, the latter background being especially important at that time because most radio and television programming originated with advertisers. When NBC approached him, he happily grabbed the reins for the network's infant television operation and almost immediately began to apply his creative thinking to this new medium, which he felt was capable of more than just copycat programming cribbed from radio. Believing that audiences would be attracted by bold concepts and quality programs, he mounted *The Admiral Broadway Revue* with producer Max Liebman, uniting for the first time a gifted musical and comedic performer, Imogene Coca, and a brilliant comedian from Yonkers named Sid Caesar. The show lasted only four months before the sponsor dropped it, but when it resurfaced the following year as *Your Show of Shows*, it was an immediate hit and became the backbone of a strong Saturday-night lineup for NBC. This was a milestone in the development of TV. Saturday night in front of the tube had not yet become a national pastime; potential viewers had to be tempted away from the theater or restaurants or the movies and, once home, had to be seduced away from the radio.

Weaver was hardly content to stop with this success. He had a vision that television could be much more than merely radio with pictures; it could bring the whole world into people's homes. He knew that 75 percent of American households ritualistically tuned in to radio wake-up shows from seven to nine every morning. So many millions of people, such a powerful habit; couldn't it be turned to NBC's advantage, by creating a wake-up show for television?

Of course, the network's affiliate WPTZ had already proven that this could be done, with Kovacs' early-morning *3 to Get Ready*. It had yet to be accomplished on a national scale, however, and this was a vastly more difficult task. But Weaver thought big; he believed it could be done; he was going to try. He conceived a program whose structure would take account of the morning activities in which he expected audiences to be engaged. Rather than trying to get them to sit down for large blocks of time in front of the TV set, this new show would emphasize auditory information: "The listener will become a viewer whenever his interest in the audio reaches a point where it interrupts his preparation for work or school and replaces it in importance to him." To host this new experiment, he hired Dave Garroway, already known both to radio listeners and to television viewers. His creation was given the working title *Rise and Shine* (taken from a successful radio wake-up show). But by the time it bowed on NBC on January 14, 1952, at 7:00 A.M., it had been renamed—for immediacy, for snappy impact—*Today*.

NBC's full-page ads in the trade magazines proclaimed that *Today* would transform the TV studio into "the nerve center of the planet" and cause "a revolution in television," but national advertisers and NBC's own affiliates were wary; daytime programming didn't even exist in some areas, and the early-morning hours clearly belonged to radio. Consequently Weaver had trouble both convincing sponsors to buy spots and getting the affiliate stations, most of which didn't begin broadcasting until midday, to begin operations early and pick up *Today*. Adding to these problems was the quality of the show in its first weeks. A far cry from the enthusiastically hyped "revolution," *Today* was a messy, embarrassing affair, its tiny studio overrun with gadgets and maps and clocks, its live reports from different cities confusing and inane. But Weaver was determined to make the program work, and NBC immediately began polishing the format and putting pressure on its local affiliates to carry the show so that it could offer national sponsors a minimum audience. By May, *Today* was breaking even.

All of this was fine for NBC, but not for *3 to Get Ready*. One of the affiliates to which NBC applied the most pressure was WPTZ. According to television critic Merrill Panitt, Philadelphia was "an important market. *Today* had to be seen here if it was to become a financial success." Ernie's contract expired on May 14, and—probably sensing what was to come—he started hunting for another job. He was actually in a fairly good position to look. WPTZ had a reputation for strong, innovative work. Moreover, its proximity to New York made it a natural breeding ground for talented people who would eventually want to move into big-league network TV; by 1952 numerous personnel from WPTZ had successfully made the leap.

And by this time Ernie himself was respected and well known around Philadelphia, and in New York he had received attention through his network shows. Indeed, there is some evidence that NBC didn't simply cast Ernie aside when *Today* came on. "The network was definitely interested in him," says Karl Weger, Jr. "I don't know whether there was some kind of consolation involved—if, because he was being taken off by *Today,* they were going to try to find a berth for him in New York. That could have been a business ploy. In any event, not too long after that he went up to New York for auditions."

In fact, in March WPTZ announced that although *Today* would replace *3 to Get Ready*, Ernie would begin a new local show on March 31 from 12:30 to 1:00 P.M. daily. But Andy McKay says that "they just wanted to throw Ernie a bone, so to speak, with another show at another hour." Ernie made it clear that this arrangement would not last long. "It is just a six-week thing to fill out the contract," he told Mitchell Swartz of the *Philadelphia Daily News* when the announcement was made.

Whether the overtures from WPTZ and NBC were serious or merely conciliatory, Ernie's growing resentment that his program was being displaced by the network's *Today* would not allow him to respond positively. "He did retain some resentments from time to time," remembers Weger. "He would not outwardly retaliate, but certainly he inwardly felt a commitment to express dissatisfaction. He often gave the feeling that the management types in authority really didn't know what they were doing."

So Ernie looked for auditions elsewhere. Not all of them went well. Already feeling "knifed in the back" (to use Weger's phrase) by his employer, he interviewed with a WPTZ rival in Philadelphia, WCAU, and the result was a handful of salt rubbed right into his fresh wound. According to WPTZ account executive Robert Jawer, "A very bright guy named Charlie Vanda was program manager for Channel 10 when they went on the air; he was given the authority to build a new station." Ernie went to see Vanda for an interview, "and when I spoke to Kovacs a day or so later," says Jawer, "he was absolutely furious. He said Vanda had said something like: 'You'll never make it on my station or anybody else's station.' He really put Kovacs down. Kovacs said,

'I'll show that S.O.B. I'll show him!' That episode was a heartbreaker to him. I think Vanda was very much an egotist too and wanted to steer his own course."

While Ernie was auditioning he was still working full-time-plus at WPTZ. *TTGR* managed to hang on until March 28, 1952, before being axed for the new *Today*. On the same day, *Kovacs on the Corner*, his detested late-morning formula show, also gave its last broadcast. He continued to do *Deadline for Dinner*, the afternoon cooking show with which he had started on WPTZ, until April 18, and he never did begin the 12:30 daily show that WPTZ had announced. By this time he had gotten an offer that he liked. Not surprisingly, it came from a rival of NBC.

Among his colleagues from WPTZ who had gone on to the networks was Dan Gallagher, a producer for WCBS-TV in New York. Gallagher found a place for Ernie in CBS's daytime lineup; within a week of his last *Deadline for Dinner* broadcast, Ernie would be at work in New York. First, however, there was unfinished business to take care of. Some accounts (written several years after the fact) say that Ernie set fire to the studio when he bid Philadelphia good-bye, but none of his WPTZ cohorts remembers this happening; the story is another one of those legends that fits what people perceived about Ernie's personality. Writer Donald Mattern, however, does recall the final episode of the tension-racked *Kovacs on the Corner:* "He used to have an audience, and we had a little bleacher set up. But on the last show, there was no audience. They cut to the bleacher, and who's there but Andy McKay, applauding." Afterward Ernie took a hammer to the sets while Bill Freeland pushed them down, according to McKay.

Others were affected by the cancellation of *TTGR* and Ernie's impending move. "They cancelled us just when we were at the height of our popularity in the ratings," lamented *TTGR*'s director, Joe Behar. "And the cancellation came about because we were an NBC affiliate and they said, "You must take the *Today* show.' There were a lot of bad feelings about them doing that to him when he was such a big hit." Weger recalls the crew feeling "definite sadness mixed with relief. We were relieved that we weren't going to have to go through this hassle every morning; we were going to get paid anyway and not have to be in early. But we did genuinely regret that *3* was going off."

Not everyone was going to be left behind, however. To smooth the transition—and perhaps out of a perceived need, as Bill Hofmann sensed, for "crutches" to help him along—Ernie chose to transplant several of his Philadelphia personnel. He invited sound man Hofmann to come to New York with him, not realizing that this might be impossible because of union rules. The unions did not make it difficult to transplant performers, however, and Ernie took with him Edith Adams, Trigger Lund, and Andy McKay, as well as his secretary, Angel McGrath. He also grabbed his old friend Eddie Hatrak from Trenton, to be in charge of the music. If he was going to plunge into a new creative environment, he would try, to the best of his ability, to re-create a situation in which he already felt some confidence.

Perhaps saddest and angriest of all about Ernie's upcoming departure were his viewers. He had acquired a large, loyal following in Philadelphia, and his fans were eager to let their thoughts be known. Merrill Panitt, who had voiced his opinion in print that WPTZ ought to try to hang on to Ernie, devoted one of his columns to letters he received regarding the Kovacs cancellation:

> Jane W. Wheeler—"We have had a lot of things forced on us by TV—football blackouts, boxing blackouts, baseball fadeouts—and now practically a Kovacs blackout. The more I see of the Gestapo methods of TV, the more I'm beginning to appreciate radio."
>
> P.B.C.—"No early morning viewer is awake enough to want reviews, newsreels, etc. Ernie's cheerfulness has started my day happily for many months . . . I'll certainly get a lot of housework done in the early morning now—to the tune of radio recorded music shows."

Mrs. Charles B. Krause wrote Panitt, "The light has gone out of the day for me! My two little boys get me up in the morning before I'd like them to. Knowing Ernie Kovacs would be in our living room to amuse them and get me started on a long day was a wonderful thing. Now I have such a bleak feeling. . . . I feel like I have said good-bye to an old friend."

PART FOUR

NETWORK ROULETTE

1952 – 1957

As the flagship station for the CBS Television network, WCBS-TV was eager to test whether Kovacs could draw as strong a daytime audience in New York as he had in Philadelphia. The station had been relying on film shows to fill its local programming hours, and hiring Ernie signaled its commitment to mounting live programming on a significant scale. Ernie and his transplanted entourage were slotted into a lunchtime period from 12:45 to 1:30 every weekday, and he was given free rein. "Should Kovacs click here," reported the trade magazine *Billboard*, "there is every possibility that he may return to haunt Garroway in an early-hour time slot."

The new offering was given the freewheeling title *Kovacs Unlimited*, like Ernie's first newspaper column for the *Trentonian*. It premiered on New York's Channel 2 on Monday, April 21, 1952, with Dan Gallagher as producer and Ned Cramer as director. Kovacs, Andy McKay, and Trigger Lund were credited as the writers, but the proceedings were every bit as unstructured as they had been on *TTGR*. As Ernie explained to the *New York Herald Tribune*'s Harold Brown shortly after the debut, "I think up three or four bits in the morning, go on cold at 12:45, and [on one of the first shows] I ended up twenty-five minutes short. We took the sets down and showed them the studio."

With Ernie and the cast having had only a week's break between the last WPTZ broadcast and their first in New York, *Kovacs Unlimited* was initially little more than a continuation of the WPTZ programs. Viewers might have seen, for example, insects walking to the sound of marching human feet, Edith Adams singing "Look to the Rainbow" or "Swinging on a Star," close-ups of Eddie Hatrak's hands playing the piano—sometimes flipped upside down or reversed, according to the cameraman's whim—or Ernie parodying the CBS late-night program *The Continental. The Continental* featured a velvet-voiced actor named Renzo Cesana romancing the ladies at home, addressing the camera directly and offering it cocktails and cigarettes from a posh apartment setting. In Ernie's version, called "The County-Nental," the video gigolo was transformed into a hayseed wearing overalls and pouring moonshine from a jug, and such seductive overtures as "Don't be afraid, darling, you're in a *man's* apartment!" became "Don't be afeared, this is only a man's silo!"

As in Philadelphia, the audience—made up primarily of housewives and children—responded to the program's blend of spontaneous zaniness and light musical entertainment. By August *Kovacs Unlimited* boasted a 3.6 Pulse rating, which put it at the top of its midday time slot and was considered a good rating in general for a local daytime program in the New York market. Naturally, a high rating drew sponsors. "Channel 2's Ernie Kovacs, the Maniacal Magyar, who a few months ago was unsponsored but unbowed, now has more 'spots' than a leopard with the measles," announced *New York Daily News* reporter Rudy Bergman in November. "With an average of nine commercials on every show, more sponsors are standing in line."

The show's success among sponsors was due, at least in part, to Ernie's hard work on their behalf. His skits for his own made-up products were thoroughly bizarre:

BESSIE MAY MUCHO'S HAIR TINT . . . SELECTION OF COLORS: GREEN, ORANGE, LAVENDER, BEIGE, AND GLEN PLAID

HIPPO-SKIN TISSUES . . . HOLD WATER, SHINE SHOES, CAN BE STRETCHED, TUGGED, AND REUSED INDEFINITELY

but his commercials for clients were often charmingly offbeat and well integrated into the texture of the show:

OAKITE LITTLE THEATER FOR OAKITE HOUSEHOLD CLEANSER . . . PUPPET NO. 1: "MY NAME IS OAK." PUPPET NO. 2: "MY NAME IS OAKIE." TOGETHER: "WE CLEAN UP LIKE CRAZY, WE'RE REALLY OAKIE-DOAKIE!" . . . THEY ATTACK PUPPET OF JOE DIRT

TRIGGER LUND EXPOUNDS ON THE LIGHTNESS OF CAKE MADE WITH SWANS DOWN CAKE MIX . . . HOLDS CAKE PAN SUSPENDED WITH BLACK STRINGS . . . EACH TIME HE TAKES HANDS OFF TO MAKE A POINT, CAKE FLOATS AWAY

"Kovacs tries to make the housewife-viewer feel she's discovering something wonderful which she really needed," reported the publication *Tide*.

The sponsors' commercials "get only the mildest ribbing; Kovacs feels there is a danger in carrying kidding so far that a potential customer may actually feel embarrassed to ask for the product for fear of letting herself in for a going over at the store or at the hands of her family when she gets it home."

Under director Ned Cramer, who occasionally alternated with Frank Moriarity or Chuck Hinds, the WCBS-TV crew quickly fell in with Ernie's penchant for the odd. Perfectly timed sound effects and fast, random candid shots (the back of Cramer's head, Edith combing her hair, a crew member walking in front of the camera) became trademarks of the show. In this way *Kovacs Unlimited* resembled the earlier Philadelphia shows, but gradually the WCBS-TV program started to acquire a character of its own. Animals—real, stuffed, sketched, toy, and imagined—became prominent, both for "breaking the telops" (cutting away from the opening credits to the first image):

OPEN . . . PENGUIN WALKING TO SPIKE JONES MUSIC

OPEN . . . PICTURES OF GORILLA NAMED MORIARITY WITH MOVING MOUTH

and as bits within the show:

SCAVOK FLY CUTTER . . . TRICK WITH SMALL GUILLOTINE

TREVOR THE STUFFED DEER IS VACUUMED . . . LAUGHS

Music also grew in importance. In addition to daily featured songs by Edith and piano solos by Eddie Hatrak, Ernie killed time with his "Illustrated Profuselies," in which he'd play a record (he favored Doris Day, Billy Eckstine, Frank Sinatra, and Nat King Cole) and draw cartoons to illustrate the lyrics. Or he would lip-sync to a recording of *I Pagliacci*, ducking out of camera range in between lines and popping up wearing different masks.

Kovacs Unlimited featured guests every day—sometimes offbeat ones, such as a Mr. Feddar, who showed crew-cut toupees, or a Mr. Blunette, who presented a Kovacs bust carved in cheese, but also the occasional actor or author plugging a new movie or book. And Ernie addressed many bits to the children watching during the midday hour. He would play children's records, bring on his daughters Kippie and Bette as guests, or open the show with neighborhood kids carrying picket signs as if protesting the show. (Ernie chased them off with a sword.) From *TTGR* he brought a character named Uncle Gruesome, who recounted tales as macabre as his name:

> ERNIE IN FRIGHT WIG AND FANGS, LIT FROM BENEATH TO LOOK LIKE SOMETHING FROM HELL . . . "UNCLE GRUESOME ARRIVED HOME LAST NIGHT, KIDDIES, AND YOU SHOULD HAVE SEEN THE EXCITEMENT! MY NEPHEWS, LOATHSOME, CUMBERSOME, AND UN-WHOLESOME, ASKED ME ABOUT THE MEETING OF THE WEREWOLF SOCIETY AND THEN DEMANDED TO KNOW WHAT I HAD BROUGHT THEM" . . . SAYS THAT HE FOUND A TOY STORE WITH "ALL KINDS OF INGENIOUS DOLLS—DOLLS THAT SHRIEKED, DOLLS THAT COULD BITE RIGHT THROUGH YOUR FINGER WITH THEIR CANINE TEETH, DOLLS THAT SLITHERED ALONG THE FLOOR, AND DOLLS THAT EX-PLODED WHEN YOU TOUCHED A REMOTE CONTROL BUTTON . . . WHAT WON'T THEY THINK OF NEXT?"

He also invented a French storyteller, Pierre Ragout, who recounted fairy tales with a Gallic twist:

> ERNIE IN SCARF AND BERET . . . BLAHS ON ABOUT HOW MOST TV SHOWS IGNORE CHILDREN, "ESPECIALLY CHILDREN WHO SPEAK FRENCH—AND MOST OF THE CHILDREN WHO WATCH TELEVISION SPEAK ONLY FRENCH OR LATIN. WE THOUGHT THAT WE SHOULD HAVE A LITTLE DEPARTMENT" FOR THEM . . . TELLS STORY OF "LITTLE ROUGE RIDING HOOD" IN FRENCH DOUBLE-TALK . . . PLAYS WOLF AS A ROUÉ: "OUI, BABY. JE SUIS LE WOLF."

Gradually, however, *Kovacs Unlimited* came to be best known for its parodies of the television shows and commercials of the time. As *NBC's Saturday Night Live* and *Second City TV* would do more than twenty years later, Ernie and his gang lampooned virtually everything that surrounded them on the tube, from news programs to dramas to quiz shows. These pieces were simultaneously silly and smart; Ernie would reduce every subject to a crude, outrageous mockery while laying bare its real flaws. The targets were sometimes taken from rival networks: the *Today* show became "Yesterday," for example, NBC's cluttered set parodied with hand-lettered wall signs reading LONDON, CLOUDY, FROWN, TRENTON, and VOTE, and the show's tendency to report on old news pointed up as Ernie held up cards announcing such hot news flashes as "Merrimac Sinks Monitor." But more often than not Ernie aimed his lance at programs from his parent network. CBS's pretentious *The Stork Club*, which broadcast live from that glamorous Manhattan nightclub with owner Sherman Billingsley as host, was transformed into "The Crane Club." Instead of champagne served in stemware, the Crane Club's house drink was beer slopped into broken mugs. Its habitués were toothless bums who spoke with *dem*s and *dose*s, and Ernie would interview pathetic made-up celebrities (including Gertrude the rag doll) while in the background one could hear crashing dishes, hysterical laughter, and the occasional stray gunshot. Similarly, the network's *What's My Line* was the basis for Ernie's "Where D'Ya Worka, John?":

ERNIE SIGNS IN AS HARWOOD BOXCAR, WEARING OVERALLS AND CAP AND CARRYING A LANTERN AND FLAG . . . PANELIST: "WHO IS YOUR FAVORITE MOVIE STAR?" BOXCAR: "LIONEL BARRYMORE" . . . "WHO IS YOUR FAVORITE AUTHOR?" "MARK TWAIN" . . . ANSWERS EVERY QUESTION WITH A TRAIN REFERENCE . . . PANELISTS VERY DUMBFOUNDED . . . FINALLY EDIE ASKS: "ARE YOU A CONCERT PIANIST?" BOXCAR: "DARN, SHE GUESSED IT! HOW DID SHE GUESS IT?" . . . PRIZE IS $3.98

From the CBS quiz show *What in the World*, in which panelists identified artworks from the University of Pennsylvania Museum, Ernie got the idea for "What in the Sam Hill?" From the network's *Mr. and Mrs. North*, in which Richard Denning and Barbara Britton played a couple who were always chancing upon dead bodies, Ernie created "Mr. and Mrs. South"—quickly, within a few weeks of the show's television premiere. (It had been a popular radio series.) Ernie's recurring character J. Walter Puppybreath, an amateur Chinese songwriter who performed awful numbers and had feathers and water dumped on his head, was born as the contestant of "Tunes for Peddle," a parody of CBS's aspiring-songwriter showcase *Songs for Sale*.

The sketches on *Kovacs Unlimited* were not always a hit. As several critics pointed out at the time, Ernie had a tendency to let jokes drag out, especially when he was improvising (which was often). His resistance to rehearsal made for a spontaneous, casual ambience that was sometimes refreshing but could also come off as amateurish. And because Ernie wasn't always a good judge of what would or would not work before an audience, his material was uneven; a stronger editorial hand would likely have benefited the show overall.

In general, however, the critics favored the program, applauding its uninhibited camera and sound work and Ernie's relaxed delivery and impudent sense of burlesque. And so, by his first autumn in New York as a professional, Ernie was riding high. He had proved his mettle by earning supportive reviews from the important New York critical establishment, a strong following among New York viewers, and a full lineup of paying sponsors (*Kovacs Unlimited* was "SRO," in the parlance of the trade). He was being handsomely rewarded for this, pulling in a reported $1,250 a week. Most important, as his confidence in his comedic vision grew, he was gradually exercising more and more control over the content and form of his program.

Not long after his New York premiere, Ernie started taking sole credit as the show's producer and writer. With the notable exception of *Kovacs on the Corner*, in his Philadelphia shows he and the cast had usually worked without a script; the most that Ernie produced ahead of time would be lists of props to be rounded up by Andy McKay, rosters of songs for which Angel McGrath needed to obtain clearances, very brief outlines of ideas for sketches that the cast would then improvise on the air. Although *Kovacs Unlimited* retained the unrehearsed flavor that had marked the WPTZ shows, Ernie now began to create scripts. Granted, often the "dialogue" consisted of no more than "Pierre Ragout tells the story of Carmen" or "Blah blah or something to close," but the fact is that he was giving an order to the show and planning skit concepts in advance, and the format he was using was slowly becoming more scriptlike. He began separating the audio and video portions on the page, as televisions and film scripts traditionally do. Then he started putting in directions to the crew. He would note where a skit might require a two-camera setup, for example, or would cue sound man Russ Gaynor on specific sound effects:

KOVACS COMES RUNNING IN . . . RUSS: SQUEAL BRAKES AS KOVACS COMES TO A HALT

UNDERWEAR GUEST . . . RUSS: GET SOME SCRATCHING NOISES

"When Trig lets go, stagehand lifts cake fairly moderate speed. Not too slow and not too fast," he would instruct the crew member lifting the Swans Down cake pan on strings. "This is a real fine tune . . . very fast . . . How about two spots, one on Hatrak and a brighter one on Edie for the foreground?" he wrote to the cameramen who were to light a musical interlude. His ideas about how he wanted his show to look and sound were clearly jelling, and his desire to see that vision realized was growing stronger. Ernie was beginning to feel his power as an artist, although he probably would have been embarrassed to ascribe the term to himself at the time.

With the exposure afforded by a successful daily television show and with favorable reviews of her vocal talents from the critics, Kovacs' featured female singer was beginning to sense her developing professional muscles as well. After moving to New York, she dropped the affected spelling "Edythe" and began to bill herself as plain Edith Adams. "I was awfully green then, and I was scared," she later recalled. But she was also eager to make a name for herself and determined not to repeat the bitter, regretful life of her mother. And so, as she had in the days when she had entered every singing contest she heard about, Edith pushed her fears aside and made the rounds of theater producers and directors, praying with each anxious visit to be given the chance to audition. This required somehow pleasing the intimidating receptionists, who determined at a mere glance whether a young hopeful was or was not the right "type" for a desired part.

One day in late 1952, an agent sent her to the office of the legendary George Abbott, who was holding auditions for the ingenue lead in a new Broadway musical he was directing. With such successes as *Pal Joey, On the Town,* and *Call Me Madam* to his credit, Abbott was considered "one of the hottest directors in the theater," said Rosalind Russell, who was set to star opposite the ingenue in the production.

Many thought the taciturn sixty-five-year-old director intimidating, although he himself attributed his aloofness to childhood shyness. He was easily bored and had no patience with the Method acting then in vogue. But this highly proper man would let down his hair when it came to ballroom dancing, especially the Latin dances that were popular in the 1950s; the divorced director was known to drive friends a little crazy when they went out for a night on the town and he insisted that they set him up with dance partners.

Abbott was then at the height of his powers. Within three years he would direct his longest-running production ever, *Damn Yankees.* The confluence of his career with that of Rosalind Russell, which was foundering, would prove critical for the dark-haired actress. Russell had a decade and a half's worth of Hollywood experience behind her, but by 1950 her film career had hit the skids. Resolved to reverse her professional bad luck, she had returned to the stage, where she had had some minor success in her twenties. Joseph Fields and Jerome Chodorov were writing a musical version of their play *My Sister Eileen*, which Russell had filmed, and they now courted her to re-create her role as the older, more practical of two Ohio sisters who land themselves in the bohemian world of Greenwich Village in the 1930s. She accepted the assignment with trepidation, worried about her lack of singing and dancing experience but tempted by the promise of working with George Abbott and with Leonard Bernstein, Betty Comden, and Adolph Green, who were writing the music and lyrics.

Despite her anxieties, Russell still had considerable pull in the project; she had already played the role successfully (if nonmusically), and she was the first choice to play sister Ruth now. Her power extended to having approval over the casting of the title role of Eileen, the younger and more innocent and romantic of the duo. "I didn't want them to pick some itty-bitty blonde with a bird-brain, one of those post-nasal drip squeaky voices," Russell told an interviewer at the time. "She had to be a pretty girl, and she had to have an exceptionally fine voice (because goodness knows I'm no singer) and the intelligence to play a giddy role with restraint; and she couldn't be too darn petite, because I'm a tall girl." Russell was also concerned about the effect the potential difference in age might have on the public's perception of her; as she confessed twenty-five years later, "I didn't want to play sister to some seventeen-year-old and have us come on like mother and daughter." (In the story Eileen was sixteen.)

If Edith Adams had known that the play's star was to have a say in the choice, she might have found the audition even more nerve-wracking than usual. As it was, Abbott's receptionist took one look at her and pronounced: "You're not the type at all." But a few weeks later, a representative from his office called and asked her to come in and sing. At this auspicious moment, an old contact had come through. Rodgers and Hammerstein's casting director, John Fernley, had remembered Edith favorably from her audition for *South Pacific* and mentioned her to Abbott as a possibility for Eileen, which was turning out to be a very difficult role to cast. "Apparently there is a right time psychologically for an actress or a singer to audition," Edith told the *Saturday Evening Post*'s Pete Martin a few years later. "By the time they saw me, Chodorov, Fields, and Abbott had seen everybody in town. There was practically nobody left. I can just imagine them saying to each other, 'Let's make up our mind on somebody.'" In another interview she said that she had been stricken by laryngitis shortly after the audition was set up, and "each time I was scheduled to appear, I was unable to show up. So at the end of each day, my name would be put at the top of the next day's list. This went on for quite a while, and what with everyone asking, 'Where's this Edith Adams?' I became a famous name even before they heard me sing. I think that was a big help."

Perhaps the timing and the delays worked in her favor, but Edith clearly possessed considerable talent, for she impressed Chodorov, Fields, and Abbott enough to be offered the ingenue lead for *Wonderful Town* after literally hundreds of actresses had been auditioned. And so on December 11, 1952, at the age of twenty-five, Edith Adams was signed for her first Broadway role. The part fit her snugly: both Edith and Eileen were innocents from the heartland of America, and both had adventurously transplanted themselves to New York to try to make it in the acting profession.

Edith went to work on *Wonderful Town* almost immediately, starting rehearsals within two weeks of signing for the role. Although she admitted to suffering terrible stage fright as late as ten years after *Wonderful Town*, Ernie's daily programs had taught her how to appear calm on stage, no matter what happened. "If I seem relaxed and unworried in *Wonderful Town*," she told an interviewer shortly after the show opened, "it's because of the great training I've been getting on Ernie's wild TV show, where it'd be a little ridiculous to feel nervous." Indeed, on the Kovacs shows she was often the only one who seemed grounded, the firm anchor to all the airy lunacy, and she came to play a similar function in *Wonderful Town*, with its Greenwich Village full of "whacks."

As far as stage work, however, Edith had almost everything to learn. Her limited experience in summer stock had hardly prepared her for the unrelenting pressures and tough routine of a full-scale Broadway musical. "I didn't know upstage from downstage," she said, "but I had George Abbott and Roz Russell as my coaches, and they taught me how to discover things for myself. I found myself saying, 'Eileen would do this,' and Roz would say, 'Now you're getting it.'" But if she lacked the experience of her famous costar, she more than made up for it in her singing voice, which was clear, controlled, and sweet. She had no problem tackling the songs, even though they required a wide range of vocal technique, from pop to coloratura. Russell, on the other hand, remained nervous about her own singing. Leonard Bernstein worked with her patiently until, she said, "I got so I wasn't too scared of the 'Ohio' duet with Edie Adams."

Edith barely had time to celebrate Christmas that year; like Ernie, she seemed to like pushing herself to capacity, and now she found herself deep in rehearsals for *Wonderful Town* and still working on Ernie's daily show. Edith remained on *Kovacs Unlimited* until she had to leave for the out-of-town tryouts in January. In New Haven, on her first opening night, she waited and waited for the makeup person to appear, accustomed to having a professional do that job for her on TV. Finally she asked for the makeup person and was astonished to find out that in the theater actors make themselves up. "We all thought she was kidding," said one troupe member. "But Roz Russell knew she wasn't. Roz took Edith back to her own dressing room and made her up, and gave her a quick lesson in theatrical make-up."

On February 25, 1953, the *Wonderful Town* troupe assembled at the Winter Garden Theater in Manhattan for opening night. To keep anxiety from overwhelming his cast, Abbott kept giving them last-minute notes: "Put the tray down with less noise," he'd tell them. "Close that door right on such-and-such a line." But who can really be calm on the opening night of a Broadway show? "Nerves like mine will never be known," confessed Edith, whose symptoms before a show often included headaches, hives, and nervous stomach. Outside, scalpers were hawking tickets at the outrageous price of $85 a pair. Inside, as the cast well knew, seven major critics were sitting in the audience. But the players had nothing to worry about. As Abbott recalled, "By the time *Wonderful Town* reached New York it was a very slick show indeed, and it deserved the big success which awaited it."

Its success was indeed enormous. Brooks Atkinson of the *New York Times* declared *Wonderful Town* "the best new musical of the season," raved about every element from the costumes to the choreography, and gushingly nominated Rosalind Russell for president. Within a week theatergoers were reserving tickets for the following New Year's Eve.

As for Edith's performance, Atkinson pronounced it "absolutely perfect" and, in a second, more detailed review, praised her as "a trained singer who can also act. In fact, she can act with a lot of nuance. For Eileen is not a simple character. Although she is genuinely innocent, she also has an instinct for subduing and annexing the predatory male. Miss Adams moves through this elusive character with the greatest of ease, keeping it fresh and sweet and adding just enough worldliness to make it palatable. Amid the bedlamite skylarking of *Wonderful Town* she gives a remarkable impression of cool individuality. She is part of the insanity without succumbing to it." He concluded: "In her first appearance on Broadway Miss Adams has won a considerable triumph of her own."

Edith's portrayal of Eileen would garner her a Theater World Award as one of the Promising Personalities of 1952–53, putting her in the company of such other young hopefuls as Geraldine Page, Paul Newman, and Gwen Verdon. *Wonderful Town* ran a year and a half, and she never missed a show, no matter how she felt. The tough and disciplined work of the stage seemed to suit Edith's talents and temperament perfectly. "I remember her as one of the best people I've ever directed for maintaining the key of a performance," said George Abbott. "When a show runs for a while, actors tend to overdo everything. That never happened with Edith Adams. Her performance was exactly right all through the [period] the show ran on Broadway."

As for Ernie Kovacs, at thirty-four he was thoroughly infatuated with Edith Adams and was not embarrassed to show it. When Edith left New York for the pre-Broadway tryouts, he joined her whenever he could. Before long, he proposed marriage (although his divorce from Bette did not become final for another year). By April, they had announced their engagement to *Philadelphia Daily News* columnist Mitchell Swartz.

But Edith was flush with her first professional triumph, and her doubts about marrying Ernie soon surfaced. To her, "there seemed many reasons why we shouldn't marry," she later reflected. "Ernie had two children by a previous marriage, and I asked myself how I could possibly give Ernie's children and Ernie and my career all I should give them. I didn't think there was enough of me to go around." The engagement was not mentioned again. Still, the proposal seemed to bring them closer together. When Edith returned to *Kovacs Unlimited* in March, after *Wonderful Town* opened, she and Ernie started performing duets on the show, light romantic songs like "Dream a Little Dream of Me." Their affection was obvious.

If he was worried that her Broadway success might take her away from him, if he felt frustrated by her refusal to marry, Ernie had to set these concerns aside for the moment. For he was about to be handed the most difficult challenge of his professional life.

Back in May 1952, it was rumored that pleased CBS officials might reward Kovacs' midday success with a nighttime network show. When the decision was finally made, however, it was to throw Ernie into the worst time slot in all of prime time. On December 22, the weekend before Christmas, CBS announced that a new, national *Ernie Kovacs Show* would be introduced on Tuesday evenings at eight o'clock, opposite Milton Berle's unbeatable *Texaco Star Theater* on NBC. The premiere was scheduled for December 30; Ernie had exactly one week to prepare. Simultaneously, WCBS decided to move the local show, *Kovacs Unlimited*, to early morning. Ernie would go head to head against the popular *Today* show starting December 29.

In public, Ernie acted relaxed about the new prime-time show, to which the network gave practically no publicity support. On *Kovacs Unlimited* he joked that CBS chairman William S. Paley had been booked as a guest on *I've Got a Secret;* his secret was the Tuesday-evening Kovacs show. But privately, the pressure could not have been higher. The vaudeville-style variety show *Texaco Star Theater* had been an almost immediate hit when it premiered in 1948, and it enjoyed the distinction of being television's number-one show for its first three seasons. Berle intuitively zeroed in on what would appeal to the fledgling audience of the new visual medium, building his brash television comedy around outlandish costumes and outrageous sight gags. Nightclub and theater attendance slowed on Tuesday nights as more and more people stayed home to watch *Texaco Star Theater.* Indeed, Berle is popularly credited as having sold more TV sets than the manufacturers' ad campaigns—hence his nickname, "Mr. Television."

For the competing networks, the Berle slot became "Black Tuesday," as one critic accurately dubbed it. Only the so-called fourth network, DuMont, had managed to make any sort of decent showing on Tuesday nights, with Bishop Fulton J. Sheen's popular *Life Is Worth Living*, and this was largely because the cleric had built a following in radio before coming to prime-time TV in 1952. By the time CBS decided to pit Kovacs against Berle, the network had tried everything from dramas to documentaries, from mysteries to old movies; it had even given Frank Sinatra a run at a musical-variety show, with no success.

In October CBS had launched its latest artillery against the Berle stronghold: a half-hour sitcom titled *Leave It to Larry*, which starred Eddie Albert as an inept shoe salesman, followed by a new half-hour comedy-variety program, *The Red Buttons Show*. *Leave It to Larry* performed weakly, and in December CBS abruptly decided to cancel it. Red Buttons, on the other hand, made the cover of *Time* magazine, and his show was widely regarded as having great promise. To give the young comedian a chance to build an audience, CBS moved him out of the deadly Tuesday-night spot. Enter Kovacs.

CBS's attempt to match Ernie against Berle with only one week's preparation seemed destined to fail. Many critics felt, with excellent reason, that Kovacs was being treated as a discardable commodity. The decision to move *Kovacs Unlimited* to the early morning, on the other hand, seemed a more considered one. In an attempt to cash in on the lucrative early-morning market that *Today* (and *3 to Get Ready* before it) had proved existed, WCBS developed a game plan in which Kovacs would play a critical part. Beginning December 29, WCBS would air a sign-on program of news and previews for ten minutes. From 8:00 to 8:30 A.M., two syndicated shows would draw the children's audience as they prepared for school: *Tele-Comics*, one of the first cartoon programs made specifically for TV, and *Time for Beany*, Bob Clampett's puppet show about a little boy and his seasick sea serpent (the precursor to Clampett's animated *Beany and Cecil* of the 1960s). *Kovacs Unlimited* would follow from 8:30 to 9:30, the thinking being that mothers, an audience who already knew and liked Kovacs, would leave their TV sets on WCBS after their kids left for school, rather than switching to NBC's *Today*. WCBS programmers were also hoping that Ernie's satisfied midday sponsors could be lured to advertise in the earlier hours, and the station was making an active effort to sell them on the new wake-up slot.

Ernie must have been eager to test his mettle against *Today*, which he viewed as responsible for ousting him from his old Philadelphia spot. He was already comfortable with the early-morning format and possessed many characteristics that could make such a venture successful. If he pulled this off on CBS's New York flagship station, it very likely could lead to bigger things; a national airing such as *Today* enjoyed was not unimaginable.

The evening program, however, was a different matter entirely. For one thing, audiences expect more in a prime-time show: more polish, more preparation, more production values, more imagination. Whereas a daytime viewer might have the TV on while vacuuming or fixing food or doing homework, in the evenings entire families gathered in front of the TV set and focused all their attention on it, expecting to receive a more sophisticated level of entertainment. The problems inherent in the "Black Tuesday" time slot were compounded by the network's failure to provide the basic kinds of support that would have given the show a fighting chance to survive. A single week—and the Christmas holiday week, at that—was unconscionably inadequate preparation time to grant a new prime-time show. Ernie requested a thirteen-week commitment, but the network would agree only to four. He needed a budget worthy of prime time, but CBS gave him virtually the same low budget he had for his daytime show (his nighttime program cost "about eight bucks less than an old movie," Ernie told one interviewer). And it provided practically no publicity. *Newsweek* called the planned premiere "one of television's most unheralded debuts," pointing out that "the network had trumpeted loudly when it cast Frank Sinatra as its Tuesday hope last season, and repeated the performance this fall when Eddie Albert and Red Buttons got the nod."

Despite the lack of resources, Ernie immediately set to work assembling his cast and crew and developing the show's format. He decided to produce and write the show himself, although, as usual, much of it would turn out to be improvised. Unlike most comedy shows of the time, *The Ernie Kovacs Show* would not have a studio audience. ("Audiences couldn't see a special effect," explained Edie Adams. "He fought them. He only put them in when they made him.") He also decreed that no laughs would be dubbed in. Canned laughter was already commonly used by TV comics performing without a live audience; to do without it was the equivalent of an acrobat working without a net.

To his regular daytime cast of Edith Adams, Trigger Lund, and Andy McKay, he added an orchestra led by Eddie Hatrak. Ernie picked the instruments—a strange combination of harp, violin, piano, bass fiddle, theremin (an electronic device that produces an unusual wavy sound) and cimbalom (a Hungarian gypsy dulcimer), plus a six-voice chorus—and then assigned Hatrak to direct it and arrange its music. "When you have a violin section or a brass section or a reed section, you write harmony for each section and then you blend the sections together. But this crazy combination, you couldn't blend!" says Hatrak. "So what I had to do was write something that was really a series of solos. Let the violinist play, and then the cimbalom player. Crazy,

Ernie Kovacs at about six months.

A 1925 snapshot. Mary Kovacs, Ernie's mother, later wrote on it: "My baby Ernie Kovacs. I took this picture of Ernie when he was 6 years old. My love."

With Mary Kovacs in Atlantic City in the early 1920s.

As Old King Cole (center, with crown) in *Mother Goose's Goslings,* 1931.

Scheduled to graduate in 1936, the year this portrait was taken the Trenton Central High yearbook, Ernie had to stay an extra to make up failed classes.

(Second from left) Circa 1933.

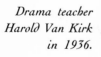

Drama teacher Harold Van Kirk in 1936.

Jane Vosper Hess and Ernie (third and fourth from left) in the 1938 Rollins Stu production of *Arms and the Man.*

*At the New
School of
Theater,
circa 1938-
1939.*

*With his first
girlfriend,
Suzanne Ludey,
in East Hampton,
circa 1937-1938.*

*The WTTM staff with
boxer-turned-wrestler
Primo Carnera (fourth
from right, next to
Kovacs) in the early
1940s. Writer Donald
Mattern is third from
left; Trenton's "polka
king," Bernie Cosnowski,
is second from right.*

h Bette Wilcox Kovacs in 1949.

*At home in Mercerville with daughters Bette (far
left) and Kippie, circa 1950.*

A station ID for WPTZ.

As Uncle Gruesome in 1950.

Cooking with guests on <u>Deadline for Dinner</u>, his first television series.

Hosting WPTZ's <u>Pick Your Ideal</u>.

Puppet capers on CBS's daytime Ernie Kovacs Show.

Teaching the TV audience how to adjust their sets.

...mbers of the Early Eyeball Fraternal and Marching Society, 1953 (from left): Trigger Lund, ...rtrude, Ernie, Andy McKay, Sandy Stewart, Bernie Leighton.

At CBS in the early 1950s.

Edie Adams, Miss U.S. Television for 195

As "The County-Nental," a spoof of CBS's _The Continental_, with Edie Adams.

Edie and Ernie as "Mr. and Mrs. South," a takeoff on the mystery series _Mr. and Mrs. North_.

CBS/Courtesy of the Museum of Broadcasting

...uthor Heats the Critics," a parody of _Author Meets the Critics_, from left: ...igger Lund, Andy McKay, Eddie Hatrak, Ernie, Edie.

Trapped in a jug as it is filled with water.

As the befuddled Eugene on the famous tilted table set the 1957 "No Dialogue" show.

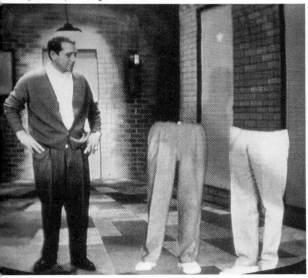

Peering through a hole in Barbara Loden head.

With Tony Bennett on <u>The Perry Como Show</u> in 1957: "Tony and I couldn't get dressed in time, so we just sent out our legs."

crazy. But Ernie was Hungarian, and he was brought up, as I was, going to Hungarian picnics," where instruments like the cimbalom were commonly played. Hatrak was of Czech background, and both he and his musician father had played Hungarian music back in Trenton. "So the violin, bass fiddle, cimbalom, and myself on piano were the nucleus of a little Hungarian combo."

Partly because of the constraints imposed by the network, but partly too because of his resistance to planning and polishing his shows, Ernie's CBS prime-time debut on Tuesday, December 30, was an almost unmitigated disaster. It started amusingly enough: people shot at Ernie for no apparent reason (perhaps a reference to his state of mind), the credits appeared in such unexpected spots as the soles of shoes, and then Ernie came onstage in a shredded rag of a bathrobe (parodying TV comedians who introduced their shows in elegant dressing gowns) and remarked, "Paley will catch cold tonight." But the rest went rapidly downhill. He fumbled with the scenery in a misfired attempt at a sight gag; he satirized various subjects, including dinnerware commercials and *What's My Line;* he twitched his features to a pizzicato recording; and every one of these bits was drawn out far too long. The only portions that didn't come off as amateurish were the musical numbers performed by Hatrak's oddball orchestra and by Edith Adams, who would soon have to leave the show to fulfill her *Wonderful Town* commitments.

Ernie was embarrassingly aware of the pathetic way this live hour was coming off. He made frequent references throughout the premiere show to his lack of budget and facilities, to the impossibly short preparation period he'd been given, to the Christmas shopping or Christmas spreeing that had kept most of his staff busy in the last week. "Friends," he appealed to the audience after one particularly bad gag dwindled to an end, "and I do call you friends because I need friends badly tonight."

Though sympathetic to his plight, the critics couldn't overlook the dismal quality of his foray into prime time. "Chalk up an 'E' for effort but little more for Ernie Kovacs in this newest attempt by CBS-TV to come up with a show that can hold its own in the hotly contested Tuesday night at 8 slot," reported *Variety.* "Kovacs' exaggerated informality, uniquely fresh type of humor and new use of special effects, while to be commended, just weren't good enough to meet nighttime standards."

As *The Ernie Kovacs Show* limped along, CBS kept Kovacs in a frustrating holding pattern, declining to give him a long- or even short-term commitment, neglecting to publicize the show adequately, and refusing to increase his budget. Finally the network gave it the ax, with the last installment airing on April 14, 1953. *Billboard* magazine pleaded, "It is earnestly hoped that CBS finds a suitable slot for Kovacs' original brand of humor, since he actually is the only comic with a mature, sophisticated type of zany horseplay in video. . . . Please, Mr. CBS, don't take Kovacs off the network; slot him opposite something less killing than Berle, perhaps in a thirty-minute version, and he could bring you good dividends yet." But Ernie would not get another chance to prove himself in prime time until a year later, and the new opportunity would not come from CBS.

In his daytime show, however, he was enjoying more success. By the end of March, WCBS felt confident enough of the early-morning drawing power of *Kovacs Unlimited* to push its start-up time back even earlier, to 8:00 A.M., thus pitting Ernie against a full hour of *Today*. In addition to his viewers at home, Ernie had developed quite a following among fellow CBS employees. According to writer John Hess, who created and wrote the CBS soap opera *Love of Life* and was married to Ernie's East Hampton friend Jane Hess, "Ernie's show was done on the floor right under ours, and I'd wander down and watch Ernie, which was a lot more interesting than my own show. What was surprising about it was not that I went to see him, but that everybody did who could spare the time. He always used to gather crowds from all over the building." Shirley Mellner, who was then unit manager for CBS's historical drama series *You Are There*, recalls that those who couldn't break away to visit the Kovacs set "would sit in the various control rooms and have Ernie piped in so we could see him. The crews and the technicians had never seen anything like this." Mellner would later work with Ernie at another network.

After he had been at CBS a year, the network scheduled him into another prime-time slot, but only as a panelist on a game show called *Take a Guess*. Premiering on June 11, 1953, at 8:00 P.M., this summer replacement for *The Burns and Allen Show* required contestants to guess secret phrases (known to moderator John K. M. McCaffery and the studio audience) by gleaning clues from questions asked by celebrity panelists. Television was already saturated with such quiz programs, and *Take a Guess* ended quietly on September 10, when the new fall season was about to begin.

One day in the middle of that summer, Ernie saw his daughters off for one of their court-ordered weekend visits with their mother. "We were dropped off at her house," remembers Kippie, who was four. She and her six-year-old sister were wearing matching outfits: blue coats and hats, white gloves, white socks, and blue shoes. Bette told them to bring their coats along, and Kippie, sucking her thumb, asked where they were going. "We're going on a trip," she says her mother told her, "a little journey." They went in a car with their mother and some other grown-ups and drove to a place where there was water and got out of the car and boarded a boat.

"It was a little ferryboat or something, but it was big to me," says Kippie. "I thought it was a weekend trip, but my instincts were telling me something more. I was scared." Elisabeth was scared, too. "I stood out there listening," she recalls, "trying to hear what the adults were saying." "Then," says Kippie, "the trip lasted for a timeless time—I don't know how long—and when it ended I knew we were nowhere near home anymore."

It soon became clear that Bette had kidnapped her daughters. The first thought was that she would have taken them to Florida. "I flew down to Jacksonville, hired a car, and began looking around," Ernie remembered. "I combed the beaches. I looked over thousands of kids. I went to a school where they had been enrolled and a teacher told me they had been taken out of that school. Every place I went, someone had seen them yesterday or last week."

Ernie's primary focus now became the hunt for his little girls. "Ernie would leave the shows to go off on these searches," said Edie Adams. "Just the slightest hint, things with really nothing to back them up, would send him out to follow up the clues." He and his father scoured Florida on weekends, and he also hired private detectives to aid in the quest. "He had this detective with a crazy name going all over the country. You didn't think it was possible; it was more like fiction—Pierre La Tooth, or something like that," remembers Eddie Hatrak. "I thought it was one of his crazy names he made up, and he said, 'No, that's his name.' I remember he borrowed $500 from me once. I said, 'What's this? Like a week's wages?' He said, 'One day.' One day. But that's what it cost him. He spent a fortune on detectives."

Three months and $6,000 in detective fees later, Ernie was at his wit's end. "To tell you the truth, I sit here crying for hours sometimes," he confessed sadly in an interview at his CBS office on West 57th Street; the reporter described Ernie as "near tears" throughout the session. Physically and emotionally drained, unable to think of any other way to recover his little girls, on October 26 he finally went to Trenton Police Court and filed kidnapping charges against Bette, her mother, Sally Shotwell, and Sally's husband, Sidney. "I hope things happen quickly," he said. "I just must have my children back with me—they mean the world to me."

Two days later, a Newark police officer and two Trenton police detectives were dispatched to the Shotwells' house in Newark to question them. When they arrived late at night, a couple they suspected were the Shotwells came out of the house and got into a car parked in the driveway. Just as the police started to move in, the driver swung into reverse; one of the detectives later he said he had to "leap for his life," and they reported that the driver allegedly tried to run them down.

While one policeman staked out the house, the others took off after the speeding car in a dramatic midnight chase. The patrol vehicle managed to keep them in sight through six red lights before losing them; the detective posted at the house later saw the wanted auto pass there. As a result of the futile chase, the Trenton police sent out an alarm for the arrest of Sally and Sidney Shotwell as well as for that of Bette Kovacs, alerting law-enforcement agencies along the Atlantic seaboard to be on the lookout.

That December, a Mercer County grand jury indicted Bette and the Shotwells on the kidnapping charges originally filed in Trenton. Suddenly, during the Christmas holidays, Ernie had a surge of hope: Sally and Sidney Shotwell were arrested while visiting Sally's mother in Jacksonville and held for $10,000 bail. But in a hearing before a Jacksonville judge, the Shotwells pleaded innocent to kidnapping, and their attorney claimed that they did not know where Bette and the children were. An attempt to extradite the Shotwells to New Jersey failed, and they were set free.

Ernie turned thirty-five that January. Alternately despondent and determined, he had no way of knowing whether he would ever see his daughters again.

So possessed was Ernie with finding little Bette and Kippie that at one point he considered quitting his shows so he could devote all of his time to the hunt. His father convinced him otherwise, pointing out that he needed the income to pay, among other bills, those of the private detectives. Perhaps Andrew also sensed that the creative work would help take his son's mind off his desperate worries and give him some much-needed focus and stability.

On his morning show, *Kovacs Unlimited*, Ernie continued to come up with bizarre blackouts for director Ned Cramer and the WCBS engineers to bring to electronic fruition:

ERNIE INSIDE BOTTLE . . . WATER POURING IN . . . OPENS UM-
BRELLA, BUT WATER THREATENS TO SUBMERGE HIM . . . HITS GLASS
WITH HAMMER . . . BOTTLE SHATTERS

BEARDED ERNIE DESCRIBES RAZOR THAT GIVES WORLD'S FASTEST
SHAVE . . . RAZOR TOUCHES FACE . . . BEARD INSTANTLY DISAP-
PEARS

With the camera's ability to flip a picture upside down, Ernie could pretend to be the magician Matzoh Hepplewhite climbing a vertical rope head-down, or he could look like a daring acrobat defying the forces of gravity as he was held up by Gertrude, the rag doll. With the help of colored filters, Ernie could ogle a picture of a woman in an evening gown and the gown would transform itself into a bathing suit. (He could also suddenly acquire a black eye.) A black patch on Ernie's forehead gave him a hole in his head, and via the electronic matting amplifier viewers could see right through it to read a newspaper seemingly placed behind it. "He would introduce me as an inventor, Professor Bernie Cosnowski," remembers Eddie Hatrak; the name was borrowed from Trenton's "polka king," Bernie Cosnowski. "And I had supposedly invented this new piano; when you played the top part of the piano it sounded low, and when you played the bottom part of the piano it sounded high." Sure enough, Professor Cosnowski would play, and thanks to the camera's reverse polarity switch, the high end would produce a low sound and vice versa.

Wearing a beret, Hatrak also played the cameraman in "Pathetic News" sketches, Ernie's tawdry parody of the Pathé and other movie newsreels of the day. Equipped with a wobbly, droopy camera jerry-built of pie tins and garden hoses—like an inept child's version of a newsreel camera—Hatrak would capture such "Pathetic News" items as balloonist Abercrombie Fisk's history-making ascent from Coated Tongue, Texas. "Pathetic News" was a regular feature on Ernie's shows for many years, as were several other sketches and characters he invented during his CBS period. On *Kovacs Unlimited* he introduced Tom Swift, whose adventures bore titles like "Tom Swift and His Electric Peach Basket" and spoofed the formal prose of turn-of-the-century novels ("It had been admitted by some that Jacqueline Forbish was not without justification when she coughed deliberately in young Tom's face, causing him to nearly expire from carbon monoxide and depositing a thin layer of soot on his handsome features"). He also created Mr. Question Man, based on the radio show *The Answer Man;* Mr.

Question Man was invariably stumped by such queries as, "If camel's hair comes from a camel, does mohair come from a mo?" And he introduced the continuing puppet caper "The Kapusta Kid in Outer Space" (*kapusta* is Polish and Russian for "cabbage"), described by one six-year-old girl as "funnier than Bugs Bunny" and by a Yale philosophy professor as "an exquisite satire." This Kovacsian version of the kids' outer-space shows popular at the time starred a little bear puppet named Kapusta, a Sicilian monkey called O'Brian (after Jack O'Brian, a critic who usually hated Ernie's work), the spacesuit-clad horse Albumen, and the fair lady Celeste:

THROUGH THE HELP OF SPIEGEL THE SPONGE HEAD, THE INTREPID ADVENTURERS HAVE ESCAPED FROM GROOTZ'S DUNGEON ON THE SQUARE PLANET . . . ALBUMEN: "I DO NOT SEEM TO SEE THE APPROACH OF SPIEGEL THE SPONGE HEAD FROM ANY DIRECTION, IN FACT FROM EITHER DIRECTION, PARTICULARLY NOT FROM THE NORTH, ALTHOUGH HE IS ALMOST AS MUCH NOT IN EVIDENCE FROM THE SOUTH."

PAUSE.

CELESTE: "WOULD YOU WANT TO RUN THROUGH THAT AGAIN FOR THE FOLKS WHO JUST TUNED IN ON THE WEST COAST, ALBUMEN?"

Kovacs Unlimited ran on WCBS until January 15, 1954, for a total of twenty-one months. It would be Ernie's longest-running series out of New York. Despite his uneven relationship with CBS, his two years there firmly established him as a well-known television personality, and when he left he was quickly snapped up by DuMont, the "fourth network."

The DuMont Television network was the brainchild of Allen B. DuMont, an electrical engineer and inventor who had found a way to convert the frail cathode-ray tube into the dependable central component for feasible television receivers. He formed his pioneering Allen B. DuMont Laboratories before World War II, and in 1946 he introduced the network, with the laboratories as the parent company.

With few affiliated stations and little money, the network had to rely on inexpensively produced shows and imaginative programming strategies to compete against the other three "webs." DuMont's innovations—soon imitated by the competing networks—included television's first soap opera, first children's series, and first regularly scheduled pro football and basketball games. The decision to schedule

Bishop Sheen's *Life Is Worth Living* opposite Milton Berle is one of TV's earliest instances of counterprogramming, a now-common strategy in which a completely different type of show is slotted to compete with an existing popular program. DuMont's cameras—along with those of ABC—helped bring Senator Joseph McCarthy's witch hunts to an end; the network's broadcasts of the Army-McCarthy hearings in 1954 would turn public sentiment against the senator. DuMont also gave a start to some of the industry's important talents, including Roone Arledge (later president of ABC News and Sports), newsman Mike Wallace, and Jackie Gleason, who introduced many of his memorable characters as well as "The Honeymooners" on DuMont's *Cavalcade of Stars* from 1950 to 1952.

CBS and NBC possessed great power partly because they had been built on the strong foundations of existing radio networks. But DuMont did not enjoy this advantage, and its principals found that attracting affiliates without the preexisting relationships from radio was a never-ending battle. During its first few years DuMont fought constantly over third place with ABC, which also had few affiliates. When ABC merged with United Paramount Theaters in the early 1950s, DuMont dropped to a weak fourth place, and its struggle to stay afloat intensified.

Searching for ways to strengthen its position, DuMont decided to push into the relatively new area of late-night programming. NBC had already proved that audiences existed: from 1950 to 1951 it had successfully mounted *Broadway Open House*, a vaudeville-style nightly show of skits, songs, and chatter hosted on alternating evenings by comedians Jerry Lester and Morey Amsterdam. (Jerry Lester's segments became famous for his interactions with blonde, bosomy Dagmar, who read deliberately dumb poems and became so popular that the far more experienced Lester left the show in resentment.) After *Broadway Open House* ended, there were other late-night experiments. On ABC's station in New York, a variety program called *Talk of the Town* was introducing audiences to a young comic named Louis Nye. In direct response to *Talk of the Town*, NBC's New York flagship station, WNBT-TV, had hired the quick-witted Steve Allen to mount an 11:20-to-midnight program beginning in the summer of 1953. WNBT's *The Steve Allen Show* was essentially a late-night version of a free-form comedy-variety-talk series that Allen had done previously at CBS, during early-evening and midday time slots. In September 1954, after a successful local run, the show was promoted to network status and given a new title: *Tonight!* (The exclamation point was later dropped.)

Eager to enter the late-night sweepstakes, DuMont's New York flagship station, WABD-TV, hired Ernie to do an hourlong weeknight series starting in April. WABD was serious about this bid and reportedly planned to put $1 million into the show on a long-term basis. Slated to air at 11:45 P.M., thereby getting a five-minute jump on the rival *Steve Allen Show*, DuMont's new *Ernie Kovacs Show* premiered on April 12, 1954, almost exactly one year from the date CBS had unceremoniously dumped Ernie's short-lived prime-time series.

For this return to glamorous nighttime TV, Ernie, who was producing and writing the show, decided that his cast and guests should make an appropriate entrance. Spoofing those extravagant movie premieres in which stars dripping with furs and diamonds are mobbed by screaming fans and flashing cameras as they emerge from chauffeured limousines, he had a remote unit stationed outside the DuMont studios to photograph the talent as they arrived in his sponsors' delivery trucks. The rest of the show was Scavokian havoc, with such TV personalities as Morey Amsterdam and Sam Levenson running about madly, Percy Dovetonsils reciting "Ode to Spring," Edith Adams and a new "boy singer" named Peter Hanley delivering vocals, and the newly formed Eddie Hatrak Trio performing musical accompaniments. Ernie reminded viewers of the industry's penchant for screening old films on late-night TV by repeating the same clip of a cops-and-robbers shootout twenty-seven times. Commercials were flipped upside down, horizontally, and vertically by the cameras. "It can safely be said that once the opening night confusions, bedlam, and uncertainties are out of the way," wrote one critic in *Variety*, "it should settle down to perhaps the most frantic hour on the video circuits. There's no pretense at making sense, and it's the only known display where the backstage clamor is more appropriately attuned to and rightfully belongs with the on-camera behavior."

Ernie spent the next year at DuMont, and, because his name had cachet, he was enlisted for two other shows. From July 1954 to February 1955 he served as a panelist on the network's *One Minute Please*, a quiz show based on a British series. Each panelist was required to expound for one minute on a given topic in which he or she was *not* expert, such as "Breeding Guppies" or "Why I Ride Sidesaddle." Its only redeeming feature was that it introduced Ernie to fellow panelists Hermione Gingold, the English actress who shared his love of a good cigar, and Marc Connelly, the playwright and former member of the fabled Algonquin Round Table, who became part of Ernie's poker circle and a close family friend.

From August to mid-October 1954, Ernie hosted the network's prime-time quiz show *Time Will Tell*, which required contestants to answer ninety seconds of lightning-fast questions. The contestant with the most right answers won, but *Time Will Tell* was really designed as a platform for Ernie's off-the-cuff interviews and remarks. Both quiz shows were precisely the sort of mindless fare that Kovacs lampooned on the programs of his own making. But they fed Ernie's need for money, which grew endlessly as he spent more and more on private detectives and on his own travels to search for his daughters; he had neither seen nor heard news of them for over a year.

As continually surprising as the quiz shows were formulaic, the late-night *Ernie Kovacs Show* served as an ideal platform for Ernie. The very character of late-night programming was, then as now, iconoclastic and inventive, even better suited to Kovacs' wild sense of humor than daytime had been. And at DuMont he was given free rein; no network executives hovered over his shoulder. Indeed, the atmosphere was so loose that Ernie and the station engineers were able to get away with a recurring practical joke for nights on end: in the control room, during the late-night movie, they'd slowly lower the sound level so that viewers would have to get up every so often and adjust the volume on their sets. At the end of the movie, they'd suddenly turn the sound way up, blasting the sleepy audience out of their beds. Then Ernie and his cohorts would rush to the window to watch as apartment lights flicked on all over Manhattan.

Ernie forged two important unions while at DuMont. The first was with Barry Shear, a staff cameraman-turned-director who had as little respect for authority as Ernie did. Shear's volatile personality made some coworkers keep their distance. He was in trouble with DuMont management for such sins as letting his shows run too long and neglecting to give DuMont a commission from the income he made off commercials; as castigation, he was assigned to do the late-night Kovacs show. Ernie, no stranger to volatile personalities, got along with Shear magnificently. They began to play poker together and formed a tight personal and professional bond that would last until the end of Ernie's life. (On the DuMont shows, Shear sometimes alternated directing duties with Frank Bunetta, who had directed Jackie Gleason on *Cavalcade of Stars*.)

Shear instinctively comprehended Ernie's comedy and how best to shoot it. "He had a great deal of energy, and he was very imaginative in terms of anything technical. But I thought his biggest contribution was understanding what Ernie wanted," says Shirley Mellner, who would work with the Kovacs-Shear team at NBC. "Ernie would write his script, and Barry knew how to give him what he wanted. Ernie would convey it to him in a couple of sentences."

The second important relationship that Ernie formed at DuMont was with a young actress named Barbara Loden, whom he added to the late-night show's regular cast on the third broadcast. Loden would work with Ernie for nearly three years, on all the rest of his programs out of New York, and she possessed that combination of relaxation, deadpan precision, and willingness to work hard that made her the ideal Kovacs performer. "She was very special. Ernie would really direct her," says Mellner. "And he used to say, 'You laugh at her and think she's just a dumb blonde, but she's going to do things.'" Loden, who married director Elia Kazan, later appeared on Broadway (winning a Tony for the lead in Arthur Miller's *After the Fall*) and directed plays and films (her independent feature *Wanda* was the talk of the 1970 Venice Film Festival). First, however, she became Ernie's regular Bessie Lou Cosnowski, appearing as a newsmaker on "Pathetic News" or as a panelist on the fake game shows, invariably responding to questions with a long, long . . . long blank stare. She would stand still for a pie in the face or an arrow through the head, and she was perfect for such electronic sight gags as "the invisible girlfriend," for which she would be dressed from head to toe in black, swathed with white wrappings, and matted into the picture frame with Ernie, who would then unwind the wrappings to reveal—nothing!

Another newcomer to the Kovacs cast was singer Peter Hanley, who made a crucial contribution one day when he brought in an odd recording titled "Solfeggio" (a *solfeggio* is a singing exercise using the do-re-mi syllables). "I thought you'd like this," he told Ernie. Ernie played the record and said, "Now, just don't talk for a second. Just don't talk." He played the record again. As he played it a third time, he started telling Hanley and Edie Adams what to do: "Okay, Edie, you sit there on the piano. Peter, you stand there." He demonstrated how he wanted them to move: mechanically, like windup toys. For the show he dressed them and himself in bowlers and overcoats and rubber gorilla masks, and thus was born the Nairobi Trio. Along with Percy Dovetonsils, the Nairobi Trio became one of Kovacs' most popular creations.

The trio made its first appearance on *The Ernie Kovacs Show* on April 21, 1954. It was a sketch of modest scale, sublimely simple and exquisite in its timing: the Nairobi Trio mimes performing "Solfeggio" as if they are mechanical toy monkeys, one at an upright piano, another at a xylophone, the third wielding a conductor's baton. At a precise moment in a recurring musical phrase, the xylophonist-ape turns jerkily to the conductor-ape and bashes him on the head with his xylophone hammer. "The manner, nuance, and mood of the clout may vary with each performance," wrote Frederic Morton in *Holiday,* but it "always dramatizes the unfathomability of fate and the treacherousness of life, and it always has the audience in stitches over seeing someone else betrayed." Over the years this "nihilistic operetta" was performed many times, with many subtle variations. Ernie almost always played the victimized conductor-ape, but different personnel were enlisted for the other two parts, including at first Peter Hanley, Edith Adams, Eddie Hatrak, Barbara Loden, and a puppeteer named Larry Berthelson and later such Hollywood friends as Jack Lemmon and Tony Curtis. Video engineer Wally Stanard, who worked with Ernie at ABC and was a self-appointed "Nairobi Trio specialist," remembers that he "could always tell if one of the apes was Edie because her arms would go all the way up and down playing the piano. Edie put a little more flair into it."

Edie Adams appeared on the late-night *Ernie Kovacs Show* until July 1954, when she left the program to prepare to go on the road with *Wonderful Town.* Her romance with Ernie had continued in an unsettled fashion, with Ernie pressing her for marriage and she remaining reluctant to make a permanent commitment. Their disagreements came to a head just as *Wonderful Town* was closing on Broadway. "I told Ernie I wasn't sure about marriage—and for my punchline I announced I was sailing for Europe," she later told an interviewer.

Ernie reacted with a dose of Hungarian high drama. "Go ahead, go to Europe!" he yelled. "Go to Afghanistan or Hightstown, New Jersey. Who cares?" But obviously he cared, and when Edith was about to sail at the end of July, he showed up at the ship laden with flowers, candy, and perfume. "It was a little broad, but touching, too," said Edie. "My heart melted a little, and a big emotional scene followed— right there in front of all my relatives. But I clung to my plans for the trip. I figured it would be our Big Test."

The test was tougher than she had anticipated. Intent on staying away from Ernie for six weeks, Edith almost immediately found herself desolate, and she spent the first three days of the trip talking to Ernie over transatlantic telephone. In a Paris flea market, as a gag, she bought him a pair of beautiful antique dueling pistols. Then, unable to bear it any longer and ignoring her vow to stay away, she flew back within a few days. Ernie was both infuriated and wounded by the whole affair.

His feelings leaked over into his television work. Eager to maintain contact with her, one night he put in an overseas call to her while he was on the air, but on the day she returned he did a bit called "Poison Pen," about marital breakup, and it seethed with ire.

But the Big Test seemed to decide matters for Edith. She was scheduled to perform in *Wonderful Town* opposite Imogene Coca at the State Fair in Dallas, and one weekend Ernie swooped down and flew her to Mexico City. There they were married on Sunday, September 12, 1954, in a ceremony presided over by William O'Dwyer, the former mayor of New York City, who had left his civic post amid charges of corruption and was now living in Mexico. The wedding vows were in Spanish, which neither bride nor groom understood, so O'Dwyer had to nudge each at the appropriate moment to answer, "*Si.*" The elopement was so sudden that friends weren't told about it; Ernie hadn't even prepared scripts for that week, and back in New York his cast had to wing it. He and Edith had a weeklong honeymoon in Mexico, during which Edith came to love the fragrant white gardenias she saw floating in bowls of water around the hotel. Thereafter Ernie would always send her gardenia bouquets whenever they were working apart.

Ernie's motto, "Nothing in moderation" (a play on the ancient counsel "Nothing in excess"), suited his new wife just fine. "Life with Ernie was totally unpredictable, and it was just what I needed," said Edie Adams. "I came from a family that had conferences about whether to cross a street; Ernie planned nothing in advance." He always seemed to be on an effervescent high: "We'd get up in the morning and he'd say, 'This is the *greatest* orange juice' or 'the most *fantastic* coffee.' Manic, you know. And he'd give gifts. He'd throw me a grocery bag filled with air, but you could hear something rattling around in it, and it would be a string of real pearls."

Ernie was besotted with his new wife and would remain so for a long time. Three years after their marriage he told an interviewer, "I look forward to a date with her the way a bachelor would. When I meet her after the theater, and I've just done a television show and millions of people have been watching me, I put on a better suit, because I'm picking her up. If I met her as a stranger at a party, I wouldn't have the nerve to go up to her and say hello." That Edith could accept and love him was a source of wonder to Ernie, who regarded himself as "not very clever with women."

The newly wedded Ernie returned to DuMont on September 20, and Edith followed a week later, her *Wonderful Town* commitments finally discharged. Although in tone they were wild as can be, the

DuMont Kovacs shows were more organized than Ernie's first programs at WCBS. His guests were better-known performers, often Broadway personalities like Zero Mostel or Geraldine Page, as the late-night time slot made it easy for them to dash over to his show just after the theater broke. And at DuMont he was scripting complex, full-blown sketches rather than limiting his writing to simple blackouts, although the blackout always remained a staple of his comedy. (A quick gag with a visual punch line, the blackout form came from vaudeville and was refined for television by Kovacs. It was later used by TV practitioners ranging from Monty Python, Benny Hill, and *Laugh-In* producer George Schlatter to video artists Teddy Dibble and Mitchell Kriegman.)

As at CBS, many of these sketches continued to spoof American pop culture. With Edie Adams and Peter Hanley supplying the voices, Ernie would shoot comic strips that parodied well-known cartoons; "Superman" became "Superclod" and "L'il Orphan Annie" was transformed into "L'il Orphan Amy" ("Shucks . . . how come, with all Daddy's zillions of dollars, I've been wearin' this same red dress for thirty-five years? Shucks."). He loved to make up silly commercials for fake products, such as Budapest Krisplies or Choco-Spin, the chocolate-covered spinach. Television shows also provided a rich source of parody material. CBS's cultural series *Omnibus*, which presented such highbrow fare as Orson Welles playing King Lear, was skewered on Ernie's "Semibus," featuring such segments as the story of the musical comb; and the popular radio and TV series *Martin Kane, Private Eye* became "Martin Krutch, Public Eye," a smart spoof of all the conventions of *film noir*, with Barbara Loden playing hard-boiled Krutch's trusted secretary Morris.

Ernie knew and loved films, and during this period he created many sketches about movies. Made up as Hollywood movie star Rock Mississippi in impossibly padded shoulders, false eyelashes, and a Tony Curtis wig, Ernie would apprise viewers of such coming attractions as "Son of Seven Year Itch" ("You will love the picture and simply adore me"). He also instituted "The You Should Have Stayed in Bed Show," a phony late-night series of bad films. Often, however, the movie sketches were lengthy, well-written miniproductions performed by the cast in full costume, with complete story lines and wacky made-up credits. The classic British mystery film, for example, was stripped down to its most ridiculous essentials—murder, questioning, and great quantities of tea drinking—in Ernie's recurring feature "Great Brit Films"; these sketches bore titles like "Arsenic and Crumpled Tweed" and starred Kovacs as Inspector Pommery, wearing a fake upturned nose.

Though Ernie preferred working without a live audience, when he did have one, he made a point of drawing it into the proceedings. The DuMont *Ernie Kovacs Show* had a small studio audience, or "23 Passing Strangers," as Ernie billed them in the credits (they were listed as part of the cast). He designed tickets printed with a shorthand self-portrait (eyebrows, mustache, cigar) and the legend ADMIT ONE PASSING STRANGER, a reference to the chance way in which studio audiences are gathered. He would have Andy McKay bring odd items for them to wrap up on the air or ask them to demonstrate the virtues of his sponsors' products or even include them in his sketches (on one installment of "Martin Krutch, Public Eye" he accused them all of being suspects while the camera closed in on each audience member in turn).

As for the audience at home, they were invited to join in his never-ending examination of the wonderful new medium they were watching. Ernie was constantly referring to television's peculiarities and building bits around them. He gave viewers a behind-the-scenes tour of the DuMont facilities; while the engineers aired a test pattern, he extemporized on its qualities; he had director Barry Shear cut to all the competing shows before returning to the final minutes of the Kovacs show, as if to imitate viewers at home switching channels. Sid Shalit of the *New York Daily News* wrote with some awe about how Ernie enjoyed "a remarkable rapport with his audience, who by some strange chemistry seem to feel they are a part of what is going on. His viewers are proud when the camera trick comes off, almost as if they had something to do with it."

Another way to involve viewers was to hold contests, as Ernie had been doing since the days of *3 to Get Ready.* For his "Plop" contest, viewers were supposed to predict the point at which a candle would burn through a string and release a baseball suspended over some borscht; Ernie kept careful vigil every night, checking on the progress of the melting candle, until finally the baseball went *plop!* "Snepshots" capitalized on the fad of photographing pictures off home TV screens. At first the "snepshots" he received were crude and distorted; to inspire viewers to greater artistic heights, he made a point of showing only the best ones on the air and giving them prizes. The shutterbugs' entries improved, until by the end of the contest people were sending him truly imaginative works of art. One contestant painted fish and air bubbles over Ernie, making him look as if he were underwater; another created a set of bizarrely charged still lifes by posing a bathing-suited model and Siamese cats before the television set, where Ernie could be glimpsed on-screen; still another printed up a large-format contact sheet with Ernie as a star over a nighttime skyline of Manhattan.

The Ernie Kovacs Show was popular, but not enough to save a financially ailing fourth-place network. Starting on January 11, 1955, DuMont made some cuts in its programming. The Kovacs show was trimmed to a half-hour (10:30 to 11:00 P.M.) and twice-weekly (Tuesday and Thursday) format. It was restored to an hour beginning March 1 and retitled *The Ernie Kovacs Rehearsal;* a new pianist, Jack Kelly, replaced Eddie Hatrak. But the rehearsal would be short-lived. The last Kovacs broadcast on DuMont was on April 7, 1955, and not long afterward DuMont Laboratories shut down its network operation. (This was just the boost that rival ABC needed; the third-place network's billings for advertising revenues rose 68 percent in 1955.) And so, a year after he had started at DuMont, Ernie Kovacs once again found himself a man without a network.

Monday, April 11, 1955, was a typically sultry spring day in Cassia, a small town in central Florida's hot, swampy Lake County. Bette Kovacs, nearly eight years old, was walking home from the old-fashioned one-room country schoolhouse she attended. Suddenly a big car pulled up beside her. Inside were her father and her grandfather, whom she had not seen for nearly two years.

Bette rushed home, which was a room in the back of a diner where her mother was working, and found her six-year-old sister, Kippie. "I said to Kippie, 'Let's have a popsicle and go outside.' Remember those lovely twin popsicles that you could share? We got one of those; I think it was lime. Then outside I told Kippie, 'Daddy's come to get us.' "

That evening, after dinner, the girls got ready for bed as usual; they shared a mattress on the floor next to a screen door, through which they could see the backyard garden of watermelons and peanuts and corn and smell the sweet fragrance of the surrounding pines and fruit trees. As they were undressing, Ernie Kovacs showed up at the door with his father, Andrew, and a deputy sheriff named A. J. Groves. Their mother "came running and saying, 'Your father's here. Your father's here. Hide in the shower,' " recalls Kippie. Her sister, as she had on the ferryboat that took her away two years before, went to the far end of the diner and tried to listen to what the adults were saying before hiding in the shower. A debate was taking place between the three men and the girls' mother. Finally Kippie turned the shower on. "I believe I wanted to let him know where I was, and I wanted to go with him, because I was living a life of misery, a total nightmare."

For Kippie, who says her mother had told her, "Your daddy's a witch, and if he gets you back, you know he's going to kill you," the nightmare ended when her father took her in his arms and brought her out to his car. "I got in the car with him," remembers Kippie, "and he turned and said, 'I see you still suck your thumb.' So I said, 'I see you still smoke cigars.' And right away it was right. There was no looking back. She didn't exist anymore."

Ernie had actually located his daughters prior to April 11, but there was bureaucratic red tape to be gotten through before he could legally take them back. First he had to have a Florida court award him temporary custody in the state; this was granted on the basis of the previous 1952 custody ruling in Philadelphia. He also had to post a bond of $1,000 to guarantee that he would return the children if the court ordered him to.

But Bette, his ex-wife, fought him for custody after he took the girls back. Deputy Sheriff Groves testified that during the grab, the girls had said "that they hated him and that they did not want to go with him," and that Kovacs had shown no feeling toward them. Agreeing with a special court officer who found Ernie's behavior during the rescue indicative of "a hardness and harshness . . . that would not commend him to the favorable consideration of the court," and perhaps also bending to the then-entrenched tendency to award custody to the mother, Circuit Judge Truman G. Futch granted Bette custody in Florida on November 14. Ernie challenged the ruling all the way up to the state supreme court but never saw it reversed. Nonetheless he never returned the girls. Ironically, the state of Florida still had an arrest warrant out for him, for contempt of court, on the day he died.

In Cassia Bette had kept the girls living in "a squalor," describes Kippie. "I remember the beatings, the bristle brush. And her telling me that my dad was a witch." According to Elisabeth, "You couldn't argue with her—the hairbrush would come out, or she'd knock you across the room." Bette taught her daughters to duck every time they saw a police car go by, a habit they retained even after moving back to New York with their father.

She had taken them first to Jacksonville, then had arranged for a job in Cassia running a diner, where there was also living space behind. Down a dirt road was a little country church, and animals seemed to be all around: wild rabbits that leaped about the garden, and goats kept by their friend Sandra, whose father had a ranch nearby, and a wild boar that once chased Elisabeth up a tree, and a variety of cats who lived in a garage.

They ate their meals in the diner's kitchen. "We would have Cream of Wheat for breakfast, and she would put blue dye in it to make it attractive," says Kippie. Only five or so, Kippie would "wash the dishes and wait on tables, and then I would get up and sing for the customers, whatever song I had heard on the radio. I loved to entertain. Then there was one scene that wasn't so entertaining. My mother had been saving a box of change, mostly pennies, and my Uncle Sid [Shotwell] was drunk. He came in angry one day and threw the box of coins all over the floor, and he made her cry. Even though she was not the greatest mother in the world, I hated him for that."

While Kippie was waiting on tables and singing, Elisabeth was seeking an education. "I had finally convinced her to let me go to school," she says, recalling her mother's initial reluctance to send her, perhaps from fear that somebody would recognize her as Ernie Kovacs' missing daughter. Elisabeth was smart and loved to learn, and soon she was allowed to skip from first to third grade, which made her very proud. But in the classroom and at the diner, she was being exposed to something new: racism. "I had black jeans, and the kids called me nigger," she says. "And in the diner, there was a window for the blacks. I used to have fights with Bette about it. In the rain they had to stand there! She said they were different."

In Florida, on occasion they would spend time with Sid and Sally Shotwell. "Sally made us Thanksgiving dresses once, and we *loved* them," remembers Elisabeth. "We demanded to bring those dresses with us when my father found us." They were pretty, pinafored little-girl frocks of floral cotton, and the special outfits included the girls' first patent leather shoes.

Then they returned to New York and moved into their father's elegant five-room apartment at 55 East End Avenue, overlooking the East River. It was "a castle," according to Kippie, "compared to where I'd lived in the back on a mattress on the floor." The castle even came with its own "perfect, golden-haired princess": Edith Adams, their father's beautiful new wife. "What more could a child ask for?" says Kippie. "The stepmother usually has the black hair, and the mother always has the golden locks. Being one of fairy tales and imagination, I just fell in love with the woman. I wanted her approval and love so desperately."

Her sister remembers their stepmother less romantically. "She was a pretty woman," says Elisabeth, and she had fascinating objects: all sorts of makeup and perfumes temptingly arranged on a dressing table, dozens of pairs of elegant shoes in the closet. "I wanted to play with her high heels and makeup," Elisabeth recalls, but then she'd get into trouble: "Have you been playing at my dressing table?" Edie didn't like their special Thanksgiving dresses from grandma Sally, "she didn't like little crinolines, she didn't like the things we had. She had to have us 'properly' dressed, in velvet dresses and stockings."

As for Edie, who had just turned twenty-eight, had always been childless, and was still a newlywed of seven months, "at first I was baffled—I didn't know what to do. So I would always answer them politely, and I got them into Miss Hewitt's and tried to straighten them out." Miss Hewitt's was a private school for girls in Manhattan, very prim and proper. Before the girls could be enrolled, however, Ernie and Edie spent a month alone with them, trying to give a new structure and civility to their lives. Elisabeth thinks this was because "we were traumatized," and this is doubtless true. But Kippie believes there was an additional reason: "The words and the bigotry from the South were well introduced into our vocabulary. The phraseology of one thing in particular . . . it's embarrassing: 'Fuckingnigger.' I thought that was a word. I didn't think there was anything wrong with it."

At Miss Hewitt's, the rules and regulations drove Kippie to distraction. "It was the most outrageously obnoxious school I've ever seen, in hindsight," she says. "We went in every day in our uniforms. Miss Hewitt would hold her pinky out, and we would curtsy and shake her pinky." As her father had been in high school, Kippie was utterly bored by academics. "We learned a little crap: 'Jack and Jill went up the hill' and all that. You learn to read and write and all that junk you can learn in five minutes and go on. I had to sit there and sit there and sit there."

Children who have been kidnapped by a parent rarely lose the feeling that the world is a dangerous and unstable place. In the case of the Kovacses, the pattern reversed itself a little bit. Elisabeth says that *she* was perpetually concerned over her father's well-being, as if he were a fragile child. "I always worried about him," she describes. "He seemed to work so hard. I would get up at 3:00 in the morning and tell him to go to bed." And to Ernie, the world would be a dangerous and unstable place from now on, for he would never shake loose the fear that his children might be abducted again. Kippie remembers being in first or second grade at Miss Hewitt's, "and I was very bored. It was very quiet, so I made this popping sound with my mouth." For punishment, the teacher promptly sent her to the library, "which was the size of a closet, and they forgot about me. I sat there all day. Three o'clock came, three thirty, and they were looking frantically all over the school for me." Her father thought she had been abducted again. After she was found, "the teacher got a bawling out."

Shortly after recovering his daughters, Ernie received an offer to return to radio and to wake-up programming. ABC Radio's New York flagship station, WABC, had hired a new general manager to revamp the entire schedule. The overhaul included replacing the morning shows with a single radio personality for a long stretch. And so on May 30,

1955, WABC's live *Ernie Kovacs Show* began broadcasting from 6:00 to 9:00 A.M. every day but Sunday. The new program had a typical wake-up show structure, with frequent time and weather announcements interspersed among anecdotes, gags, one-man sketches, and occasional records. Newscaster Charles F. McCarthy provided capsulized news reports every half hour, and the Buddy Weed Trio played jazz. The job required that Ernie rise at 4:30 A.M., but the payoff was a reported $95,000 a year by his second year on the job.

The difficulty of awakening so early was softened by the fact that Edith, too, was working an early-morning show. In 1953, while doing *Wonderful Town*, Edith had been the regular "girl singer" on the daytime *Jack Paar Show*. As of March 1955 she was back with Paar again, in a 7:00 to 9:00 A.M. weekday slot on CBS, after a bit of a personnel scandal. Adams had been asked to replace Paar's vacationing singer, Betty Clooney (sister of Rosemary), for just two weeks, but Clooney returned to discover that Edith had been offered the job permanently. Rumor had it that Clooney was fired because of her romantic involvement with Paar's Cuban orchestra leader, Pupi Campo, who was separated but not divorced from his wife. Paar's stated reason, however, was that Edith gave his show a necessary "lift." The television host admitted publicly that the decision was "cruel" but rationalized, "Is there a nice way to give anyone notice?" (Clooney was immediately hired by Robert Q. Lewis.) Edith was paid a handsome $800 a week for about fifteen hours of work. She was also finding lucrative jobs performing in television commercials.

While Edith was working on the Paar show, Ernie received an offer from an unexpected quarter: NBC Television. Tom Loeb, the network's national program manager, had seen Ernie on DuMont and had also been in contact with director Barry Shear about another project. Loeb went to Pat Weaver, who had by now been promoted from television operations head to president of NBC, and told him, " 'This is wild. Let's do something about Ernie Kovacs.' And he looked at him and he loved him," remembers Loeb, "so we signed him for something like $25,000 a year. It was nothing. But Ernie never went in for money. He didn't think that $25,000 meant anything. He wanted to experiment. He was terribly inquisitive, and he was like an inventor."

NBC put Ernie under an exclusive television contract but did not immediately find a slot for a Kovacs show. This was not an uncommon practice then; according to Loeb, "We signed many people ahead of time in hope that we could find a place for them. We paid him for exclusivity, to lock him up." Still, Ernie's work was so offbeat that

NBC was hard-pressed to know how to use him. Weaver had comedy on at 8:00 P.M. seven nights a week, mostly revues hosted by comics, such as *The Colgate Comedy Hour*. "I had great hopes for Ernie because he was so funny," recalls Weaver, "but that very undisciplined structure made it difficult to figure out just where to put him. Somehow, the material he was doing and—as I gathered in just slight talks with him—his determination to do his thing, which was so different from everybody, made it unlikely that he could be set up in a revue format like most of the comedy stars could." Not knowing quite what to do with Ernie, NBC did almost nothing for a long time. Occasionally he would pop up as a guest on various NBC shows, but it would be many months before Ernie had a series of his own on NBC.

This lack of a permanent television slot, however, allowed Ernie to spend time with his newly re-formed family. In June, he and Edith sublet the East End Avenue apartment and moved the family into a seventeen-room duplex in the El Dorado, at 300 Central Park West, where their neighbors included comedienne Imogene Coca and writer Herman Wouk (Wouk's novel *Marjorie Morningstar* opens in the El Dorado). Built in 1931, the El Dorado's modest sandy-colored facade belied the grandeur of its interiors. One entered a dramatic green-and-gold Art Deco lobby and took a semiprivate elevator up to the eighteenth floor, where the Kovacses occupied a two-story penthouse surrounded by long terraces with spectacular views. On one end of a terrace a portable pool was installed for the girls; in the mornings, Ernie and Edie would relax there and watch the boxers and wrestlers do their roadwork around the reservoir in Central Park. During the day, one could gaze upon the full sweep of Frederick Law Olmsted and Calvert Vaux's romantic manmade landscape, lush in the summertime and fairyland white in the winter. After dark, the sounds of the buses and taxis stopping and starting between 90th and 91st streets floated up from below; Bette, an urbanite at heart, found comfort in this city sound that went on all night long.

Ernie and Edith set about making the duplex into a real home. They scoured auction houses and antique shops and filled it with a potpourri of antiques. Animals would find their way into the family, including Edie's little Yorkshire terrier, Pamela, and a marmoset named Howard, whom Ernie adored. Everything in the duplex was done on a grand scale. In the living room, whose walls were painted a dramatic deep brown, there were great expanses of wall-to-wall carpeting on which Ernie liked to sprawl his six-foot-two frame for a quick nap; the table in the formal dining room could seat eight or ten with ease; in the master bedroom, Ernie and Edie shared a king-size bed, and at its foot were not one but two television sets, equipped with separate ear jacks. Ernie now had room to collect objects he liked in quantity: he began acquiring beautiful Chinese ivory figurines, and the dueling pistols Edie had jokingly bought him in Paris became the basis for an extensive collection of antique weaponry—medieval suits of armor, pistols and rifles, sabers and daggers. For the enormous, expensive Havana cigars he loved (he was smoking twenty a day, a habit that would eventually cost him some $13,000 a year), Ernie placed four humidors around the house and devised an elaborate ritual by which he would start his new cigars off in humidor number one, let them age a bit, then move them to the next humidor and the next, until finally, by the time they reached humidor number four, they were aged to precisely the point at which they would produce the most satisfying smoke.

Fascinated by gadgets, Ernie quickly transformed his new home into a sort of domestic laboratory for electronic experimentation. He installed five television sets (including the two in the master bedroom), complete with remote controls, which were a rare feature then. He had a Louis XV commode fitted up with hi-fi equipment and one of the TVs, and hi-fi was piped into each room. An intercom network enabled family members to communicate electronically from room to room. The many telephones around the house were operated by push button, also a rare feature at the time.

No expense was spared for the happiness of Edith, Bette, or Kippie. If Edith wanted to buy Louis XV chairs or a Mainbocher dress or a topaz necklace, she had only to charge it; Ernie took control of all the money in the family, and his wife never even saw the bills. If Kippie and Bette wanted to see their favorite musical, *Peter Pan,* over and over and over again, they had merely to ask. "We saw every play there was, practically," remembers Kippie. "I loved every time. *My Fair Lady. South Pacific. Oklahoma! Pajama Game. Damn Yankees.* I went to them all."

As for Ernie, driven as he was by memories of his lean, difficult days—the days when he had survived on cheap spaghetti dinners or been near death in a Welfare Island hospital—now he wanted only to enjoy every moment to the fullest. Like Auntie Mame, Ernie had appetites that were larger than life; money was great because it enabled him to satisfy them. If, for example, Ernie found that he was running out of cigars, he would simply fly the whole family down to Havana for the weekend. "We would fly to Havana all the time. Once we even flew in a transport plane with gutted interiors; he needed cigars and this was the only thing available," says Elisabeth, miming how they all scrunched up on the floor of the plane, the thrumming din of the motors right in their ears. "It was lovely with my father there. We would go bicycling in Old Havana, snorkeling, swimming. At the hotel restaurants they had entertainment, and every night he'd take Edie out dancing, and we would watch them from a table. He always said he didn't dance, but Edie would know all the new steps."

To create a stable family routine for the girls, Ernie and Edith made a point of sitting down to dinner with them every night. They hired a Brussels-trained cook, "an expert in sauces and genius in pastry," according to Ernie, and they were served by a dignified butler in their formal dining room, which was decorated with a grand crystal chandelier and wallpaper showing steamboats puffing up a river. On Sundays the whole family attended a Presbyterian church, and Kippie and Bette were also enrolled in Sunday school. But this institutionalized form of religious training made less of an impact on them than their father's own day-to-day example, which both remember with great clarity. "He never took off his St. Christopher medal" except when he was going to bed, recalls Elisabeth, and "every night he'd say an Our Father and personal prayers. In his behavior I was guided to be a spiritual person." Kippie, too, recollects that "he used to get down on his knees every night and pray. Every night. He wasn't really a churchgoer, and neither am I. I don't have to go to church to pray."

When the girls came home from school, they were watched over by "a constant governess," says Kippie, who didn't like the woman because she was "strict, and I don't like anybody who tells me what to do." She never rebelled, however: "I was always the good child, sickeningly—a real little people pleaser. My sister was the one who was outspoken. I used to be very quiet, quiet as a mouse." Ernie would be writing one of his shows, sometimes upstairs in his wood-paneled den, which was filled with antique firearms and books, and at other times downstairs "on the floor, lying down writing—he had no set place. And he would take time out to play with us. He was always there for us." Kippie and Bette would perform scenes from plays, one of their favorites being *Peter Pan*, and their father would set aside whatever he was doing and provide an attentive audience. "We used the living room as the stage, and Peter Pan flew, so I had to fly," recalls Kippie. "I would use those Louis XIV chairs, or whichever Louis it was, and jump on top of them and fly off of them. Edie didn't know about it back then. My dad never told her, I guess. And he got a kick out of it. When my dad was home, he'd watch. When he was busy, my grandmother would watch. She seemed to visit a lot, and she was marvelous with children. She just seemed to appear at times."

In typical lavish fashion, Ernie hired a New York cabbie, Lou Pack, as a private driver for his family. Pack drove the girls to Miss Hewitt's in the morning and picked them up in the afternoon, and he was always on call. Ernie gradually came to depend on Pack for more than just driving. After *The Jack Paar Show* was moved to the afternoons, for example, and Edith didn't need to get up before dawn anymore, Pack became his employer's breakfast companion. Six mornings a week, just after 5:00 A.M., Pack would unlock the door of the Kovacs apartment with his own key and go into the kitchen to fry up bacon and eggs for two. He was soon joined by Ernie, freshly shaved, and they would eat and read the morning papers before driving to the ABC Radio studios.

When she wasn't working, Edith seemed to be trying hard to feel her way into a loving relationship with Ernie's children. At first they called her by her first name, but one day they asked their father whether they could call her "Mother." "I had the feeling that it would work out better if it was their own idea instead of something they were told, or forced, to do," said Edie. Bette went one step farther, according to her father: on the first day of school, she pulled him aside to request that he call *her* "Edith" in front of her classmates. "They're trying to grow up in Edie's image, and they want to dress like her, and talk like her, and look like her," Ernie beamed to *Cosmopolitan* interviewer Hyman Goldberg, who described him as "openly impressed and deeply moved by this development." (Elisabeth, however, says that "if I did that it was because I was humiliated that my parents were divorced. I didn't want the kids in school to find out.") Goldberg also observed that "both girls obviously adore [Edie], for they constantly throw themselves in her lap or hug and kiss her." Kenneth McCormick, the editor-in-chief of Doubleday, befriended Ernie and Edie a couple of years later. He remembers that around the girls, Edie "would do anything that would amuse them. She was really a sort of pixie and tremendously attractive. And Ernie was just crazy about her. So what started as a love affair ended up as a home for these two children."

In an episode of Edward R. Murrow's live interview show *Person to Person* broadcast in June 1955, shortly after Kippie and Bette were recovered, the four appear as the classic mid-1950s nuclear family. Ernie refers to Edith as "Mother," as do the girls, who are wearing long nightgowns in preparation for bedtime. Kippie is shy; she politely greets "Mr. Murrow" but won't look at the camera. Bette is laughing and seems less reserved than her little sister. They mention that they liked

Peter Pan, and Ernie comments that they set a record for *Cinderella*, having seen the musical five times. Edith looks very young and uneasy with the impromptu situation; despite several years of television and stage experience she giggles much too much. Ernie is clearly the calm center of this family. Surrounded by the women he loves, he is completely relaxed, modest, and happy.

That same month, Ernie took Bette and Kippie to see their grandmother Mary, who had been hysterical when they were kidnapped. Mary was living in New City, in suburban Rockland County, just outside New York City, in a house Ernie had bought for her several years earlier. During the two years his daughters had been missing, Ernie had filled the house with presents and decorations each Christmas in the hope that he would be reunited with his little girls in time for the holiday. "He had made a Christmas house for us," remembers Elisabeth. "And when we went out to the house, it was summer, and there were still candy canes and stars on the ceiling in the room where we were to sleep." The candy canes and stars remained in the house for all the years that their grandmother occupied it.

NBC put Ernie to work briefly late that summer, but not on his own show. From August 29 to September 13, 1955, he substituted for Steve Allen, his former late-night rival, as a guest host on *Tonight!* The network finally found a permanent slot for Kovacs in December, and even then it was daytime rather than prime time. But at least it would give him national exposure, something he hadn't enjoyed since the quiz shows at DuMont.

The new *Ernie Kovacs Show*, premiering on December 12, was scheduled from Monday to Friday at 10:30 A.M. NBC hoped to steal some viewers away from Arthur Godfrey, who had had a daytime TV version of his successful radio series *Arthur Godfrey Time* on CBS for three years. Joining Ernie on the air were Edie (as she now billed herself) Adams, singer Matt Dennis, and pianist Archie Koty and his orchestra. His new announcer was Bill Wendell (who would become David Letterman's announcer decades later). The cast was eventually expanded to include Barbara Loden, folk singer Dylan Todd, and actor Henry Lascoe.

As he had in Philadelphia, now Ernie was responsible for creating a superhuman amount of original programming each week: eighteen hours for his ABC Radio show and, with the new NBC series, an additional two and a half hours for TV. This time, however, he elected to delegate some of the responsibilities that he had fulfilled himself in Philadelphia. The initial director of the television series, Jacques Hein, was also installed as producer, a function Ernie normally carried out. In April Ernie brought director Barry Shear over from DuMont (putting his own job on the line to do so, according to Shear, who said that NBC hadn't wanted to meet his agent's asking price until Ernie went in and threatened to tear up his own contract). That month Hein left the show, reportedly after Ernie put a bucket on Hein's head during a skit. For his new producer, Ernie approved the appointment of Perry Cross, a young NBC unit manager who was being promoted as of the Kovacs show.

He also worked with a staff of writers for the first time since *Kovacs on the Corner*. Unlike his staff writers on that show, however, these three new writers were all handpicked by Ernie. Indeed, because it had been his idea to hire them, his relationship with them was far more companionable than that which had plagued *Corner*'s Donald Mattern and Marge Greene. He originally hired all three to work on the radio show, which was consuming copious amounts of material, and when the daytime television program started, he asked them to write for it as well. Rex Lardner (nephew of the sports writer and satirist Ring Lardner), Louis ("Deke") Heyward, and Mike Marmer stayed with Ernie for most of his tenure at NBC. (Ernie also tried out a writer named Alan Robin for a short while, "but he didn't fit in with the rest of the group," says Rex Lardner.) Ernie continued to write material as well, and all four were credited on the TV show, with Ernie first. But this period when he collaborated with three other writers produced the only Emmy Award nomination for writing that any Kovacs series ever received. And their influence on Ernie's work was felt beyond the shows with which they were directly involved, for he would continue to draw on sketch ideas, characters, dialogue, and images developed during this time until the end of his life.

During this period Ernie was constantly being approached by writers who wanted to work for him. "There was a cachet in writing for Ernie—you were different," says Deke Heyward. "You could dare to do anything. We did not know what television was incapable of doing." When Heyward heard that Kovacs was about to be hired by NBC, he churned out a hundred or so pages of material and obtained a meeting. (The writer had been free-lancing for up to fourteen shows a week; the credit that most impressed Ernie was *Winky Dink and You*, a cartoon show with which kids could interact via "magic crayons" and a special plastic sheet over the TV screen.) "One of the first tests Ernie gave writers was: 'Tell me a joke about a Hungarian,' " remembers Heyward. "Now, understand that Ernie hated people who repeated jokes by rote. He admired people who could create a joke, just by doing inversions, making absurd situations—it didn't even have to have a payoff to it. But he would not converse further with people who gave either one of these jokes in answer to his question 'What's a Hungarian?': 'A Hungarian is a guy who goes into a revolving door behind you and comes out in front of you.' Or if they said, 'How do you make chicken paprikash? First, you steal a chicken.' He'd say, 'Out! Out!' They were not Hungarian jokes to him. He also hated stereotypes, and this he felt was stereotyping Hungarians."

Heyward was of Hungarian background, "so, with my limited vocabulary, when I presented my scripts the first time I said, '*Jó napat,*' which means, 'Good day.' He didn't blink; he just kept reading. So I said, '*Hogy van?*' which means, 'How are you?' And then I threw in '*Baszd meg,*' which means, 'Fuck you.' And he said, '*Te senkiházi*'— his way of saying 'You're a countryman,' which was nice. He spoke it better than I did. And then he looked at my material, and we started a love affair." (Both Heyward and Lardner felt that Ernie identified himself strongly as a Hungarian ethnic. Heyward would bring in Hungarian treats made by his mother—meaty stuffed cabbage, terrible heartburn-inducing cookies—and Ernie "would wolf his way through these things." According to Lardner, "He had deep roots in Hungary. A lot of his humor was Hungarian-type humor. He had a character named Miklos Molnar, who would make *bor*, a kind of Hungarian wine. During the Hungarian revolution, when the Soviets clamped down on the Hungarian population and murdered their leaders, Ernie was very disturbed by what was going on.")

Another important addition to Ernie's NBC team was Shirley Mellner, who had worked on *You Are There* and *Studio One* at CBS. According to Heyward, who helped her get a job as Ernie's associate producer, "Shirley was one of those superinspirational people, always available day or night. If Ernie was in a low period, she was in a low period. If Ernie was in a high period, she was in a high period. In addition to being one of the brightest people I've ever worked with, she was terribly underestimated because in those years to be a woman was a curse. Shirley was capable of exhibiting great brilliance, then someone would say, 'Oh, by the way, would you mind typing up all that stuff? And then bring us some coffee.'

"She also had one of the greatest figures in the whole world at the time, and she wore tight dresses, and this may have mitigated against her," he continues. "But she was a solidifying force on the show. In the control room Barry Shear would go crazy, and she'd bring him back down to earth by saying, 'Barry, cool, cool, cool. Let's protect Ernie. Get a camera on him.' In terms of Ernie, she was more important than most of us. She did personal things for Ernie, she acted as a critic for Ernie; he wanted her approbation. He respected her enormously. He also delighted in her great figure."

The format of the new *Ernie Kovacs Show* did not differ markedly from his previous shows at DuMont. "At ten thirty in the morning, Ernie just did what he did. He didn't change anything," says writer Mike Marmer. The only thing really new, besides some of the personnel, was the permanent set. When the show was being planned, Jacques

Hein had asked Ernie what sort of atmosphere he wanted to create. "Something different," Ernie smiled. "A dungeon, maybe, or a nice torture chamber. Perhaps a slaughterhouse, or even——"

"No, too gloomy, too sad. We need something nobler," Hein entreated.

"Very well," said Ernie. "Then I would like a castle." And a castle he got: a little boy's splendid medieval set, with trompe l'oeil stone walls and barrel-vaulted ceilings, a massive-looking door to withstand enemy attacks, an iron-studded desk decorated with fleur-de-lis and lion's-head reliefs, a standing suit of armor and, on the wall behind Ernie's tall and elaborately carved wooden throne, heavy draperies pulled aside to reveal crossed spears and a warrior's shield.

The writers worked out of the Kovacses' apartment, where the decor was also informed by Ernie's medieval interests. Mike Marmer recollects the duplex as "quite big and nicely appointed in all I can say is an Ernie fashion. Ernie always did everything in a large way. He had a lot of armor in that apartment; I remember wood paneling and armor. I have no idea why armor intrigued him, but it seemed to go with Ernie."

The dining room was converted into a workroom for the writers, who arrived every morning around nine. The atmosphere was "glorious—total chaos," says Heyward. "First there would be offerings, things like"—he pretends to have a handkerchief—" 'Saw something last night where you take a handkerchief and you turn the handkerchief into a rabbit.' And I would go through this, or Rex or Mike would go through whatever they had discovered. It wasn't offered as food for the show so much as social intercourse, but eventually it turned into food for the show. 'Oh! You can make a rabbit out of a handkerchief? Let's switch it into——' Ernie wouldn't arrive until later. He was doing the radio show. And Edie was sleeping. She always made grand entrances; she looked gorgeous. It was always sort of a torture for us to see her coming down the stairs in a peignoir!"

After the offerings, the writers did "whatever we felt like doing. There was no organization to this," he says. "If I wanted to do an Albert Something, the World's Something Clod, I would do that. You did whatever pleased your fancy and whatever you felt like you were capable of doing, and then somehow you'd find a balance for the show later." The finished pieces were organized by Rex Lardner, who passed them on to Ernie with his own recommendations. "Rex was very good as an editor, and Ernie trusted him implicitly," says Heyward.

Then, recalls the writer, "Ernie would breeze in, full of the joys of spring. Now remember, he'd been up since four in the morning. 'And hi-hos, and hi—!' He loved writers, and he loved being in their atmosphere. Ernie would say, 'Hey, this is good, we're going to use this, use this, use this here, I want you to use these pieces,' but he'd never throw anything out. Everything was filed, and I'm sure there are great files somewhere."

While the writers were at Central Park West generating material for both the TV and the radio shows, over at NBC the *Kovacs Show* production team was busy readying the day's telecast. Kovacs depended a great deal on Shirley Mellner's organizational abilities. "Sometimes I would have to stop by the radio studio to get any last-minute changes, but I'd certainly talk to him, and then I'd get to the studio, because we didn't have much time for preparation," says Mellner. "I'd make sure everything was ready for him that I knew he wanted, that his desk was set up, that the props were there, that I had all the music for the orchestra, that the ushers were there—whatever had to be done. And by the time Ernie arrived at the studio, Barry had talked to the technicians and the cameramen, so they were ready. Everybody on the show had to be attuned to Ernie, so they could improvise all along the way. He used people who understood him. Everybody was on the same wavelength."

When the show went on "it was exciting, it was interesting, it was terrifying because we used to work live," says writer Mike Marmer. "There were times when he would walk in and say, 'I don't like this,' and we were ready to start the show, and we would have to write a new sketch and put it on the TelePrompTer! And he saw it for the first time while we were on the air! He would rehearse when it was important to rehearse; the big sketches were rehearsed. I think for the most part, though, he improvised to some degree, but he'd improvise around written material."

After the show there was a meeting at NBC to discuss subsequent shows, although they were never planned more than a few days in advance. In the afternoon Shirley Mellner went to the duplex for another meeting, this time with Ernie and the writers. Even after everyone else was done for the day, Ernie kept working. "He would call me up at all hours of the night to see if I thought something was funny," remembers producer Perry Cross. "He would wake me up. And I'd say to him, 'I can't stay up all night. I have to be in in the morning to work.' But he'd call me with a list of things he needed—sound effects, props, records, costumes—while he was writing. He would stay up all night." When he wasn't writing new material, he went over what his writers had turned in that day. "We'd come in in the morning," describes Heyward, "and on our desks were the pieces we had done for three shows up, with a little comment here, a little comment there— he was very courteous about editing. But he was stronger than all of us. I mean, we'd go *home* after the show."

For a break from work, during the day he took steam baths at the New York Athletic Club, often with friends. "Ernie used to love taking Perry and Barry to the New York Athletic Club because they didn't take Jewish members," remembers Shirley Mellner. Or he would have Mellner set up a "meeting," as she refers to it, with his poker cronies; there was also a regular weekly game at Ernie's duplex, during which "Edie would disappear," says Rex Lardner. "The only thing I ever could relax with is cards," Ernie once explained. "Tennis I love, and swimming, but I always feel I ought to be working instead. But with poker I don't feel guilty, because— well, I tried to analyze it the other day. Maybe because it's one way to catch up on my friendships. I can't be a one-cocktail-every-three-months friend. If a guy is a friend and he's around, I want to poker it out with him one or two nights a week."

During this period, at first he would "poker it out" in "nickel-dime games; that I played with a little bit," says Deke Heyward. "Barry played a lot; I think Perry did. Then it got to be very heavy, and he worked his way into people who had more money"—people like Dave Garroway and playwright Marc Connelly and Marty Kummer, Kovacs' agent. "When it got to be the heavy-stakes game, I know a lot of people got hurt. Barry at one point lost $3,000 in one night, and it was a major tragedy—that was two-weeks-plus salary for him." When he couldn't get Heyward to play, Ernie would pick up one of the countless decks lying around the house, deal out a sample poker hand, then inform his writer, "Here's how much you *could* have won, you schmuck, you, if you had played." "He would force you into a game of blackjack for no stakes," Heyward recalls. "And Ernie was a bad poker player. He would hear voices from the great beyond saying, 'You're going to get another fill-in-the-blank when you draw the third piece.' He would not play a logical game of poker. It was a mystical game. 'Something wonderful is going to happen.' It doesn't!"

Rex Lardner, who played in Ernie's regular poker game for a while, remembers that Ernie just bet people out of the game. "He was a bad player in the sense that he wanted action," Lardner says. "I guess he knew he had a terrific future in show business, either in movies or television or something, so money was no problem with him. Whereas some of the rest of us, maybe directors and other writers, had to worry a little bit about how much we lost. So Ernie would win a lot of pots just by betting a lot of money. He wouldn't always bet on the high end, but often he would be in hands he had no business being in, and he would be very optimistic about the cards he would draw. But Ernie loved to gamble. It wasn't then a compulsion. All he wanted was the fun of it and the action and the conversation. He didn't care about winning or losing. He liked the people."

The attitude with which Ernie approached poker—that taking wild risks in a game among friends was one of life's greatest sources of pleasure—carried over into his work. "We all were young, adventuresome people with a lot of spirit and a love of experimentation. He tuned us into that," says Perry Cross, Ernie's producer at NBC. "He stimulated us to be different and to have fun while we were doing it. And I think the reason the daytime show started to catch on was that everybody realized we were all enjoying what we were doing and it came across that way."

These shows do indeed come across as though everybody is on a mad lark. At any moment anything might happen: real goldfish might gossip about the audience (in Ernie and Edie's voices), random gunshots and "Teddy Bear's Picnic" might come wafting out of nowhere, the camera might flip Ernie upside down to the sound of a scream, or Ernie might stick a goatee on the camera's zoom lens and warn, "You'll have to shave that zoomar before you come in here from now on!" (The goatee, a blurry splotch to viewers, stayed on the lens through an entire number.) In one show from this period, Ernie is blahing about nothing in particular, and Archie Koty's orchestra suddenly starts making weird sounds. Ernie spontaneously flares his nostrils, wiggles his eyebrows, blows a raspberry, all in sync to the bizarre nonmusic; he really gets going as the camera moves in for a close-up. Then, just as suddenly, he simply cracks up. "That," says one cast member, "was the climate in which we worked." The bedlamite tone was carried through to the end credits, which featured such artwork as a dead-looking fellow with his tongue hanging out and an arrow through his head (producer Perry Cross), a lunatic shouting through a bullhorn, sweat beads flying (director Barry Shear), and the THIS HAS BEEN AN NBC PRESENTATION card painted to look like cracked glass.

Wedged into this ongoing delirium were the written sketches, most of which were built around the thwarting of expectation. Many of these were simply structured—a setup, and then a twist:

BARBARA LODEN MADE UP AS THE COTY GIRL IN A PERFECT REPLICA
OF THE COTY COMMERCIAL SET . . . GETS HIT IN THE FACE WITH A
PIE

EDIE ADAMS AS HILDA DIMPLES, CHILD STAR, IS ABOUT TO MAKE
HER SINGING DEBUT IN "THE LOLLIPOP EXPRESS" . . . THE DIREC-
TOR STANDS BY . . . THE CAMERAS ROLL . . . EDIE SINGS "BYE,
BYE, BLACKBIRD" . . . OUT COMES LOUIS ARMSTRONG'S VOICE

HAROLD FOOFNIK HAS COLLECTED STAMPS ALL HIS LIFE . . . TO-
DAY, ON HIS EIGHTY-THIRD BIRTHDAY, HE WILL BEGIN TO MOUNT
THEM INTO ALBUMS . . . OUTSIDE, A SNOWSTORM; INSIDE, A TABLE
PILED HIGH WITH STAMPS . . .ERNIE COMES IN AS HAROLD FOOF-
NIK . . . WIND BLOWS THROUGH ROOM AND TABLE FALLS . . . THE
STAMPS STAY IN PLACE IN FRONT OF HAROLD FOOFNIK

BARBARA LODEN DRESSED AS THE WHITE ROCK GIRL, POSING ON A
ROCK BY A STREAM EXACTLY AS IN WHITE ROCK AD . . . FALLS INTO
WATER

"Ernie was the master of the switch," says Mike Marmer. "He set up
a picture that you felt totally comfortable with, and he took care in
setting it up with great authenticity. For the Coty girl there was a marvelous, beautiful, picturesque setting that was exactly like the commercials. He made you believe what he was doing. You'd say, 'Jesus, that
is *exactly* right!' And then he'd switch it—the Coty girl gets a pie in
the face, the White Rock girl slides into the water. I learned from Ernie
that the more real it is, the more shocking the switch will be."

The payoff to a Kovacs gag, according to Deke Heyward, was exactly the opposite of what one would write for another comedian. "You
did everything upside down when you worked for Ernie," he says.
Someone would write a bit, for example, about the World's Greatest
Chess Player—"and I'm talking about thirty seconds' worth of bit,"
explains Heyward. "Ten chess tables set up. Ten guys behind each one
of the tables. And the World's Greatest Chess Player is going to play
them all blindfolded. Ernie makes his appearance blindfolded, and you
know he has got to bump into that first table. Anybody else would do
that. We don't do that. Blindfolded, with great surety, he walks to the
first table, second table, third table, tenth table, makes a move at each
one of the tables, and then looks to the audience through the blindfold
and walks off—at which point all the tables collapse without anybody

touching them. That's the difference! Thirty seconds I'm talking about. They're precious little thirty seconds you do.

"You lead somebody to expect something and then deny them what they are expecting," Heyward says. "Ernie called this 'the humor of anomaly.' It was totally anomalous, and he loved words like *anomaly*." Many of the anomalous gags ended with the camera moving in for a close-up of Ernie's face, looking for all the world as if he had "a question mark in the center of each eyeball—which he could do!" says Heyward. "It's like, 'What the hell is going on here? Why is this happening to me?' ":

> ERNIE WILL DEMONSTRATE THE SUPERIORITY OF ERADICATO, "THE
> BETTER PENCIL ERASER" . . . "HERE IS AN ORDINARY PENCIL.
> I WILL ATTEMPT TO ERASE THE WORDS ON ONE SHEET OF PAPER"
> . . . FIRST ERASER IS SHELLACKED SO IT DOES NOTHING . . . "NOW
> I WILL TAKE ERADICATO AND SHOW YOU HOW IT ERASES" . . . SEC-
> OND PIECE OF PAPER IS DAMP . . . ERNIE TEARS HUGE HOLE IN IT
> . . . CAMERA PANS UP TO ERNIE'S FACE . . . HOLDS FOR ONE BEAT

"That's on the negative side," says Heyward. "But he could also conjure up the same look to work on the plus side, where this bewilderment would occur":

> ERNIE SITS ON A TREE BRANCH . . . CASUALLY SAWS OFF THE LIMB
> . . . THE TREE FALLS . . . HE LOOKS UP AT CAMERA IN GRINNING
> WONDERMENT

The tree gag exemplifies another important aspect of Kovacs' humor. "He took a forlorn, lost soul and made him into a hero in certain aspects of his comedy," describes Heyward. "You'd get the total idiot, who'd look blankly into the camera—and I would discuss this with Ernie—and he was almost patterned along the lines of the Talmudic innocent." The Talmudic innocent might be walking down the street as a safe was hoisted above him; the rope would break, but "the Talmudic innocent down below would be unscathed because it would crash behind him, in front of him, or whatever," says Heyward. "Buster Keaton, also a non-Jew, instinctively went to the Talmudic innocent. When a building crashed in its entirety around Buster Keaton, not a fleck of brick came near him; he went through everything unscathed. And this was a substantial part of the comedy Ernie was doing."

There is a quietness and an innocence—a sense that one is watching a protected fool—about some of Ernie's comedy that is indeed reminiscent of Keaton; in spirit the two comedians are very close. The gags differ, however, in their scale and in their settings. Working for the enormous motion picture screen, Keaton put himself through oversized, complicated, very physical, very lengthy routines, often placing himself in an outdoor space made to seem endless through the traveling power of the camera. Keaton would be chased through the streets of the city by 500 desperate-to-be-married women. He would step into a boat, the camera taking in the huge lake all around him, and stand there while the vessel gradually sank. He would struggle mightily to maintain control of a Civil War steam engine while racing through the pine woods of Georgia.

A Kovacs television gag, by contrast, was deliberately compact, modest in concept and in scale of execution. It almost always took place indoors (or in an obviously fake outdoor setting, so that the sense of the indoors remained). It required only minimal physical movement, and it was elegantly tailored to the essentially private nature of video space:

ERNIE IS READING A NEWSPAPER . . . HEARS DOOR OPEN, SOUND OF GALLOPING HORSE . . . ERNIE'S EYES FOLLOW SOUND ACROSS THE ROOM . . . WE HEAR DOOR CLOSE

A door opens and closes; in between a horse gallops. On TV, Ernie could build an entire bit around these two simple sound effects. He would return to his newspaper, but before long you'd hear a door open and the horse would gallop across the room the other way, Ernie following the sound with his eyes. Now the door shuts, but Ernie is prepared for the next entrance. He sets up a little hurdle and sits down to wait. Sure enough, we hear the door open, and the invisible horse gallops through once again, Ernie's eyes following it as it jumps the barrier and races out the door one last time.

Even though such a bit is perfectly suited to TV, few comics do anything like this on television today, nor did they then. "He did things with sound effects that nobody will do today because nobody will *wait* the time that it takes to do those things the way Ernie saw them," says Mike Marmer. "He would take the time; if it was a three-minute sound-effect bit, he would play a three-minute sound-effect bit for one laugh. It was a much more leisurely paced kind of comedy, but Ernie was very interested in buildup before he got to the piece." Sometimes he spent too long on the buildup and diluted the impact of the payoff, as many critics have noted. "There was nothing you could write for Ernie for six minutes that he wouldn't stretch to twelve," Marmer says. "But he insisted on the buildup, and he had the patience to do it. People may have argued with him on the basis that to them nothing was happening. Nobody's laughing while you're in the setup. Ernie always wanted the setup. That was important to him."

Kovacs was so aware of how his visions played on the small screen that he would watch the monitors continually during a broadcast. "When I first came in, I used to watch the stage to see what everybody was doing," remembers Marmer. "And Ernie said to me, 'You don't watch the stage. You watch the monitor. That's the show that comes out. What they do down here on stage doesn't mean anything. It's only what you see up there, because that's what the audience sees.' That's why Ernie could create all these bizarre things—because he knew what the pictures would look like on the tube. He knew it instinctively."

The small-scale Kovacs television gag reached its quintessence in the recurring adventures of Howard, the World's Strongest Ant. First introduced on DuMont, Howard didn't even physically exist; this whimsical conceit consisted entirely of Ernie bending down to talk to a tabletop, with Edie offscreen supplying Howard's teensy-weensy voice. But viewers fell in love with Howard, and he became the most popular character on Ernie's NBC-era shows.

At the height of Howard the Ant mania, *The Ernie Kovacs Show* was receiving about three dozen gifts daily from all over the country, insect-size offerings often made by hand especially for Howard; the donors' names would be announced and the objects used on the program. There were miniature false teeth, tiny tool kits, easels and paintbrushes, space suits and tuxedos; there were cars and champagne and loaves of bread, an igloo and an ice-skating rink, a Lilliputian gymnasium and a mink-lined swimming pool. One viewer sent Howard a mate, Henrietta Ant, complete with her own diminutive wardrobe; another supplied a full array of wedding gifts, including a toaster, flowers, money, candy, and a book of poetry. Howard had tiny Texas longhorns for his den, a stagecoach and a covered wagon, a locomotive with a track, and his very own yacht club. For thank-you letters, one fan made him monogrammed stationery. He could even play poker with a microscopic deck of cards sent to him by nine-year-old Victor Mary of Grand Rapids, Michigan.

Every day, says Deke Heyward, "Ernie would come in with *a lot* of junk that had come through the mail, which turned into pieces for Howard. Little pitchers of milk—viewers sent him thousands of these.

Little cups and saucers this big"—he holds his fingers apart half an inch—"and that would inspire you to do something where you had a walking cup and saucer that Howard couldn't catch up with. Or we'd get teeny-weeny cars, and in response to the teeny-weeny cars, we'd make teeny-weeny garages out of cardboard."

Indeed, little objects (Howard-related and not) were often the inspiration for bits. "We had a magnificent view of Central Park, and we had our little typewriters, and the most important things we had were cardboard and X-Acto knives," says Deke Heyward. "The prop man can only do so much, and without a budget it's hard. So we'd buy balsa wood, and we'd have cardboard, and we'd say, 'Hey! What if we had a thing that articulated like this?' And we'd put a Band-Aid on it and bend it over, 'and then suddenly this part jumps up,' and we'd make little things." In such a way they figured out how to make Howard's vehicles appear to move. "We were playing with a little tin cutout that we made from a beer can," remembers Heyward, "and we put it on top of a piece of cardboard with a magnet below it. And then we realized that if we drew a path below, we could set obstacles above, and the ant could be articulated to move from point to point." The tiny creations were shown to Ernie "once they were brought to moderate fruition. Then he would participate, once he believed it could work. It was not hard convincing him, because he was a fairyland-type character. It was like *Peter Pan:* 'I believe! I believe! I believe!' He believed everything would work."

Virtually any object might become the source for a bit. "There was a magicians' supply house called Louis Tannen," says Heyward, "and they got out a catalog every year. Even though we really didn't have the budget from NBC, we'd say to Ernie, 'Here's something stupid that looks like it could work. Give me $15 to send to Louis Tannen.' And we'd get a lot of things that way—foolproof card tricks that actually did work, but that we would rig so they wouldn't work for Ernie." Sometimes Ernie and Deke went downtown to an army-navy surplus store around East 12th Street. "Oh, there was wonderful garbage there: pieces of bombsight motors, prisms, refractors, strange optical lenses which you would use at the slightest provocation." Inside the store Ernie became like "a baby in a toy store at Christmas. He loved mechanical things, he loved electrical things," says Heyward.

Gadgets weren't the only thing that produced wonder and fascination in Ernie. "Strange materials affected him," remembers the writer. "They were going to re-cover some of the chairs in the house, as I recall, and he was looking for materials, and he found a velvet stretched out on a table in the upholsterers' place. There was a penny on the velvet, and he discovered that by scratching the velvet he could make the penny move forward. He spent twenty minutes playing with the penny on the velvet! But later we turned that into a means of locomotion for one of our little skits."

Part of the reason that army-surplus gadgets and pennies on velvet and things made of cardboard were useful was that an enormous quantity of material had to be generated for Kovacs during this period. "The radio show ate up a lot of material," points out Lardner. Many of the television bits that relied on language rather than visuals—Martin Krutch, Pierre Ragout, Uncle Gruesome, Tom Swift, Percy Dovetonsils—were adapted to the radio shows as well. "The Kapustas, strangely enough, were also done on radio," remembers Mike Marmer. Most of the radio bits were short, "ongoing, monologue-type things, with a lot of sound effects. You had to go down and get sound-effects records and music that went with it. You put it together and then Ernie would look at it. Most of the stuff he performed by himself with these sound effects."

Many recurring bits were created specifically for Ernie's radio show, including "Contrary to Popular Opinion," "Embarrassing Moments," "What's Your Vocation?," "Hip Dialogue," and "Movie Dialogue" (dialogue for a prehistoric film: "Can I have the keys to the dinosaur tonight, pop?"). New characters were born as well, such as the mystical Great Kowloon, the Roman newscaster Lucius Flavius, Jr., and Armand du Clef, French chef extraordinaire. (Both the television and the radio pieces abounded with silly names, many used only once: Asbury T. Pimslit, Arthur Grommet Higgins, Francophile Z. Etras, Armand K. Frechette.) Rex Lardner invented "Strangely Believe It," a bit that parodied the syndicated "Ripley's Believe It or Not" cartoons; soon they were all writing "Strangely Believe Its," which doubled for the radio and the TV show:

QUAGMIRE T. QUONSET, INTERNATIONAL MAN'S SINGLES PUSH-UP CHAMPION FOR THIRTY YEARS, COULD DO 950 PUSH-UPS AT ONE SESSION. ONE FACTOR IN HIS FAVOR WAS THAT, WHILE HIS ARMS WEIGHED 170 POUNDS, HIS BODY WEIGHED ONLY 11 POUNDS.

According to Lardner, "Sometimes we'd announce that we were going to do some 'Strangely Believe Its,' and we would each turn out a page of them." They would work fast, generating the bits stream-of-consciousness fashion. "Of course, when you turn out a page of that stuff, maybe one or two are going to be good. So we would pick out the best ones and give them to Ernie."

Eventually the "Strangely Believe Its" and some of the other material found its way to yet another medium: print. In 1952 Harvey Kurtzman had founded *Mad* magazine, a comic-book-format compilation of wacky humor. Initially Kurtzman wrote, designed, and laid out the magazine himself, but eventually *Mad* became a forum for many talented visual and verbal satirists. "I was a fan of Kovacs, as he was a fan of ours," says Kurtzman. Ernie used to like to take copies of *Mad* with him to the posh 21 Club and ostentatiously whip one out at just the right moment. One time he invited Kurtzman and *MAD* publisher William Gaines to be guests on his radio show "at something like 6:00 A.M. on New Year's Day," remembers Gaines. "I don't think anybody in the world would have been up then except us." Eventually, says Kurtzman, "I asked him if he could do something for us. He had material in his file drawer that he whiffled through, and he came up with something." In the late 1950s Kovacsian humor adapted from the television and radio skits came to grace the pages of several *Mad* numbers. Ernie also wrote the introduction to the 1958 compilation *Mad for Keeps*, in which he explained to readers of the book, according to an ad of the time, "why you're crazy to go on!"

In May 1956, a year after recovering his daughters, Ernie took the family on a holiday to Switzerland, Italy, and France. Before he left, there was talk at NBC that the network might offer him a prime-time summer replacement show. But Kovacs was frankly cynical about the prospects. "I've had so many big deals," he told columnist Earl Wilson in the *New York Post,* describing how once he had been on vacation in Bermuda when he got a call from CBS programming chief Hubbell Robinson. "He wanted me to come right back and start a big program with a million-piece orchestra," Ernie said. When Kovacs returned three weeks later, he rushed in to see Robinson, who came out of his office, casually inquired, "Hi, Ernie, how are you, Ernie?" and walked on. "So many things had happened in those three weeks that the program he'd been thinking about had been entirely forgotten."

But the NBC executives did not forget. In mid-June, after Ernie returned from Europe, they announced that a new, prime-time, hourlong *Ernie Kovacs Show* would air that summer three out of every four weeks. The program would occupy the well-watched 8:00 to 9:00 P.M. slot on Monday, replacing the respected *Caesar's Hour* until the fall.

The personnel for the new show stayed fundamentally the same as for the daytime series. Behind the cameras were producer Perry Cross, director Barry Shear, writers Kovacs, Lardner, Heyward, and Marmer, and associate producer Shirley Mellner; on screen Ernie was joined by Edie Adams, Barbara Loden, Henry Lascoe, Peter Hanley, and Bill Wendell. But for the first time Ernie had a substantial budget and the support necessary for a prime-time show, including ample rehearsal time and the stage of the spacious Century Theater rather than an inadequately small studio. A large orchestra led by veteran conductor-composer Harry Sosnik was added, as was a group of dancers, the Bob Hamilton Trio. In fact, this was be the best opportunity Kovacs would ever have for making an impact on prime time. "That was Ernie's big hurrah," says Mike Marmer. "It was the biggest show he'd ever done; it was the biggest show any of us had ever done. The budget was bigger than any he'd ever had, so we could do major sketches on a big scale. That show probably made Ernie a star more than anything else."

Television's fourth *Ernie Kovacs Show* premiered on July 2, 1956, in Sid Caesar's Monday-night spot. At the time producer Perry Cross said, "While we're not abandoning the tested, tried-and-true features of a comedy-variety show altogether, we're going to break a lot of rules and see what happens." Today Cross describes the show as deliberately "antiform." Prime-time comedy-variety shows always featured big-name guest stars, for example; on the *Kovacs Show*, "the guests were treated in a way that was different, like when Boris Karloff, who was very popular as the Frankenstein monster, came on and read the alphabet dramatically." Other shows had "crystal-clear announcers," says Cross; the *Kovacs Show* had Al Kelly, a vaudeville comedian who spoke unintelligible double-talk. "It was just typical of what Ernie and all of us cooked up. He was the regular announcer, and the sponsors were going crazy," says the producer. "Even when Al Kelly talked straight you couldn't understand him."

Because of pressure from the sponsors, whose product pitches couldn't be understood, Kelly was soon replaced by Bill Wendell as the announcer. But then, says Cross, "We used Al as an executive from NBC in charge of programs. Every time he came out, we dropped him through a trap door in the floor. The first time we introduced him as [NBC national program manager] Tom Loeb and said he wanted to welcome us on the air, and we dropped him. The second time he wanted to answer some complaints, and we dropped him. Then he started showing up in the middle of skits. If we were in the jungle doing 'Leena, the Jungle Girl' [played by Kovacs in drag and a blond wig], he would show up and we'd drop him."

Other programs did straightforward Broadway- or vaudeville-style dance production numbers, but Perry Cross recalls that "Ernie and Bob Hamilton, the choreographer, used to consult, along with the writers and myself, about doing a different kind of dance production if we were going to do a dance. And ideas would come out of conferences between Barry and myself. We'd do the top halves of bodies dancing on the bottom halves of other bodies, or on parts of a horse. It was really lunacy." In one number utilizing special effects, dancers dressed in chess costumes disported around a chessboard; as they danced, the camera changed black to white and white to black, so that the chess pieces had to scurry to find their proper spots. Another number featured a big chorus line of men in top hats, white ties, and tails, tap-dancing up a huge set of elegant columned steps. "I remember the cost-control people at the network screaming at me that it cost so much to build these steps, but I did it anyway," says Cross. "The whole thing started out with the meticulously produced look of a Fred Astaire movie of the 1930s. They started climbing the steps, and when they got into a gigantic pose, the steps collapsed and they all slid down, about fifty of them. They just fell down all over each other."

Ernie, says Perry Cross, "loved big introductions, and he loved to introduce famous people who weren't anybody." At the beginning of the show he would give a lengthy buildup to "a racecar driver who had set a land-speed world record. He has his record-breaking car here; it had gone 260 miles an hour in 35 seconds. We cut to the car and he can't get the damn thing started. Then we cut back to Ernie and he goes on and introduces the next number." Later in the show the driver is glimpsed again, always having some sort of trouble with the car; finally he gets it started, only to crash into a wall. The writers referred to these as "teasers," quick running bits interspersed throughout the show:

DURANTE TEASER: ACTOR MADE UP AS JIMMY DURANTE DOES STAN-
DARD DURANTE ENDING . . . WALKS AWAY FROM CAMERA INTO
POOLS OF LIGHT . . . AT LAST POOL FALLS THROUGH TRAPDOOR

Long satirical sketches remained a staple on the prime-time program. They might be spoofs of genres, such as this Kovacsian version of a television game show:

ON THE QUIZ SHOW "WHOM DUNNIT," ERNIE AS DR. HARVEY
SERENE, CURATOR, MUSEUM OF PORTUGAL, GASPS OUT CLUES AS
THREE PANELISTS TRY TO GUESS WHO HAS JUST SHOT HIM IN THE
ABDOMEN . . . MODERATOR: "I'M SORRY, PANEL, BUT YOUR TIME
IS UP. THE CONTESTANT IS DEAD."

or this twisted movie saga of sweet child actress Vivien "Baby" Dimples, portrayed by Edie Adams in a Mary Pickford wig and a fluffy Shirley Temple dress, and her director Houston Crane, played by Ernie clad in jodhpurs:

VIVIEN: "YOU COULDN'T DIRECT TRAFFIC ON A SIDE STREET DURING YOM KIPPUR . . . DON'T FORGET, HOUSTON, I'M STILL YOUR STUDIO'S BIGGEST MONEY-MAKER."

CRANE: "I'M NOT FORGETTING IT, KID . . . AND I WANT TO KEEP IT THAT WAY . . . I WANT THAT SWEET, SMILING, UNSELFISH YOU, THE REAL YOU, TO SHINE THROUGH THIS MASS OF TINSEL THAT IS HOLLYWOOD."

VIVIEN: "WELL, THAT SWEET, SMILING, UNSELFISH ME IS SMILING HERSELF RIGHT OUT OF THIS NUMBER . . . EITHER WE SHOOT THIS TURKEY MY WAY OR WE STUFF IT FOR THANKSGIVING . . . CALL ME WHEN MY JAGUAR IS READY, FATHER."

Other times they parodied specific films and TV shows. Since TV art instructor Jon Gnagy emphasized how easy it was to draw by breaking down every shape down into cones, squares, and triangles, Ernie dressed up as John Magee, in a striped smock and wearing a squashed bathcap for a beret, and pitched his book *Cones, Squares, and Triangles:*

ERNIE AS JOHN MAGEE ASKS, "HOW DO YOU KNOW YOU CAN'T DRAW? SEND FOR MY BOOK 'CONES, SQUARES, AND TRIANGLES' . . . SOON YOU'LL BE AN ARTIST AND BEAUTIFUL WOMEN WILL BE BEGGING YOU TO DRAW THEIR PORTRAIT, JUST AS THEY ARE BEGGING ME" . . . HE OFFERS JOHN MAGEE CARDBOARD CUTOUTS OF CONES, SQUARES, AND TRIANGLES, SPECIAL JOHN MAGEE PAPER "PERFECTLY SQUARED AT THE EDGES," THE JOHN MAGEE PICTURE FRAME ("ONE OF JUST A FEW FRAMES MADE OUT OF GENUINE WOOD"), AND JOHN MAGEE WIRE FOR "HANGING ALL YOUR OWN FRAMED PICTURES IN GARAGE, ATTIC, AND STOREROOM."

EDIE ENTERS AS ARTIST'S MODEL . . . ERNIE: "I'M GOING TO DRAW ONE OF THESE BEAUTIFUL WOMEN WHO HAVE BEEN BEGGING ME ALL DAY" . . . QUICKLY SKETCHES HER . . . HOLDS UP DRAWING . . . IT IS MADE UP OF CONES, SQUARES, AND TRIANGLES

Besides poking fun at content, Kovacs and his writers also parodied the formal aspects of television and film. "News Analyst" exaggerates newscast producers' attempts to add excitement to their shows by varying the camerawork. Opening with heavy kettledrums and a fireworks display under the word NEWS, which fills the entire screen, Ernie comes on as newsman Leroy L. Bascomb McFinister, wearing a newsprint tie and a huge chrysanthemum in his lapel:

WIDE SHOT OF SET . . . "GOOD MORNING. THIS IS LEROY L. BAS-
COMB MCFINISTER" . . . PICTURE IS WIPED INWARD, LEAVING TINY
VERTICAL SLIT IN MIDDLE THROUGH WHICH WE GLIMPSE ERNIE
. . . "WITH THE NEWS" . . . WIPE WIDENS TO FULL SET . . . "BE-
HIND THE NEWS" . . . PICTURE TILTS RIGHT . . . "NEWS FLASHES
AND NEWS HIGHLIGHTS" . . . TILTS UPSIDE DOWN . . . "EVENTS OF
THE DAY, EVENTS OF THE NIGHT" . . . PICTURE SPINS 360 DEGREES
TO LEFT . . . "BROUGHT TO YOU" . . . PICTURE SPINS TO RIGHT,
ENDS UPSIDE DOWN . . . "AS THEY HAPPEN" . . . PICTURE SPINS
UPRIGHT . . . "WHEN THEY HAPPEN" . . . TILTS TO RIGHT, THEN
BACK . . . "NEWS" . . . TILTS TO LEFT AND BACK . . . "FROM ALL
OVER" . . . SHOT OF SPINNING WORLD GLOBE . . . A HAND
REACHES IN AND STOPS GLOBE

There are fast zoom-ins and zoom-outs, loud drumrolls and cymbal crashes, a battery of teletype machines, exactly sixteen seconds' worth of film clips of "four different fast sports activities," and such hot-off-the-wire news items as the forty-eighth birthday of Arnold P. Glantis of Newark, New Jersey (reported three days after the fact and accompanied by a crazily spinning picture of a mild-mannered middle-aged man). This whole complex sketch—like everything else on the show—was performed live.

According to Perry Cross, the show "had a tremendous instantaneous acceptance by the audience. Ernie was enjoying being Puck right in front of the television camera, and people knew that. They never knew when anything was going to happen, when there would be a switch." As in the daytime program, which was driven by a frenetic sort of camaraderie, "that same spirit and energy came through in the performances and in the elements of the summer show and in him. Here was this big ostentatious show, and we didn't take it seriously. That was the reason it was funny. We didn't get overwhelmed by the fact that we had money now."

Although the production team did have money, their budget was not unlimited. One friend remembers Ernie saying, "I'm paying no attention to the cost of the show I'm doing and spending more money than I'm earning, because I feel this is a great opportunity." Writer Rex Lardner says that Ernie "was willing to spare no expense or effort to get a laugh. He told me that if a gag had died and he desperately needed a laugh, he would take his cigar and put the wrong end in his mouth, just to make sure that the audience reacted in some way—which illustrates, metaphorically, his attitude toward gaining an audience's laughter and approval. For the same reason he was very profligate in the amount of money he wanted to spend on sets and gags. His prime motivation was to be amusing and original, and to hell with the money."

In that quest for the laugh, budget restrictions were for the most part ignored. "We didn't pay any attention to them. I didn't," recollects Perry Cross. The producer, however, knew instinctively when the spending might be too blatantly unjustifiable, and he controlled it. "Sometimes I said to him, 'I can't do that.' He understood that." When they went overbudget, Cross had to answer to network executives, "but that was okay. The people who were in charge of NBC then were also young and aggressive. They were all good people, and they were all pulling for him. And we didn't spend the money wastefully. It was always for a good reason, like the dance steps."

The summer replacement show just about doubled Ernie's income, but it also added to his already enormous work load. "The burden was very, very tough on him," says Lardner. "I kept urging him to drop the radio show because getting up at that time was murder on his health." (Lardner even remembers Ernie as having had something of a collapse during this period.) But the ABC Radio deal was "a very tough contract to get out of," says the writer. Instead, he dropped NBC's daily *Ernie Kovacs Show*. The last morning segment aired on July 27, 1956, enabling Ernie to spend the rest of the summer concentrating all his television efforts on the big prime-time show.

During summer vacations from Miss Hewitt's school, Kippie and Bette stayed with their grandmother Mary at her house in New City. "I loved that house very much," says Kippie, who had her own pony there, a palomino rented for the summer, just as Ernie had when he was young. "I would tie her up outside, just like a cowboy in the old West, and I would ride her up in the hills in the back. There was a lot of acreage back there. Then we had this Doberman pinscher. He would wait until you got in the house with a stranger and closed the door and then pounce on you. He was my dad's dog. I named him Rocky because I taught him to put his foot on a rock."

Like her son, Mary Kovacs loved to spend time with children. "My grandmother was marvelous with children," Kippie says. "She gave us something that not many children have: she gave us the ability to live in a world of fantasy." In the home in New City, "she created a room that was like a whole house for children. It had a miniature living room, a miniature bedroom, a miniature kitchen. She made it herself, every-thing miniature." Mary was always sewing wonderful costumes for them or playing the piano or entertaining them with stories, most of them her personal versions of reality: stories about her poverty-ridden child-hood, about her miserable marriage, about their beloved father, about how she had discovered Kippie and Bette in Florida by driving around and showing their picture to strangers. "Oh, she could weave a story," recalls Elisabeth. "And add to it and subtract from it, I'm sure."

Elisabeth says that her grandmother "was a genius, brilliant with her hands. She could make a hat in two seconds or a dress in four seconds. She'd say, 'Oh, I think I'll paint today,' and then she'd take out the oils." Her ceramic pieces, which she baked in her oven, "were odd; some were crude, and some were very refined. She was brilliant with no education."

Her lack of education and manners, however, sometimes caused Kippie agonies. "I was embarrassed to be around her when my parents were around. And I feel bad about it now," she says. "I felt, instinc-tually, that she was not educated—I am putting into words now what I think I felt then. I just was embarrassed for her tactlessness, for everything. She would belch in a movie theater—I'm not talking about a small burp—and she'd snore. It was embarrassing." And the unso-phisticated Mary was never able to comprehend her son's work. "She got him the education, but she never understood those very bizarre things he did," says Elisabeth. Ernie was aware of it: "I know my mother doesn't have the faintest idea what I'm doing, but she enjoys it," he told one reporter.

With her new daughter-in-law, Mary got along no better than she had with Bette Wilcox Kovacs. "My grandmother wanted him all to herself," says Kippie. "Terribly possessive. She was out to get my fa-ther everything and anything he wanted and to make him everything he possibly could be. And she did not like any woman who was around him." In Mary's eyes, Edie Adams was simply a rival for her only son's affections—and an unworthy one, for what woman could ever be wor-thy of her son? "But he understood that she loved him," says Kippie. "That's why he always protected her. He had all the years of suffering with his mother and not with his wives." George Kudra, Ernie's furrier friend from Trenton, remembers that during this period, "I made furs for his wife and also for his mother. I made a mink coat for his mother." As he had back in his Trenton days, when he had bought his friend Marion Shapiro violets and duplicated the gift for Mary, Ernie tried to safeguard her—and himself—from her own uncontrollable jealousy.

To those of Ernie's colleagues who occasionally encountered Mary Kovacs at the duplex in Manhattan, she seemed a rough, peremptory, frightening character. When she wasn't there, she would telephone Ernie constantly. "He used to be on the phone," remembers Rex Lardner. "I think she was making some kind of demands. He was sometimes quite disturbed when she called." Elisabeth, however, says that he was adept at calming her down. "She could be handled. She would call every five minutes while he was working. 'Goddamnit, mom, I'm in the middle of—. I love you. Let's talk later.' Grandmom we loved and tolerated."

While the girls were in New City, Edie remained in Manhattan with Ernie, working with him on the evening show. In videotapes from this period, she exudes little personality when she sings. Her voice, however, has grown in power; the phrasing is controlled and evocative, the tone rich and full. When Edie sang, it wasn't unusual for the camera to cut briefly to Ernie; he would be sitting off to the side of the set, watching her, and when she finished he would comment warmly, "That was beautiful." Writer Deke Heyward says that "Ernie totally totally totally adored Edie. And this was almost obsessive. He cried very easily; his emotions were raked up. She did one song, I think it was 'Scarlet Ribbons,' and whenever he heard it—I get goose pimples talking about it—he would just keep looking at her, and the tears would be coursing down his cheeks. She could tear him apart by singing that song."

If as a singer she hadn't yet found a way to project a strong personality, as a comedienne she was letting loose with some inspired wackiness. With Ernie, Edie felt it was permissible to explore her silly side; she also had an excellent teacher from whom to learn about timing, accent, costume, gesture, facial expression, and other elements of comedy. Gradually, on her own, she started experimenting with funny imitations. At parties she would make people laugh by pretending to be Marilyn Monroe singing nineteenth-century German lieder. After a while she began doing the bit on *The Jack Paar Show*, wearing a fur stole, heavy lipstick, and a tousled blond wig. Eventually she was imitating Monroe reading Shakespeare. She did Monroe when she played a monthlong engagement in March 1956 at the Persian Room of the Plaza Hotel, headlining in an act that mixed straight singing and comedy. "Ed Sullivan came to the Plaza and saw me and asked me to do Marilyn on his Sunday-night show," Adams remembered. "It was on the Sullivan show that it became really big. It brought so much mail I had to repeat it two weeks later."

In the Philadelphia-era shows Edie's comedy duties had consisted mostly of acting as "the master of the ten-second fill," as she called it. In New York, however, she was blossoming into a true comedienne. In the Kovacs shows' "dizzy mock commercials," for example, Edie would do "a perfectly wonderful imitation of that simpering smile worn by all those girls when they're demonstrating the shampoo," wrote John Crosby in the *New York Herald Tribune*. From material created by the writers, she was also developing her own recurring characters, such as Clowdy Faire, the Weather Girl, who would sexily muddle up her weather reports, and Zaza Esterhazy, a sort of Gabor-sister composite inspired by her father-in-law Andrew's thick Hungarian accent:

"THE ZAZA ESTERHAZY SHOW" . . . EDIE AS ZAZA WEARING LOTS OF FLASHY DIAMONDS . . . "ZAZA HAD A VERY DULL VEEK . . . NO VEDDINGS, NOT VUN . . . I BOUGHT A DIRTY BOOK" . . . BOOK IS SHAKESPEARE, FIRST FOLIO . . . "ZAZA IS LOVING SHAKESPEARE . . . HE'S SO— SO— *HUNGARIAN!*" . . . HUNGARIAN VIOLIN MUSIC PLAYS UNDER TITLES: "ZAZA'S JEWELRY BY JOLIE ESTERHAZY . . . ZAZA'S SCENT, EXTRACT OF ESTERHAZY . . . ZAZA'S GOWN BY GIGI ESTERHAZY . . . ZAZA'S CHAPEAUX BY SAM OF LONDON"

According to Rex Lardner, "She had tremendous admiration for him, and he had tremendous admiration for her, as artists. He was crazy about her singing and her comedic talents. And I guess he also respected her dramatic talents, but she never got a chance to use them except in *Wonderful Town*. But she was a very good comedienne, and he liked it when we put her in skits and things." Deke Heyward says that they would write solo skits for Edie because "there was this goofy generosity in Ernie. He was the star of that show, there was no other star. But he so delighted in allowing Edie to do something of a solo nature. We did the weather girl with her, we did 'Stock Market Analyst'—whatever stupid idea you could come up with. I did 'Stock Market Analyst,' and he loved it."

Away from the television studio, when Edie and Ernie were together at home, "I saw nothing but love. She would do little things for him," describes Heyward. The kitchen was on the writers' floor, and "she would find a piece of something that he particularly liked—I believe it was chicken kidneys—and even though we were in a session, she would come into a story meeting to give it to him. To have a story meeting broken up for chicken kidneys is kind of strange, but it was a measure of their love."

At around this time, a musical version of Al Capp's popular cartoon strip *Li'l Abner* was being prepared for Broadway. Michael Kidd, who had staged the jazzy dances in *Guys and Dolls*, was set to choreograph and direct. Edie had heard about the project when she was doing *Wonderful Town* and had set her sights on landing the lead role of Daisy Mae. Then she heard that the producers wanted Marilyn Monroe. "I thought, If they want Marilyn, maybe they'll take a first-string Monroe imitator," she said. So she called Al Capp and Michael Kidd and asked them to watch her second Ed Sullivan appearance. The ploy worked; she won the part. In the title role they cast a strapping young newcomer, Peter Palmer, who had played tackle for the University of Illinois in the 1952 Rose Bowl.

With *Li'l Abner* due to open at the St. James Theater on November 15, Edie was gearing up for the show by late summer. The role of lusty Daisy Mae, whose primary goal is to nab Li'l Abner on an antic Sadie Hawkins Day in Dogpatch U.S.A., was about as far a cry from her old dreams of opera as any could be. Edie had already begun to shed her fresh-from-the-heartland image; when playing the Persian Room she had posed for ads in a glittering evening gown and heavy Dietrich-style makeup, her hair blonder and more sophisticatedly styled than before. Now she let her tresses grow long and bleached them completely platinum. She also lost weight in order to fit into costume designer Alvin Colt's raggedy-hemmed short shorts and low-cut, shoulder-baring blouse—very true to Al Capp's cartoons, skintight and revealing. As work proceeded on the musical, her appearances on the summer *Kovacs Show* diminished. For the final episode of Ernie's series, she filmed a Marilyn Monroe sketch in advance because her schedule didn't permit her to appear live.

That fall, during the trial runs of *Li'l Abner* in Boston and Washington, Ernie saw the show "about fifteen times," according to Edie. After the show opened on Broadway, the Kovacses saw it "about twenty times, at least," remembers Kippie. "And I loved every time." The family would meet for dinner before Edie had left for the theater, and then "Edie would come in about two or three in the morning, after her show. We were sleeping. She would sit us up and braid our hair for the next day, and we'd go back to bed," says Kippie.

Like her husband, Edie seemed happiest when she was pushing herself to capacity. During the day she enrolled in acting classes at Lee Strasberg's Actors Studio. Three evenings a week, she was allowed a late call for *Li'l Abner* so that she could attend the Traphagen School of Fashion. Her contract with the musical prohibited her from taking on regular TV assignments, but she was negotiating with NBC for a three-year contract that would include a pilot for a situation comedy and guest appearances on the network's TV and radio shows.

Just as Edie was stepping up her professional activities, Ernie was winding his down. The effort of mounting a live radio wake-up show six days a week, for three hours a day, was taking its toll. In August it was reported that he was negotiating an end to his ABC Radio contract, although it had nearly four more years to run and provided a substantial income. "It's become a matter of survival," he said. "I can't physically do it anymore." He finally succeeded in getting out of the contract, and ABC Radio's last *Ernie Kovacs Show* aired on August 24, 1956. He entered into discussions with NBC about the possibility of doing a shorter, less frequent radio program for the network, but no agreement was reached.

Now the summer replacement show—or "The Gravy Train Show," as one script referred to it—was nearing the end of its run. Although Ernie and his staff were outdoing themselves to make *The Ernie Kovacs Show* the best that they could, NBC offered Ernie no encouragement that the series might be given a permanent slot in the fall. He was becoming irritated by well-intentioned people who kept saying, "Gee, if you click on this replacement series, you'll really be set, eh?" "I'll be set? Set for what?" he complained. "NBC has promised me nothing in the way of a nighttime spot for the fall, and even if they wanted to give me one, where on earth would they put me? There just isn't any room. I've been trying to make this show the funniest I've ever done, but let's not go overboard on what it means to my future."

By September 10, when the final installment of the prime-time *Ernie Kovacs Show* was to air, it was clear that the network was not going to continue the show. "The summer show was a beautiful combination of Ernie's experimentation abilities and of formal entertainment in the variety medium," says Perry Cross. "We almost did a satire of a variety show, only for real. I think had there been some way to do that show right away again, or reasonably right away, it might have been the vehicle that would have propelled him to where I think he should have been." Cross believes that Kovacs never did reach the pinnacle he might have reached on TV. "He wanted to do things, and there were always budget problems or there was always something—and it plagued him. Had he had his opportunity around '56, '57, to do a large, upscale show his way, without budget restrictions, I think that would have propelled him."

The show did, however, finally bring him a measure of serious recognition in the television industry. The summer replacement for *Caesar's Hour* certainly was the highest-quality show Ernie had ever done. Given a supportive network, a proper budget, a high-visibility prime-time slot, and a handpicked staff perfectly attuned to his comedy and his way of working, Kovacs was able to prove to the business that he was a heavy hitter, the equal of Sid Caesar and Milton Berle, Jackie Gleason and Lucille Ball. The industry responded with respect. The summer *Ernie Kovacs Show* received an Emmy Award nomination for best new series for 1956. Ernie was also nominated for best continuing performance by a comedian in a series, competing against Jack Benny, Sid Caesar, Robert Cummings, and Phil Silvers. Edie Adams was nominated for best continuing performance by a comedienne, competing against Gracie Allen and Lucille Ball. And Kovacs, Deke Heyward, Rex Lardner, and Mike Marmer were nominated for best comedy writing in a series; their fellow nominees included Nat Hiken, Goodman Ace, Mel Brooks, Neil Simon, and Larry Gelbart. (*Caesar's Hour* swept the Emmys that year, however, and Ernie's work would not receive an Emmy Award until after his death.) Kovacs and his writers were also honored with the prestigious Sylvania Television Award for outstanding comedy show of the year.

But the kudos came later. First, there was a tiny piece of revenge to be exacted—on the air. "I believe that Ernie believed that whatever monies we saved on the production—because we were given a big budget for the Sid Caesar replacement—would accrue back to him," says Deke Heyward. "I believe he found out on the last show that he was not getting any money back, and NBC was getting the money, and he didn't want NBC to get anything. If he wasn't going to get it, ain't nobody going to get it." Ernie's solution? To do "the biggest goddamn production number in the world," Heyward says. "Now, these were our instructions. And we were spending money like crazy. We had twelve midgets. We had three fat women. We had a number of elephants. We had a number of camels. We had a guy dressed in a Roman toga riding across the stage in a whatever the Romans rode across the stage in. I think at one point Ernie was in the center singing something wonderful, amplified, and the orchestra had additional pieces—every penny that could be spent was spent." For the grand finale, "with possibly a hundred-something people on stage, everyone had little axes and chopped the scenery to pieces! And it was total chaos, and it was live." While everyone chopped up the set, Ernie sauntered back and forth across the stage, smoking his cigar and "looking on with great glee," remembers Heyward, "great delight, at the destruction going on."

16

By 1956, the name Ed Sullivan had become synonymous with Sunday night. Sullivan, whose CBS variety show had premiered in 1948 under the title *Toast of the Town*, was an ex-sportswriter and gossip columnist with an excellent nose for the newsworthy. His television credo was "Something for everybody," and his briskly paced *Ed Sullivan Show* had acquired an enormous audience by bringing the world's hottest entertainers into families' homes week after week.

That spring NBC, casting about for a strong program to schedule opposite Sullivan, decided to offer the slot to Steve Allen on the basis of his success with the *Tonight* show. "Suddenly somebody came to me and said, 'Hey, why don't we put you in there?' and I said, 'Fine, I won't stop you,' " remembers Allen. "In my youthful energy and naivete, I thought I could do both shows and do justice to both." The Sunday-night *Steve Allen Show*, which premiered in June, was built around "pure comedy, wild sketches. The only thing like it in today's world is *Saturday Night Live*. Big sketches. Big stars. It was hard work; every week we had to put on the equivalent of a Broadway musical comedy revue, and sometimes on Broadway it takes them a year and they close in one night. That was quite a time-consuming and demanding assignment." Before long, Allen realized that he couldn't continue to do both shows, and he asked NBC to release him from his late-night duties. "They said, 'Oh no, please,' and so we compromised," says Allen. "I cut down to three nights a week."

Allen was scheduled to host *Tonight* Wednesday through Friday. For Monday and Tuesday nights, NBC planned to run old *Tonight* kinescopes (shows shot off a TV monitor with a film camera), and the network put Roger Gimbel, a young associate producer from *Tonight* and the daytime *Home* show, in charge. "They were going to use Gene Rayburn, who was the sidekick for Steve Allen, to be the host," remembers Gimbel. "He'd just sit in a sound studio with one camera—I was directing it—and he would talk and introduce segments from old shows of that year.

"The problem was that there just wasn't time to edit these things and find the kinnies and so forth," Gimbel explains. "After a few weeks, it was perfectly clear that we couldn't go on. So NBC gave me those two nights to program. They said, 'Why don't you just try out some people?' Suddenly I had a live show on my hands. I didn't have a clue how to put it together."

Gimbel began testing different hosts, mostly stand-up comedians, including Henry Morgan, Tony Randall, Jerry Lester, and Jack Paar. "We tried dozens of people on the *Tonight* show," says Gimbel. "I was desperate because I had to put together a hundred-minute live show two nights a week. These were people I either had worked with or knew about from the *Tonight* show, because we used stand-up comedians all the time. And Steve Allen was sensational. He's the only guy I've ever known in the business who called me up and said, 'Roger, I'm sending you all the files on how the *Tonight* show was started, in case this will help you find a replacement.' Most guys would say, 'Good luck, and I hope you fail. I'm the only guy who could make it.' "

Gimbel wanted to use Jack Paar. "He was, I think, the best we had. I loved him. But the sales department at NBC did not want to use Jack Paar because they said they couldn't sell a commercial with him. So we kept trying." Kovacs had guest-hosted for Allen's *Tonight* the previous September, and his Caesar replacement show was nearing the end of its summer run. NBC offered him the job, but he vacillated.

"I'm not keen on doing the show permanently," Ernie said in August, three weeks before the final installment of his prime-time *Ernie Kovacs Show*, "because I don't know whether it would be the right thing to do. It's a very informal kind of show, and I've done plenty of informal shows in the past. I'm bent on getting my own spot once a week, if only so there would be a lot more time to prepare sketches and things."

But his own weekly spot was not forthcoming from NBC. Still under contract to the network, and lacking any better offer that would make it feasible for him to turn down *Tonight*, Ernie finally accepted the assignment. ("I know that Ernie did a lot of things because he needed money," says writer Mike Marmer. "I forgave anything Ernie did because I know he went into debt looking for his kids. And the other part of it is that Ernie liked to live very high.") Ernie became the official Monday-Tuesday host of the *Tonight* show on the October 1 broadcast. He, Lardner, and Marmer were the credited writers; Barry

Shear took on directing duties; and Shirley Mellner continued as associate producer. Perry Cross (who later produced *Tonight*, when Jack Paar became permanent host) was replaced on this show by Roger Gimbel, although Gimbel says that "Ernie did it all. I may have been producer in name, but Ernie was the guy. He was very organized and knew precisely what he was going to do."

The cast, a familiar one to Kovacs aficionados, included Bill Wendell, Peter Hanley, and Barbara Loden. Edie, however, for the first time since *Wonderful Town*, was prevented by her Broadway contract from working on the show. In a massive search for a replacement, 300 aspiring "girl singers" were tried out, and auditions were held both in New York and Hollywood (on Ernie's first trip west, accompanied by Barry Shear and Shirley Mellner). Maureen Arthur, a twenty-two-year-old singer from St. Louis, was working in Los Angeles when she heard about the auditions. "In a way, it's because of my admiration for him that I happened to go to the audition," said Arthur, who was subjected to more than she had bargained for in the tryout. "First I was asked to sing. Then I read a comedy script. Then I had to recite in eight different dialects. Then I had to do all eight dialects in one little monologue."

More than Arthur's musical abilities, Ernie was impressed with her "intuitive feel for comedy," he later said. "During her reading she stopped once, evidently realizing she wasn't getting the lines quite right. She started over again and this time was fine. And she has just the right amount of inexperience— Maureen doesn't have to unlearn anything." As he was able to do with Barbara Loden, Kovacs sensed that he could "really direct" Arthur (to borrow Mellner's phrase), and the blond, blue-eyed singer won the job.

Not surprisingly, Kovacs' *Tonight* show bore no resemblance to the ad-lib and chat format that Steve Allen had instituted. Instead, Ernie grafted the structure of sketches, blackouts, and songs from his previous programs onto *Tonight*. "It was an opportunity for him to practice things. I think that's the way he looked at it," says Roger Gimbel. Each show opened with a teaser:

MAN WITH STUBBLE BEARD IN FRONT OF MIRRORED MEDICINE CABINET . . . OPENS DOOR . . . BARBER INSIDE SHARPENING RAZOR

ERNIE WEARING SANDWICH BOARD: "WAVE TO YOUR FRIENDS AT HOME, 10 CENTS" . . . BARBARA, PETE, AND MAUREEN WALK

THROUGH AUDIENCE HOLDING OUT POTS AND PANS . . . SOUND OF
CLINKING COINS

"He liked to have these teasers in the beginning like two oxen pulling
somebody apart," remembers Gimbel. "A man would whip the oxen,
and then it would say, THE ERNIE KOVACS SHOW. He got these wild
ideas, and then one of us would go out and chase down the oxen. Or
he would open with the Nairobi Trio. There were a a lot of things he
could fill in with." This was followed by the traditional Kovacsian mixture of movie and television parodies:

ERNIE IN LEDERHOSEN, SCARF, AND TYROLEAN CAP AS WOLFGANG
SAUERBRATEN, THE GERMAN DISC JOCKEY . . . WEARS ROMAN SAN-
DALS AND TOGA OVER HIS USUAL OUTFIT . . . PLAYS LEAD IN "VAS
YOU DERE IN 44 B.C.: DER AZZIZZINATION OF JULIUS CAESAR"

and bizarre characters:

ERNIE IN LOUD, PADDED JACKET AS HOLLYWOOD COLUMNIST
SKODNEY SILKSKY . . . SOUND OF TELETYPE MACHINE . . . DE-
SCRIBES NEW MOVIE "ABBOTT AND COSTELLO MEET THE KING AND I,"
STARRING ELVIS PRESLEY AS "I" AND HOWDY DOODY AS THE MAD
DOCTOR . . . "ONE OF THE TENSEST MOMENTS EVER FILMED IN A
MURDER FLICKER COMES WHEN DOODY LUNGES FOR ELVIS, BRAN-
DISHING A HONED PUTTY KNIFE, AND PRESLEY SINGS THE HIT TUNE
OF THE SHOW WHILE HE FLAILS DOODY TO DEATH WITH HIS KNEES"

and camera trickery:

ERNIE AS SUPERCLOD (ALIAS CLARK BENT) CONFRONTS SOME HOODS
. . . "DON'T TRY ANY FUNNY STUFF . . . REMEMBER, I HAVE X-RAY
EYES" . . . CLOSEUP OF ERNIE'S EYES . . . CUT TO HOODS . . .
DISSOLVE TO WHITE SKELETONS . . . ERNIE: "I THINK MY PUPILS
NEED AN ADJUSTMENT. THEY'RE A BIT TOO STRONG"

and musical interludes by Maureen Arthur, Peter Hanley, and LeRoy
Holmes and his orchestra.

To Roger Gimbel, "His was the easiest show I ever did, in the sense
that Ernie did the work. And he did it so easily, it seemed, because he
had this endless reservoir of material. Some of the things had been on
the summer shows, and some were new. We did sketches with people

coming to life out of armor, a lot of medieval stuff—there were people inside, or voices. It was unusual; nobody thought about doing those things. Anyway, it didn't even seem like he was sweating to do ninety minutes in the evening. And he was the most relaxed performer." That's not to say, points out the producer, that Ernie didn't give thought to the show; "that's all he thought about," he says. "But Ernie wasn't in show business, to me, at all. He was in Ernie business. He was in his own world and thinking about different things."

To production assistant Mitzi Matravers, however, Ernie's attitude toward *Tonight* seemed unprofessional. "Ernie would be in a smoke-filled room playing poker with a lot of NBC executives and directors, and I would knock on the door as production assistant and say, 'Ernie, we don't have any scripts for tonight.' He would go to a file cabinet and pull out an old script—we had new material too, but he was too lazy to work on the scripts. The old scripts would come from other shows he had done." His lack of discipline, she felt, hurt the comedy itself. "There were some brilliant things, but they demanded special effects for which there was no budget and no rehearsal time either," she said. Often a sketch would be leading to a "great finish" but "would be so badly timed that the point would be lost in the middle of the station break—the whole thing would be kaput. The skits were hysterically funny when they came off. But he was ill prepared and wasn't putting in the time, and the money was slight."

The production staff had offices on the twenty-eighth floor of the RKO Building, in Rockefeller Center. "The drama department was next to the comedy department; we all had little offices up there," recalls Gimbel. "And Ernie had a lot of poker games going on up there. It was quite a place. Barry Shear had piranhas in a tank; half the thing was finding food for Barry's piranhas. It was a stunt. He would feed them my fish or somebody else's fish. He would do things to shock the secretary." Ernie would sit in his office with the door wide open, clacking away at a typewriter and smoking a huge Havana. "He could be eating and talking and writing at the same time. It was amazing," says Gimbel.

As in his Philadelphia days, Ernie did little in the way of rehearsal for *Tonight*. "Rehearsals would be: 'Here is the platform, I'm going to be the captain, you're going to be this, and so forth,' " describes Gimbel. More important were the production meetings, to which Ernie would bring vast, detailed lists of props and costumes. "Ernie was very big on props and wardrobe, and the production meeting was unlike any production meeting I've ever been in," says Gimbel. "Usually the producer, me, sits there and says, 'We need two cups and three pens.'

Ernie would run the meetings, and he'd sit there and say, 'I need two olives six millimeters long, bread this size. I need two cups of cotton. I need a tiger. And wardrobe, I need a bow tie. I want a toothpick. What size toothpicks do you have?' It was a meticulous list, very specific. Precise. You could leave the production meeting and come back, and he'd still be talking about the length of the trousers."

Because of Ernie's emphasis on props, says Gimbel, "the prop man was his best friend. And the crews he really treated well. He depended on them. They were his team." A crucial member of his team was director Barry Shear, who would man the control booth during the show and drink one Coke after another; at the end of a broadcast, all the Coke bottles would be lined up in a long row. "He was a rough, gruff, sassy kind of director," remembers Gimbel. "A very talented man, extremely clever with matting and early things. These were all live shows. He was very, very good with tricky stuff, and he could do it instantly. The two of them really had a synergy; they loved to invent things."

The *Tonight* show was broadcast from the Hudson Theater on West 44th Street near Broadway, a short walk from the production offices. The theater was "a great audience house and very suitable for comedians," Roger Gimbel remembers. "It seated about four or five hundred people. But it wasn't always full for Kovacs, because there wasn't a big thing to see. You'd have to look at the monitors to get it."

For some sketches, Ernie set up screens at the front of the proscenium so that the audience couldn't see the action onstage and would be forced to watch the monitors. "He had one sketch where he was a baseball player, and he hit the ball and it went out of the park and around the world. You saw Eskimos looking at it, you saw all these things," describes Gimbel. "But he would hide it. He was doing what he was going to do. He didn't care whether you had an audience there or not. The ideas were so terrific. But we judged our successful nights when the house went crazy, and it was a very mild reaction, which made us nervous."

Despite the audience reaction, Kovacs' *Tonight* show made two significant contributions to the history of TV. One was the creation of a new character, a mute blithe spirit who wanders about in an ill-fitting hat and a too-tight plaid jacket, perpetually bewildered by the absurd world around him. At first he had no name; eventually he was christened Eugene. "He, too, is the Talmudic innocent," says writer Deke Heyward. He made his first appearance on October 15, 1956, in a sketch titled "Library Bit."

As elegantly spare in concept as the Nairobi Trio, "Library Bit" is

simply about the torture and perplexity of having unexpected, uncontrollable sounds come out of one's body and one's actions. Eugene
enters a quiet library. As he walks his shoes squish loudly. He pulls a
book off the shelf; we hear a rasp drawn over metal. He opens *Camille*, and the book emits a delicate cough; he opens *The Swamp*, and a
frog croaks. Finally he sits down, takes out a tiny Chiclet, and drops
it; it sounds like a four-by-four hurled downstairs. He fills a cup with
water, and waterfall sounds stream forth. He sharpens his pencil, and
we hear a machine gun. This is the last straw for his fellow library
patrons, Peter Hanley and Maureen Arthur; they get up and leave in
disgust. The camera closes in on Eugene's face. He blinks, and we hear
iron pipes clang.

The following week, Eugene showed up in a ship's dining room:

> EUGENE BITES OLIVE, PRODUCES LOUD CRUNCH . . . APOLOGETI-
> CALLY PLACES OLIVE ON PLATE, IT ROLLS AWAY . . . TAKES AN-
> OTHER OLIVE, IT ROLLS AWAY TOO . . . CLOSE-UP OF SOUP, SOUND
> OF GURGLING LAVA . . . EUGENE OPENS HIS MOUTH, WE HEAR
> LOUD SHIP HORN . . . MAN AND WOMAN LOOK AT HIM, ANNOYED

The olives were made to roll by means of the second important *Tonight*
show contribution: a set built entirely at an angle, with all the furniture
and decorations securely nailed down. A prism on the camera lens cor-
rected the tilt, so that everything appeared upright on TV. But the
tilted set transformed the normal consequences of gravity into something anarchic and strange:

> EUGENE PUTS ANOTHER OLIVE ON TABLE . . . CAMERA FOLLOWS AS
> IT ROLLS DOWN THE TABLE TO A SNARE DRUM CLIMAXED BY THE
> CRASH OF CYMBALS AND A TRIANGLE'S *TING!* . . . BAFFLED, EUGENE
> KEEPS PUTTING OLIVES ON THE TABLE . . . CAMERA FOLLOWS EACH
> ONE AS IT ROLLS AWAY TO PERCUSSION SOUNDS

For an actor, working on a tilted set demands perfect muscular control;
every action must be performed sideways in order to appear straight in
the camera. "It was hard, because it was as steep as they could do it,"
remembers Roger Gimbel. "Everybody had splints to hold them
straight." Ernie, however, sometimes moved around on the set, and
without the aid of splints, he had to angle his body exactly right and
yet not appear to be straining.

Eugene, the "Library Bit," and the tilted set became recurring staples on the *Tonight* show, with little additions and variations. "We used to do a lot of silent stuff on our show; what noise there was came out of total silence," says Roger Gimbel. "The library sketch we did endlessly. You could always put up the library shelves; that's the kind of thing Ernie could fill time with. And we had a lot of fun with the slanted set. We'd sit around and say, 'What if you're pouring water? If you're pouring water, it pours over here.' Then we'd say, 'Instead of using the water, what happens if we do this?' When you're doing the show a couple of nights a week, you could practice these things. You would try it three or four times."

Not surprisingly, Eugene has often been compared to Buster Keaton and Charlie Chaplin. (Perhaps Ernie knew of a tilted set used by Chaplin in his 1917 film *The Immigrant*, in which the deck of a ship and the interior of its dining room are made to rock back and forth.) But Eugene also bears a correspondence to another quiet man: Monsieur Hulot, the fictional alter ego of French filmmaker Jacques Tati. "Jacques Tati was one of Ernie's idols," recollects writer Mike Marmer. "He always mentioned Jacques Tati. Tati used a lot of sound effects with visuals, that slow pace to the comedy. I don't think Ernie got it from Tati; he just liked it because they were both doing the same things. But I know that he was one of his heroes."

Indeed, in spirit and in the form their comedy takes Eugene and Monsieur Hulot might be cousins—the one bumpkinly American, the other solemnly Gallic. As one critic has written of Tati's gentle creation:

> Hulot is a situational, not a personality, comedian. Hulot does not go out and make funny things happen. He is a magnet which attracts *contretemps* to himself. Tati says Hulot is, as it were, invisible, and it is for the audience to find him and to decide whether or not he is their friend, or just someone they would pass unnoticed in the street.
>
> "Hulot is not a doer," says Tati. "He is perhaps more childish. He does not dare. He is not necessarily funny to everybody. Some spectators do not laugh at him."

Not everybody laughed at Eugene. The bits involving olives and books and oddball sounds were little jokes, subtle jokes, perfect for the small screen but destined to be lost in the space of a Broadway theater. "He was trying things that didn't seem like big jokes, and they were funny in a totally new, different way. Sort of avant-garde, experimental television," Roger Gimbel says. The problem was that experimental TV did not draw the sort of ratings expected from a network show. With regard not only to Eugene but to all of Ernie's comedy, "the general feeling was that we had a very, very good show, but it wasn't catching on with the audience," remembers Gimbel. "The reaction in the theater was a bumpy thing for us, because we felt that if people weren't coming, it wasn't what the *Tonight* show was supposed to be. Heavier comedy, more stand-up material, sketch material worked great. Ernie's sketches were entertaining and wildly imaginative, but they didn't always get big laughs."

In the meantime, Steve Allen was becoming wearied by the effort of mounting his full-scale Sunday-night show every week while continuing to host *Tonight*. "Look, it was a compromise," he said to NBC management. "It's still not working. Doing a Sunday-night show and doing it great—which is what you want—takes all the time I've got and all the creativity." NBC finally agreed to take Allen off *Tonight* in January 1957 so that he could focus all his energy on the prime-time hour.

If, in retrospect, it seems odd that a performer would have given up hosting the *Tonight* show, the reasons seemed clear-cut in 1956. The Sunday-night show opposite Ed Sullivan "had about ten times as large an audience," explains Allen. "America basically goes to bed at eleven o'clock at night. Those late-night show ratings are very small, whereas in the early evening you can have thirty million people looking at you. Also, the money was about five times more than I was being paid for the late-night, because it was prime time. It was that simple. Oddly enough, in those days none of us connected with the *Tonight* show thought it was a big deal at all. It's amazing. It seems a big deal now. It's now part of the national psychological furniture."

Faced with the loss of Allen as *Tonight*'s permanent host, the network quickly put all its resources into the development of a splashy new late-night show, featuring live remote segments from different cities and to be titled *Tonight! America After Dark*. Ernie "must have been aware that NBC was putting enormous effort into a new midnight show tentatively scheduled to debut that January," pointed out Mitzi Matravers, the *Tonight* show production assistant. And there was only one way he could read it: as a sign that NBC was not interested in retaining him as a permanent late-night host.

This could not have come as any surprise to him, of course. Kovacs and *Tonight* had been uneasy bedfellows from the start. "It seemed to me that he was uncomfortable with the traditions of the show," says

Roger Gimbel. "There's no way to keep the *Tonight* show going without using talk. Every time we tried to get him to do that he'd say, 'Oh, I'm uncomfortable with that.' It was the wrong spot for him. He wasn't interested in other people. He was interested in how to create things."

Ernie hosted his last *Tonight* broadcast on Tuesday, January 22, 1957. But the preceding Saturday he had made a special appearance on TV that would redirect the course of his career.

In 1946 a Catskills comic named Jerry Lewis and an Italian-American baritone named Dean Martin had decided to form a team and try to climb together out of the small time. Their first engagement as partners, at Atlantic City's 500 Club, was an instant success. Audiences loved the way the smoothly relaxed, handsome Martin was always being interrupted by the frantic antics of the goofball Lewis, and by the end of the 1940s Martin and Lewis were the most popular comedy duo in the country.

Martin and Lewis worked in the nation's top nightclubs, on stage, and in television (they were among the principal rotating hosts on Pat Weaver's *Colgate Comedy Hour* for the entire run of the show, from 1950 to 1955). They also starred together in sixteen films, most of them forgotten today but all of them financial hits. In 1956, however, Martin and Lewis announced that they would part ways. NBC negotiated a deal to feature each one in his first solo television appearance. These appearances were much publicized and eagerly awaited; Martin without Lewis and Lewis without Martin were still among the hottest draws imaginable (although the French had not yet crowned Lewis "Le Roi du Crazy").

Jerry Lewis, who was slated to go first, agreed to mount an hour-long special. NBC, however, scheduled Lewis to do a ninety-minute show: *Saturday Color Carnival*, the network's weekly color "spectacular" (as specials were then called). But Lewis, who was in a position to call his own shots, would not do half an hour more than he had agreed to do, nor would he follow anybody else; he wanted to do the first hour of the ninety-minute showcase. (In fact, these are reasonable demands that any other comic would have made.) NBC was in a panic; where would they find someone willing to follow one of the most heralded solo comic debuts in TV history?

NBC approached Ernie, who had only a little time left before his *Tonight* hosting duties were to end. Some have speculated that NBC was taking advantage of Kovacs' still being under contract. Unable to figure out a proper way to showcase his talents over the long run, and with supportive network head Pat Weaver on his way out due to disputes with NBC's parent company, RCA, now the network seemed to be throwing Kovacs into the breach out of desperation, just as CBS had done when it had needed somebody to pit against Milton Berle.

But Ernie had an idea and, offered the leftover time period, he saw it as a welcome opportunity to call a few shots of his own. He discussed his idea with some of his closest confidants. Shirley Mellner advised him, "If you have enough time and enough money, and nobody's standing over you, then it's a good idea. But if it has to be done the way we did the other shows, there isn't enough time or enough money." Ernie told NBC that he would accept the assignment on one condition: absolutely nobody from the network could interfere with what he wanted to do. He had to have a good budget; he had to have enough rehearsal time; most important of all, he had to have complete creative independence. NBC was desperate. They had to agree.

Ernie put together a script and then showed it to Bob Sarnoff (the son of RCA chairman General David Sarnoff), who had been appointed to succeed Pat Weaver as president of NBC. "Bob Sarnoff discussed it with me at lunch and said he didn't think it was so good," said Ernie. "I didn't say anything, but later I called NBC's film department and told them to get a half-hour Western show ready. That did it. I got the word to go ahead with my original script."

What Ernie wanted to do was a wildly adventurous gamble for prime-time network TV: a half-hour show entirely in leisurely paced pantomime, with only sound effects to augment the gentle action. (Following Jerry Lewis, whose fast, riotous comedy depended heavily on motion and noise, the concept seems even more radical.) Ernie's attitude was that he was "being put in a spot where I'll sink or swim"; he might as well take the most perilous risk that he could conceive. In fact, remembers Deke Heyward, "We had talked about doing the silent show for some time, but nothing ever happened." Now that he was in a position of some power over the network, Ernie could set forth on his grand, avant-garde (although he would not have called it such) experiment.

Not everything went exactly as planned. An early notion to hire Harpo Marx as a guest star was never brought to fruition. And although some of the commercials were mute, Ernie's desire to run silent commercials exclusively was ignored by several sponsors. (*New York Journal-American* critic Jack O'Brian, normally negative toward Ernie's work, even came to his defense in this regard. "Having once bought Kovacs' speechless whim, the commercials should have gone along with the mute notion for the simple purpose of making the show all of an impertinent piece," he wrote. "But antique radio techniques still plague TV, and talk must thunder out at regular intervals.") But Ernie's great gamble paid off. His January 19, 1957, *Ernie Kovacs Show*, directed by Barry Shear, produced and written by Kovacs, and starring Ernie as the Talmudic innocent Eugene, is now regarded as one of the classics of television comedy.

"No Dialogue" or "The Silent Show," as it has come to be called, opens with a teaser: As Harry Sosnik's orchestra plays, a musician is poised to pound a kettledrum. But he drops his stick, and it descends into a pasty muck inside his instrument.

Now Ernie comes on to explain the show's gimmick. By way of demonstration, he offers this bit:

A STUFFED SQUIRREL IN A FOREST SETTING HAS COTTON IN ITS EARS . . . TREE FALLS . . . NO SOUND . . . ERNIE REMOVES COTTON . . . WE HEAR TREE CRASH

The half hour includes a singer named Mary Mayo performing a hummed vocalise—no words—of a Gershwin medley, accompanied by Sosnik's orchestra; Betty Colby in a perfect parody of Jackie Gleason's "Away we go" girl taking an unexpected pie in the face; and the Nairobi Trio, who closes the program with a sort of calypso number.

The heart of the show, however, belongs to the sweetly perplexed Eugene. Eugene enters a stolid men's club, his feet squishing like sponges. He sees a shelf labeled "Dirty Books"; he is bewildered when he finds no dust. He opens the book *Digging the Panama Canal;* the sound of steam shovels and mosquitoes fills the air. He opens a book on Thomas Edison and is blinded by a flash of light. He picks up a copy of *Camille;* a woman's cough issues forth.

Now Eugene takes a drink. We hear the sound of a bathtub filling. He wiggles his pelvis mischievously; we hear water sloshing as if in a galvanized tub. When he walks by the Mona Lisa, she chuckles mysteriously.

Eugene dials a telephone, and we hear a pneumatic drill. He cracks each knuckle to the bang of a kettledrum. He has an hourglass to tell time, but it is ticking loudly, so he puts it in his pocket to muffle the sound. All this noise is beginning to annoy the staid club members.

Eugene decides to eat lunch. He takes an olive out of his lunchbox, and it rolls down the table. He ties an olive to a string, and it hangs at an angle. When he pours milk from his Thermos, it misses the cup and hits the table. He can't quite comprehend it. Suddenly it occurs to him to move the cup to the left. He pours again, but the cup and Thermos keep sliding away.

Frustrated, Eugene stands up. He pushes down mightily on one end of the table. The whole room appears to tilt sideways; his mouth opens in a silent, triumphant laugh. Eugene has finally figured out a way to beat the bizarre forces that rule his world.

Some of these ideas had been tried out before on *Tonight*, and some were new. But Eugene had never been performed as the long centerpiece of an entire show. He had never been given meticulous rehearsal and production attention. (Some fifty-second shots—such as when the camera follows an olive down the table—were rehearsed for an entire afternoon; for the live broadcast the sound man was in his own roped-off area with nine turntables of precisely cued sound-effects records.) Most important of all, Eugene had never before appeared on a prime-time show. That meant, as Steve Allen pointed out, that Eugene was being seen by an audience about ten times larger than any he had ever enjoyed before.

This first color Kovacs broadcast uses color with great sensitivity. (It would be the only color show Ernie ever produced.) Ernie is costumed in an exceedingly loud plaid jacket in browns, plums, and oranges; it clashes nicely with his light blue shirt and a red-and-white checkered tie. The Nairobi Trio, performed by Ernie, Peter Hanley, and Maureen Arthur, appears very rakish wearing purple overcoats, purple and green derbies, and yellow scarves and gloves. They play against a background of solid red, and Arthur sports a pair of 1950s cat's-eye rhinestone glasses. The titles, too, are enchanting— little stylized animated figures, including a little Ernie, that stretch and float in space to the tune of the Gershwins' "Summertime." Animated live during the show by John Hoppe and his Mobilux Title Effects in a process that used mirrors, "these tiny, moving abstractions [are] beautiful beyond words," wrote Harriet Van Horne in the *New York World-Telegram and Sun*. "Imagine minute mobiles of the Calder school, dancing in some sunny limbo and changing form as they dance. . . . That's what the 'Hoppes' look like."

The reaction to "The Silent Show" was spectacular. Congratulatory telegrams flooded NBC, and the network's switchboard lit up immediately after the show and did not go dark until some 200 complimentary calls had been logged. "He always had kind of an underground of people who watched him and loved him. But it wasn't like after Eugene," remembers Shirley Mellner. "It was live, and as soon as he went off the air the phones started ringing with people calling from all over who had apparently been fans of his but hadn't said anything about it. Now they were being very vocal. It was wonderful for him. And for all of us—we worked hard and were thrilled with it. But that was definitely all Ernie."

In retrospect, it may be said that Jerry Lewis was fortunate not to have followed Ernie Kovacs on the evening of January 19, 1957. Lewis' much-awaited solo television debut was a disaster, universally panned for its agonizingly long sketches, for his heavy borrowing from other comedians, and for his generally embarrassing performance. Jack O'Brian, who titled his review in the *New York Journal-American* "Lewis: No; Kovacs: Yes," observed that "from the looks of Jerry Lewis' first TV solo he needs Dean Martin badly. Very, very badly. It was a program almost entirely empty of imagination, fresh material or techniques, even taste. . . . From almost any angle it was a perfectly dull performance, dolefully produced, sluggishly directed, and stupidly written."

Over Ernie, on the other hand, the critics were ecstatic. "Where Lewis relied on noise and frenzy, Kovacs' equally unsubtle humor was fresh and wildly inventive. . . . Look on, Lewis, and learn something," wrote one critic in the *New York Daily News*. Harriet Van Horne agreed: "In technique, sophistication, and charm, the Ernie Kovacs 'dumb show' was light years ahead of the Jerry Lewis spectacular. Coming as it did right after this tedious and costly hour, it was a gem of the purest ray serene." The *New York Herald Tribune*'s John Crosby called the Eugene sketch "reasoned nonsense much like that of *Alice in Wonderland*" and concluded that "it was all pretty weird and wonderful and—though Kovacs won't approve of this appellation—avant-garde." Ernie's "Silent Show" became the only television program presented by the United States at the 1958 Brussels World's Fair, and his script was nominated for an Emmy.

At the time Tom McAvity, NBC's vice-president in charge of programs, had referred to "The Silent Show" as Ernie's "audition," although it is hard to imagine why the network felt it had to audition him after having had him under contract for nearly two years. "If his rating is good," McAvity said, "we hope to sell him as TV's big new comedy talent next fall." But—aside from the Caesar summer-replacement show—NBC never came up with a satisfactory showcase for Ernie. Network television is a numbers game, a thing of high stakes and repetitious formulas. Kovacs' work, ironically, was totally indigenous to the medium, but as it became more and more offbeat and original, it fit less and less into television's increasingly conservative game plan. "His work did not seem to indicate that he wanted ratings above all," says Pat Weaver, who notes that such an attitude put Kovacs on the fringes of TV comedy: "He was working his own territory and would always be different from the other major artists in the comedy field." Working one's own territory might make for inspired TV, but "it stops you from being a very popular star," Weaver points out. Still, the problem did not all lie with Ernie's attitude. Today the former NBC president, who admired Kovacs' work, admits, "We never utilized him properly."

Certainly Ernie was aware that he was not being utilized properly. The fact is, the creative control he achieved for "The Silent Show" was hard-won and something of a fluke for him. As his ideas veered toward the experimental, Ernie was finding himself increasingly frustrated with the strictures of television, increasingly stifled in what he viewed as a closed, unimaginative industry. His success with "The Silent Show," however, had been noticed in many quarters, including quarters in Hollywood. Suddenly Kovacs was hot. And so when Columbia Pictures chief Harry Cohn, last of the big-time movie moguls, offered Ernie a four-year contract at $100,000 per picture and second lead in a service comedy he was preparing with a young actor named Jack Lemmon, Ernie jumped at the chance.

The offer from Columbia Pictures possessed an important symbolic value for Ernie: it signified that his creativity was being rewarded, that somebody regarded his talent as valuable rather than discardable. A movie lover for many years, now Ernie was eager to plunge into the world of filmmaking, a world where he hoped at last to find the creative freedom he craved. He intended to learn as much as he could about the craft so that eventually he could write and direct his own films, exercising the total artistic control that seemed to be eluding him in TV. He also, as Edie Adams later told a reporter, dreamed of being a movie star.

Operation Mad Ball was one of a slew of popular armed-services comedies that Hollywood was turning out in the mid- to late 1950s. With World War II now a memory, moviegoers were ready to respond to such lighthearted looks at the military as *Mister Roberts* and *Teahouse of the August Moon*. Adapted by Arthur Carter, Jed Harris (who also produced it), and Blake Edwards from an unproduced stage play by Carter, *Operation Mad Ball* centered on the amorous activities of the GIs and military nurses at a U.S. Army hospital base in France in September 1945, immediately after the war. Ernie was cast as their commanding officer, Captain Paul Lock, a martinet bent on squelching all romance among his subordinates.

Kovacs would leave for Hollywood that spring to film *Operation Mad Ball*. Before going, however, he was approached about a completely different sort of project, one that would prove important to his development. The publisher Doubleday had enjoyed success with books written by such celebrities as Oscar Levant and Ilka Chase. Kenneth McCormick, Doubleday's editor-in-chief, was married at the time to a woman "who was crazy about Ernie, and we would watch his show together. He just fractured me," says McCormick. The editor contacted Kovacs and made a date to visit him at his Central Park West duplex.

When they got together, McCormick asked him, "Have you ever thought of writing a book?" Ernie responded, "Well, I really have. I've never written a book, but I have got a kind of crazy idea to make a book out of the expansions in TV. And I even have the title: *Zoomar*." McCormick asked what that word meant, "and he said, 'It comes from the zoom lens, which is new.' And so I instantly thought, That's perfect."

Ernie had already put together some sample pages—"I don't know whether in anticipation of our date or not," says McCormick—which he showed the editor. "He had written that *Trentonian* column, so he knew that he could write. And then he realized that from the kind of life he was leading, he could create a character, and he had the idea of writing a novel in which he would be the principal character." Ernie was offered a contract and an advance, "probably five thousand dollars, something like that," says McCormick. "Not big. But he was just dying to be discovered" as a literary talent.

"I think the contract excited him," says the editor. "He told me once, 'I feel that my career is just starting.' And in a sense it was, because, although the column was good, that wasn't what he wanted ultimately to do." The column had been ephemeral, just as the TV shows he was making were ephemeral. A novel, Ernie felt, would be a concrete legacy. And he was a voracious reader himself; he respected literary talent. "He was interested in publishing, he was interested in everything," remembers McCormick. "He wasn't intellectual, but he was an absolutely fascinating person."

As Ernie's work proceeded on *Zoomar*, he kept in close contact with McCormick by phone, and his editor would drop by to check on his progress. "He was so funny, and I enjoyed him so much. I was just fit to be tied by him," McCormick remembers with obvious affection. "He had a very soft voice, and he really was gentle. And he was so excited about the idea of writing a book." With Edie performing most nights in *Li'l Abner*, Ernie had uninterrupted chunks of time in which to write. "I think she had dinner at six o'clock or something like that and was down dressed and ready for the show," recalls McCormick. "Then they would go out somewhere after the theater, and their hours were theater hours. Usually I would see him in the afternoon." Ernie turned in pages to his editor as he went along—fairly well written pages that didn't need much editing, says McCormick, "because he was very professional. He worked very hard."

Zoomar is a caustic, enjoyable, rather adult novel about a rising young TV executive named Tom Moore. As a sponsorship vehicle for a shoe polish company, Moore creates *The Miss Wipe-Ola Beauty Hunt*, a TV show that becomes a hit. (The zoom lens of the title is used only for close-ups of women's busts.) Despite the patent dumbness of his show's concept, Moore manages to maintain his integrity and even to wind up in a position where he can make uplifting reforms in the system. The novel has an insider's flavor, not only in its story line but in such details as a description of restaurateur Vincent Sardi's diplomacy in seating celebrities according to their level of power.

In *Zoomar* Ernie vivisected everything he hated or couldn't understand about commercial TV: the misdirected network brass decision-making, the stupidity of sponsors, the schlocky shows, the political game playing, the Byzantine cost-accounting systems, the ridiculous pampering of the stars. To Tom Moore, Ernie's alter ego, "The people who earn enough money to buy expensive television sets aren't idiots. They have responsible jobs in life." They are our pilots and priests, our cab drivers and scientists, our architects and electricians, and for entertainment they deserve something more than inane game shows featuring "a row of people standing in isolation booths with their brains getting sucked out on close-ups." They deserve the best of which the medium—a device "so miraculous in its function that it is thousands of years ahead of its time"—is capable.

At the end of the novel, Tom Moore confronts his boss, Peter Garnett, who is preparing to sign a contract promoting Moore to an important position on the West Coast. Tom puts his job on the line, making a final-hour appeal for more intelligent and imaginative programming, programming genuinely worthy of this "miraculous" medium in which they work. "What are we going to be?" he asks. "Little Orphan Annies, wearing the same red dress for thirty-six years?" He then tells Garnett, "Don't sign it, Pete. Unless you want the guy who will stand for everything you just heard. . . . In fact, with a freer, stronger hand, I will put into effect every possible thing I can to bring the public adult entertainment."

At this, Garnett considers Tom for a long moment: "He wanted to see him as he was for the last time before signing the agreement that would place this man in a position where ideals were harder to hold by. If Tom could hold on to what he was now," Garnett thought, "he was a man to be envied." Naturally, Garnett approves the appointment. It is a grand Kovacsian fantasy. Ernie places his alter ego squarely in the center of the network structure, where he is in a position to fight it and also to dignify it with his own scruples. In fiction—as he never had the power to do in his own life—Ernie found a way to triumph over the system.

Zoomar was fairly well received when it was published in October

1957. "The principal fascination of *Zoomar*," wrote Martin Levin in the *Saturday Review*, "is that it is so preeminently an inside job by an operative who knows his ground. Only the names of the players are (slightly) changed, but the pressure-cooker atmosphere in which they machinate is so palpable that the author could bottle it." Wanting to surprise Edie with his literary achievement in all its printed-and-bound glory, Ernie did not let her see his book until it was published. He opened the volume with a loving, if awkwardly worded, dedication: "To Edie, my dear wife. It is difficult to say, in this dedication of a book which, to be so dedicated, should be a collection of fine poems or at least prose of deep tenderness, how much I thank you for your love and the great kindness and happiness you have given me. This is hardly a private place to say very much. So for here, at least, on your reading this as you open the first volume, know that without you, there would have been no book, ever."

Unfortunately, however, Edie's reaction to *Zoomar* was "chilly," as Ernie later described it. In the novel Tom Moore is happily married to Eileen, a woman he clearly loves and admires. But there is also a subplot about Tom's fantasies concerning his eminently attractive and dedicated assistant, Karen Loeb. Loeb is the sort of woman whose "body held a scintillating conversation with all males present as she walked the length of the bar," and she is also smart, compassionate, efficient, funny, and twenty-two. She and Tom finally make love, and afterward she tries to sort out the confusion they are both feeling.

"Would you understand me if I explained how I'm in love with you?" Karen asks him. "I'm in love, first of all, with Tom Moore, the man whose problems sometimes I've shared and the man with whom I spend most of my day. I love you as that part of my life. I'm not in love with you in the 'Be my Valentine' sense." She admits that she intended them to make love "just this once." Then she completely absolves him of his infidelity: "If I can tell you that this happened tonight because I was determined it would happen . . . if I can make you believe that, so that you will not have lost any of your fidelity to Eileen, then this will have been perfect." Another grand Kovacsian fantasy. The trouble, according to editor Ken McCormick, was that Edie "was absolutely sure" it was taken from a real-life incident, "and it wasn't."

This suspicion drove a wedge between them that lasted a long time, and at first Ernie didn't even know why it was there. Among friends "Edie always acted very strangely whenever [the book] was discussed. She seemed very cool toward the whole thing, and I could never figure out why until she confessed recently," Ernie said two years after *Zoomar*'s publication. "Now if you read the book, you'll recall there was some pretty wild stuff going on between the main character and his secretary, and with some other dames. Edie figured all of it had happened to me."

But Ernie wanted Edie to be openly proud of his book, not secretly jealous over its subplot. Her conviction that the infidelity had really occurred was "one of the things that hurt him, and it came up subtly between them," remembers McCormick. Tom Moore encounters many women in the course of his work and has sexual thoughts about some of them, although actual infidelity makes him extremely uncomfortable. Ernie wrote the character with a sophisticated understanding of the subtleties of adult thought and emotion, a sensitivity to the complicated tangle that always exists between sexual attraction, fantasy, and marriage. But because Tom Moore had started out being an autobiographical character, "that became a trap," his editor says. "Edie after a while wouldn't believe that he wasn't writing his story and his extramarital life. He got tired of explaining, 'I was writing a novel and I'm not even a character in the novel. Anybody like that would have a girl around as an assistant.' "

Ernie did indeed enjoy a deep—if platonic—intimacy with women throughout his life. He was comfortable around women, he trusted them, and he respected them as intelligent human beings (even as he took pleasure in "appreciating a pretty pair of legs," as his daughter Elisabeth says). And women responded to him as well. "He was enormously attractive to them, first, for his genius," observes writer Deke Heyward. "Second, his madness, which set him aside. Third, his demeanor. He carried himself with great surety. But he was not a player-arounder, so far as I know." Even if the infidelity Ernie had written about in *Zoomar* was fictional, the closeness he felt toward some of the women in his life was real. While it is not necessarily a betrayal to share one's most secret and personal side with more than one person, it can feel like a betrayal to a spouse. Edie's reaction was reminiscent of Mary Kovacs' responses to Ernie's involvements with "other women." Eventually, Ernie said, "I think I've got her convinced now [that Tom Moore] was two other guys."

Despite Edie's reaction, Ernie was very proud of *Zoomar* and publicized it whenever he could. He took to telling interviewers that he had written it in thirteen days: "I ad-libbed that novel. I did the thing in thirty-six-hour stretches, some forty pages at a time. I remember writing the last page—and it's a fairly big book, maybe a hundred thousand words—and I was rushing down to Edie to tell her I'm finished, when I looked at the calendar. It was thirteen days after I'd written the first line." The feat of writing a novel in thirteen days became part of the Kovacs legend, and some of Ernie's closest associates never doubted his account; in general he worked quickly and with intense focus. "I had my doubts that he would ever get it done, but he just sat down and wrote it. I don't think he ever rewrote any pages," says Rex Lardner. "He just did it in his crazy typing style and had somebody else type it up for the publisher. He had a great gift of concentration." But Ken McCormick disputes Ernie's thirteen-day tale. "I kept reading along" as Ernie was turning out pages, says the editor. Nonetheless, he recollects, "I think that he really did write it in about two months."

Ernie always seemed to enjoy impressing people with the swiftness and ease of his writing. With regard to his script for "The Silent Show," he bragged to one reporter: "Now they call it a classic, dirty names like that. The whole thing took me eighty minutes to write, not much longer than my Philly stuff." In another interview he said that he wrote it in an hour. Nowhere did he mention that many of the gags had already been worked out previously, nor that other people had been involved in inventing them. In fact, according to Edie Adams, "The one thing that Ernie always wanted to be known for, first, last, and always, was being a writer. It was very important to him." Ernie loved to lose himself in the creative and solitary act of writing. "My greatest pleasure," he told Hedda Hopper, "is to sit at a typewriter with a sheaf of blank paper and start putting down ideas." To Ernie, being a writer meant being the originator of ideas; ideas were the root from which all his other accomplishments sprang.

Because this was the strongest component of his professional self-image, he was eager for the world to identify him as a writer, too. Rex Lardner remembers that Ernie became very excited when an *Encyclopaedia Britannica* editor asked him to contribute a piece of comedy writing for the 1957 *Britannica Book of the Year*. A script for "Welcome Transients," a parody of the radio and TV show *Welcome Travelers*, appears under "Humour of 1956." "This was written entirely by Ernie, and it was a great piece of humor," says Lardner. (The following year Ernie contributed a banal bit with talking mice, from a guest appearance on NBC's *Producers' Showcase*.)

Recognition as a writer was so important to Ernie that it created a weirdly ambivalent relationship between him and his own staff of writers. On the one hand, "he was very close to his writers," remembers

Perry Cross, his NBC producer. He treated them with the same gentleness and protectiveness he exhibited toward his little girls. "Ernie was faced with a number of personal problems during this period that he protected us from," describes Deke Heyward. "It may have been the business with the kids, the kidnapping; it may have been problems with the ex-wife. We did not know what they were." Nevertheless they were aware that Ernie was having problems, "because despite the fact that he liked being with us, the writers, and he would rather be with us, the writers, than anyone else during this creative period, he would disappear into a private room somewhere and do whatever was necessary in his own privacy." Heyward remembers discussing this with Lardner, and "Rex, who had a deep insight into Ernie's thinking, said Ernie was afraid that if he shared external problems with us, it would take us out of the fairyland in which we were living, in which all good things were possible."

On the other hand, Ernie—a man who was always quick to credit crew members' and performers' achievements on the air—liked to project the illusion that he wrote all of his own material or just made it up as he went along. In August 1956, for example, when he was employing Lardner, Marmer, and Heyward to write both his television and his radio shows, he told one interviewer, in reference to the radio program, "I used to write scripts, but now I just talk." Reams of the writing that he used to "just talk" on this radio show are on file in the Kovacs Special Collection of the University of California, Los Angeles. While Ernie had a talent for improvisational gab, by this period he was improvising around great quantities of prepared material. "Ernie worked from written material," remembers *Tonight* producer Roger Gimbel. "If he ad-libbed, there were some guidelines around. He would improvise within a given piece of material." Perry Cross, who produced the daytime and prime-time *Ernie Kovacs Shows* at NBC, says that "it was hard to delineate who did what. My gut feeling is that the writers did more than appeared. I think they fed a lot more material to him than he would have liked to admit in those days."

Zoomar dovetailed with Ernie's new career scheme in a couple of ways. First, in writing the novel he had given expression to all that he felt was frustratingly wrongheaded about the television industry. Since he believed this aspect of the book to be the truth, now he had to face the possibility that, for him, network TV could only be a creative dead end. The movie offer, posed at just the right moment, opened up a new and (he believed) ultimately more satisfying career path. In addition, Ernie intended to write and direct a screenplay based on *Zoomar*. Were this to come true, it would be the grandest Kovacsian fantasy of them all: Ernie exerting total creative control in one artistic medium in order to exact his revenge on another artistic medium that had denied him this power. Kovacs talked widely about a *Zoomar* film at the time. He chatted about the project in interviews; he told his editor, Ken Mc-Cormick, "about this deal that hadn't been consummated"; in a letter to a *Redbook* editor he mentioned that he was set to direct the project. This, however, may have been more Kovacsian fantasizing. It is unlikely that anyone with no prior experience directing movies—or even acting in them—would have been signed to such a deal. In any case, his dream of filming *Zoomar* was never realized.

In April 1957, shortly before *Operation Mad Ball* was to begin shooting, Ernie set up a bachelor's home away from home at the Beverly Hills Hotel. In New York, Ernie had been comfortable and relaxed in his role of the loving and protective family man. In faraway Hollywood, however, separated from his wife and children, he felt lonesome at first and possibly a little shy. That month he appeared on the cover of *Life* magazine, a sure sign that his star was on the rise. The show business community was inviting him to one party after another, but he was uneasy about accepting these famous strangers' invitations. "By then, he really was in demand," remembers Shirley Mellner, who had moved to California after "The Silent Show" to work for Desi Arnaz and Lucille Ball at Desilu. "Everybody wanted to meet him and know him and talk to him."

Finally, however, he said yes to an important invitation from Frank Sinatra to join him at a party at the home of producer Bill Goetz, one of Hollywood's first serious art collectors, and of Goetz's wife, Edie, the daughter of MGM mogul Louis B. Mayer. An invitation to the Goetzes' was considered a Hollywood rite of passage. Edie Goetz was "the undisputed social queen of Hollywood for decades," according to society chronicler Dominick Dunne. "Her chef knew no peer in the community, and her guest lists were as carefully honed as fine ivory. No outsiders in Edie Goetz's drawing room, ever."

Ernie invited Shirley Mellner to accompany him. From the moment they arrived, the whole event seemed like an absurd exaggeration of the stereotypical Hollywood party. Kovacs and Mellner started giggling as soon as they got out of their rented Cadillac. The white Georgian mansion was huge; the parking lot surrounding it was huger. They were met and introduced around by Sinatra himself. After cocktails they were ushered into Edie Goetz's famous drawing room, which was designed by a silent film star turned interior decorator, William Haines. The lights went dim, Picasso's *Madonna and Child* went up, and a movie screen slid down in its place while Ernie and Shirley watched in disbelief. When Bill Goetz pushed a button, *Strategic Air Command* came on in VistaVision. After a while Goetz offered, "If you don't like this one, I'll put on another," and on came an Alfred Hitchcock movie. "Excuse me, Mr. Goetz, but do you have any UPA cartoons?" Ernie finally inquired. "Why no, Ernie, I don't," his host replied. "Then we'll have to leave," Ernie informed him, and he grabbed Shirley and walked out.

They could hardly contain their laughter until the front door was shut. This was like something out of a Rock Mississippi sketch, not real life as lived by serious people. Ernie started the Cadillac, emerged from the Goetzes' parking lot, and drove into the driveway across the street. "What are we doing here?" Shirley asked. "I want to see what's playing at this house," Ernie said.

If the Goetzes' party had been the epitome of Hollywood extravagance, Ernie's new employer, Columbia Pictures, was the very definition of shrewd Hollywood thrift. The studio was founded in 1924 by Harry Cohn, his brother Jack, and their partner, Joseph Brandt. Harry Cohn was ruthless and uneducated, with an unerring eye for creative talent, a tongue for profanity, and a despotic nature that earned him the nickname White Fang (courtesy of screenwriter Ben Hecht). He built Columbia up from a nickel-and-dime studio on Hollywood's Poverty Row to a major producer of some of the industry's most profitable and artistically outstanding motion pictures. Columbia's vast output included the great Frank Capra films of the 1930s (*It Happened One Night, Mr. Deeds Goes to Town*), Howard Hawks's frenetic screwball comedies (*His Girl Friday*), Rita Hayworth's star vehicles (*Gilda, The Lady from Shanghai*), and such moody '50s dramas as Elia Kazan's *On the Waterfront*, Fred Zinnemann's *From Here to Eternity*, and Nicholas Ray's *In a Lonely Place*.

When Ernie came to Columbia, Harry Cohn had only one more year to live. Their first meeting was auspicious. Kovacs was on the set shooting the climactic party sequence "with lots of drunken GIs and lots of pretty French girls," as he later described it. To get his performers into the proper "mad ball" mood, director Richard Quine staged it as a real party, beginning at midnight and featuring a torrid jazz combo, gallons of champagne, and a catered feast of lobsters and roasts. At about four in the morning, Ernie said, "this character comes up to me and says: 'I hear you've been having a ball chasing these pretty starlets around the set all night.' Actually, that's what I was supposed to be doing in the scene, but I figured it was none of this guy's business, so I just told him 'to go to hell.' " Ernie was later informed that "this character" had been Harry Cohn. "For some reason, Harry and I became great friends after that. Don't ask me why."

Operation Mad Ball also introduced Ernie to two men with whom he would become extremely close both personally and professionally. The first was Jack Lemmon, who in 1955 had won the best supporting actor Oscar for his portrayal of the antiauthoritarian Ensign Pulver in *Mister Roberts*. Lemmon was cast in another antiauthoritarian role in *Mad Ball*, as Captain Lock's principal nemesis, Private Hogan. Lemmon already admired Kovacs from television. To get his hero's attention on the set, the mischievous Lemmon would sneak around nailing his cigars to tabletops so that whenever Ernie tried to pick one up he'd get a crumpled mess of tobacco. Ernie, of course, had pulled similar pranks all his life, but as the target of this one he was less than amused. Concerned about the difficulty of obtaining his favorite Havanas in California, he chewed his costar out. "Then I didn't nail them down anymore, and I tried a couple of them," Lemmon later told an interviewer. "Jesus, I think they were soaked with dynamite—the roof of my head went off."

At thirty-two, the Boston-born, Harvard-educated actor had just a handful of films under his belt. Before coming to Columbia in 1954, Lemmon had worked in New York, performing in radio soap operas and taking all sorts of parts in live TV, including starring roles in two now-forgotten situation comedies, *That Wonderful Guy* and *Heaven for Betsy*. "Television was like instant summer stock, some of it very good, a lot of it junk. But the training ground was incredible; you just can't get that today because television is too important," he explained. "Every film and every part in television or anywhere else is too important; you open your mouth and they want somebody who's already had experience. Whereas back then, you might get ten lines one week, or you might have the lead the next time in a comedy, drama, halfbaked musical, whatever. It was terrific. You were rehearsing one while you were shooting another, just like stock."

In New York Lemmon had a friend who would get him and his actress-wife, Cynthia Stone, onto the CBS show *The Stork Club* (the target of Ernie's old "Crane Club" sketches). "Sherman Billingsley, the famous owner of the Stork Club, was petrified of television, but his own ego refused to let somebody else be the host of that show," recollected Lemmon. The young actor possessed a plaid dinner jacket ("in those days some people wore them"), and thus costumed he would appear with Cynthia on the show. "We were both starving to death, and we would sit as part of the dress in the replica of the club room. We would be served a bottle of lousy champagne—the good stuff was on camera—and get a free meal and just sit and pretend to talk. You know, just mouth the words. I would keep clapping my hands, trying to bring head waiters over to my table every time the camera swung toward me, anything to be seen. I damn near got thrown off because of that."

The other *Operation Mad Ball* colleague with whom Ernie would become close was director Richard Quine. A year younger than Ernie, the son of an actor, Quine had spent his childhood singing, dancing, and acting in vaudeville and on radio. In his teens and twenties, he had played many supporting roles in films, but by the early 1950s he had turned to directing and screenwriting. Some of his best movies were adaptations from the stage, such as *The Solid Gold Cadillac* and the remake of, ironically, *My Sister Eileen,* on which he had worked with Jack Lemmon in 1955. "He knows the camera backward and forward," said Lemmon, "and is absolutely marvelous with actors. There isn't an actor who ever worked for him who doesn't think he's absolutely tops. If he can be faulted at all it's that he gets overly sentimental and romantic at times."

Richard Quine and Jack Lemmon were already buddies when they met Ernie, and they soon took him under their wing. Lemmon was recently divorced from Cynthia Stone; within a year Quine would be separated from his second wife, Barbara Bushman (granddaughter of silent screen star Francis X. Bushman). When they were together, they led the lives of men without women. "We engulfed Ernie into our little group, and we did a lot of stagging, actually," described Quine. "He and Lemmon and I used to buzz around a bit, and Ernie and I would end up playing cards damn near every night. We had a running game that lasted for years."

Lemmon and Quine's attentions were touching and significant to Ernie, a man to whom friendships were vital. "It was one of those immediate things. We were just on the same wavelength right away," remembered Lemmon. Kovacs was on the same wavelength with Quine, too: "He's a member of the fraternity," he said of his new director friend. "I mean he knows, too, that the world's really at an eighteen-degree angle. Dick and I play poker right on the set, even while they're putting makeup on me." They would all be intimate comrades until the end of Ernie's life. "For a long, long time afterwards," said Lemmon, "I would catch myself saying, 'Oh my God, wait till I tell Ernie about this,' and it would be three years after he had died. The man had an incredible presence—the great ones do, very often. Without pushing, his personality and his character were pervading in the best possible way."

But new friends could not compensate for Edie's absence. (During the shoot, not wanting to take off his wedding ring, he covered the wide gold band on his finger with tape.) They soon developed a routine that suggests how much they meant to one another. Every Saturday night, immediately after *Li'l Abner* broke at around 11:00, Edie was whisked by hired car to Idlewild airport. At 12:30 A.M. the plane took off; she was in Los Angeles by 6 A.M. and at the Beverly Hills Hotel by 7:30. There she and Ernie would have Sunday to themselves. Mostly they would hang around the hotel's pool, where producers and agents wheeled and dealed in waterside cabanas and starlets arranged to have themselves paged. Then they would eat dinner together, and by 11:00 Sunday night Edie was back on a plane, bound for New York.

Often Edie brought with her a valise full of fresh Havanas. Ernie had taught her to buy cigars the way connoisseurs do, rolling them between her thumb and index finger to check the crispness of the leaf, sniffing for the proper fragrance, identifying whether there was any filler. Edie spent $500 to have a jeweler make Ernie a little gold box in which to keep wooden matches, which he preferred to lighters. A match, he claimed, "gives you time to light up properly while it burns. I like to light a cigar without putting it into my mouth at all until the ash has eaten an eighth of an inch into the tobacco. Then when I puff it, it's the greatest fragrance in the world."

Ernie also brought Kippie and Bette out to Los Angeles to visit during the shoot, beginning a tradition that he would practice on all his movie shoots. The girls stayed with him at the Beverly Hills Hotel, and he took them to Disneyland, which "he loved," remembers Elisabeth, "except for all the Coca-Cola signs. He felt the advertising spoiled the fantasy." Kippie, who later became an actress, remembers the first time she set foot on a sound stage at the age of eight, surrounded by massive cameras and brilliant klieg lights and overhead microphone booms: "I was mesmerized by the whole thing. I felt like I belonged." On the set, Ernie would introduce his daughters to his colleagues. " 'This is Kathy Grant [who played Lieutenant Bixby, Private Hogan's love interest]. This is Jack Lemmon. This is So-and-so. These are my kids.' I just felt very comfortable," says Kippie. Then he would leave them to their own devices. "He didn't show us around," she explains. "He just said, 'Take a look around, kid.' He never said, 'Now come here and sit here and do this and that.' It was, 'Go ahead. Have a ball.' " At home he was the same way. "He trusted us with everything," says Elisabeth. "He'd carry around $500, and he'd peel off $100 and give it to me so I could pay the cab driver. When I was ten, twelve, I was making plane reservations for the whole family."

Compared to the frenetic TV and radio pace to which Ernie was accustomed, movie making felt like a guilty, easy pleasure. "I change my suit, take five minutes to look at the script, and then play gin rummy with the director. Hours later, they shoot five or six lines and I'm done for the day," he told the *Philadelphia Inquirer*'s Harry Harris. To *New York Herald Tribune* columnist Marie Torre he said, "This is like retirement! While I'm earning a good living—and believe me it's good—I get to the pool every day, play tennis. I look twenty years younger, and I feel like a kid again. They'll never get me back in that grind again." He declared to Torre that he had decided to have nothing to do with weekly TV. "Four or five shows a year would suit me fine," he said. "That way, I could live here in California six months out of the year and continue with picture work. Oh, have I got ideas for movies. I've already made plans to film my book, *Zoomar*. It's great to have the time to plan things."

Despite his flippant description of movie work, Ernie took his acting very seriously. As Captain Paul Lock, he got to play the sort of man he loathed, and he threw himself into the role with gusto. Exploitive of his subordinates, unctuous toward his superiors, the pompous, power-hungry Lock doesn't make a move without consulting his mental rulebook. His office bears a sign reading DO IT NOW AND DO IT RIGHT; his chair is like a gilded throne. He is unimaginative, unyielding, and universally hated within the little world he commands. *Operation Mad Ball* posits gaiety, laughter, and romance as the natural order of things and Captain Paul Lock as an unnatural force that must be overcome.

Operation Mad Ball opened to enthusiastic reviews in the fall on 1957; Ernie's performance in particular was singled out for praise. *Variety* called *Operation Mad Ball* "noteworthy for transferring Kovacs from TV to pictures" and predicted that he would "undoubtedly rate numerous calls for his services in future films." In the *New York Post*, critic Archer Winsten observed, "It is Ernie Kovacs, truant from TV, who stands out as the happiest comic discovery the movies have made since it was proven in England that Alec Guinness could be uproarious merely by acting with utter conviction. That is what Kovacs does." And in the *Saturday Review*, Hollis Alpert wrote, "Arthur Carter's screenplay . . . offers Kovacs the best opportunity he has so far had to display his talents, and maybe the TV boys had better take a look at this movie to see what sort of material he ought to have on the smaller screen."

But the "TV boys" were not going to have the chance to redeem themselves with Kovacs. "I discovered a whole new way of life in Hollywood. It was a great revelation to me," he said. "For the first time in my life I realized that it was possible to make a whole lot of money without working yourself to death."

Ernie finished shooting *Operation Mad Ball* in May 1957. By June he was happily lounging around the duplex back on Central Park West, granting interviews while sprawled across a chaise longue on one of the outdoor terraces, stretched out on an oversize sofa inside, or lying flat on his back on the floor while puffing a cigar. He told everyone how much he loved Hollywood and the relaxing life of a movie star.

"When I first got out there," he described to one journalist, "it upset me to see how they worked. Instead of all getting together to hash over what had been done and to plan the next day's work when that day's work was finished, people would look at their watches and say, 'I'm due at a party at So-and-so's,' or 'I'm going to wander home and lie around the pool,' or something like that. For a couple of days it drove me frantic," he confessed. "But then I fell right into the *mañana* lifestyle. After I'd been there three days, it was different. I'd be sitting out in the sun at the hotel where I was staying, and I'd say to the man from the studio, 'Just put my check under my whiskey sour, so the wind won't blow it away.' "

It wasn't just the casual pace and attitude that appealed to Ernie. The moviemaking experience had caused him to reassess certain values, particularly with regard to his family. "It used to be that even when I was spending time with Edie or our daughters, or when I was supposed to be relaxing and getting away from it, at a party or in the movies or in a nightclub, I'd still be working, looking for material in everything that happened or that anyone said." He recalled telling Bette and Kippie a bedtime story. "I was making [it] up as I went along. I called it 'George and the Little Drop of Water.' Right in the middle of the story," Ernie said, "the thought suddenly occurred to me: 'Why am I wasting this story, it's a wonderful story, instead of wasting it like this, I should be sitting down writing it and making money out of it.' And you know, I started to get up, to go to my typewriter, and I just caught myself in time. What a terrible way to live." (In a few years, however, Ernie would create a lengthy television bit tracing the life of a drop of water.)

Ernie's contract with NBC was up for renewal that June. The network was eager to keep him on, but Ernie raised the stakes impossibly high: his asking price was now a quarter of a million dollars a year. (Jackie Gleason, who had enjoyed far more success in the ratings, was reportedly being paid $100,000 a year by CBS.) There were reports that he was unenthusiastic about another long-term commitment to NBC. Ultimately, he decided to go free-lance, although he told NBC he would be available for guest appearances.

Ernie was now busy fantasizing about a new life, one in which he, Edie, Kippie, and Bette would move to Hollywood for part or all of the year, and he would do movies interspersed with an occasional television project—all strictly on his terms. He told one reporter he'd do "four or five TV shows a year but not as an actor—I'd like to go into producing and writing for television" without the acting responsibilities. To another interviewer he said he wanted to limit his TV work to highly paid guest appearances. "Look, I'm not knocking TV. It's a great paying medium," he said. He had decided that "it doesn't take any genius or brains to be a big success in television. All it takes is a lot of time spent working."

Such fantasies were fine for Ernie, but Edie was still gainfully—and enthusiastically—employed in New York. Her contract for *Li'l Abner* ran until November, and it would have been impossible for her to get out of the hit show any sooner. Besides, Edie was very happy living in Manhattan. She told one reporter, "I did not want to move to California. I love to work in the theater. Ernie loathes the theater, to go to or work in."

Moving to Hollywood, she feared, would plunge her into a languid and glitzy life-style with which she would quickly become discontented. "Ernie loved California with a passion," she said. "My only problem was, I'm a dyed-in-the-wool Easterner." And like most dyed-in-the-wool Easterners, she simply could not take seriously Hollywood and all that it stood for in her mind. In the New York theater world Edie felt grounded, creatively challenged, successful; in a move to California she stood to lose a great deal. Her career was on the rise in New York, and unlike her husband, she had no expressed interest in making films. In New York she could continue to study at the Actors Studio. She was becoming part of the established theatrical community, and she was being offered projects that afforded her terrific visibility. In January 1957, for example, for the American Theater Wing's annual show, she had mounted an act parodying movie stars of the 1930s. Oscar Hammerstein II had caught the act and offered Edie the part of the worldly, practical Fairy Godmother in an updated version of the musical *Cinderella* that he and Richard Rodgers were preparing for prime-time TV. The highly publicized, elegant color show broadcast over the CBS network that March was watched by 25 million households.

Besides these opportunities, the late 1950s was an exhilarating, fast-paced, richly creative period in the history of the Broadway stage. During the time that Edie was performing in *Li'l Abner*, theatergoers could also see Julie Andrews and Rex Harrison in Lerner and Loewe's *My Fair Lady*, Jason Robards and Fredric March in O'Neill's *Long Day's Journey into Night*, and Judy Holliday in Comden and Green's *Bells Are Ringing*. Ethel Merman, Maurice Evans, Cyril Ritchard, and Gwen Verdon were all appearing on Broadway that season; Moss Hart, George Abbott, and José Quintero were directing; plays by Lillian Hellman, Jean Anouilh, and Frank Loesser were being performed. She did not want to leave. In the fall, just before her contract was up, it was reported that Edie had been signed to her first straight dramatic role on Broadway, in Coe Bridges' new drama *The Love Vine*, due to open in February.

Ernie, too, was receiving offers to work on Broadway, as a director. Perhaps because he knew that Edie wanted to remain in theater, he gave serious consideration to some of these projects, including a musical version of *Jekyll and Hyde* and *Solomon Grundy*, a musical comedy about a mad scientist who builds a machine to create a human being with a seven-day life-span. But in truth he was taking a curmudgeonly attitude toward the stage, calling it "overrated" because "there is just as much lousy, mediocre stuff in the theater as there is on television and with less excuse," because "the hour of the theater is all wrong" and it "fouls up the whole evening," and because "the theater is just as bad for the performer as for the audience. If you're in a bomb that closes, it's hardly been worth all the trouble, and if you're in a big hit, it's a long, boring drag." Ultimately he did not accept any of the directing assignments.

Edie's dramatic debut in *The Love Vine* did not come to fruition either, although she was certainly primed for it: her portrayal of Daisy Mae in *Li'l Abner* garnered Edie the Tony Award as best supporting or featured actress in a musical for 1956. "Before the curtain went up on opening night [of *Wonderful Town]* in New Haven," Rosalind Russell had commented a year or two earlier, "I said to her, 'One of these nights, Edie, I'm going to be sitting in the audience in a Broadway theater, and the curtain will come up, and the star will come out on stage, and the star will be you.' I haven't changed my mind. Edith Adams has it, and she's going to be one of the great ones of the Broadway stage, just as Ethel Merman is one of the really great ones." As Edie Adams stood on the stage in April 1957 and accepted her Tony Award along with fellow winners Judy Holliday, Rex Harrison, Margaret Leighton, and Fredric March, it did indeed look as if Russell's prediction was coming true. Sadly— and at least in part because of her marriage to Kovacs— Edie would never fulfill the promise Russell perceived. Her Tony Award triumph would turn out to be the zenith of her Broadway career.

Following the success of "The Silent Show," Ernie had suddenly found himself much in demand as a guest star on television programs. While still under contract to NBC he appeared on such shows as *Tonight! America After Dark* (the replacement for the *Tonight* show, featuring roving reporters and remotes from many cities) and the Emmy Awards telecast. In July, after his contract with NBC expired, he substituted for Ed Sullivan on CBS's *The Ed Sullivan Show.* (When his impending appearance was announced, the program was reportedly deluged with letters requesting a performance by the Nairobi Trio.) By that fall, while marking time waiting for Edie to finish *Li'l Abner*, he was popping up on such light variety programs as *The Perry Como Show* and *The Polly Bergen Show*, sometimes singing a duet with his wife.

Ernie generally put little effort into these assignments; on his *Ed Sullivan Show* appearance, for example, one critic complained that he had merely "warmed over some of his coldest, oldest bits." Guest appearances posed no creative challenge for Ernie, who responded to them as he had to the classes that had bored him in high school. He was accepting these jobs for one reason only—the money—and he readily let everybody know it. "For one guest shot," he explained to the *Philadelphia Inquirer*'s Harry Harris, "I can get 50 percent of what I got for a spectacular. For one guest shot I can get what I earned for nine weeks of *Tonight*. Do six guest shots and you've earned a year's salary. It's much more desirable that way, and much less work."

His need for money became amply clear when he announced his

first permanent commitment after quitting NBC and completing *Operation Mad Ball*. On August 11, 1957, Ernie joined gossip columnist Dorothy Kilgallen, actress Arlene Francis, and publisher Bennett Cerf as a panelist on the Sunday-night quiz show *What's My Line*, which Ernie used to lampoon in his "Where D'ya Worka, John?" skits. He filled the seat vacated by the death of the crusty humorist Fred Allen, earning $750 for each appearance. "It requires no preparation whatsoever," he said. "You go in about a quarter to ten on Sunday, and you're through at eleven. It's not performing. You just sit there. I have no idea how to play the game. If I hit on anybody, it's just pure luck." So casually did he view this job that, although he was supposedly hired as a regular panelist, his agreement with CBS specified that he need appear "only if I'm in town and I feel like it," he said. The first three weeks he preferred to take Edie out to dinner because "you get so little out of being alive; then suddenly one day you wake up and say, 'I wish I'd enjoyed myself more.' Edie and I are enjoying ourselves right now."

Despite his new vows to relax and enjoy life, money was much on Ernie's mind. Around this time he began to complain that taxes and other bureaucratic obligations were leaching his income down to nothing. "On paper, I'm in the big numbers now," he said, "but when you're in the 65 to 67 percent tax bracket, plus state taxes and legal and agent fees, it doesn't seem too much different from the old days. I only made $40 a week in radio, but it was net." It is true that he was in a tax structure that required him to give two-thirds of his income to the government. But it is also true that no matter how much money he made, he always seemed to need more. He assiduously kept this from Edie, feeling it was his duty to shield her from such mundane stresses; whenever she asked whether they could afford something, he'd say, "Don't worry about it. I've got plenty of money put away." But other people noticed his financial worries. "He had just gotten his kids back when I was there," recalls writer Rex Lardner. "He used to tell me stories about going to Florida with his father and looking around for the mother of these kids. And he got terribly in debt with the government because he used tax money to pay private detectives." In fact, in 1955 Ernie had neglected to pay his taxes because he had channeled all his income into the search for Kippie and Bette. He hadn't done it deliberately to deceive the government; he simply didn't have the money when the time came to pay taxes. This debt—and the attendant laissez-faire attitude—would catch up with him later, with more awful consequences than he would have foreseen.

In the fall, he was finally offered a television project that captured his interest. On September 26, 1957, he made his dramatic television debut on the CBS anthology series *Playhouse 90*. Ernie was cast in the title role in *Topaze*, Marcel Pagnol's play about a meek, honorable schoolteacher who becomes a corrupt politician's puppet and, finally, a ruthless powermonger himself. He was excited about the challenge—and sensitive to the fact that some perceived his talents as limited to comedy. "I don't believe there's that much difference between comedy and drama," he declared. "If you can do comedy it means you understand people and are sympathetic. This is essential for drama, too. I saw Maurice Chevalier in *Love in the Afternoon*, and Chevalier, never a dramatic actor, came over great because he has these qualities. But as far as publicity goes—that I'm pulling a 'Pagliacci'—that's just too much. It's a job I want to do, and I've been thinking about it for over a year."

Live dramatic anthologies formed their own large genre in 1950s television programming. *Studio One, Alcoa/Goodyear Theater, The Best of Broadway, The U.S. Steel Hour, Ford Theater, The Motorola TV Theater*, and *The Elgin TV Hour* were among the many series that helped give this period its reputation as the golden age of television drama. Of all the anthologies, however, CBS's high-budgeted *Playhouse 90* is generally considered the most prestigious; it drew some of the best writers, directors, and performers of the era into its fold. In its first season, 1956–57, *Playhouse 90* earned the Emmy Award for best new series of the year (beating out, among others, Ernie's prime-time summer replacement show on NBC). For Ernie, it was a high-profile opportunity to show off his acting muscles, which he had just begun to flex in *Mad Ball* for the first time in almost twenty years.

The producer of *Playhouse 90* was Martin Manulis, who had been Leighton Rollins' assistant back at the Rollins Studio in East Hampton before the war. According to Manulis, Kovacs was cast partly because he had a name; "the name was part of the policy of the shows," he says. "But if he hadn't been good, we certainly would not have cast him in such an important dramatic role. His instincts as an actor were very good. Also, it was kind of the style then to cast comedians in dramatic parts. We had Ed Wynn doing a dramatic role in *Requiem for a Heavyweight*, Mickey Rooney in *The Comedian*, Shirley Jones playing an alcoholic in *The Big Slide*. For the audience, it was refreshing to see. And suddenly we could get people we otherwise wouldn't, because we were offering them roles they didn't otherwise get to play." After the show, Ernie made a sweet gesture to his old friend from summer stock. Manulis recollects that "this was not a time when people gave lavish gifts in television. But Ernie gave me some beautiful cuff links set with topazes."

The critics were divided both on Ernie's performance and on the production as a whole. Jack Gould, writing in the *New York Times*, called the whole show "a wildly infantile shambles"; as for Kovacs, "by now he must be pleading for reinstatement in the Nairobi Trio." But the *New York Herald Tribune*'s Marie Torre had high praise. "Jack-of-all-trades Ernie Kovacs revealed another facet of his manifold talents with an impressive performance in *Topaze*, a gentle French romp," she observed. Calling Kovacs' portrayal "something of a tour-de-force," she added, "*Topaze* is a talky piece with dull stretches which might have become unbearable if not for Kovacs' vivid portrait. His transition from the meek, bullied schoolteach [*sic*] to tyrannical tycoon was accomplished with ease, believability, and a subtle sense of comedy."

Ernie followed up his *Playhouse 90* assignment with a brief return to NBC. On November 10 he appeared, together with many other luminaries, on the network's documentary series *Wide Wide World* in a segment entitled "The Fabulous Infant," which traced the story of network television. He and Edie were engaged in discussions with the British commercial network about doing six weeks of television shows in London, possibly following these up with trips to England every few months to shoot kinescopes ahead of time for a weekly series. But this plan, like so many others, would never come to be. Instead, when Edie's contract with *Li'l Abner* ended that month, she and Ernie accepted a lucrative deal to present a nightclub act at the recently opened Tropicana Hotel in Las Vegas. From their monthlong stop in that gamblers' paradise they would not return to New York but would continue west, to California, their new home.

THE
RAINBOW'S
END

1957 – 1962

Ernie and Edie opened as headliners at the Tropicana Hotel on Las Vegas' burgeoning Strip at the end of November 1957. Kippie and Bette sat in the audience every night watching the show. At the time, Edie said they brought the girls along "mainly to keep Daddy away from the tables." But according to Kippie, "We used to gamble, are you kidding? The pit boss would say, 'Come on, you guys, get out of here'—they knew us so well." She and her sister played the slot machines "just a little bit. It was fun."

The Kovacs-Adams act, a potpourri of sketches and songs, was written by Ernie and framed by Monte Proser's *You Gotta Be in Love* production, about a strawhat troupe on its way to Las Vegas. Ernie presented some of his television characters (Percy Dovetonsils, Skodney Silksky), did a sketch in a Pullman equipped with a private blackjack dealer and Vegas dancer, and tried his hand at some magic tricks. Edie combined serious singing (*Porgy and Bess*) with comic impersonations (Marilyn Monroe's whispery " 'S Wonderful," Marlene Dietrich's "Hey There" in pause-laden German). Together they performed a "Forty Years of Celluloid" sketch as well as the Nairobi Trio, with dancer Neile Adams as the third ape.

The critic for *Variety* felt that the act had potential but that it should have been broken in before they got to the Tropicana, "the biggest of the bigtime." The reviewer reported that "They are as promising a team for saloons, revues or musicals as has come along in many years," but their sketches needed "judicious scissoring" to eliminate overdrawn or otherwise weak portions. "Opening night the show ran 101 minutes and the headliners were on for at least fifty-five minutes. It was obvious that they could be cut a minimum of twenty minutes to their and the show's benefit."

Christmas was spent in Beverly Hills, where the family rented a house at 619 North Canon Drive, in the area south of Sunset Boulevard known as the flatlands. Canon Drive was an unusually wide residential street lined with tall old palm trees and a motley conglomeration of large, well-tended pre- and postwar houses. Like many of its neighbors, the two-story house was of an indeterminate architectural style, its sides partly sheathed in wood siding and beige stone, with two shallow bay windows and such stuck-on decorations as fake shutters and a nonfunctional balcony. "It was a furnished house other people would just die for, but they hated it because it was not in very good taste," remembers Kippie.

Unlike winter holidays in New York, where the girls could go ice-skating and play in the snow, Christmas in these California flatlands was hot and foreign. Even the Christmas tree seemed alien and phony; provided courtesy of Columbia Pictures, "It was a horrible white tree with pink balls," recalls Elisabeth. "I hated it." For a few months she and her sister attended a public school nearby, where Kippie was teased about her weight. "In childhood I was always too fat, and I was constantly reminded of that by Edie and by my classmates. And also I was very introverted, extremely shy. I hated that school especially. But she was just looking for a private school to get us into, to be 'educated' correctly—proper manners and all that jazz."

While Edie was searching for a private school, Ernie began work on his second film, *Bell, Book and Candle.* The John van Druten comedy, a hit on Broadway, was being brought to the screen by producer Julian Blaustein (*The Day the Earth Stood Still*) and Oscar-winning screenwriter Daniel Taradash (*From Here to Eternity*), whose independent production company had a financing deal with Columbia Pictures. The partners hired Richard Quine to direct the picture and cast Kim Novak as the melancholy witch who falls in love with a handsome publisher, played by James Stewart.

Ernie was set to play Sidney Redlitch, a bourbon-swizzling author of best sellers about witchcraft. "As I recall, he was the only choice for the part," says Julian Blaustein. "He didn't look to me as if he were a trained actor. He was an instinctive actor, very intelligent—a clown. But anybody who thought the clowning around was all there was would be wrong. Very sweet man, I never saw him angry." Kovacs dropped from the third billing he had received in *Operation Mad Ball* to fourth billing here, underneath Stewart, Novak, and Jack Lemmon, who was to play Novak's warlock brother. (There was also a cameo by jazz musician Pete Candoli, who would become Edie Adams' third husband in 1972.)

Quine agreed that Ernie was "an intuitive actor. He was an extremely sensitive man, and everything I ever worked on with him, he required very little direction. He was always quick to find that extra little schtick." For his entrance, Ernie was supposed to come into Jimmy Stewart's office after having waited in an outer room. "I didn't tell Jimmy—we were just going to rehearse it—but I told Ernie, 'When the secretary tells you to go in, just walk in talking. Start before you get through the door, no hellos, nothing, just start talking.' And he grabbed it like a hungry trout. Stewart looked so astonished at this absurd entrance, it cracked him up."

Though Sidney Redlitch is a peripheral character, Ernie makes the most of his limited time on-screen. Redlitch is defined by the nature of his books, his physical appearance, and his body language. His volume *Magic in Mexico*, comments Kim Novak, was "completely phony," but James Stewart points out that it "sold like the Kinsey report"; the author is a crackpot, but he knows what the public wants, and this makes him valuable. Visually, everything about Redlitch is rumpled and wrong-sized. His mustache hasn't been trimmed in months, his hair looks like a tornado swept through it, his clothes fit poorly and the patterns clash; he slouches when he stands and slops over the sides of the chair when he sits. To play against his outrageous appearance, Ernie gives Redlitch an unexpectedly subdued temperament and a quiet voice. He speaks very little, mostly to ask for another drink or to make witless attempts at jokes. (When Stewart says, "Keep in touch," Ernie responds with a chuckle, "I'll touch you for an advance—ha, ha, that's a play on words.") He makes an earthy, messy contrast to his sleek publisher, whom *New York Times* critic Bosley Crowther described as James Stewart playing "himself, highly lacquered."

"John van Druten had described this character who was like an un-made bed, and Ernie built on that," explains producer Julian Blaustein. "This character was already a sight gag when he walked into the room, with the hair in disarray and the disheveled clothes and the cigar. And always drinking but never really drunk." Blaustein recollects that Ernie "had pretty free rein" in creating the character rather than being given precise instruction by Richard Quine. "My memory of Dick is that he was not that kind of director," recalls Blaustein. "A very easygoing guy, very sensitive, fully understanding of the script."

Tall, balding, soft-spoken, and thirteen years Kim Novak's senior, sweet-tempered Richard Quine had directed the actress in her first feature film, *Pushover*, in 1954, when she was twenty-one. They would eventually carry on a romance for several years, with the Hollywood gossip columnists periodically querying them about marriage and No-vak tossing off cryptic comments like, "This is romance and this is friendship, but who knows where it will go?" Through her relationship with Quine, Novak was drawn into Ernie's sphere of friends in Hollywood.

Bell, Book and Candle is an intensely pleasurable film to watch. Every image is rich and gorgeous, from Novak in her perfect Jean Louis outfits to the homburg that James Stewart tosses off a skyscraper in wintertime Manhattan, the camera following its joyful arc all the way to the ground. But the movie received mixed reviews when it opened in the winter of 1958. At the center of a potentially captivating story, Novak gave a bloodless performance that was universally panned. Most of the other elements were praised, however, including Ernie's portrayal, which *Variety* called "a comedy standout." The paper's prediction of "good b.o. [box office] despite bad miscasting of Kim Novak" proved to be correct.

Upon completing *Bell, Book and Candle*, Ernie packed up his family again and returned to Las Vegas. He and Edie were due to replace headliners Jayne Mansfield and Mickey Hargitay, the actress' muscleman husband, in producer Monte Proser's *Tropicana Holiday* revue on April 15. They arrived in time to celebrate Easter Sunday on April 6; Barbara Quine, Richard Quine's wife, accompanied them on the trip. (In May the Quines announced that they would separate.)

This second Las Vegas engagement blended sketches from the Mansfield-Hargitay act, material that Ernie and Edie had already tried out in November, and some new material written by Ernie, including a skit in which Edie played a waitress trying to impress movie producer Kovacs. She scored with her impersonation of Jayne Mansfield's own satirical creation, the flashy sexpot movie star Trixie Devoon. They were backed by a dance troupe that included a young George Chakiris.

This time, the stay in Las Vegas went on and on. The Kovacses moved into the Tropicana, and the girls were enrolled for three months in a local public school where "there were bats in the hallway," remembers Kippie. When Ernie wasn't working, he was gambling his earnings away. "We had to walk through the casino, and as a gambler it was like giving a drunk a walk through the hooch plant," said Edie. One night, in a streak of luck, he won $2,000; he happily decided to present the money to Edie as part of a down payment for a new house in Los Angeles. The next night, hoping to win again, he lost the $2,000 and a great deal more. "It was a terrible sensation," Ernie later said. "I got deeper and deeper in hock and all I could think of was that I had to keep playing to get it back for Edie. Of course I didn't. It was breakfast time when I quit—very tired, very unhappy, very broke."

Much later he told his wife, "I lost a lot of money." "Well, how much and where are the commas?" she wanted to know. Laughing, he confessed, "I think it was $10,000." "So," said Edie, "I went out and bought myself a chinchilla coat for exactly the same amount. And then he'd gamble and I'd find out again. I bought a harpsichord, and he said, 'Well, we can't afford that.' And I said, 'Well, then stop gambling. It's very simple.' " But he could never stop entirely. "He would sort of reduce it down," described Edie. "And now that I know about it—I've read all the books on gambling—it's something that you don't say, 'Stop.' It's like to a drunk you don't say, 'Stop drinking.' It's a psychological problem. It's, I guess, a self-destructive thing, it's just a little slower. So instead of taking these big poker games he would do gin games, and they were still pretty big games, but he really couldn't help it."

For the final night of the show, Kippie and Bette, who had taken voice and tap dance lessons in New York, were to perform in the act. Kippie planned to do Marilyn Monroe singing " 'S Wonderful," costumed in Edie's fur stole, while Bette would imitate Marlene Dietrich singing "Hey There," wearing Edie's trench coat and slouch hat. "We watched the act and learned from her," explains Kippie. The girls did their imitations, and then Ernie and Edie joined them so they could all sing "Inchworm" together. "It was so beautiful, all of us together on-stage, I started to cry," Elisabeth remembers.

On March 26, just before leaving for Las Vegas, Ernie and Edie had bought a house in Beverly Hills. Located at 2301 Bowmont Drive, a narrow, winding street deep in the hills surrounding Coldwater Canyon, the $62,000 purchase made them the neighbors of Frank Sinatra, Charlton Heston, and Peggy Lee. If the duplex on Central Park West had been an exaggeration of the lavish Manhattan life-style, the Bowmont house represented casual Southern California living on its grandest scale. The facade was modest enough, California ranch style done in whitewashed brick and white columns, with diamond-paned windows to let in the morning light from the east. But from the front door to the northern end of the lot, the house rambled on and on: a big living room and a smaller family room and an office and a lanai, a formal dining room and a breakfast room and a kitchen, bedrooms for Kippie and Bette, a master bedroom suite with its own bath and two dressing rooms.

Next to the driveway was the garage that Ernie would eventually turn into his private den. Down at the end of the steep rise on which the house was set, a dense, high hedge and an electronically controlled wrought-iron gate provided privacy befitting a movie star's household.

In the back was the requisite pool, and beyond the house was a large roller-skating rink. One day, inspired by the signs on Mr. Toad's Wild Ride at Disneyland, the girls decided to paint the rink's white walls with signs saying things like GO BACK. "My sister instigated the idea," Kippie says. "We were alone for some reason at home, which was truly a rarity because of the fear that my real mother would come back." They were painting their signs when they heard their father's car drive up, and they hid. "I didn't know what we had done, but I knew it was wrong," Kippie recalls. "My dad was just scared to death. He went out and saw all this weird painting and thought we had been kidnapped." Finally they came out from where they were hiding. "He was furious because we had scared the hell out of him. But he could never stay mad. Actually, he was grateful that we were okay. When our father was alive, our biggest punishment was one week of not watching Andy Hardy."

Because Ernie had to have the best of everything for himself and his family, the house was soon expanded. "We would need a new kitchen and wind up with a new steam room," remembered Edie Adams. "Another time we needed a new hot water system. We got a Japanese garden with a waterfall built into the hillside." The rooms were quickly filled with a distinctive combination of Ernie's electronic gadgets and Edie's antiques. "I'm just one of those guys who has to have everything new that comes along," Ernie said. "Edie is just the opposite. She's got to have everything antique." The house was remodeled so much that he lost track of how many rooms it had. By 1961 the residence was widely reported to be worth $600,000.

Mary Kovacs, Ernie's mother, moved to California too; the house Ernie had bought for her in New City was given to Andrew, Ernie's father. Mary lived for a period with Ernie, Edie, and the children at the Coldwater Canyon house, but her relationship with Edie was perpetually strained. At one point Edie's mother, Ada Enke, moved in as well. "She was a schoolteacher, and she did not like us," remembers Kippie. Nor did she like Mary; when they clashed—which was virtually all the time—they were "just hell on wheels," Kippie says. "It was a battle every night to see who got to cook in the kitchen. They were both strong old women." Eventually Ada Enke returned to the East, and Ernie obtained an apartment for Mary in Hollywood.

Once he was settled in, Ernie threw himself into his new, relaxed California life-style. "I don't think I could take it, to live in Manhattan again," he declared to one New York reporter. "I couldn't stand to be so closed in. I've discovered space." He announced that he was glad to have left behind the formality of Manhattan, glad to be rid of the burden of dressing every night for dinner and being attended by a butler and a cook and a private taxi driver. To Hedda Hopper he raved, "I lost thirty-five pounds after I came here. Now when I get home tired after the movie day, we toss some steaks on the barbecue and sit around in sports things while they sizzle." Before long, however, he would hire another butler, a cook, a private secretary, and others to care for him and his family in California. And now that he had severed all ties with the networks, he had gained freedom to pursue whatever work he wished but also had lost a structure that sustained him. Personally and professionally, his life in Hollywood would take on an increasingly erratic shape.

Ernie's next movie took him to New England with his buddies Jack Lemmon and Richard Quine. As in his first film, he was back to playing a villain: Harry Foster Malone, "the Meanest Man in the World." Originally titled *That Jane from Maine* but eventually released as *It Happened to Jane*, the film starred Doris Day as Jane Osgood, a feisty New England widow who runs a mail-order lobster business, and Jack Lemmon as a principled but passive lawyer who's in love with her. Richard Quine both produced and directed. As the ruthless railroad baron Malone, Ernie again provides a pivot for the movie's action. When Jane sues his railroad for having allowed one of her lobster shipments to perish, she sets off a rancorous battle that forms the core of the story.

In homage to Orson Welles, makeup artist Clay Campbell used Charles Foster Kane, the newspaper magnate of *Citizen Kane*, as a visual model for Harry Foster Malone. Although Ernie had refused to shave his mustache for *Operation Mad Ball* and *Playhouse 90*, he now shaved his whole head. (The mustache stayed, as did the oversize cigar, which he brandished throughout the movie like a scepter.) That June Ernie was shorn at a Seventh Avenue barbershop in New York, an event that was touted as a "photo opportunity" by the film's publicists and was even made into a promotional short and screened on the *Today* show. In July, while making the movie, he appeared on *The Ed Sullivan Show* wearing his Harry Foster Malone makeup and conducting an entire orchestra of Nairobi apes.

To render his already large frame even more imposing, Ernie gained forty pounds. His newly heavy and hairless look "was really upsetting to me," says Kippie Kovacs. "I was devastated by the way he looked;

it wasn't my father. Besides, he had a weight problem all his life, and that was all he needed. He was always dieting. And he was very strict when it came to doing a movie. He would not drink any alcohol, and he would barely eat."

Most of the movie was shot on location in Chester, Connecticut, which doubled for the fictional Maine small town in which the story was set. Ernie, Richard Quine, and Jack Lemmon roomed together in a seventeenth-century house with oak-beamed ceilings. "At three o'clock every afternoon, Dick Quine would let us off for the day—whether Columbia ever found out I don't know," said Steve Forrest, who played Jane's virile newspaper boyfriend in the film. "There was a beautiful trout stream nearby, and the trout were absolutely teeming. So most of us would go trout-fishing. Jack wouldn't. He would go home and play the piano." Lemmon had had an electronic piano with earphones installed so that his playing would not disturb his housemates.

One of the most interesting aspects of this minor film is its perceptiveness about how powerful television was becoming in the formation of popular opinion. In Norman Katkov's screenplay (based on a story by Katkov and Max Wilk), the frustrated Jane finally decides to publicize her case against Harry Foster Malone on the airwaves. For these scenes, Jane appears on real television shows of the day, and there are cameos by such contemporary TV personalities as Bess Myerson, Jayne Meadows, Garry Moore, Henry Morgan, Betsy Palmer, and Gene Rayburn. Jane is questioned on *Youth Wants to Know*, an NBC public affairs show in which teen-agers interrogated newsmakers. She is interviewed by Dave Garroway in the middle of Times Square. She even pops up as a mystery guest on *I've Got a Secret*, her secret being "I'm Fighting the Meanest Man in the World." (Asked by a panelist whether the thing she is fighting is human, she responds, "He most certainly is not." "Well then," the next panelist queries, "is he a baboon or a snake?")

Whereas Ernie grounded his portrayals of Captain Lock and Sidney Redlitch in comic realism, he plays Harry Foster Malone as a deliberate burlesque of the old-time capitalistic robber baron. Constantly surrounded by yes-men, pretty women, and servants, all of whom he treats like faceless slaves, the loathsome Malone barks and snarls and threatens and insults his way through the film. He is a railroad-magnate cartoon, stepping to the sound of "I've Been Working on the Railroad," a patriotic red-white-and-blue train decorating his boardroom, his bedroom a luxuriously upholstered replica of a Pullman sleeper. Once again Ernie uses his whole body to convey the character, slouching like a

Percy Dovetonsils.

e Nairobi Trio.

Helping Bette (left) and Kippie put the final touches on a jack-o'-lantern in the early 1950s.

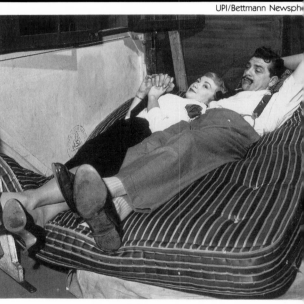

Wirephotos of Kippie (top) and Bette were published in newspapers when they were kidnapped by their mother in 1953.

Backstage with Edie at DuMont, just after their Mexico C wedding, 1954.

formal family dinner at Central Park West, 1957.

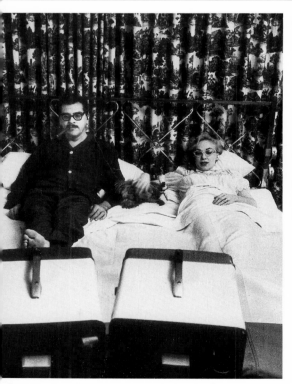

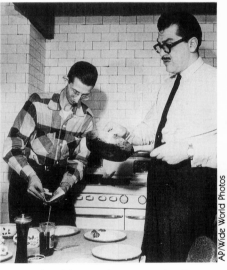

Fixing breakfast with Lou Pack, the Kovacses' private cab driver, at home in New York in 1956.

AP/Wide World Photos

their New York duplex, Ernie and Edie kept twin TV at the foot of their bed.

Preparing to play "the Meanest Man in the World" in the 1959 film It Happened to Jane, with costar Jack Lemmon.

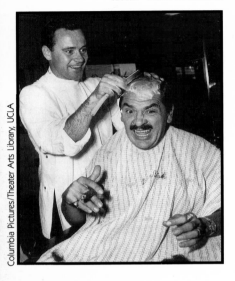

Edie and Ernie's Las Vegas nightclub act, 1958.

Dressed as a germ for an ABC special, with Jolene Brand, 1961.

As the martinet Captain Paul Lock in his 1957 f... debut, Operation Mad Ball, with Jack Lemmon ... Kathryn Gra...

OFFICER'S

THE ROAD TO YESTERDAY

...roducing Silents Please from the den
...his home, 1961.

As the boozy writer Sidney Redlitch in the
1958 movie Bell, Book and Candle, with
...rom left) Elsa Lanchester, Jack Lemmon,
Kim Novak, James Stewart.

Romancing Cyd Charisse in the 1961
black comedy Five Golden Hours.

With Jo
Morrow
and Alec
Guinness in
the 1960
thriller
Our Man in
Havana.

Playing poker in Hollywood (clockwise from left): Jerry Gershwin, Tony Curtis, Milton Berle, Kovacs, Billy Wilder, Dean Martin.

With Edie and newborn Mia Susan in June 1959.

With (clockwise from left) Edie, Kippie, Bette, and Mia in his Coldwater Canyon den, 1961.

the Forest Lawn funeral, Edie (center) is flanked by her
ther, Ada Enke, and Andrew Kovacs, Ernie's father.

acs' gardenia-covered coffin is taken from church by (clockwise from left) Jack Lemmon,
rvyn LeRoy, Joe Mikolas, a funeral director, Frank Sinatra, Billy Wilder, Dean Martin,
cond funeral director.

Ernie Kovacs.

moral slob as he walks, gesticulating regally with his cigar to claim space for himself, doing a funny, tortured twist when he finally forces himself to be nice to Jane.

At the end, however, Malone is made to go through an inexplicable change of heart, as bizarrely off-key as if Mr. Potter had suddenly taken a liking to George Bailey in *It's a Wonderful Life*. And the film overall, while enjoyable, is ultimately too saccharine to be believable. Despite these flaws, most of the critics responded positively when the movie opened in the summer of 1959. Ernie's farcical performance was consistently, if briefly, complimented; *Variety* called his scenes "skits of considerable humor." The audiences seemed to know better than the critics; *It Happened to Jane* was a box-office disappointment both in its first run and in its 1961 reissue (with a new title, *Twinkle and Shine*).

Edie Adams' career slowed down considerably once the family moved to Hollywood. In 1958 she performed only occasionally, appearing with Ernie in *Showdown at Ulcer Gulch*, a promotional short for the *Saturday Evening Post* featuring Bing Crosby, Chico and Groucho Marx, and Bob Hope, and playing a nightclub dancer down on her luck in "If I Die Before I Live," an episode of NBC's *Suspicion* series. "As long as somebody was making the money, I didn't care who it was," she told an interviewer in 1981. "He was making a lot of money, so I had nothing to worry about."

But at the time Edie seemed to relish the idea of making good money of her own. Having left the theater behind, she was reassessing her attitude toward television series work, which presented lucrative possibilities. "I never thought much of doing a TV series," Edie said to Marie Torre of the *New York Herald Tribune* that February. "Then, a while back I spoke with Jackie Cooper, who has a series of his own, and you might say I had an awakening. Jackie told me the kind of money he will make from the re-runs, here and abroad, and it staggered me. I never would have believed it. Jackie says that for the first time in his life he has security, and he owes it all to his TV series."

Other than working as a singer on *The Jack Paar Show*, Edie had never done any series work without Ernie. (Indeed, her TV career was so associated with her husband's that television listings often included a parenthetical "Mrs. Kovacs" after her name during the 1950s.) With her new openness toward TV, however, she was discussing a possible series with CBS and Hal Roach Studios. "We're almost set to begin work on the pilot film," she said to Torre. "I like it because it would give me a chance to sing and do comedy." But the only series assignment she would get for a long while was a short summer replacement for NBC's *The Dinah Shore Chevy Show*. While her husband worked on *It Happened to Jane*, Edie joined John Raitt and Janet Blair as the musical hosts of *The Chevy Show*, emanating from NBC's Burbank Studios. The comedy was supplied by Stan Freberg and the young team of Dan Rowan and Dick Martin; George Schlatter, who later produced *Laugh-In*, booked the show's talent.

In September, Ernie and Edie celebrated their fourth wedding anniversary in New York. They were spotted dancing and chatting their way across the floor at the Club Mocambo, Ernie's hair just beginning to grow in, his breast pocket crammed with a battery of plump cigars. The next month there was good news in the family: thirty-one-year-old Edie was pregnant. "My production this year was the baby," she later told Ken McCormick, Ernie's editor at Doubleday.

With a new baby on its way, Ernie went into a frenzy of work. During the first quarter of 1959 he performed in several network anthology shows, guest-starred on CBS's *The Jack Benny Show* (sharing his collection of mustaches with Benny), and acted as ringmaster on ABC's *High Spots of "The Greatest Show on Earth,"* a televised version of the Ringling Bros. and Barnum & Bailey Circus. He groused about the latter: "Every time I go to the circus, things happen to me—all bad. I buy a miniature chameleon. It dies. I buy my kids some cotton candy. It sticks to my clothes. I buy a whip. It breaks. I buy balloons. They burst." He hadn't taken his daughters to a circus for three years, he claimed, and the thing he had liked best about that one was "the end."

The majority of the dramatic anthology roles were uninspiring, done primarily for the money: an old miner in "The Salted Mine" (a pilot for a projected Western series to be titled *Shotgun)* on *Schlitz Playhouse;* a private eye attempting to find a kidnapped elephant with his powers of smell in "I Was a Bloodhound" on *G.E. Theater.* Only one of these parts really challenged his acting abilities. In February he starred in Ernest Kinoy's "Symbol of Authority" on CBS's *Westinghouse Desilu Playhouse*, playing the meek proofreader Arthur Witten. Arthur leads a cramped, repressed existence; his life acquires a much-needed purpose when he purchases a stethoscope at a pawnshop and pretends to be a doctor. "Everything about Arthur breaks the heart just a little. His innocent pleasure in strolling the hospital corridors on his day off, his $3 stethoscope around his neck, only endears him to us further," wrote Harriet Van Horne in the *New York World-Telegram and Sun*. "By stern critical standards it was a trite story, watered-down Walter Mitty at best. But Ernie Kovacs made the little proofreader a dear and lovable fellow."

In the midst of making these guest appearances, Ernie was preparing for his next film role. After moving to Hollywood he told one reporter, "We don't read scripts. We read locations. It's great." But he regarded the location of this new project as less than "great"—indeed, as worrisome. He was scheduled to shoot in Cuba, which had just undergone a revolution.

Kovacs' new film project was *Our Man in Havana*, a melancholy satire starring Alec Guinness as a Cuban-based vacuum cleaner salesman who becomes entangled with the British secret service. Ernie was cast as the cold-blooded Captain Segura, a Batista-regime head of the political police who carries a cigarette case of human skin and is known as the Red Vulture. Graham Greene had adapted the screenplay from his own 1958 novel. Carol Reed was producing as well as directing, under the banner of his newly formed Kingsmead Productions, and Columbia Pictures would release the film.

Best known for his atmospheric, skillfully plotted thrillers and dramas, the London-born Reed was a meticulous worker with a keen eye for detail and tremendous powers of concentration. He and Greene had already collaborated successfully on *The Third Man* and *The Fallen Idol* and had spent two weeks in 1958 scouting locations in Havana for their new film. The region's growing political unrest, however, had forced them to find backup locations in Spain, and when Fidel Castro's small band of bearded guerillas toppled the dictatorship of General Fulgencio Batista in January 1959, the decision about whether to shoot in Cuba was still up in the air. Indeed, the commitment to go ahead to Havana was not made until the beginning of March, six weeks before the shoot's scheduled startup.

There was no time to waste. On March 13 production headquarters were established at Havana's Hotel Capri, which Alec Guinness has described as "very gilded." Sound and lighting equipment, cameras, and film stock had to be shipped into Cuba from London and New York; a wardrobe had to be created; the police force, labor union, and increasingly powerful Artists' Syndicate had to be met with; and dozens of matters of logistics had to be worked out. After Reed and the cast arrived in mid-April, the production team adhered to a rigid six-day-a-week schedule (Reed arranged for tea to be served on the set twice a day). At the end of the day, the work was not yet over, for there was so much ambient noise on the streets that synchronized voice recordings had to be made each evening in a local studio. All this was accomplished in the wet swelter of spring in the tropics, where temperatures reached the nineties by midmorning and worsened under the intense heat of the movie lights.

While the rest of the cast flew in from various locations, Ernie took a train from Los Angeles to New Orleans and from there made the hop to the Cuban capital. He had developed a hatred of flying and avoided it as much as possible, says his daughter Elisabeth: "He was afraid of it. It reminded him of his own mortality." Kovacs found the old, familiar Havana in an ecstatic uproar. "The city was full of excitement and chaos. Rich American businessmen were withdrawing rapidly, and there were no tourists," remembered Alec Guinness. "Men in the streets would often stop us, pull up a trouser leg to show scars from electric shock torture inflicted by Batista's police, and then laugh, saying, '*Viva Fidel!*'"

During the day, the hot streets of Old Havana were dotted with stands bursting with ripe papayas, mangoes, and bananas and with carts piled high with exotic flowers—golden acacias, white *diamelas*, red-and-black *pensamientos*. In the warm evenings, Habañeros strolled the seawall along the Malecon, music wafting out of nearby hotels. Underneath the gaiety, however, lurked a frightening violence. "My father was deeply concerned during that film because of the takeover," remembers Elisabeth. Guinness recalled that "what looked like tumbrils made their slow way through the streets; they were in fact farm carts or battered lorries with cages of chicken-wire imprisoning shocked and puzzled peasants on their way to be interrogated." Everyone seemed to be carrying firearms, and hundreds of executions were being carried out.

Nervous over Havana's political unrest, anxious about working in the illustrious and potentially stuffy company of the English (the cast also included Noel Coward and Ralph Richardson), Ernie reverted to outrageous schoolboy behavior. Journalist Robert Emmett Ginna, who visited the set for *Holiday* magazine, reported that when he wasn't on camera Ernie "was every instant the jolly joker of his television fame." "The first day Ernie and I worked together," described Guinness, "he deliberately got his head stuck in the clapper-board, kept up a hilarious, foul-mouthed commentary on all who were watching, and I thought, 'Oh, hell! This is going to be an endless music-hall turn and we shall never complete the film.' And it was exhausting." Carol Reed "was tolerantly amused, which is more than some directors would have been" by such shenanigans.

But as Kovacs relaxed and his frenzy diminished, Guinness came to grow "very fond" of him, finding him rash and extroverted and, "in a Goonish way, just about the funniest man I ever met." (BBC radio's comedic *Goon Show* had spawned such talents as Peter Sellers.) For Ernie's part, his daughter Elisabeth recalls, "he *loved* Alec Guinness"; he especially admired the British actor's subtle sense of humor, which he told one interviewer was "better than innuendo." The unlikely pair often went for walks together, making stops at Havana's countless bars. "One evening," remembered Guinness, "I was touched when he suddenly said, 'You know something? I was dreading working with all you toffee-nosed Brits: *Sir* Carol Reed, *the* Noel Coward, *Sir* Guinness. There'll never be a laugh, I thought; but you're the ones who laugh with me—not all those American broads and clapped-out bores.' "

Ernie's hotel suite was on the same floor as Alec and Merula Guinness's, whose suite resembled "an ante-chamber at the court of Louis XVI." One afternoon the actor was walking down the corridor when he noticed that Ernie's door was open. "He was sitting at a desk typing furiously, a vast cigar jammed in his face," described Guinness. "He spotted me and waved in a 'I'm terribly busy' way, but somehow I sensed it wasn't quite real. Then I noticed there were about half a dozen lovely girls, all totally naked, sprawled about the room reading magazines."

Guinness tactfully asked, "Shall I shut your door?" "No! For heaven's sake! What would people say?" Ernie responded. "They'd say Kovacs is in that room with a bunch of naked broads. And they'd think the worst. With the door open they can see for themselves it's all perfectly innocent." Alec Guinness later recounted the story to Jane Hess, Ernie's old friend from East Hampton summer stock. "What he'd done was hired a whole lot of girls just to take their clothes off and sit around the room," says Hess.

Initially Ernie's role required that he grow a beard. In Castro's new regime, facial hair was regarded as a badge of revolutionary fellowship. When he first appeared in the streets, a buzz ran through the crowds. A little boy called excitedly, *"Miren a Ernie el barbudo! El es uno de los nuestros!"* ("Look at Ernie the bearded one! He's one of us!") But the government intervened, declaring that only heroes, not villains, could wear beards in the Cuban capital. To play the Batista officer, Kovacs was required to shave.

Ernie told one reporter that he liked strutting about in the blue uniform of the despised Batista police. "Especially crossing streets," he said. "Stopped traffic both ways. It was great fun until I found myself staring into an automatic rifle with the safety catch clicked open by the bearded soldier behind it. 'Movie! Movie!' I started shouting and gesturing. After that I never left the set without two guards." It was in fact dangerous for Ernie to be impersonating a Batista sympathizer, for these people were being imprisoned and executed daily. Kippie Kovacs remembers her visit to the set clearly: "That was the heavy-duty one. My dad dressed up in a uniform, and we were in a car with him. People were throwing rocks at the car. I believe this particular visit was cut short because of that."

Despite his off-camera antics, Ernie "showed himself on camera to be a professional who could perform in this league," observed *Holiday*'s Robert Emmett Ginna. During a crucial nightclub scene in which Captain Segura is doused with a siphon by Maureen O'Hara, Ernie demonstrated utter professionalism as Reed ordered retake after retake. "Between each take he had to take his uniform jacket off and put on a spare while the other was dried and pressed," described Ginna. "He was patient, but director Reed was not enchanted with the accuracy of the attack. He stood there, hands behind his back, rhythmically clenching his teeth."

Finally Reed got the shot to his satisfaction. Finished for the day, Ernie went off to change, then returned to say good-bye to his fellow actors, taking a seat off-camera. "Softly," wrote Ginna, "Sir Carol ordered it to roll, and out of nowhere a huge stream of water smote the freshly dressed Mr. Kovacs, who leaped to his feet with a bellow." Reed's camera captured the authentic surprise on the faces of his performers, which had been his goal. "Very nice, Ernest," the director said, "hope you didn't mind; I needed that reaction, you know. You were first-rate."

In Greene's novel Captain Segura is a shadowy background figure. By his existence and his power he affects people's actions, but he only occasionally appears in person. (One notable exception is a long scene that later became well known from the movie, in which the vacuum cleaner salesman tries to get Segura drunk in a game of checkers played with little bottles of bourbon and Scotch; whenever one of the men captures a piece, he must drink its contents.) Greene enlarged the role in his screenplay, but it seems to make no difference. Perhaps told by Carol Reed to play the threatening role with restraint, Ernie holds back so much that he establishes little on-screen presence for his murderous police captain. During interrogations, his words promise danger but he does not; trying to seduce a woman, he flounders, mechanical and unconvincing. (Alec Guinness, on the other hand, communicates flirtation magnificently with no dialogue, using just his eyes and face.) Kovacs' emotional tenor never changes; he conveys the Latin's rigidly controlled surface but not the complexities behind it. (He also affects an accent that is more Eastern European than Cuban.) When the film opened in January 1960, the critics saw it as a chilling portrayal, but this may be more because of what the other characters say about Segura, the way they must bend to his authority, than because of Ernie's performance, which was the weakest he would ever give in a film.

The location shooting for *Our Man in Havana* was completed in May, but another, longer shoot, for studio interiors, was scheduled to begin shortly in London. Before traveling to England, however, Ernie returned to Los Angeles. He had been offered a new television project to produce: a prime-time special for his old parent network, NBC.

In order to mount this new special, Ernie was given a lavish budget, plenty of rehearsal time, creative freedom, and a choice prime-time slot, on a Friday night, May 22, from 8:00 to 9:00. For the first time, he would shoot ahead on tape, giving him total control over the final product. He decided to take as his theme a favorite subject—music— and invent many variations around it, calling the program *Kovacs on Music.* In its structure, quality, and level of ambition, *Kovacs on Music* anticipated the highly polished half-hour specials he would produce at ABC in his final years.

Ernie enlisted Shirley Mellner and his director friend Barry Shear, who had also moved to Los Angeles, to work on the new special. With André Previn as musical director, Ernie cast himself, Edie, James Darren, double-talking Al Kelly, and Louis Jourdan. (Shear ingeniously shot Edie so as to camouflage her eight-month pregnancy.) Ernie produced it under his and Edie's new E. & E. K. Enterprises banner in association with NBC. He also wrote it, creating a minutely detailed script that mixed blackouts and longer sketches—all relating to the subject of music—with musical numbers and dance.

Unlike his earlier shows, where he had eschewed rehearsal in favor of flying by the seat of his pants, Ernie now used his rehearsal time to try everything over and over again until it was perfect. On the last day before shooting, he and the rest of the cast wound up a long day of practice at the NBC lot in Burbank. Ernie, Edie, Shirley Mellner, and Barry Shear decided to walk over to the big studio where André Previn was rehearsing. "We walked in, and there was André Previn with a sixty-piece orchestra," remembers Mellner. "We looked at it and we looked at each other, and Ernie said, 'This smells like big time.' And we sat down on the floor—there were big mats there—and we cried."

In *Kovacs on Music*, Ernie undertakes to "explain" every facet of music he could think of, from Tchaikovsky's *Swan Lake* ballet (performed with utmost grace by a corps of gorillas in tutus) to the origins of song (with Ernie and Edie as Urg and Ula Cro-Magnon and James Darren as Urg, Jr., who suddenly breaks into "Gidget" in the middle of the prehistoric sketch). Ernie's opening monologue sets the tone: "I have never really understood classical music, so I would like to take this hour to explain it to others. There most certainly should be a definite place in television for this type of program, as I have a crying need for money."

The special is filled with Kovacs' trademark irreverence:

TITLE "KOVACS ON MUSIC" . . . MAN'S FEET STOMP ON A STRADI-VARIUS . . . SIGN NEXT TO DEMOLISHED VIOLIN: "$25,000"

ERNIE INTRODUCES AL KELLY AS PROFESSOR OF MUSIC . . . KELLY BABBLES ABOUT MUSIC IN DOUBLE-TALK . . . EXPLAINS WAGNER . . . TOTALLY UNINTELLIGIBLE . . . ERNIE LISTENS AND NODS SERIOUSLY

ERNIE IN AN OLD BED, WEARING PAJAMAS AND COVERED WITH A QUILT . . . "ALL THE SHOWS TODAY ARE SO CASUAL. WE TRIED TO GET A ROCKING CHAIR OR A STOOL, BUT CROSBY AND COMO HAVE RENTED THEM ALL FOR THE YEAR"

He also utilizes some electronic tricks:

THE BIRTH OF "CHOPSTICKS" . . . DANCERS JUMP AROUND ON GIGANTIC PIANO . . . CHASE EACH OTHER AROUND GIANT OLIVE AND GLASS . . . ONE DANCES WITH GIANT PAPER CLIP . . . ANOTHER CLIMBS INTO A SANDWICH . . . ERNIE AT PIANO TAKES A BITE OUT OF SANDWICH

ERNIE ELEGANT IN WHITE TAILS . . . PACES BACK AND FORTH AS HE SPEAKS . . . WHEN HE CROSSES MIDDLE OF SET, TAILS TURN BLACK . . . RECROSSES AND TAILS TURN WHITE

EDIE SINGS VILLA-LOBOS' "BACHIANAS BRASILEIRAS NO. 5" ACCOM-PANIED BY EIGHT CELLOS . . . CELLOS APPEAR MATTED INTO PIC-

TURE WITH EDIE . . . VIA ELECTRONIC SWITCHER, THEY SEEM TO
UNDULATE TO MUSIC, AS IF GIVING VISUAL FORM TO THEIR MUSICAL
VIBRATIONS

Not all of Ernie's ideas for *Kovacs on Music* were carried out, probably because of budget and time limitations. For the opening titles, he
envisioned an elaborate sequence shot from a helicopter, with the camera
zooming in and out on the credits as they were painted onto the side
of a building by several men with paint rollers. He also wrote a sketch
that would have engagingly mixed live action and animation, in which
Ernie and Edie's heads would be matted onto a cartoon cowgirl and
cowboy playing and singing songs about flies while an animated fly in
top hat and tails acted out the lyrics.

And not all the pieces that *were* produced worked well. The Cro-
Magnon sketch dragged, for instance, and the idea behind the "Chopsticks" dance seemed derivative of Busby Berkeley. Three sketches stand
out memorably, however. The first is the hilariously surreal *Swan Lake*
ballet excerpt: Odette-Odile's dying scene is performed completely
deadpan by ten gorillas, with pirouettes, lifts, pas de bourrée, and all;
there is even a gorilla hunter with bow and arrow, and at the end Odette-
Odile accepts a banana bouquet. The second is a long, mostly pantomimed, courageously slow-paced sketch about the making of a singing
commercial, very reminiscent of the work of Ernie's hero Jacques Tati.
Louis Jourdan plays a blatantly gay tenor, Edie Adams a teeth-gnash-
ing soprano, and Kovacs the white-haired maestro at whom Jourdan
keeps making eyes; at the end they are joined unexpectedly by a 120-
voice chorus that sings one brief line: "Buy gum!" (For Ernie, the joke
was making the network spend money on a huge choir to sing just two
words.) The third outstanding piece is the grand finale, eight minutes
long and an inspired piece of perfectly choreographed satirical chaos:

ITALIAN TV STATION ENNA-B-C HAS JUST GONE ON THE AIR . . .
WILL PRESENT ITS FIRST PRODUCTION, AN AMERICAN OPERETTA
COMPANY . . . ERNIE DRESSED AS CANADIAN MOUNTIE SINGS
"MARIE" IN NELSON EDDY BARITONE . . . WAGNERIAN CHORUS
KEEPS INTRUDING WITH "RIDE OF THE VALKYRIES" . . . CAMERA
CAN'T FOCUS, SHAKES, RUNS INTO THINGS, KNOCKS DOWN PARTS OF
SET . . . EDIE IN JEANETTE MACDONALD WIG SINGS "AH! SWEET
MYSTERY OF LIFE" . . . WALKS THROUGH TRELLISED ARCH,
HAT GETS CAUGHT . . . CREW MEMBERS GET IN THE WAY . . . EDIE
PULLS VINE, CUPID FOUNTAIN FLIES UP . . . WATER IS COMING

FROM CELLO, PIZZA DOUGH FROM KETTLEDRUM . . . EDIE KNOCKS
DOWN WATERMELON CART, GAMELY CONTINUES SINGING . . . RAN-
DOM BACKDROPS GOING UP AND DOWN WILDLY—MISSISSIPPI RIVER-
BOATS, U.S. CAPITOL . . . VALKYRIES STILL SINGING . . . ERNIE
STILL SINGING . . . EVERYTHING IS FALLING APART AND THERE IS
WATER EVERYWHERE

During the production of *Kovacs on Music,* Shirley Mellner was
given her usual title of assistant producer. But when the show was being
taped, an NBC executive saw the credit and told Kovacs he could not
give it to Mellner, lest other women at the network start asking for
similar titles. Ernie fought for Shirley's credit, but the executive would
not budge; finally Mellner said she didn't mind having it cut. A week
later Ernie presented her with a heavy gold bracelet dangling a big gold
heart. On one side the heart was engraved with a loving cup and "Assistant Producer"; on the other side was an obscenity directed toward
the NBC executive.

Almost immediately after completing *Kovacs on Music,* Ernie traveled to England to shoot the interior scenes for *Our Man in Havana.*
Ernie had always become nervous over the birth of his children; now
his anxiety was intensified by the fact that he had to spend his days at
the Shepperton Studios outside London instead of by his pregnant wife's
side. With Edie thousands of miles distant and due to deliver at any
moment, Ernie whiled the time away doodling potential baby names,
all for girls, on his script: Kay, Julie, Susan, Penny, Teresa, Tess, Margaret, Patricia. In between shots he roamed restlessly about the set,
cigar in hand, trying to round up enough men to join him in a hand of
poker. Even when there weren't enough takers, he refused to ask women
to play, considering it strictly a man's game. "Poker players never play
with women. If you win it's impossible to take their money, and if you
lose the woman will take your money, so it's impossible to come out
ahead," he said. "Anyway, Edie is in Hollywood about to have a baby,
and if I could be with her I wouldn't want to play poker to pass the
time away."

Finally he was called back to Los Angeles; on the night of June 20,
Edie had given birth to a seven-pound, seven-ounce baby girl at Cedars
of Lebanon Hospital. Named Mia Susan, the little girl took after her
mother, with a tiny nose and a rosebud mouth set into a fine-boned
oval face and surrounded by fine blond hair. Ernie joined Edie two
days after Mia's birth and happily escorted the new member of the
family home from the hospital on June 28.

For ten-year-old Kippie, Mia's homecoming presented a distressing dilemma. She loved her new baby sister, but she also felt that Mia's birth caused her stepmother, whose regard she craved terribly, to pull away. "*Mia* means 'my own,' and Edie made sure to tell us that," remembers Kippie. "All my life all I had wanted was her love. My sister and I used to fight in the car for who would sit behind Edie." After her half sister's birth, she says, "I felt I was shut out from Edie almost totally."

The change in Edie's feelings did not occur gradually or subtly, as Kippie perceived it. "She totally disengaged herself from my sister and me, absolutely when she came home from the hospital." She and Bette were not allowed to go near their new baby sister; Edie told them, "You can see her through the window outside." Kippie says, "There was a glass sliding door leading to the Japanese garden. We could take a look at her through the window when she was breast feeding, that's it. Couldn't come near her, because children have germs." Ernie seemed oblivious to the new strains that Mia's birth was causing. "He was working," says Kippie. "These were her orders. I can't say for sure, but I don't think my father involved himself with these things. Whatever she wanted . . . whatever she wanted. He loved us, and he showed us his love. But I still yearned for her love, and it was even less than before."

When Edie had first become pregnant, she and Ernie decided to add a nursery to the northern end of the house. What started out as a nursery soon became an entire two-story wing, costing a reported $200,000 and covering the roller-skating rink where Kippie and Bette had played. Downstairs were a baby's room, a bath, and a room for the full-time nursemaid; on the second floor were sewing and rehearsal rooms for Edie. She also had built "a closet about the size of one of Sears Roebuck's smaller warehouses," as Ernie joked, which she stocked with her ever-growing collection of gowns and furs and shoes. The northern wing was a self-contained little world, far from the center of the house, and as the months passed Edie would spend more and more time sequestered there, designing and sewing clothes or practicing her music; it became her personal domain.

The summer after Mia was born, Kippie and Bette decided to live at Disneyland for a month. "Every summer, ever since we came back from Florida, my dad would ask, 'What do you want to do for the summer?' " says Kippie. "We chose to live in Disneyland, in a hotel." Their father was too busy to live with them at Disneyland, "so grandmom took us. She was the poor soul who had to go every day to

Disneyland." They got to know everybody who worked at Disneyland and had a glorious time. "My sister and I dressed up as two of the Mousketeers, and everybody believed it," remembers Kippie. "People came up to us and asked us for autographs. For the few years that my dad was alive, we had a trippy, wonderful childhood."

While Kippie and Bette were living at Disneyland, Ernie was preoccupied with trying to earn money. By 1959 he was back to working on radio, but with a far less stressful arrangement than he had had in New York. Instead of being responsible for his own program for eighteen hours a week, he was contributing a weekly segment to NBC Radio's *Monitor*, a flexible forty-hour weekend show that featured a potpourri of music, remotes, interviews, news, and comedy. He hired his old New York writer Mike Marmer and also wrote some of his own material. To the familiar characters and recurring bits were added such new creations as "Life Of" (the life of a shark, the life of a worm), "Comeback Story" (about bizarre imaginary comebacks), and monologues on offbeat subjects ("Sound Waves," "Olive and Pimiento," "Space"). But *Monitor* hardly provided enough income to keep his household going in the high style to which he had become accustomed. Consequently, when he was approached to do what he had vowed never to do again—a weekly television series—he had to give the offer serious consideration, and ultimately he had to accept it.

CHAPTER

20

In the late 1950s, the third-rated ABC Television network, still struggling despite the demise of its competitor DuMont, had purchased a quiz show called *Take a Good Look* from independent producers Irving Mansfield and Peter Arnell. The pilot, with Mike Wallace as the host, was dreary but had possibilities. At the same time, an advertising man named Bob David, from the agency Erwin Wasey, Ruthrauff and Ryan, was looking for a television vehicle through which his client the Consolidated Cigar Company could promote its Dutch Masters cigar label. ABC suggested *Take a Good Look*, David took the show to Consolidated's senior vice-president of marketing, Jack Mogulescu, and together they decided that it might work if they could get a celebrity host who was well known for smoking cigars. George Burns was uninterested but suggested Kovacs, who saw the pilot and balked. But he was being offered $5,000 a week for a game show that he perceived as requiring very little work. It was only a matter of time before he agreed to do it.

Privately he was humiliated; taking a weekly game show made him feel like a failure, and he would always harbor some resentment toward *Take a Good Look*. Ernie set about to publicize the show in interviews, but he could not hide his ambivalence. He declared to the *Philadelphia Inquirer*'s Harry Harris, "I *hate* panel shows," then talked about his desire to take artistic risks: "It's no fun if you play it safe all the time. I can do a stock variety show and make a lot of money. But I don't want to get to the point where I'm satisfied to do a 'nice' show, any more than I want to eat boiled meat or look at ugly girls. You only have one short life. . . . I want to do something good on TV. Not artsy-craftsy, with a 'message,' but something I can take pride in."

But then he had to find a way to explain his participation in *Take a Good Look*, in which he felt he could take no pride. He told Harris he hoped it would not be "just another panel show. . . . I'm trying to make it as interesting as possible." Finally, he made it clear that he would invest the least possible emotion and effort in the new show: "I'm budgeting my TV work deliberately, and I want to do stuff that's easier. . . . I don't want to do a weekly variety show, because I'd get enthusiastic and want to write it and sit up all night long."

It was obvious to everyone close to him why he was doing *TAGL*, as it came to be known. "There was a period when Ernie was not as innovative as he might have been," says Mike Marmer. "*Take a Good Look* was not the most innovative thing that he's ever done. That was this—" he makes a money sign with his fingers. Certainly there was nothing innovative about the format. "What we did," recalls Rex Lardner, whom Ernie brought to Hollywood to help write the show, "was dig up somebody who was reasonably celebrated, but not so celebrated that you would recognize him, and get him there as a guest." There would be three such contestants during the half-hour show, and a celebrity panel would try to guess their identities by asking yes-no questions and by deciphering prefilmed "clues" acted out by Ernie and a tiny cast.

Take a Good Look premiered on the ABC network on Thursday, October 22, 1959, in the 10:30 to 11:00 P.M. slot, following the new Desilu series *The Untouchables.* For this first segment, Ernie hosted, Barry Shear directed, and Janet Leigh, Hans Conried, and Cesar Romero acted as panelists. The theme song was composed by Ernie, who had joined the composers' association ASCAP in 1957, registering such original works as "The Irving Wong Song" and "Hotcakes and Sausage." (His "Take a Good Look" lyrics, evidently unused on the show, were about a husband telling a wife to take a good look because he was leaving her.) At the end of the program, Ernie's face was matted into the famous tableau of the old Dutch Masters, smoking a cigar and sporting long hair and a big Dutch collar.

The program was shot at the ABC lot in Hollywood, in what was then Studio E (later Studio 55), "the same stage where Al Jolson shot *The Jazz Singer* and where *Phantom of the Opera* was shot," says Robert Kemp, one of the cameramen on *TAGL*. "You can still see the old sets of *Phantom of the Opera*. And I think that history meant something to Ernie. I always felt he liked that idea." There were a number of personnel changes over the run of the show. Hans Conried and Cesar Romero became regular panelists, but the third spot was filled at various times by Edie Adams, Ben Alexander (of *Dragnet* fame), Carl Reiner, and guest celebrities. Producer Irving Mansfield's wife, the aspiring actress and future novelist Jacqueline Susann, appeared on occasion.

At first the skits were acted out by Ernie, a gorgeous singer named Peggy Connelly, and the diminutive blond actor Bobby Lauher. Before long they were joined by a beautiful, dark-haired actress named Jolene Brand. (Ernie always employed dazzlingly attractive women for his comedy. He claimed that it was because a pretty woman getting hit with a pie was funnier than the same gag with a man; but it was also because he enjoyed being around good-looking women.) Bobby Lauher and Jolene Brand became regulars in the Kovacs troupe, working with Ernie on his final series of specials. "Peggy Connelly wanted to be a singer, and she was more interested in furthering her singing career than doing this show with Ernie Kovacs," recalls Brand. Brand's husband, George Schlatter, had worked with director Barry Shear, and Shear took to calling Jolene in to substitute. "She wouldn't get up at six in the morning, and I would get a call from Barry at four thirty or five in the morning asking, 'Will you come in and sub?' Barry would call me up so mad; he was such an explosive character."

Brand had already worked briefly with Kovacs, in a blackout on the NBC special *Kovacs on Music*. "I had to do a kissing scene with Louis Jourdan," she recollects:

JOLENE BRAND AND LOUIS JOURDAN ON SOFA . . . THEY ARE KISS-ING PASSIONATELY . . . SHE IS RUNNING HER HANDS THROUGH HIS HAIR . . . SUDDENLY THEY STOP . . . JOLENE TURNS TO CAMERA, CLUTCHING HER TEMPLES: "GONE-A. GONE-A. MY HEADACHE IS A-GONE-A!"

"Barry got me on that one too," says Brand. "It was a takeoff on the old Bayer aspirin commercials, where they said, 'Gone. Gone. My headache is gone!' And the reason my headache was gone was I was kissing Louis Jourdan." For the *TAGL* skits, which were shot prior to the show, "we actors were there as props. That was it. Toward the end, once the shows kind of took shape in his mind, we started having rehearsals in his den. But in the early ones, often there wasn't even much dialogue. We actors were not important to what he wanted to convey. We were just bodies that had to fulfill a function in his electronic comedy." But Brand remembers her time with Ernie as "the job I enjoyed the most. Just knowing Ernie was the best. He inspired confidence. The more you hung out, the more he encouraged you."

Another personnel change involved director Barry Shear. "He was a hard-liver," recalls Brand, "a very wound-up guy. He smoked incessantly and loved to gamble with Ernie. They were very, very good friends. And Ernie was a man's man. He liked to drink and gamble and be with his buddies and have lots of laughs." Shear was constantly clashing with the crew, most of whom disliked him intensely, and the dissension reportedly led to his removal from *TAGL*. (He was replaced by the more even-tempered Joe Behar, who had been Ernie's director in Philadelphia and had come to California with NBC's *Wide Wide World*.) And writer Rex Lardner, who had left his family behind in Long Island, worked on *TAGL* only six weeks or so before personal considerations made him return East.

Take a Good Look is often dismissed in discussions of Ernie's work, partly because as a quiz show it lacked prestige and partly because Ernie himself resisted doing it. But *TAGL* was very important to Ernie's career. First, it marked the beginning of an enduring relationship with Consolidated Cigar, the only sponsor that ever nurtured Ernie's inventiveness and granted him complete artistic freedom; with Consolidated backing him, Ernie eventually produced some of his most sophisticated television work. Second, *TAGL* brought Kovacs together with a very special production team at ABC, with whom he forged a deep and empathic relationship and who made possible much of his best work. Finally, much as he complained about *TAGL*, he quickly found a way to bend the format to his own artistic ends. Ernie used the filmed clue segments as an excuse to create the blackouts and sketches and special effects that he loved, and it mattered not a whit to him that nobody could ever guess what they were supposed to mean.

"Ernie had tremendous insight and had all these sneaky ideas and things that he wanted to do, and he wouldn't let anybody in on it," remembers *TAGL* cameraman Bob Kemp. "He would sit in a restaurant, have an interview, have some bread and some wine—what did that mean? It would end up meaning something about a hippopotamus, and nobody knew why. Ernie knew why. Nobody ever guessed the answer, of course, but there was some meaning in it, and it was very funny." ("They're not supposed to be understood," Ernie told an interviewer at the time, shaking his head as if amazed that anyone could make such a dim-witted assumption. "They're supposed to be laughed at.")

The clues were truly bizarre and often bore only the thinnest, if any, relation to their alleged subjects. For a well-known rodeo champion, the following hints were offered:

ERNIE AND PEGGY CONNELLY DRIVING AT NIGHT IN BIG CAR . . .
CUT TO TOY CAR . . . THEY START NECKING PASSIONATELY . . .

TOY CAR GOES OFF ROAD INTO WATER . . . CUT BACK TO ERNIE
AND PEGGY INSIDE CAR . . . FISH SWIMMING OVER THEM

BOBBY LAUHER IN ROWBOAT . . . FACE OF DORIS DAY . . . SUR-
PRISED WOMAN EMERGING FROM BEHIND SHOWER CURTAIN: "OH!"

The car sketch was supposed to signify "steer"; the second little montage meant "row-day-oh." For a contestant pertaining to the navy, Ernie offered this informative skit:

BOBBY LAUHER DRESSED AS NAVAL COMMANDER . . . ERNIE ENTERS
AS HUNGARIAN CHEF MIKLOS MOLNAR . . . BOBBY TELLS HIM THE
MEN ON BOARD ARE COMPLAINING ABOUT MOLNAR'S HEAVY COOK-
ING . . . MIKLOS ARGUES . . . TAKES OUT A MUFFIN: "NOW WHAT'S
WRONG WITH THIS?" . . . PLACES MUFFIN ON TABLE AND ENTIRE
TABLE COLLAPSES . . . CUT TO BATTLESHIP SINKING INTO SEA

Although he invented many gags for *Take a Good Look*, Ernie was intent on making his $5,000 a week and remaining emotionally uninvolved with the show. And so he took, on occasion, to recycling material from his old New York shows. "Some of the things that we did here had already been done," says ABC special-effects chief Bobby Hughes, who worked on virtually all of Ernie's shows at the network. Hughes remembers recognizing sketches on programs about Kovacs made after Ernie's death and hearing them described as having come out of the pre-ABC shows. "Whole routines that he had done before and was redoing," he says. "I guess he felt that he didn't have a large enough audience to make a difference, so redoing them didn't bother him. We didn't know that they were redoers at the time."

Nonetheless, a decent portion of the material was new, and among the clues were some of the blackouts for which Kovacs would become most famous:

ERNIE SITS IN PLANE DRESSED AS PILOT . . . BOBBY LAUHER SPINS
PROPELLER . . . ENGINE ROARS . . . "CONTACT!" . . . PLANE
TAKES OFF, LEAVING ERNIE BEHIND

BOARDROOM FILLED WITH CORPORATE TYPES . . . BOBBY STANDING
AT HEAD OF TABLE GIVING SPEECH . . . TAPS ON DRAWING OF DAM
BEHIND HIM . . . DAM BREAKS, FLOODS THE ROOM

ERNIE IS USED-CAR SALESMAN . . . SLAPS FENDER OF CAR TO DEM-
ONSTRATE DURABILITY . . . CAR DROPS THROUGH GROUND

This last extremely brief sight gag cost ABC's special-effects department somewhere between $3,000 and $12,000 (depending on which report is to be believed), and it could be done only once, because the car
was destroyed. "It seemed like some of the biggest gags were not for
the later specials," says Bobby Hughes. "They were for *Take a Good
Look*. Like the drop in the car, I'm quite sure, and the breaking of the
dam, taking off with the airplane. And there was a huge one, which
I've never seen since, in which a tugboat fifteen or sixteen feet high
crashes through the wall of a house. These things were never rehearsed.
They were only shot once. And we never got a chance to test anything,
because there wasn't time to rebuild it if it didn't work. So everything
was built, and you crossed your fingers, and Ernie got in, and we
did it."

Because there was no opportunity to rehearse the special effects,
hugely complicated gags sometimes failed completely. "I remember one
that just made me sick, it was so horrendous," Hughes says. "It was a
takeoff on *Zorro*. Any time Ernie took a sword and made a Z motion
toward a wall, he wanted a Z to appear on the wall, but without him
touching it." Hughes figured out a way to precut the Z out of the wall
and then recast the hole with plaster, embedding a cable inside. "You
put a big handle on that cable, and when you jerk it, it pulls out a little
piece at a time, like it's being drawn," he explains.

"But I had a conflict with the art director on the scope of the thing,"
Hughes continues. "He liked things big, so the Z's were sometimes
huge, five feet high. For one pull, because of the length of the Z, we
had to open up the doors and run clear out of the studio with a cable.
And when we did it, the whole wall shifted and vibrated because it
wasn't braced properly. Little pieces of plaster were flying everywhere.
It was not what you would call successful."

Ernie's reaction? "He got a kick out of it. What he liked was the
attempt. And for that show, it didn't really matter if it was good quality. He would much prefer it that way, but if you gave it your best
and did everything you could, that's all he'd ask for."

Not long after *TAGL* started, Consolidated's Jack Mogulescu decided to hire Edie Adams to make a series of commercials for another
of the company's products, Muriel cigars. Sheathed in a slinky gown,
her hair in a bouffant bubble cut, Edie would do a vampy takeoff on
Mae West: "Why don't you pick one up and smoke it sometime?" At

the time she declared, "These commercials have given me the best exposure I've ever had." In her fifties and sixties, many years after Eileen and Daisy Mae were forgotten, Edie Adams was still remembered by most as television's sexy Muriel cigar "girl."

From the beginning of *TAGL*, Consolidated also hired Ernie for commercials. He developed a series of spots for Dutch Masters cigars that were completely pantomimed, set to the strains of a Haydn string quartet. These wry, slow, perfectly paced little sketches were among his most conceptually elegant work, and eventually they would earn him a Clio award, the advertising industry's equivalent of an Oscar:

> ERNIE DURING INTERMISSION AT CONCERT . . . RETURNS TO SEAT, STARTS TO LIGHT A CIGAR, AUDIENCE TURNS AND STARES AT HIM IN ANNOYANCE . . . SLOW PAN UP TO STAGE . . . THE MUSICIANS ARE SMOKING DUTCH MASTERS CIGARS

> ERNIE IN FRONT OF FIRING SQUAD . . . HIS FINAL WISH IS TO SMOKE A DUTCH MASTERS CIGAR . . . HE LIGHTS UP . . . FIRING SQUAD DROPS RIFLES . . . SOLDIERS CROWD AROUND HIM TO INHALE WONDERFUL AROMA

> ERNIE UNDERWATER OPENS BOX OF DUTCH MASTERS CIGARS . . . CIGARS ALL FLOAT AWAY . . . HE MANAGES TO GRAB ONE AND LIGHT IT . . . SMOKE BILLOWS OUT OF HIS MOUTH

For this last skit, Ernie told his special-effects men that "he wanted to smoke his cigar underwater, and they came up with the idea of filling his mouth with milk," remembers Bob Kemp. "So while he was underwater he would move the cigar and blow out the milk, and it looked just like smoke."

By this point in his career Ernie had become very outspoken about his contempt toward sponsors; to him sponsors and network executives were cut from the same cloth, both interfering, penny-pinching, anticreative forces to be overcome or avoided whenever possible. "With sponsors he was horrible—if they came in a room he would leave," said Edie Adams. But one day, while Edie was working on her first Muriel cigar commercial and Ernie was with her, in walked a quiet man carrying some volumes of Bertolt Brecht. "My god, who's the guy with the Brecht?" Ernie asked. He was utterly shocked when Edie told him it was Jack Mogulescu, the vice-president from Consolidated Cigar. Mogulescu, who always maintained a hands-off policy toward Ernie's artistic endeavors, became the rare sponsor who won his respect. He also remained close to Edie after Ernie died.

Take a Good Look performed poorly in the ratings, but sales of Dutch Masters cigars swelled at a time when cigar sales overall were soft. "It was a struggle to keep the show on the air," remembered Mogulescu, "because I don't think ABC ever understood what he was trying to do. The fact of the matter is, in *Take a Good Look* there was no question about it—it confused us sometimes, it confused the public, it confused the critics, and unnecessarily so." But the show accomplished its ultimate goal as a vehicle for selling cigars, and despite its low ratings it ran for two seasons on ABC.

While Ernie was working on his first season of *Take a Good Look*, he made two more movies in quick succession. *Strangers When We Meet*, a drama about adultery in a white middle-class suburb, was considered daring for its time. Starring Kirk Douglas and Kim Novak as lovers unhappily married to others, the film was adapted by Evan Hunter from his own novel. Ernie was cast as Roger Altar, a best-selling author who commissions Douglas, an architect, to design a house for him. Unlike the disheveled Sidney Redlitch in *Bell, Book and Candle*, Altar is a serious dramatic role, the only one Ernie would ever play in a film.

Ernie's role is secondary but significant in *Strangers When We Meet*. Roger Altar and Kirk Douglas' Larry Coe, the architect with whom Roger forges a brief friendship, are mirrors for each other. Commercially successful men, they remain artistically unfulfilled; lonely men, they feel trapped by relationships in which love has died or never even existed. The house that Coe designs becomes the movie's central symbol. Modernistic and beautiful, with a Japanese-inspired profile, it is fashioned of such natural materials as unpainted wood and water (in a Zenlike foyer and a pool) and is cantilevered out over a bluff with an unobstructed view ("We'll have to anchor it to a cloud," Larry Coe says). The structure seems simultaneously to root itself deeply in nature and to soar as high as the spirit can reach. For Roger Altar and Larry Coe it becomes a metaphor for the artistic freedom that each craves. While it is being built Roger keeps visiting it, as if spending time in this structure aborning brings him closer to his true inner path.

Working once again with Richard Quine, who produced and directed the film, Kovacs turns in a moving, well-shaded performance. We first see him with the trappings of his writerly success—well-cut clothes, an expensive apartment, a costly convertible, pretty women at his beck and call. But inside he is gripped by anxiety. He knows his books are shallow but is terrified to write what he really wants. He aches for love but treats the women with whom he surrounds himself as objects of contempt. *Strangers When We Meet* is the first film in which Ernie was able to create a character who undergoes a complex transformation. He captures Altar's fear that his new house will be too avant-garde, his mixed-up anger toward the critics, his tortured self-doubt as he awaits publication of the noncommercial novel he's finally written. The book is well received, but then he has nobody with whom to toast his success; his life is fundamentally empty, a fact that he at last sadly confronts.

There is an anxious edge to *Strangers When We Meet*, as if beneath the glossy color surface, a lot of churned-up repressed emotions are on the verge of exploding. Adultery, marital discord, and sex in general are treated with candor, a radical notion for Hollywood at the end of the 1950s. Because it is, at core, a soap opera (a devalued genre aimed at women and thus not taken seriously), *Strangers When We Meet* was pretty much dismissed by the male critical establishment when it opened in June 1960. But it is compelling for its complicated passions, for the charged physicality of the love scenes, and for its poignant examination of the pains that well up in a disintegrating marriage. And Kovacs was singled out for praise; *New York Times* critic A. H. Weiler saw his performance as proof "once again that he not only is an eminent comedian but also is an actor of stature."

In his next picture Ernie received top billing, but he was back to playing another captain. *Wake Me When It's Over* was an armed-services comedy about a group of air force men, bored and restless after the Korean War, who build a successful resort hotel on their remote Pacific island base. (The film bore more than a passing resemblance to the 1956 *Teahouse of the August Moon.*) Ernie was cast as Captain Charlie Stark, the slightly wacko commanding officer; the film also introduced comedian Dick Shawn as a charming bumbler who spearheads the building of the Hotel Shima.

Ernie is marvelous as the boisterous Stark, cheerful and uncouth and out of control. He talks as loudly as possible, obliviously sprays beer all over himself, flings his huge body down on a couch to laugh until he's gasping for air. For the first time he plays the love interest in a film, and he is sweetly convincing as the confused man who must suddenly rein himself in to please a cool, by-the-book lieutenant (Margo Moore), who considers him an unreliable "sky tramp." To woo her, Stark stops flying, begins to wear his uniform, and abandons his buddies; one can see just how alien and helpless he feels. Finally he reverts to his old self and turns the tough chauvinist ("You just run your end of the stove. All you have to do is sit around looking pretty, rack up a few babies, and keep some cold cans of beer in the icebox"); this being 1959, she relents and smiles happily as the romantic music swells.

Wake Me was directed and produced for 20th Century – Fox by Mervyn LeRoy, who had first gained attention in the early 1930s for *Little Caesar* and *I Am a Fugitive from a Chain Gang;* these movies made stars of Edward G. Robinson and Paul Muni and helped establish the tough tone and hard-driving realism that characterized the Warner Bros. films of that era. The Oscar-winning director enjoyed surprising his actors during shoots. Near Christmas 1959, the cast and crew were preparing to shoot a scene in which an ammunition dump was supposed to blow up outside Captain Stark's office, actually a little set raised six inches above the floor on blocks. Ernie and fellow actors Jack Warden and Robert Strauss were prepared for the explosive sound, but not for what LeRoy had instructed his stagehands to do.

The second the blast went off, the blocks were yanked out from under the set; as it dropped to the floor the stagehands violently rocked the walls. "The four performers looked terrified," described one observer. But they continued with their dialogue:

"Holy mackerel, what was that?" cried Strauss.

"You think it was the ammunition dump, Cap?" asked Warden.

"It better be," said Kovacs. "If that was our beer supply that just blew up, somebody's in REAL trouble."

LeRoy yelled "Cut! Print it!" and the shaken performers came sputtering off the set. "What are you trying to do to us, Mervyn?" Ernie demanded. "Just what I did—get a good scene," smiled LeRoy. "You were ready for the explosion, but, boy, did you react when the floor dropped!"

A more physically demanding sequence involved Captain Stark parachuting onto the patio of the hotel and getting caught on a flagpole. Ernie performed his own stuntwork for this scene. Strapped into a parachute harness that was in turn attached to an enormous construction crane, he was hauled 150 feet above the ground. At a given signal the crane quickly lowered him until his parachute caught on the pole; there he hung, wearing a jet pilot's helmet emblazoned with a lightning bolt, delivering his lines with perfect aplomb.

Released in the spring of 1960, *Wake Me When It's Over* is a long-winded mishmash, so bad that Mervyn LeRoy ignored it completely in his autobiography. The reviewers were divided both on the film and on

Kovacs' performance. The *New York Times*'s Bosley Crowther found Ernie's portrayal "perhaps the most witless" in the film: "As the mad captain of the radar station, he performs acrobatics with his cigar and howls crude and arrogant comments with the finesse of a clod." But the *Variety* critic wrote that his "comic strength is appropriate for the role of the island's commandeer. He is excellent."

Neither *Wake Me When It's Over* nor *Strangers When We Meet* brought Kovacs closer to his goal of writing, directing, and producing his own films. Nor did they catapult him toward the star status of which he sometimes dreamed; instead of being cast as a leading man, Ernie kept getting character roles, doomed by his ethnic look and by Hollywood's insistence on perceiving him strictly as a comedic talent. (Of his straight dramatic performance as Roger Altar in *Strangers When We Meet*, *Variety* reported, "Ernie Kovacs' sole function is to supply comedy relief.") "There was no popular Hollywood actor who had a big black mustache, and Kovacs was too specialized a talent to carry any picture himself. A Tyrone Power he wasn't," explained Ed Henry, Ernie's film agent at MCA. "It was my feeling with Ernie that he was a personality, rather than a romantic image, and if you wanted to hold a picture you had to have a romantic image."

In particular it chafed Ernie to be typecast over and over as a captain. "I don't want audiences seeing my pictures ten years from now and saying: 'Oh, yes, I remember him—the guy who always played fat captains.' So I diet between roles. I lost forty pounds for *Havana*. That shows I can play thin captains, too," he joked to one interviewer. Privately, he didn't feel it was a joke. His daughter Kippie remembers his endless frustration: "He'd say, 'Another fucking captain's role!' Excuse my language, but that's it."

"I think what happened was that Ernie came out here and was seduced by the thing he always loved, which is money," says writer Mike Marmer. "He became a movie star, and he may have lost contact with what he did the very best, which was to innovate. In movies, he was just a character who looked like a Cuban and could play it because of the mustache, or he could play a general because he looked authoritative. But he loved directing, and he loved writing. He told me he wanted to produce and direct and write and act in movies. He wanted to be the Renaissance person of his time."

As if to counter the limitations he felt were being imposed on him by the film industry, Ernie joined the Directors Guild of America, and he also began working on his second novel. Titled *Mildred Szabo*, this new book would trace a Hungarian family for several generations, from its origins in the old country through its life in America. "I have wonderful letters and documents for background," he excitedly told Hedda Hopper. "It'll be a long book, but I think it's worth it."

Doubleday had an option for Ernie's next book, and his editor, Ken McCormick, encouraged him. Inspired by the project, Ernie immersed himself in the history and customs that had shaped his own family's past, poring over hundreds of period magazines, pictures, and books, accumulating masses of notes. Within six months he had gathered several trunkfuls of research and had begun writing. But he could work on the novel only sporadically, in between projects that paid immediately. As the pressure to make money increased, he was forced to set *Mildred Szabo* aside more and more often. "I knew he was not progressing as well as he wanted," remembers McCormick, who says that Ernie never signed a contract for *Szabo:* "Maybe he didn't want to commit himself." At the time of Ernie's death, the novel remained unfinished.

Having portrayed two writers in films, now Kovacs was cast as a writer in a television drama. In April 1960 he starred as the successful mystery writer Maximilian Krob in "Author at Work," a production of NBC's *Alcoa/Goodyear Theater.* Essentially a two-man play, George White's English adaptation of Friedrich Duerrenmatt's drama was talky and boring. The goateed, elegantly grayed Maximilian Krob is visited by a student of his works, who has deduced that the crimes in Krob's novels have in fact been committed by the author. Krob decides to murder him, saying, "You must understand, dear man, I'm doing this purely for financial reasons." The same may be said for Ernie's appearance.

That spring he was back in uniform, too, for a cameo role in *Pepe,* a splashy Technicolor production starring the gentle Mexican comic Cantinflas in the title role of a ranch hand who travels to Hollywood in pursuit of a racehorse he has raised like a son. The Columbia film was an attempt to follow up on Cantinflas' high visibility as Passepartout in the 1956 box-office hit *Around the World in 80 Days;* like that film, *Pepe* contains cameos by countless celebrities. Ernie plays an immigration officer who interrogates Pepe when he crosses the border; he is fine, but it is a tiny turn, intended strictly for audiences to enjoy recognizing him in the part.

In this period Ernie also performed for the first and last time with another genius of television comedy, Lucille Ball. In an episode of *The Lucy-Desi Comedy Hour* (the post-1957 incarnation of *I Love Lucy*) titled "Lucy Meets the Moustache," Edie Adams, who had recently become pregnant again, and Ernie play themselves as the neighbors of Lucy and Ricky Ricardo. When Ricky gets depressed because he hasn't had any work lately, Lucy disguises herself as Ernie's chauffeur—complete with mustache—in order to convince Ernie to give Ricky a job.

Ernie and Edie's appearance carried with it several sad ironies. In "Lucy Meets the Moustache," Ernie and Edie supposedly had their own major television show; but in actuality the couple's only regular gig was the low-rated *Take a Good Look*, whose first season would end in July. Kovacs was in no position to give a job to Desi Arnaz, who was becoming a wealthy man from his judicious management of Desilu. Moreover, this episode marked the final performance of Lucille Ball and Desi Arnaz as Lucy and Ricky Ricardo; their stormy marriage of almost twenty years was coming to an end. The atmosphere around the set was tensely cordial. Edie remembered that "every time they wanted to film a funny scene, Lucy would break down and cry. Nobody could stand to watch it." The day after they finished filming, Lucy filed for divorce, claiming that married life with Desi was "a nightmare." That same month Edie suffered a miscarriage. And in the saddest irony of all, the outwardly perfect union of Ernie Kovacs and Edie Adams was heading toward the same fate as that of Desi Arnaz and Lucille Ball.

Ernie could often be found sequestered in his den, the former garage that he had remodeled into a three-story hideaway and furnished, as director Billy Wilder once said, in the style of early Wallace Beery. Separated from the main house by a brick arch spanning the driveway, anchoring the southern end of the property just as Edie and Mia's wing anchored the northern side, the den was Ernie's personal domain. Outside he installed a sign reading NOT NOW, and by flicking a switch to light it up, he could enjoy unalloyed privacy for as long as he wished.

The entrance was on the uppermost level, an eighteen-by-twenty-foot room whose main feature was an inlaid card table that Edie had given him as a present. "It was in a little alcove," recollects ABC cameraman Robert Kemp, "and they played cards endlessly, it seemed"—"they" being virtually anybody Ernie could talk into playing, although the regulars included Jack Lemmon, Richard Quine, Billy Wilder, Dean Martin, Tony Curtis, and Eddie Fisher. Against the wall were a bar and refrigerator, and off to the side Ernie had added a bathroom and a steam room to which he might retreat several times a day.

The middle level, the library, was reached via a staircase whose banisters were made of antique sabers. This dark-paneled space was cluttered with hundreds of books and thousands of records and $40,000 worth of vintage weaponry. "He had some in display cases," says ABC special-effects man Bobby Hughes, "and some of them were on racks on the walls. It was a beautiful collection—Indian-type blunderbusses, antique inlaid guns, sabers that you could take out and look at." There were rare shields and helmets and suits of armor; in this room he taught his daughter Bette to shoot an air rifle.

The library was a comfortable space, with an indoor waterfall cascading into a small pool, a huge polar-bear rug, and overstuffed leather furniture surrounding a firepit topped by a funnel-shaped chimney. (When he was remodeling the den, Ernie built a miniature scale model of everything he wanted, with little windows and little bricks and a little funnel over the fireplace.) This room also held the electronic heart of the Kovacs home: Ernie's mammoth desk, custom-built especially for his frame. ("I finally got things licked here," he said. "Everything is too big, for a change.") The desk held tape decks, an oscilloscope, editing equipment, a typewriter, and a control panel from which he could regulate his battery of gadgets—the turntable he had built into the driveway so cars could turn around, the hi-fi systems and television sets, his steam room, the swimming pool, the telephone answering machine, the intercom network that connected him to the rest of the household.

By lifting up a rug and descending through a trapdoor, one entered Ernie's wine cellar, which he stocked with the best wines and champagnes money could buy. "It was kind of a spooky place with creaky wooden stairs," remembers Bob Kemp. "You felt a little funny about going down there." When the wine cellar was being built, Ernie enlisted the talents of some of his ABC crew. "He had everybody involved in it," says Bobby Hughes. "The art directors designed the interiors, and I think some people from the carpentry shop veneered the walls, to make them look more dungeony. Then we built the latch for the big handle that locked the door, with bolts that went out and down like a bank vault. He didn't want just a plain old knob on it. And we cobwebbed the whole place, using a machine that spins out a material like rubber cement, and we dusted it with fuller's earth. Made it look ancient. He used to like to take his dinner guests down there and have to break through the cobwebs to get at the wine."

In this completely controllable environment, Ernie would spend hours and days immersed in his two favorite activities: writing and gambling. When he created, he needed total isolation, so he would turn on the NOT NOW sign and throw himself into his work, his only companion his young pet donkey, Piccolo. "I'd wake up at three or four in the morning, go out and say hello to him," recollects Elisabeth Kovacs. "He'd be alone at the typewriter. I think it was hard for him to go to sleep because he was constantly creating." When he wasn't working he was holding marathon poker or gin sessions. "Those poker games, these I really didn't need," said Edie. "All those men would come to the house and the game would go on for days."

But the game that had begun as an amusement when he was eleven had become, by the time Kovacs had reached forty-one, a compulsive behavioral disorder. Gambling wasn't recognized as a disorder by the psychiatric community until almost twenty years after Ernie's death, but many of the now-identifiable symptoms apply to him. Ninety-six percent of all compulsive gamblers begin gambling before the age of fourteen, for example, and their average intelligence is high (120 IQ or higher). Compulsive gamblers typically admit to high energy levels and often have trouble sleeping. They are extravagant with their money—always picking up restaurant tabs, for example, and lavishing gifts on others (traits for which Ernie was known)—and they frequently exhibit other compulsive or addictive behaviors, such as workaholism and smoking.

Compulsive gamblers like other people who gamble; Ernie sometimes inquired whether somebody was a card player before even asking his name, and most of the men with whom he became deeply involved gambled with him to some extent. Compulsive gamblers experience a high that has been likened to the high from cocaine. It is a progressive disease, like alcoholism: the longer it continues unabated, the more of the addictive substance or activity the person needs to reach the same high. Whereas in Trenton Ernie had kept his gambling out of the workplace, by now he was gambling not only at home but in studios, on long-distance phone calls, on cross-country train trips, and in limousines.

Experts have pointed out that gambling can meet certain emotional needs. "The crux of the gambling really is the need to control the uncontrollable. Money is something that they control, or think that they can control," says psychiatrist Richard J. Rosenthal, head of the California Council on Compulsive Gambling. Fantasy and escape can also be strong elements of the compulsion. According to psychiatrist Robert L. Custer, a medical adviser to the National Council on Compulsive Gambling, the activity "relieves all fears, frustrations, disappointments, worries, anger—temporarily. It allows one to escape from reality into a world of fantasy."

Most admitted compulsive gamblers are men; for their wives, the addiction can be emotionally as well as financially ruinous. It's not unusual for a woman to be attracted by the gambler's carefree attitude toward money, as Edie had been. That attraction, however, eventually turns to helplessness, confusion, and rage. As the wife's resentment intensifies, she might isolate herself from family and friends. She can become the villain of the piece because she is often the one who tries to impose some structure on things.

The dynamics in the Kovacs family changed in complicated ways after the move to Hollywood, partly but not entirely because of Ernie's gambling. Edie told one interviewer that "suddenly we were out every night, we never sat down, we never used the dining room except at

Thanksgiving. Something was wrong. We can't keep going out, out, out, but Ernie loved it." Elisabeth describes their lives in Hollywood as "somewhat dissipated, compared to our family life in New York," but she adds, "I always heard from my father that my mother was the one who liked to socialize."

"It's hard to swallow, that she didn't like it," agrees Kippie. "I know that she loved to party. She was the one who wanted to go to all the parties. But he did like to go out to dinner, and he and Edie were always going out to dinner." Kippie thinks that their lives changed "for many reasons. Partly it was because my dad was now doing movies. It wasn't a steady schedule. It wasn't like dinner together; it was like dinner when we could. Things were different. And Mia was born, and then things were really different."

By this time Ernie and Edie were being identified by the press as members of the Rat Pack, a group of revelers that usually included Frank Sinatra and Lauren Bacall, Tony Curtis and Janet Leigh, Dean and Jeanne Martin, Anne and Kirk Douglas, Sammy Davis, Jr., and Peter and Pat Kennedy Lawford. But Ernie denied the association. "The members of the Rat Pack are, individually, good friends of mine and Edie's," he told a reporter. "However, nothing would embarrass me more, personally, than to think I was a member of a little group. This would eventually lead to our all wearing identifying beanies with 'Rat Pack' on the front and a local tavern as a sponsor on the back of our sweat shirts."

At home on Bowmont Drive, however, an open-house policy seemed to prevail day and night. "There were millions of people in the house," says Kippie. "Not parties; once in a great while they would have a party, and I don't think he initiated the idea. This was more like friends hanging out. They'd go into the den or the steam room, and they'd talk or listen to music or work on his new gadgets. Fun. Play. Little boys. Or the girls. Liz Taylor and Eddie Fisher, Natalie Wood— they all enjoyed being around him. They were all buddies." (Elisabeth remembers that one of her father's buddies, Shirley MacLaine, "helped me to do dance exercises in the swimming pool, because she knew I was interested in dance." Elisabeth later became a dancer and choreographer.)

When he wasn't with friends at home, Ernie was on the telephone talking to them. Jolene Brand, who performed on Ernie's ABC shows, remembers that "Ernie would call George and me two or three times a week, maybe at two-thirty in the morning, maybe at five in the morning, just to tell us what he'd been doing. It was usually playing cards.

He'd tell us who he was playing with, the latest joke. For years afterward when the phone rang in the night I would think it was Ernie. There was such a bond between the three of us." She and her husband "would see Ernie a lot on our own. Edie was always sewing or whatever. We didn't see them together as a couple much, except at parties." But Ernie once confided to Jolene, " 'I just hate parties!' I said, 'You're kidding.' And he said, 'No, I just hate them. I come in and everybody says, "Oh, there's Ernie Kovacs! I just love you! Say something funny!" And I always do something awful, either say a four-letter word or something embarrassing.' He liked to be with his own close friends."

As for Edie, she just seemed to want to go further and further away. "I've sometimes thought of a one-room apartment somewhere for an escape hatch," she told an interviewer, "but it might look a little strange with all those rooms as home." Edie felt that Ernie's refusal to discipline his daughters and his undermining of her own attempts at discipline were harmful. "We'd come back and they'd be looking at a movie at two in the morning when they had school the next day, and I'd say, 'My god, get in there and go to bed!' and Ernie would say, 'Oh, let 'em finish the movie,' " she recalled. "They just did anything they wanted. He was such a kid himself."

But Kippie thinks the lack of discipline "didn't hurt. His nondisciplining, if that's what it was, left a lot of room for creation." And both girls experienced him more as a father than as a playmate, as Edie perceived. "I would still connect with my father, always," remembers Elisabeth. "He would tell me how his day was and listen to everything I said. We'd have some private dinners; he'd barbecue a steak and we'd eat it with tomatoes and onions. He always had time for me." Ernie would sometimes play the piano, "and he and Kippie and I would sing," says Elisabeth, who learned to play Erik Satie's *Gymnopédie no. 2* as a surprise for her father. "This piece was something he admired—the simplicity of it."

Elisabeth also remembers her father being very involved in her schooling. When she was twelve or so, she wrote "an original piece about a raindrop named George" (perhaps not realizing that her father had told her a similar story about George and a raindrop in New York). "I wrote 'a *troupe* of raindrops,' and the teacher thought my father had written it because of the way I spelled *troupe*. He showed up the next day at school," instantly ready to defend his daughter. "He was always there—every parents' day, every school play."

Finances were becoming a particular stress, although Ernie assiduously kept the increasing monetary problems from Edie. "I never had to worry about mundane things like bucks," she said. "He treated me like a little girl, and I loved it—women's lib be damned!" Ernie's protectiveness came partly out of a deep urge to take care of the people he loved. Just as he tried to protect his mother from her own jealous fits and his writers from his personal entanglements, Ernie wanted to keep those around him safely ensconced in a land of make-believe. And it was normal in those gender-conscious times for the man to retain control of the family finances. But the setup would also prove to be ruinous. Gamblers often control the family's money and hide the true state of affairs from their kin. The protective cocoon in which Ernie had so carefully encased Edie would soon be ripped into shreds, and he would be powerless to do anything about it.

By June 1960 Ernie was at work on his eighth feature film, a period Klondike comedy directed and produced by Hollywood veteran Henry Hathaway. Originally titled *Go North* but released as *North to Alaska*, the 20th Century–Fox production starred John Wayne and Stewart Granger as Alaskan gold rush partners; Ernie had third billing as Frankie Canon, a suave con man and gambler who tried to swindle the men out of their claim. Once again, his part was peripheral; the center of the film is a romantic triangle between the partners and a classy prostitute (Capucine) with whom the virulently antifemale Wayne falls in love.

When shooting began at a waterfront site in Point Mugu, some sixty miles north of Los Angeles, John Wayne was worrying over preparations for the premiere of his own independent production *The Alamo*, and Stewart Granger had just been sued by Jean Simmons for a divorce he reportedly did not want. Ernie, however, seemed to be having his own private party, chatting happily or napping in a beach chair facing the Pacific. "This is great," he told a visiting *New York Times* journalist. "I've been here since nine this morning and we're behind schedule, so I haven't even put on my costume. I didn't do anything during the actors' strike and now I'm back at work and I'm still not doing anything. It's a great way to make a living." The night before, some technicians had carefully piled a raft with equipment and left it on the beach. The tide had pulled it all out to sea, and Ernie was finding "vast amusement in this minor catastrophe," according to the reporter.

Actually, not all his days were so relaxed. *North to Alaska* features three lengthy fight sequences, and Ernie appeared in two of them. The first was set in a hotel saloon and took seven days to shoot. In the

THE RAINBOW'S END 273

midst of a chaotic slapstick fight, with gallons of beer exploding out of kegs, Ernie calmly observes the proceedings, walks over to a gaming table, and silently pockets everybody's money. Director Henry Hathaway used up 300 gallons of beer—which gets sticky and odorous as it dries—because he had decided that no substitute liquid looked realistic enough.

Ernie's second fight sequence was far more complex to shoot, and in it he is the loser. The climactic scene in the picture, it takes place in a mud-filled street and involves collapsing facades, escaping goats, a seal, the Salvation Army, and many people being knocked out to birdsong sounds, as in a cartoon. "I had about five suits made by my own tailor at $500 apiece," said Ernie. "Henry Hathaway sometimes would complain that the neck didn't fit just right or that the cuffs were too long. The tailor would laboriously work the suit to perfect fit. Then Hathaway would okay it and I would walk into the scene and Wayne would immediately shove me into six feet of mud. This went on for a week."

Ernie does the most physically demanding work of his career in this scene. He is hurled around repeatedly, falls flat on his face, has a barrel roll over him, and suffers John Wayne dragging him by the collar—all in gallons of mud. By the end of the fight, he is completely covered with it. "You got a match?" he asks as he is arrested, utterly unrecognizable, putting a soggy cigar in his mouth. When Mary Kovacs saw *North to Alaska*, she wept over the scene: "They made you do that?" "He just laughed. 'It's okay, Mother. It didn't hurt,'" remembers Kippie.

Ernie is dapper and smooth as Frankie Canon, his elegant hats, ruffled shirts, silk ascots, and finely cut jackets setting him apart from the rougher characters clad in work clothes. Every inch the gentleman gambler, Canon is fast and ruthless, good with the dice and the cards, always on the lookout for opportunities to cheat the unsuspecting or to steal outright from the successful. Kovacs plays Canon as the smart, cool con man, but he gives him just a bit of a buffoonish edge. He speaks too loudly and laughs too jovially when he tries to befriend John Wayne, for example, and he makes the mistake of trying to pawn off a fake diamond on him, with the result that he gets punched.

When *North to Alaska* was released in November 1960, *Variety* observed, "Wayne and Kovacs share comedy honors. Wayne displays a genuine flair for the light approach, [and] Kovacs, apparently sensing instinctively that the shortest path to humor is to seem to be playing it seriously, is the best of the lot." The film overall is misogynistic, carelessly structured, overlong, and filled with Three Stooges–style burlesque. Most critics loved it.

Ernie was scheduled to shoot a new film in England and Italy at the end of the summer. ABC had picked up *Take a Good Look* for a second season, so in order to go on location, he shot some episodes of *TAGL* that July for broadcast starting October 27. Kovacs' ninth feature would be the only film he would ever carry as the male romantic lead (even in *Wake Me When It's Over*, where he had top billing, Dick Shawn's was the central character). *Five Golden Hours* was a black comedy that starred Ernie as professional pallbearer Aldo Bondi, a sympathetic man who offers more than just business services to wealthy widows. Bondi meets his match when he falls for the Baronessa Sandra (Cyd Charisse), a beautiful and cunning widow pretending to be on the brink of financial ruin. It was directed and produced by Mario Zampi, a Roman-born filmmaker best known for a series of sly, oddball British comedies he made in the 1950s. The title refers to a scheme devised by the Baronessa's late husband for doubling investments by taking advantage of the five-hour time difference between the stock exchanges in Rome and New York.

As Aldo Bondi, Ernie is on-screen in virtually every scene, and he gets his first and only chance in a film to create a fully rounded character around whom the story revolves. Ernie plays Bondi with a great deal of nuance; he lives as a con man but is basically good-hearted and sweet. He makes his widows very happy, showering them with an affection that restores them in their time of grief; what he gets from them—expensive clothes, a beautiful apartment—is given out of real appreciation. When he meets the Baronessa, he becomes the boyish innocent in love, doing a gleeful little kick when she allows him to trim her rosebushes, accidentally tumbling down her stairs after being invited into her bedroom and then happily declaring, "Glad I made you laugh!"

Five Golden Hours contains lengthy scenes that show the subtle and complex acting of which Ernie was capable. To con one widow into putting money into a five golden hours scheme (so he can secretly raise funds for the Baronessa), he feigns resistance to her desire to invest while simultaneously trying every wile in his power to get her to do it. In another sequence he plays both himself, drunk, and his greedy alter ego, with whom he struggles over the idea of killing all the widows for their money. When he finally takes them for their last drive, he is utterly nervous and miserable; after he shoves the car over a cliff, he is immediately stricken with remorse, tries to hold it back, has to let it go, weeps, and tries to throw himself over the edge, overcome with horror.

Five Golden Hours has the lighthearted, urbane spirit one associates with the films of Ernst Lubitsch, although it lacks the German director's irony and virtuoso structuring, and the humor is somewhat more broad. It is absolutely delightful until halfway through, when Hans Wilhelm's screenplay veers off on an unexpected and protracted course, eventually bumping along to an anticlimactic end. But even with its structurally flawed script, *Five Golden Hours* possesses a charm and an offbeat wit that are unusual among Kovacs' films.

The film was released in the spring of 1961 to generally tepid reviews. *Variety* complained that "too much onus is flung on the shoulders of Ernie Kovacs, a talented comedian, but one who is more acceptable in smaller doses." Only the *Sunday Times* of London praised it, calling the movie "a wicked, happy little surprise" and "an excellent black joke of a sort rare in the British cinema" and also noting that, "most important, it has Ernie Kovacs, a player whose comic vitality hasn't been staled."

There are some parallels between Hans Wilhelm's story and Ernie's life. The Baronessa's husband killed himself by driving off a mountain cliff; it turns out that he had been gambling away his friends' investments, and "that was the only direction left for him to go." To try to keep the Baronessa's house from being attached by creditors, Aldo Bondi himself gets deeply into debt, taking the money he made from his widows' investments and handing it over to the wily Baronessa, who promptly disappears. When Aldo is finally committed to an insane asylum, his new roommate, the continental Mr. Bing (George Sanders), instantly pronounces, "I know from one look at you that your trouble was debts. I have the same disease myself." Mr. Bing has a neat cure for Bondi's ailment: "You merely draw a curtain between yourself and your creditors." But for Ernie, there would be no such simple remedy.

One day, men from the Internal Revenue Service showed up at the Kovacs house and asked to talk to Ernie's business manager, who was there working. After a while the IRS men came out and informed Edie that the family was being put on an allowance. Her husband had neglected to pay income taxes, they explained; now the IRS was limiting what they could spend, to ensure that the agency was paid what it was due. Edie was totally baffled. She turned to the business manager for an explanation; he told her she would have to resume working full-time. "Why?" she pressed him, still not understanding. Finally, he was blunt: "You and Ernie are broke."

Ernie had first ignored his income taxes in 1955, having used up most of his money that year in his search for his kidnapped daughters. In 1956, 1957, 1959, and 1960 he had again underpaid or completely neglected to pay them. By this time, his income had increased to the point where 91 percent of it was supposed to go to the IRS. (This structure has since been changed.) To Ernie, this was worse than unfair; he had earned it, so he could spend it, couldn't he? And spend he did. "After you pay the taxes, the thrill is gone. I'm in the 91 per cent bracket, so if you don't at least live well, what's the point?" he said. His Trenton friend George Kudra remembers that "about 1960 Ernie told me it cost him $15,000 a week to live. He had that whole entourage, governesses and all."

There were ways to get around the killing 91 percent bracket; others in the entertainment industry, for instance, were incorporating or putting their money into tax shelters. Ernie understood that these options were available. "It has become necessary for the financially short-lived to incorporate to legalize his keeping a couple more bucks," he had complained to the *New York Herald Tribune*'s Marie Torre back in 1958. "It's rather discouraging to realize that when the smoke blows away from the gold print on the corporate door, the professional people of today really have no desire for all these business ramifications as such. They are merely trying to hold on to some of the original money they made as boxers, actors, and singers."

But Ernie seemed incapable of translating his understanding into effective action. "Ernie had nine corporations and then he'd gone to Canada to get a few more like the Bazooka Doopa Hikka Hooka Hocka Company," recalled Jack Lemmon. "He had it so screwed up that [the IRS] couldn't figure anything out, so they started attaching everything. They said, 'None of this can be, we can't understand it.' "

According to director Barry Shear, "It was the first time that I'd ever seen Ernie really worried about it because he realized that there was no way out of it. He was doing everything and anything, like fish-market openings, anything to get money to pay for the tax. He was grossing $800,000 a year, but I doubt if he was keeping a hundred— he kept going back into hock."

Now Ernie was trapped on a treadmill. The more he owed, the more he had to work; but the more he earned, the more he would owe. In fact, he had accepted *Take a Good Look* because of the pressures from the IRS, and he felt demeaned by having to do so. It seemed that he would never catch up—much less get ahead. His desperation mounted. Still he continued to spend—on himself, on Edie, on the children, on friends like Richard Quine. Nor would he stop gambling. The major financial problems, the desperation, the insistence on extravagant spending and on gambling in the face of mounting debt—all these are common behaviors among compulsive gamblers.

"The IRS didn't hold with Ernie's idea that if he made it he could spend it," said Edie, who went back to work immediately, taking any jobs that were offered. She was terrified once she understood the extent of the trouble they were in. "At the time they were attaching things in our house. They were attaching furniture. They were attaching everything and taking our salaries." Now the situation between her and Ernie grew "really, really bad," she said. "We both felt the strain, and nothing was ever really the same again."

22

ABC canceled *Take a Good Look* near the end of its second season; the last show aired on March 16, 1961. Consolidated Cigar, however, was eager to retain Kovacs as a company spokesman, so it asked him to host a summer replacement show called *Silents Please* beginning the week after *TAGL* ended, in its same Thursday 10:30 P.M. slot.

Silents Please showcased classic silent films (trimmed when necessary to fit the thirty-minute format) that starred such artists as Douglas Fairbanks, Laurel and Hardy, and Lillian Gish. Ernie would research, write, and perform short introductions to the movies and also close the show. *(Silents Please* had aired the previous summer season, but without a host.) "There's a complete lack of need for me to be involved in the whole thing, but I was shoved down the producers' throats," he told one reporter. "I like silent films. I have a good background in them and I have an affinity for them. It's not an illogical association. But I don't think my involvement is worth an interview."

To save money and time, Ernie's introductions were all shot ahead, over a period of a few days, and were set in various parts of his den, whose medieval decor would lend atmosphere to the show. One day he and the crew were shooting in the steam room, with steam coming out for effect. "Ernie and I had a couple of signals," remembers Norm Silvers, one of Ernie's regular ABC cameramen. "If he wanted me to back up, he would blink his eye twice, and I would do a pullback. I never knew what he was going to do, but I knew what he wanted by the signals." Outside, in the remote truck, three women—assistant director Maury Orr, a wardrobe woman, and a makeup woman—were watching the take on a monitor. Inside, Silvers had his camera pointed at the door of the steam room. "Ernie opens the door and comes out and slowly walks toward the camera. When he gets to where I've got him full length, he blinks his eyes. I do a slow pullback and he slowly walks up to the step. When I stop, he slowly opens up his bathrobe, and he's stark naked. All you heard was screaming in the truck," says Silvers. "I had to take my headset off."

Ernie's deal with Consolidated Cigar called for *Silents Please* to be interrupted once a month by a Kovacs half-hour special. Consolidated gave him carte blanche, but at the start of the project he was as unenthusiastic about the specials as he was about hosting *Silents Please*. "I asked them not to call them anything," he said. "A half-hour show isn't a Special and it isn't a Spectacular. For a while the sponsor wanted to call them *Kovacs Unlimited*, but I asked them how, for the amount of money I'm budgeted for the whole thing, they could call them *Unlimited*." Despite his complaints, the eight specials Ernie produced for ABC under Dutch Masters' sponsorship were the most sophisticated work of his career, beautifully polished anthologies that melded everything he had learned and thought about in twelve years of working in television. With regard to these specials Ernie was a true auteur, accomplishing what he would never get to do in the movies.

With E. & E. K. Enterprises as executive producer, Ernie's black-and-white Dutch Masters specials began airing on April 20, 1961, and continued monthly (with a break in July and August) until January 23, 1962. He produced them, wrote them, and codirected them (mostly with Joe Behar, his old Philadelphia director). Bobby Lauher and Jolene Brand, who had worked on *TAGL*, were recruited for the cast, joined by the pretty blond actress Maggi Brown and Joe Mikolas, a tall, good-looking gambling buddy of Ernie's. Kovacs would act in them as well, but only minimally; by now he preferred to stay behind the cameras, figuring out ways to bring form to his surreal visions.

The basic structure of the specials was a refinement of the loose format he had devised for the 1959 *Kovacs on Music*. With eight or ten related blackouts popping up throughout the half hour, viewers would get a mixed bag of two or three longer sketches, some unrelated blackouts, and one or two lengthy "sound-to-sight" pieces, the highlights of the show. Flawlessly planned and executed, these synchronizations of images and music were Ernie's pride and joy. "Actually there is a purpose to this program, even if it doesn't seem so to the naked eye, if I may use that expression on TV," he explained in his introduction to the second special. "The inherent love that I have for music is really why I'm here. The money means nothing—the money IS nothing, consequently it means nothing. But it is a desire to illustrate music, sound to sight more or less." All the specials ended with thematic credits that formed their own series of running gags (in one he spoofs old-time damsel-in-distress serials; in another all the names float to the surface from underwater).

With his ABC specials, Ernie had come full circle from the un-planned chaos of his earliest TV shows in Philadelphia. "This wasn't just fly-by-night comedy," says Maury Orr Demots, Ernie's assistant director at ABC. "Most of his stuff was very well thought out, and he was very organized. My hunch is that most everything turned out the way he saw it in his mind's eye. He knew what he was doing." Al-though he relied on his crew implicitly, he was no longer following their lead, as he had in Philadelphia; now he knew exactly what the medium was capable of and what he wanted to accomplish.

With the luxury of a month to plan a single show and absolute freedom granted by his supportive sponsor, Ernie was able to concen-trate on working out his private visions to the tiniest detail. Isolated in his den, working for twelve- to eighteen-hour stretches at a time, he would start by listening to dozens or even hundreds of albums in order to discover the pieces of music that inspired pictures in his mind. "I've spent as many as eight days just listening before getting the music for a show. You've got to wait for the ideas to come," he said. Then he would play his selections over and over, timing different sections and noting the corresponding visuals on gigantic sheets of paper. He would write scripts with minutely specific descriptions of music, sets, cos-tumes, and visual images, every shot and every movement of every object timed down to the second. (A single prop might elicit several single-spaced pages specifying exact dimensions, how certain parts should move, which portions were to be operated mechanically and which manually, and even the precise shades of gray it was to be painted. In case verbal descriptions weren't enough, he sometimes attached rough sketches.) For the sound-to-sight pieces, he would create storyboards, indicating each new shot on a separate panel, like a cartoon. By the time he was finished, he had the whole piece preedited in his mind— every cut, every fade-out, every wipe. "All my rehearsals are on paper. If I am wrong, I am really wrong," he told one interviewer. Most of the time, he wasn't wrong:

THE 1812 OVERTURE ISSUES FORTH AS A FAT BALLERINA STAGGERS TOWARD THE CAMERA . . . CUT TO RANKS OF TOY MONKEYS BEAT-ING TINY DRUMS IN TIME TO THE MUSIC . . . CYMBALS CRASH AS EGGS ARE DASHED INTO SKILLET . . . CELERY SNAPS TO THE ROAR OF CANNON FIRE . . . VICTORY BELLS TOLL AS A COW'S HEAD SPINS WILDLY . . . CAMERA ZOOMS IN AND OUT OF HORN PLAYED BY TOY MONKEY TRUMPETER . . . KNIFE CHOPS THE CELERY INTO BITS AS

THE SCALE RIPS DOWN ITS FINAL STACCATO DESCENT . . . FADE OUT
ON SKILLET SWIMMING WITH BROKEN EGGS

Ernie enlisted his special-effects man, Bobby Hughes, to operate the toy monkeys for the *1812 Overture.* "I bought a record and memorized the whole *1812.* I can tell you every note of it," says Hughes. "Ernie brought in the little monkeys. And I took them home and rehearsed with them for days so that I knew every beat of that thing and I could get those guys just right. But all the ideas were Ernie's—he had it all written out."

WITH NO HUMANS IN SIGHT, AN OFFICE COMES ALIVE TO THE RO-
MANTIC STRAINS OF THE "JEALOUSY" TANGO . . . FILE DRAWERS
SLIDE IN AND OUT TO TROMBONES . . . SWITCHBOARD LIGHTS UP
TO A PIANO ARPEGGIO . . . AS CHORUS SINGS, LITTLE PHONE CORD
PLUGS START TO SWAY . . . MUSIC CHANGES TO "SENTIMENTAL
JOURNEY" AS A PENCIL SHARPENER LAZILY TURNS ROUND AND
ROUND . . . TYPEWRITER KEYS MOVE, CUPS SHOOT OUT OF DIS-
PENSER, PHONE DIALS ITSELF, ALL IN TIME TO THE MUSIC . . .
RADIATOR EMITS STEAM TO SOUND OF TRAIN WHISTLE . . . GLASSES
CLINK TO THE BEAT

By setting pictures to music, Ernie was creating some of the precursors to music videos. In Ernie's world, an upbeat Deems Taylor piece suggested a sardine chorus line and a dancing roast turkey; Satie's *Three Gymnopédies* accompanied a "documentary" on the life of a drop of water; and Bartok's Concerto for Orchestra inspired a moody visual drama following many different types—a thug, a fruit vendor, a mother, a cop—on a New York street from dawn until nightfall.

As with any experimental work, not all of these pieces came off. Sometimes Ernie got carried away with sentimentality, having a clown fall in love with a prostitute, for example, to music by Bartok; other times the ideas were merely weird, such as when he had a group of people jerkily eat dinner in time to an obscure Soviet folk march. "A lot of them were zany and crazy, and they weren't all great," remembers Bob Haley, another of Ernie's ABC cameramen. "It was just the idea. They came from his heart and soul so much."

Interspersed among these sound-to-sight pieces were blackouts and sketches, many featuring very dark humor:

ERNIE IS PAINTING BOBBY LAUHER DRESSED AS LITTLE BOY IN
BUSTER BROWN OUTFIT . . . ERNIE ERASES HEAD . . . CAMERA PANS
BACK TO BOBBY . . . HEAD IS GONE

ERNIE AS BARBER TILTS CUSTOMER'S HEAD BACK AND PUTS RAZOR
TO HIS THROAT . . . CLOSEUP OF ERNIE AS HE SNEEZES . . . SOUND
OF HEAD THUMPING ON FLOOR

JOLENE BRAND AS HOUSEWIFE ADVERTISES JIFFO, "A SUREFIRE
METHOD OF MAKING SURE THAT THOSE LITTLE HOMECOMING FEET
AFTER SCHOOL WON'T RUIN YOUR FLOORS ANYMORE" . . . LITTLE
BOY APPEARS . . . JOLENE TAKES OUT JIFFO GUN AND SHOOTS HIM

Others depicted strange things happening with people's bodies: a man
drinks from a fountain, only to have water squirt out the top of his
head; a hand emerges from a bathtub drain; as a man bends down to
tie his shoes, the camera cuts to one foot, a second foot, and a third
foot.

Often the bits had to do with the simple inability to make ordinary
objects work right. In one series of running blackouts, Joe Mikolas,
dressed as an Indian, struggles to shoot an arrow. He pulls back the
bowstring and it breaks; he lets go an arrow and it splits; he draws
back the string again, and the bow stretches like rubber; he lets go the
arrow and it shoots a flag reading BANG! At last he launches the arrow
with no mishap, but then he gets hit in the face with a pie.

The arrow gags and other running blackouts gave the specials continuity and also allowed Ernie to build up and play on the audience's
expectations:

TO "MONA LISA" SUNG IN POLISH, JOLENE TAKES A BUBBLE BATH
. . . SHE LIGHTS CIGARETTE, MATCH FLAMES UP IN WATER . . . SHE
STICKS HER FEET OUT OF TUB, THEY ARE AT THE WRONG ANGLE
. . . A SEA DIVER EMERGES AS SHE CONTINUES TO BATHE . . . PERI-
SCOPE COMES OUT OF WATER, IT IS A GERMAN SUBMARINE . . . CUT
TO BOBBY IN GERMAN UNIFORM: "DUMBKOPF! VE ARE OFFEN ZE
COURSE! SUBMERGE! SUBMERGE!"

ERNIE INTERVIEWS DR. EWING, INVENTOR OF MOTORCYCLE SO
SMALL IT CAN'T BE SEEN BY NAKED EYE . . . MOTORCYCLE DRIVES
OFF BY ITSELF . . . ERNIE AND DR. EWING GO AFTER IT . . . WE
HEAR CYCLE GO BY PICNICKERS, SEE IT PLOW HOLE IN CAKE . . . IT
FALLS OFF DOCK, DR. EWING SEARCHES UNDERWATER WITH A

FLASHLIGHT . . . CYCLE GOES BY JUNGLE NATIVES, DR. EWING PUR-
SUES WITH PYTHON AROUND NECK . . . ESKIMO FOLLOWS SOUND
OF CYCLE CIRCLING ROUND HIM, FALLS THROUGH ICE . . . ON THE
MOON, WITH NO SOUND, SPACE-HELMETED DR. EWING CONTINUES
TO LOOK

Ernie also created some pieces that were purely abstract, reminiscent of the kaleidoscopic bits he had first improvised on his early-morning
3 to Get Ready. To the strains of "Mack the Knife," Ernie brushed a
line of white paint, which promptly turned into an oscilloscope showing the sound waves of the music; in time to various pieces of music
(including his theme, "Oriental Blues"), he played the piano, manipu-
lated candle flames, or swished around finger paint, all through a kaleidoscopic prism.

Some of the funniest sketches in these specials spoof contemporary
culture, including poetry, modern art, and, of course, TV. "There's a
standard formula for success in the entertainment medium, and that is:
Beat it to death if it succeeds," Ernie informs us in one show. There
follows a series of sketches satirizing the then current trend among TV
producers of varying the traditional Western form in order to draw
audiences. Ernie gives us an "arty Western" done from the point of
view of a bullet, a psychological Western with the villain on a psychiatrist's couch, a monster Western with a gigantic chap-clad leg stomp-
ing on a miniature Western town set, a *Twilight Zone* Western featuring
fog, fanged cowgirls, and a gun that shoots bananas, and a new foreign
Western, "Das Einsam Aufseher" ("The Lone Ranger," in butchered
German), with the principals dressed in lederhosen and cowboy hats
and speaking in German double-talk ("Guten Tag, Kemo Sabe").

Ernie's method of producing these specials was as extreme as his
creative process. Instead of scheduling his shoots for, say, two consecutive Sundays, as ABC wanted him to do, "We'd come in at seven
in the morning and just go on until seven—two days later!" remembers
cameraman Robert Kemp. "We'd never leave the studio," says cameraman Norm Silvers. "But no one ever complained. No one ever said,
'Let's stop. I can't go any further.' There wasn't a damn thing we
wouldn't do for that man."

There were many reasons why the crew never complained. For one
thing, they were all making golden overtime, and many of them suspect
that Kovacs kept the shoots going in part so that they would get paid
well. For another thing, Ernie made these sessions into gigantic work
parties. When everybody was ready to collapse, he would have a full

feast catered in from one of Hollywood's finest restaurants, most often Chasen's (for chili) or Villa Capri (for Italian food). "There were probably forty or fifty of us on the crew," remembers Norm Silvers, "but there were always two or three hundred people eating—gardeners, guys from the carpentry shop, people from other stages and all over." Silvers remembers being in Ernie's dressing room when somebody asked, "Ernie, why don't you turn those guys in to the company? You're spending a fortune for all that food." Kovacs replied, "When they walk out of here, they like Ernie. Don't worry about it."

During these marathon sessions, recalls cameraman Bob Kemp, "ABC management would come in and say, 'No no no, they're going home, the overtime's killing us.' And Ernie would say, 'No. They're going to shoot.' We wouldn't shoot right then, but we still got paid; he wanted us to get paid." If ABC complained that they weren't supposed to be eating on the set, Ernie invited everybody into his dressing room. "Ernie went out of his way to make sure there were no barriers," explains Kemp. "If management put up a barrier, he'd tear it down." During breaks Ernie would play cards with director Joe Behar or actor Joe Mikolas or his friend Jack Lemmon, who would visit the set, "and the rest of us would sit around and wait. An hour, a day—however long they wanted to play. ABC cared, but the crew didn't. It was a lot of money to us. And Ernie had some idea; it must be important, so we just waited."

While waiting, they could help themselves to the quantities of excellent liquor or boxes of expensive cigars that were always available, "because the star wanted you to make yourself at home and have a good time," says cameraman Bob Haley. "That's the only time in the history of television you could do that." Ironically, the cigars were not Dutch Masters. "Oh, no," says Haley. "Cuban. It was always the best of everything. He wouldn't smoke a Dutch Masters." According to special-effects man Bobby Hughes, Ernie never fought with Dutch Masters "as long as they didn't make him smoke the cigars. He smoked them on camera, but off camera he had his Cubans."

As he had demonstrated with friends like Helen Wilson and Edna Vine back in Trenton, Ernie made those around him feel special, and "he seemed to have a different relationship" with each member of his ABC crew, according to Bob Kemp. Kemp had recently bought a 35mm still camera and was learning to shoot photographs, and "Ernie took an interest in that. He bought a lot of my pictures, but he also offered his opinion and gave me this long story about *his* early days taking pictures someplace in New York. That became a bond between us." Kemp would bring his camera on the set, and Ernie would say, "Get me one before the makeup," and then, "Get me one with this makeup, this is great, I want this." Other photographers would come on the set, "but they couldn't really compete with me because Ernie was close to me, so nobody bought their pictures, and they eventually went away."

Ernie was also very respectful of his crew's abilities. "Ernie always believed in the people around him, perhaps more so than any other professional I've ever worked with," says Maury Orr Demots, his assistant director at ABC. "If he thought you knew what you were doing, he trusted you implicitly. He'd never say, 'No, I don't have time to talk to you now.' He felt that if you had something to say, it was important enough that he should listen. He had a wonderful sense of what the tube could do, but the crew was very valuable to him for their technical ability."

Although Ernie drove ABC management wild with his overspending, he got away with it because the whole industry was much looser then. "The attitude then was to create something, and time wasn't as important as it is now," says Bob Kemp. "Now it's a factory—we have to finish nine shows before four o'clock or whatever. In those days we just had to get the close-up that day. None of us really knew what we were doing. It was just called television, and we had to create a show. So Ernie'd say, 'Here's what I want to do, guys, how do we do that?' 'Gee, I don't know. We've never done that before.' And together we'd figure it out." Then the Kovacs crew "would be heralded as innovators. 'Guess what they did on Ernie Kovacs last week! Wow! Never been done before!' My friends at other networks would say, 'God, how did you guys do that?' Sometimes it was a secret: 'Oh, no, I'm not going to tell you.' Other times we were so proud we'd be glad to share it."

Besides creating a party atmosphere on the set, Ernie threw real parties for his crew at places like the Villa Capri. "He would be at the door, greeting everybody by name—he knew every one of us," recollects video control operator Wally Stanard. "You can go for years and a lot of people who perform won't even know who you are." Bob Kemp remembers them as "exciting parties, lavish! Anything you want, everything paid for. On other shows we'd have little wrap parties, but they weren't like that, and the talent didn't stay very long. But here Ernie threw the party, and he'd come over and sit at the table with us and the spouses or girlfriends or boyfriends of the crew! 'Hi, how're you doing? and chat chat chat.' And it wasn't like he was 'seeing' everybody; you didn't feel like he was doing the obligatory parade of sitting at your table." Edie Adams sometimes attended, and she and Ernie would seem "a little reserved," recalls Kemp. "Might have been

a little strained. They were polite. There seemed to be an in-joke between them all the time, something they shared that we didn't quite
understand. A wink or a nod worked with them—there was that communication. I'm not sure, but it seems like Edie would go home earlier
than Ernie."

Cameraman Bob Haley, who used to trade fine wines with Ernie,
remembers one particularly expensive party Ernie threw for his crew at
the Villa Capri. He said to Haley, "Bob, go around and tell everybody
to drink doubles, drink triples, go ahead and get sick, throw up, go
back and drink some more—and get the best." "So I went around the
tables—they were drinking Chianti or something—and I said, 'No,
get the bottle of this, get this, get the better wines. Spend more money,
the more the better.' He said, 'That way, the word will get around
Hollywood that not only do I drink but my friends drink too.' " Ernie
spent $5,000 on that party, according to Haley. "That's not much money
in today's world, but the equivalent would be $20,000 or more. Be-
cause we had the best of the best." To reciprocate, Haley organized a
special party just for Ernie and Edie. He went around and collected ten
or twenty dollars from each crew member and reserved a flamenco club
called the Matador on La Cienega, which was then Beverly Hills' restaurant row. "We didn't invite any people but the crew and Ernie and
his wife. No ABC people allowed."

But if Ernie had an affectionate relationship with his crew, he hated
ABC management with a passion. Cost considerations were a constant
source of friction between him and the network's money men. On the
Dutch Masters specials, Ernie was acting as a packager: ABC set a budget, Consolidated Cigar paid Ernie that set price each time he delivered
a completed show, and then ABC rebilled Kovacs for their below-the-
line costs, such as studio time, camera rental, wardrobe, and special
effects. But Ernie was going vastly overbudget on each show, with the
result that he owed money to ABC as well as to the IRS.

Ernie was forever complaining that he was underbudgeted on his
specials. But in fact this was true only on his first special, when he was
given the inadequate amount of $11,000. He spent $25,000, and ABC
reasonably raised his next budget to a little over $25,000. But on his
second special, he ran up costs of nearly $35,000; a hefty $5,400 of that
was in penalties for overtime, the result of shooting nonstop for twenty-
hour stretches rather than breaking the work up over two or three days.
"The shows were getting wonderful reviews," says Maury Orr Demots, the assistant director, "and he was going bananas on the budget.
He always had his coterie of fans, and the stuff was technically fresh
and inventive. It was good television, but how long it would take to

shoot, how expensive it was to create—that was a problem. On one show, I had a paycheck where my overtime was more than my salary."

ABC was on his back not only for monetary reasons but because it was concerned about the health and the efficiency of the crew, who, after all, had to work on other shows; indeed, the marathon sessions violated state and federal regulations limiting work hours. But the more ABC tried to curb Ernie, the more he dug in his heels. For his third special in May he started to shoot at midnight on a Saturday and wrapped at 6:00 A.M. on the following Monday—this despite on-the-set attempts by his TV agent, Marvin Moss, his associate producer, Milt Hoffman, and ABC production coordinator Scott Runge to force him to quit after twenty-four hours and carry over to the following weekend. The three men literally did everything short of shutting off the power, but Ernie was adamant that he would lose continuity if he stopped in the middle.

Ernie felt that shooting nonstop made it possible for him to get every element perfect. "When you're shooting you have a momentum, and it's very difficult to get that back," explains Wally Stanard, the video control operator on the Kovacs shows. "Sometimes, if you do ten takes, you know so much that on your eleventh take you make it superb. That's it for a comedian. You just can't come back and recapture that whole moment." And the timing was very important on the sound-to-sight pieces, which were for the most part edited in the camera, with fades, cuts, and dissolves put right onto the tape as they were to occur on TV.

Despite the party atmosphere he created on the set, Ernie worked very hard and with great concentration during these shoots. He set up a bank of monitors on the stage so that he could see what each camera was shooting and direct from there. "He'd have little high signs for the director that meant this or that," says Bob Kemp, "or he would pull on his ear or have signals like a catcher in a baseball game." Wally Stanard remembers that after a take, "he would immediately ask for playback to the floor and watch the monitor and hear the audio. The videotape man would wind it back and play it to Ernie, and then Ernie would say, 'I'm going to do another one.' Ernie was a perfectionist for the correct tape. He would just keep doing it over until he felt it had the element he wanted. The bit in the office with the file drawers we did over and over again."

Despite the fact that Ernie was losing tremendous amounts of money on his shows, he protected his crew from that knowledge. "We had no idea," says Bob Kemp. "It was something he wanted to do, it was his little playground: make a television show. Little did we know that was forcing Ernie into bankruptcy! If he'd said, 'Gee guys, I'm in trouble,' everybody would have put up money and paid off every single bill he had, and nobody would have batted an eye."

But it was no secret to the crew that Ernie despised ABC management. "There were a couple of guys from ABC whom Ernie did not want to have in the studio at all," remembers Wally Stanard. "Any time they came around, he just kicked them out. He didn't even want to see any money people at all." Bob Kemp says he "knew he had trouble at ABC because the president of ABC would write letters urging Ernie to cut down expenses and begging him to take it easy. Ernie would go into the men's room, get a piece of toilet paper, and write his answer. And it wasn't a very pleasant answer."

Continuity or not, Ernie was running himself into the ground with these specials. Financially he was on the losing end, owing several thousand dollars to ABC after each production. The stress of combat with the network and the worries over money were draining him emotionally. Physically he was pushing himself to exhaustion. One journalist, visiting the set, observed Ernie's arrival in his two-toned Rolls-Royce to begin shooting: "It is eight in the morning, and Kovacs is already courting total collapse. He has played gin rummy until 6:00 A.M. with a dogged literary agent who would not go home the loser." To keep himself going he would take a quick nap face up, sprawled out on the floor, his head in Jolene Brand's lap, before resuming work; "back in the booth," wrote the reporter, "the pace never slackens."

After two nonstop days and nights in the airless studio, he would leave with terrible headaches. At home he took steam baths, "which kept him, he thought, alive," says Maury Orr Demots. "He'd stay up all night playing poker. And he'd take his steam, wouldn't sleep, and then would come to work. He beat his body to death. I think it was a combination of the poker, which he loved, plus the image of the creative genius at work, which he really began to believe." Despite the stress, however, "he was never angry or testy or irritable at the studio, because he loved what he was doing; he was seeing his baby come to life." Demots thinks Ernie had "sort of a purge complex about steam bathing; you sweat out all the impurities and start all over again. But it can be very debilitating, especially at the scale he used it. He would sit for hours and hours. He worked too hard and he didn't sleep enough and he used the steam room and he just exhausted himself so that he had no stamina. Your body can do that just so long."

During this period, one of Ernie's most memorable creations came to an end. While Ernie had been out of town, cameraman Bob Haley decided to welcome him back with a practical joke. Haley excelled at imitating Percy Dovetonsils. "Haley loved Percy Dovetonsils so much because it was so different from Haley's character," remembers Demots. So the cameraman dressed up "in the smoking jacket with all the froufrou, and I fixed my hair with little bangs in front and wore those crazy glasses. I wrote a Percy poem welcoming back Ernie and Edie: 'Ernie gained a pound, but he's not to be found,' little quibbles like that. The last line was, 'Here's to Ernie and Edie so hearty. Let us all return to the Villa Capri for another party.' "

The plan was for one of the other cameramen to tape Haley's performance on the standing Percy Dovetonsils set; the tape would then be played back to the unsuspecting Ernie during a normal session. Everybody on the crew was in on the joke. "It's a pretty big thing for someone who's supposed to be behind the camera. I had Jack Daniels before, to get up enough nerve," remembers Haley. "Then I taped it, and they all died laughing. But it wasn't as good as I wanted because I had only one take, and Ernie showed up early. I was scared to death."

When it came time for Percy Dovetonsils, Haley had a camera on Ernie to watch his reaction. "He did Percy Dovetonsils and said, 'We have to play it back, because it was a blooper.' And we were all watching the monitor. Upstairs, they put my tape on right away. It was fantastic. He just sat there and he looked at it and he watched it and he looked at it and he said, 'Well, when did we do that?' For a full minute he didn't know, because I timed it."

But Wally Stanard, who was sitting next to Ernie in the control booth, saw a different reaction. "He's sitting back against the control room walls, in the director's chair," Stanard remembers. "And he leans back, and now the skit starts, and he pulls forward and looks at the monitor. And I think what he said was, 'That's not me.' Ernie recognized that this was somebody else, and it infringed upon his territory. Looking at his face, it was not that funny. But he tried to cover it up: 'Let's get on with it.' "

"At the time it was something good, I guess, but he didn't make anything of it," says Bob Haley. "But I'll tell you a little secret: the last Percy was the one I did. He said, 'The camera's getting into my heart, into my insides.' He said that was scary. In other words, understand, he's the only one who does Percy Dovetonsils. Because of that invasion, he never did another Percy again."

As of February 1961 Ernie had been set to costar in *Sail a Crooked Ship*, based on Nathaniel Benchley's novel about some bumbling burglars who steal a Liberty ship out of a mothball fleet, rob a Boston bank, and escape by sea. But the new comedy got bogged down in script development and did not go into production until late spring.

In *Sail a Crooked Ship* Kovacs was cast yet again as a captain (indeed, on the credits he is listed only as "The Captain"): Captain Bugsy F. Foglemeyer, an inept small-time crook who heads the gang of robbers. Ernie dropped to fifth billing here, the lowest he'd ever had, below Robert Wagner and Dolores Hart as a young couple who get shanghaied on the ship, Carolyn Jones as Foglemeyer's sweet-tempered moll, Virginia, and Frankie Avalon as Rodney, the captain's nephew. Worst of all, Ernie was working for only $9,000, because 91 percent of his $100,000 fee had been attached by the IRS before he even started filming.

Producer Philip Barry, Jr., and the film's first writer, William Bowers, had an offbeat idea for mixing live action and animation throughout the film, "which turned out to be so far ahead of its time that it scared the hell out of the front office at Columbia," recalls Barry. "Our plan was that you would never see a long shot of the ship; we would cut back and forth between a cartoon ship and a live interior. For example, in one sequence Ernie would try to get to the porthole, and you'd cut outside and see a cartoon porpoise taking off toward the cartoon ship, and then you would cut back inside, live, and he'd open the porthole and a porpoise would run himself through the porthole. It would have been wonderful with Ernie Kovacs, but the front office got scared."

Bruce Geller (who later produced the TV series *Mission: Impossible*) was hired to do a rewrite, but Columbia was still unsatisfied. They called in director Irving Brecher, whose background was as a writer. "They told me they had a script that was not really what they wanted, but they had to do something," says Brecher. "As I recall—and this came later—one of the issues was that they had Kovacs under contract, and he had gotten advances from them of quite a bit of money. They wanted to wipe that off by making him work."

Brecher was nervous about the project. "I'd heard Kovacs didn't really want to do it," he recalls. "He had a favorite director, Richard Quine, and he didn't know who the hell I was. That didn't make me feel any more comfortable, because I had a high regard for him as a creative comedian." When Ernie appeared for his first day on the shoot, "he was less than cordial," recalls Brecher. "I had the feeling that I was on trial. I also felt that there was a little boy in there who needed a security blanket. He carried around a box of cigars—enormous box, it looked like a skating rink—all the time except when he was shooting.

"He was professional, he didn't sulk," continues Brecher. "We would rehearse the scene, he would respond. But all the time I got the feeling that he wished there was someone there he was more sure of." After that first day, however, Brecher says, "I made some adjustments that he responded to, and he changed. He'd slap me on the back and say, 'How are you, buddy?' and we'd play gin rummy when the cameras were setting. He was a truly funny, bright man. During the shooting on more than one occasion I was invited to his home, where he had scores of cars."

Instead of investing in mixing live action and animation (the only animation in the final film is a cartoon ship in the title sequence), Columbia poured $50,000 into building a thirty-foot-high replica of a Liberty ship inside two sound stages. The script (which was being rewritten nightly by Brecher and screenwriter Ruth Brooks Flippen) relied heavily on physical comedy, mostly performed on this ship set during a manufactured hurricane. "They built enormous dump tanks on high scaffolds with chutes," remembers Philip Barry, Jr., who more or less distanced himself from the project when his concept was changed. "To get a shot they would take an hour to load all these tanks with water. They'd do one take, and all the water would be dumped, and then you'd wait around for two hours while they reloaded the tanks to get the next shot. There was plenty of time for Ernie to play cards," which he did with Brecher or Robert Wagner or "three or four people who would come to the set. He had a big gang of hangers-on. Poker buddies."

After a day of shooting "he used to go out for drinks with me," says Barry. "I know he was drinking off the set, a lot." On the set, recalls Brecher, "he kept to himself quite a bit, in his dressing room, when he wasn't shooting." This was new behavior for Ernie, who previously quite often hung around the public areas of the set between scenes. He also did something new one day when, during an interview with a newspaper reporter, he poured himself a big glass of liquor on the spot. Barry sensed that he was going through "kind of a depression."

He hid the depression while working, however. "I didn't think he came there knowing his dialogue that well," says Brecher, "but he would grab it quickly from the script clerk or from me, and it had a freshness when he did it." Philip Barry, Jr., recalls that Kovacs and Carolyn Jones practiced their scenes together in private, and these segments are among the best in the film. "Edie used to drop in on the set," says Barry. "She obviously adored him. I think Edie was somewhat jealous of Carolyn because she played his girlfriend."

After the *Sail a Crooked Ship* shoot ended in June, Ernie sent Irving Brecher a thank-you present "that stunned me," says the director. "There was a thing like a leaning trellis in the form of an easel, and on it were more bottles of different kinds of expensive liqueurs and whiskey than I'd ever seen in one place! It looked like a Roman funeral."

Although the depression doesn't show in his performance, Ernie plays Captain Bugsy F. Foglemeyer somewhat mechanically, giving him the boisterous goofiness of a warmed-over Captain Charlie Stark, but with a softhearted side. We quickly see why Foglemeyer is a failure as a crook: he's simply too nice. When a fellow burglar (Frank Gorshin) decides to kill the young kidnapped couple, Foglemeyer tries to talk him out of it, and when Gorshin sends the pair out to sea in a lifeboat, Bugsy is appalled that he could set "those two kids" adrift with a hurricane coming. Once in a while Ernie lets loose with some funny moments; in one scene, for example, he does a manic sort of dance with Virginia while Rodney croons in the background (occasionally he shrieks, "Sing it, Rodney!"). But it is a workmanlike performance only; his heart doesn't seem to be in this role. He looks jowly and a little tired. Released in February 1962, *Sail a Crooked Ship* was his last film.

Even though the IRS was attaching his wages, Ernie continued to spend as though he had all the money in the world. He bought Edie a classic 1937 Bugatti (they already owned, among other cars, a Rolls-Royce, a Bentley, an MG, and a Corvair station wagon). He thought nothing of making transatlantic and cross-country calls several times daily, running up phone bills of $1,000 a month. The Havanas had become more expensive after Castro's government came into power, but he was still smoking up to twenty a day (they were made for him by an old Cuban cigar maker who had immigrated to Miami after the revolution). He and ABC cameraman Bob Haley liked to exchange wine knowledge, and Haley remembers, "I'd tell him about a good wine, and he'd send me a case. I'd give him a bottle, and he'd give me a case. I don't know how many cases of wine he gave me."

That June, he and Edie bought a commercial complex at 3084 Motor Avenue in Los Angeles; it included a health club, a dress shop, a beauty salon, and several bars, and it made the Kovacses responsible for a mortgage of $1.6 million. An undertone of impatience was beginning to creep into Edie's public statements: "Ernie likes to live well. He has never cared about money and probably never will." Privately, the quarrels were escalating. One close friend of Ernie's thought that they were arguing about money and that the marriage wouldn't last another year.

Through all this, the gambling never ceased. "I sat and held gin for forty minutes once before he finally could get gin," recalled Jack Lemmon. "I just sat and held it just to see how long it would take him. He was down to the last card in the deck and he's still going in there." Another person who sometimes gambled with Ernie remembers, "I was bad but he was worse. I think he had a death wish. Never paid his losses—he'd always say, 'Put it on my tab.' He may have owed other people."

Friends who had known Ernie well in New York were beginning to notice changes in him. Doubleday editor Ken McCormick, who always visited the Kovacses whenever he traveled to Los Angeles, perceived that "he was clearly a hounded man." Kovacs kept his troubles private, but "I was aware of it. I was somewhat depressed when I saw him in Hollywood because it seemed to me that he'd turned into a different kind of person. He would say slyly how he was chasing Marilyn Monroe around and everything. He was just somebody else." Back in New York, he never would have done that: "No, he was in love with Edie there. But by that time, I was never too sure that things were very good between them." Ernie told Ken McCormick of times when Edie had been out of town working, "and he said he used to sleep on the floor outside her bedroom," an act that seemed to signify "love or repentance." One day, McCormick recalls, "Edie and I were talking and I said, 'Edie, I have to tell you something. You don't know how dedicated Ernie is to you,' and I told her this whole thing. She looked at me and said, 'You're kidding me.' I could read it in her face that she didn't believe it. I said, 'I really am not kidding. Ernie is dedicated in his fashion, and you're the one.' She looked a little skeptical at this."

The problems were becoming obvious to their friends in Hollywood as well. "It was evident. He was running away," says Jolene Brand. "They had a rough time for quite a while there. He wasn't the kind of guy who would tell you this, that, and the other, but there was this sadness about him. And I understand it, some men are that way; they just don't want to face up to a problem." Brand thinks that Edie "was trying to make him face up to some problem, and he didn't want to. It's not that he wanted to giggle his way through life, but he didn't know how. But we could see he was torn. She was very self-sufficient, or at least she appeared that way, whereas he was just vulnerable. 'No, she's up in her room, busy with her sewing, busy with her singing.' And he was just . . . not banished to his little room, but making his hours go by."

In the meantime, fourteen-year-old Bette was going through her own adolescent troubles. For a short time she went to a Catholic school called Notre Dame. Her father was going to be out of town when school was scheduled to start, and he asked his friend Jack Lemmon to accompany her on her first day. "So Jack Lemmon took me—bleary-eyed, the poor man, because you had to be there at the crack of dawn," remembers Elisabeth. "I was touched that he cared enough to shuttle his friend's kid to school, and also that my father didn't want the chauffeur to drive me; he wanted his friend there." But "I never got along with the sisters, and genuflecting was getting to me. I hadn't been told all that stuff before—that heaven was a little cottage and all."

She decided she would be happier at a boarding school because "I had read all the Nancy Drew books and seen a lot of '30s and '40s movies, and there were always girls' dormitories where they had dances and the people were fluffy and happy." But the one she chose to go to, in Pasadena, turned out to be "hideous, terrifying. I sobbed when my father and Kippie dropped me off. It was a weird place, abusive, and I was lonely. Two girls tried to commit suicide while I was there." She tried to convince her father to let her leave, but he told her, "Edie wants you there, and there's nothing I can do. If anything happens to this marriage, I will lose custody of you because of the court ruling." A divorce could have left him vulnerable to a custody challenge, and the possibility of losing his daughters again "panicked him," says Elisabeth.

In August, Ernie accompanied Edie on a lengthy trip back East, where she was to perform in summer stock. He told one intimate, " 'If

I don't go see her . . .' In other words, there had been some sort of ultimatum." By this point the gossip columns had reported tensions in their marriage. Now columnist Earl Wilson spotted them in New York, dining "luxuriously and happily at the Four Seasons, making fools of columnists reporting them busted."

Ever needing money, Ernie used his time on this trip to "knock off" (in his phrase) two books. Since 1959, he had been pitching quickie book ideas to editor Ken McCormick in order to earn some fast bucks: a volume of short humor pieces to be titled *John Has Fungus* (John was Kippie's pet turtle), a collection of ball-point pen sketches that had taken him five or ten seconds each, a compilation of Percy Dovetonsils poems. "They were usually things that wouldn't stand development," recalls McCormick, who tactfully turned down these desperate projects while continuing to encourage him on his novel *Mildred Szabo*. After the last rejection, however, Ernie had become so discouraged he had stopped writing for months, even putting aside the Hungarian family saga about which he had once been so excited.

Now, however, he managed to interest McCormick in *How to Talk at Gin*. Dictated over four and a half days, this breezy guide to gin playing is rambling and not particularly amusing. Edie's displeasure over his card playing was evidently much on his mind, for he devoted two chapters of this slender volume to the subject of that nemesis of the gin player, the wife. Here he describes "The Perfunctory Type":

> This is the woman who greets his friends with about as much enthusiasm as a *Hausfrau* being informed of her thirteenth pregnancy. She has learned to put into "Hello" both a greeting and a reminder of how late they stayed the last time. Most wives do this with the effective grace of a hippo with double hernia. . . . This wife never leaves sandwiches or tidbits for the men. If she *did* decide to supply them with food, she would prepare something terribly continental to show them the contrast of her complex accomplishments as opposed to their stupid game.

Despite the thinness of the concept, Ernie received a $5,000 advance against royalties for *How to Talk at Gin*. He made illustrations for the book and consulted with his daughter Bette about which ones should be on the cover. "He would do ink drawings reminiscent of Egon Schiele—a lot of ink on ink, and then the form would emerge," she describes. "He showed me four drawings and said, 'Which one do you think would be best?' And he used the one I chose instead of the one he had picked. I think he respected the child's point of view."

The second book produced on this trip East was *Please Excusa da Pencil,* a dismal collection of imaginary letters from historic personalities that took him one weekend to write: "Cleopatra to girl friend, dated March 15: 'Well, today is the day I'm going to marry Caesar. Then I'll be queen and take care of some of those characters, like Cicero and his pals.' " *How to Talk at Gin* was published posthumously in 1962 by Doubleday, but *Please Excusa da Pencil* never saw print.

When he returned to California that fall, he immediately went back to work on his ABC–Dutch Masters specials. In a *TV Guide* article titled "10⅝ Years Ahead of His Time," critic Dwight Whitney heralded Kovacs' forthcoming shows: "They may well be among the most important events of the new season. TV has been starved for some comic invention worthy of the name."

Most of the specials followed the format he had established in the spring. But for his November special (the sixth)—partly because Consolidated Cigar's Jack Mogulescu had been complaining that Ernie was writing himself out of these shows—he mounted a new version of his famous "Silent Show" of 1957. Although in substance the redone Eugene sketch relies heavily on the earlier script, Ernie varied many of the old gags (using gunshots when Eugene opens his lunch box, for example) and added some new elements, including a magical hall of statues in which lovers pant and *The Thinker* mumbles and an introductory section in which a maid vacuums with an invisible vacuum cleaner, a TV repairman fixes a nonexistent TV (switching a cowboy-and-Indian movie on and off out of thin air), and a spiked dog collar—without a dog—tugs at its leash and growls underneath a sign warning BEWARE OF GNARF. Ernie also found a way to incorporate the "Mack the Knife" rendition he liked:

EUGENE IN LIBRARY TAKES OUT TINY TURNTABLE AND TINY RECORD
. . . PLUGS TURNTABLE INTO OUTLET IN HIS STOMACH . . .
SPEEDED-UP GERMAN VERSION OF "MACK THE KNIFE" PLAYS . . .
HE SNAPS HIS FINGERS AND SWAYS HIS HEAD

The second "Silent Show" earned Kovacs and Joe Behar a Directors Guild of America award for best television direction of 1961. Ernie's series of Dutch Masters specials also garnered the only Emmy Award any Kovacs shows would ever get, for the most outstanding achievement in electronic camera work of 1961 (the Emmy was shared by technical director Gene Lukowski and the engineers and cameramen on the crew).

Another reason that Ernie may have decided to remount the "Silent Show" was that around this time he was working on a screenplay for a feature film, *Eugene*, in which his fey hero would fall in love with a movie star. Intending it as a starring vehicle for his friendly acquaintance Alec Guinness, he hoped that this project would launch him into what he really wanted to do—writing, directing, and producing motion pictures. "After Alec read the treatment of my picture he sent me a four page letter dealing with his feelings about it," Ernie told Hedda Hopper excitedly. "I told Alec I was pretty sure I could get private financing and that he must ask for his regular salary plus a percentage of the gross. He told me: 'Oh the gross doesn't matter. If I want to do something I don't care if it pays only $100—I'll play it.' . . . The moment Guinness read it he wanted to do it and I think it will be made as one of the four he's agreed to do at Columbia." Guinness, however, no longer remembers anything about Ernie's *Eugene* treatment. Either his memory has faded with the passage of thirty years, or Ernie misread Guinness' enthusiasm to begin with—or he was exaggerating to Hedda Hopper for the sake of publicity, although there is no doubt that he intended to pursue the project.

A third reason for Ernie's repeating the "Silent Show" suggests itself as well. Depressed by the ceaseless financial pressures and the strains of his marriage, physically drained by overwork and unhealthful habits (his weight, usually hovering around 215 or 220, had dropped to 195 pounds), Ernie's imagination was simply wearing thin. On December 3 he taped his eighth special, due to air on January 23; low on fresh material, he decided to repeat the Bartok "Street Scene" sound-to-sight piece, and instead of the usual eight or ten running gags, he devised only four unrelated blackouts. And the script for the ninth Dutch Masters show, which would never be produced, was one of the dullest he had ever devised.

Written at around the time of the quickie books, while Ernie was clearly uninspired, it does away altogether with the blackouts, the running gags, and the sound-to-sight pieces. Instead, it is one long prison-movie spoof called "Ex-Con," and it bears little resemblance to the wickedly satirical movie sketches he had done for years in New York. Ernie wrote himself in as Vaseline-haired speakeasy owner Rotten Louie, whose crime is that he has too much money, so much that somebody suffocates in it and he winds up in jail. At the end, released from prison, he is hired to work at a bank, handed the combination to the bank vault, told to take home millions of dollars to count over the weekend, and winds up on a yacht with two pretty women, being served drinks by a private steward and tossing around handfuls of bills to the music from *Gone with the Wind*— a pathetic Kovacsian fantasy.

As his life fell apart, Ernie tried to regain some sense of stability by drawing a few trustworthy people close to him. His ABC special-effects man, Bobby Hughes, recalls that "he tried to get me to quit ABC because he wanted to form his own production company. I never had to make the decision because it never quite got to that, but he did ask me if I would leave ABC and go with him." He also said to Hughes, " 'For next season, think about square bubbles.' He'd like to zing you every once in a while with ideas. I've been thinking about square bubbles ever since. That would have been the only time he ever completely stumped me."

George Kudra, Ernie's furrier friend in Trenton, says that Ernie invited him to come to Hollywood and stay for a month, "all expenses paid," but Kudra did not take him up on it. He made a similar offer to his former next-door neighbor Helen Wilson, who had seen Ernie during his trip back East in the fall. "We had dinner in Trenton—the Cregars and ourselves and Ernie," Wilson recalls. "He wanted Dean and me to come out and work there for him. He said he would give us a home." Wilson sensed that her old friend had become jaded "about the fast crowd and the fast living. I think at that stage he just didn't know whom he could and couldn't trust. And I had never seen Ernie drink like he did that night. I think he was not as happy as he had been with his life."

Wilson also suspected that his health was poor. But he told her, "Helen, I will never, ever go back to a sanitarium again." "You can't burn the candle at both ends, up all night and playing cards. Physically you can destroy yourself," she warned. "Oh," he said, "life is short." But he also told her, "I just don't sleep as well." Wilson remembers, "I had a feeling he was really concerned about his health. I asked him, 'Why don't you have a checkup?' And he said, 'Oh, sure.' But I think he was a little scared of what they were going to tell him. I told my husband later that I had a funny feeling. That was the last time we saw him."

Elisabeth Kovacs remembers that period too. "I dreamed I lost my father two weeks before he died," she says. "I had this terrible dream that he was never coming home. I was sobbing and sobbing—then I woke up."

Edie, who had never wanted to leave New York, was now pressing

Ernie to return there, at least to work. Right before New Year's, she told one interviewer, she issued an ultimatum: either they would fix what had gone wrong with their lives, or she would seek a divorce. She said that Ernie broke down in tears. On New Year's Day 1962, Ernie announced that he would go East with Edie in February to direct some Broadway plays. He had had offers periodically since moving out to Hollywood but had always turned them down. Once his old friend Jane Hess had flown out to California to try to convince him to do a play her husband had written and in which Edie was evidently interested as well; she had even enlisted the aid of Harold Van Kirk, Ernie's beloved mentor, but to no avail. "I don't think he wanted to do the theater at all," says John Hess. "I think the idea of doing the same thing night after night was appalling to him." But now he made a commitment to direct two stage productions: *The Happy Medium*, a satire on television by Ronald Alexander, and a James Lipton musical based on the lives of two Prohibition agents, *Izzy and Moe*.

The final project of Ernie's actually to come to fruition, however, was for television, and it teamed him with none other than Buster Keaton. Ernie had long been an admirer of Keaton's work, and in the 1920s the silent star had achieved the creative control over his films that Ernie hoped to attain someday too. But these two talented men were brought together for a terrible project: a Western series, *Medicine Man*, in which Ernie would play a snake-oil salesman named Doc and Keaton his mute Native American sidekick, Junior. The pilot episode, "A Pony for Chris," has lots of canned laughter augmenting a silly plot about a Confederate-money con scheme. The only thing that can be said about Ernie's role as Doc is that it was more dignified than that of Buster Keaton, who was reduced to being the butt of racist jokes throughout the show.

The only reason Kovacs (and presumably Keaton as well) accepted *Medicine Man* was because he was desperate for money. One night during the second week of January, while he was working on "A Pony for Chris," Ernie met Jack Lemmon and his fiancée, Felicia Farr, for dinner at one of their favorite haunts, Dominick's. "I took a look at him, and he was wiped out," recalled Lemmon. "And maybe I just imagined it, but there was also a terrible kind of look in his eyes that I had never seen before. I mentioned to Felicia, after he left the table, that it was the first time I'd seen him where he might feel like giving up."

Friday morning, January 12, dawned sunny, smogless, and cool. Ernie got up early to drive to Griffith Park, where he was scheduled to spend the day shooting "A Pony for Chris." After work, he stopped at the ABC Television studios in Hollywood for an engineering session with his technical director, Gene Lukowski; they spent a couple of hours putting the final touches on the eighth ABC special. Later in the evening he was due to meet Edie at a party. Milton and Ruth Berle had just adopted a little boy, and Billy and Audrey Wilder were throwing a shower in their honor.

But Ernie seemed reluctant to go; he preferred intimate get-togethers with just a few friends. He phoned Jolene Brand and invited her and her husband, George Schlatter, to meet him for an early dinner at Dominick's before he had to go to the Wilders'. They declined, feeling that the evening would be too rushed. "He wanted to be with his buddies whenever he could," says Brand. "But it just seemed like he was dragging; it was too much to go tearing over there and be crammed into an hour or so. That was not normal for him. Normally we would have a whole evening with him." Instead, he grabbed a quick dinner with his poker friend Joe Mikolas before going home to change for the party.

When he got home, around 8:30, "he did not want to go to the party," remembers Kippie, who was sitting on her father's bed watching TV. "He was preoccupied and swearing. He went into his dressing room and was grooming his hair with two brushes. He took some shiny patent leather shoes off his rack, and he was putting on his clothes and getting ready, and he was swearing the whole time: 'This goddamn party I have to go to, I don't want to go.' He'd just finished work; he had to work the next morning. I asked, 'What's wrong, daddy?' And he said, 'I don't want to go to this goddamn party.' He finished getting dressed and gave me a big kiss and a hug and said, 'Bye, baby. See you later.' And he left."

"He was furious at having to go," recalls Elisabeth, who talked to her father in his den, where he went to get a bottle of champagne to take to the party. "He was crazed, and he said Edie wanted to go. He'd been working all day and he was miserable, exhausted, he had bags down to here"—she points way down on her cheeks. "I asked him to please come in and say good night, and he said that he would, but he didn't. It was the only night ever that he didn't do that."

Edie was already at the Wilders' apartment on Wilshire and Beverly Glen when he arrived in his Rolls-Royce; she had driven the family's white Corvair station wagon. Such Hollywood friends as Dean and Jeanne Martin, Kirk and Anne Douglas, and Lucille Ball and her new husband, Gary Morton, were in attendance. Kovacs hid his fury at having to be there. "Ernie was in great form at the party. He was

clowning at high speed, and the Kovacs cigar was in great evidence,"
said Gary Morton. "He had just finished this Western pilot film and
was in high spirits." Ernie told Jeanne Martin that he had found the
secret to long life: "All it takes is three steam baths a day, lots of good
brandy, about twenty cigars, and work all night."

By the time he and Edie were ready to leave, around 1:20 A.M., it
had started to drizzle. Yves Montand was staying at a nearby hotel,
and Kovacs offered him a lift, but Montand decided to ride with the
Berles. When an attendant brought the Rolls-Royce first, Ernie told
Edie to drive it home, knowing she disliked the Corvair. He took the
latter himself, waving good bye to Kirk Douglas as he drove off to
meet Mikolas for a nightcap at the club PJ's.

And now, Ernie took a peculiar route; nobody has ever been able
to explain adequately why he was around the 10000 block of Santa
Monica Boulevard, half a block southwest of the Beverly Hills Hotel,
on a stretch of street that was not on the way to PJ's from the Wilders'
apartment. But there he was, driving too fast as usual, the air misty
and the road slick with oil that the rain had brought to the surface. He
decided it was time for another cigar, and, as was his habit, he took his
hands off the wheel to reach into his pocket.

The Corvair station wagon, its weight heaviest in the rear where the
engine was, went into a spin, jumped a median, and a moment later
had wrapped itself around a utility pole. Ernie's skull was fractured,
his ribs were broken, his aorta was ruptured, and he was bleeding from
his ears; somehow he managed to pull himself partway out the passen-
ger door, but by the time the police ambulance arrived at 2:15 A.M. he
was dead. They found him with his left hand stretched toward an unlit
cigar that had dropped to the ground. In ten days he would have turned
forty-three.

Edie knew nothing of this; she started to worry an hour after she
got home. A reporter called and then—realizing she didn't know about
the accident—got off the phone quickly, suggesting she call the West
Los Angeles police. She did call but was told only that there had been
an accident. She kept calling until, finally, she heard the policeman put
his hand over the receiver and say, "It's Mrs. Kovacs. What'll I tell
her? . . . Jesus God, he's on his way to the coroner's office." They
sent an officer over to the house to give her the news in person. She
refused to believe it until Jack Lemmon telephoned from the morgue,
having identified his best friend's body. (A toxicology report showed
Ernie's blood alcohol level to be 0.11 percent, just a hair over the legal
limit of 0.10 percent later adopted by most states.)

Kippie, too, had an unexpected call, from a girlfriend who asked,

"Are you all right?" "I said, 'Yeah, I'm fine, I was sleeping.' Then she realized I didn't know: 'Oh, oh, okay, I'll talk to you later.' " Soon there was a knock on her bedroom door; it was the girls' pediatrician saying, "Your mother wants to talk to you." Kippie put on her robe and followed him down the hall, where they were joined by her sister Bette. "Actually, I had another fear in mind: that Edie was pregnant again. Because I had already lost that much of her," says Kippie. "She was in the secretary's office, sitting in the corner of the leopard-patterned couch, and she was red and crying. I said, 'What's wrong? What's wrong?' She said, 'There's been an accident.' I said, 'Are you okay?' And she said, 'Your daddy's gone.' Everything from that moment was gone. His life was gone and my life was gone, my sister's life—everything had changed in one moment. Because of a party. Because they switched cars."

Elisabeth remembers being told, " 'Your father's been killed.' My reaction was: 'Who? Who did it? I'll get them!' Then there was great crying. The doctor gave us tranquilizer shots. Edie and Kippie went to sleep in one bed, but I didn't want to. I knew otherwise I'd have to go through it later." The house was starting to fill with people—Jack Lemmon, Kim Novak, Buddy Hackett, Sondra and Barry Shear, Billy Wilder, Richard Quine. "Everybody started coming," remembers Kippie. "I couldn't even count the people. You could name anybody and they were there." After Kippie and Edie were put to bed, Elisabeth says, "I walked around all day and talked to Dick Quine a lot; he was a great comfort to me that day. Everybody was so tender to me and Kippie." One family friend remembers walking into the master bedroom and seeing little Mia, two and a half, playing by herself; her feet were encased in her daddy's enormous shoes. (Ironically and horribly, Mia would die in a car accident in 1982, sustaining injuries similar to those of the father she barely had known.)

Sometime on Saturday, Mary Kovacs, Ernie's mother, "came up to the house and she was told and she made a big scene," says Kippie. "I remember my grandmother being thrown out of the house, unfairly." According to Mary, it was Edie who had her thrown out. Mary was apparently also barred from attending the funeral of her only son. Richard Quine said that this was because "Edie was terrified" that Mary "would throw herself in the grave," a normal funerary tradition in some countries. In any case the decision seems an unduly harsh one to have made on behalf of a grown woman. So broken up was she by Ernie's death that Mary, who was "very religious," says Kippie, "stopped going to church forever."

Ernie's older half brother, Tom, had been in Bermuda that week. "I knew something was going to happen," he said. "I felt restless. I couldn't wait to get home. And then we got the news." He and his wife, Mabel, left for Los Angeles immediately. Andrew Kovacs heard of his son's death on the radio. He flew to Los Angeles on Saturday afternoon, looking pale and near collapse when he arrived along with Edie's mother, Ada Enke. When Andrew tried to talk to reporters, he broke into uncontrollable sobs.

By Monday, the day of the funeral, the rain had stopped and the sun had emerged again. A memorial service was held at the Beverly Hills Community Presbyterian Church, to which Edie belonged. Hundreds of mourners from the film community filed into the church: Edward G. Robinson, Jack Benny, George Burns, Sam Goldwyn, Groucho Marx, James Stewart, Kim Novak, Danny Thomas, Donna Reed, Jayne Mansfield, Buster Keaton, Greer Garson, William Wyler, Milton Berle, Kirk Douglas, Janet Leigh. Only a few of Ernie's ABC crew members came; most of them couldn't stand the sadness, and those who were there have blocked out the details. (Ernie's final ABC special aired as scheduled on January 23, his birthday; in his honor, Dutch Masters replaced the commercials with a clip of the Nairobi Trio.)

After the service, hundreds of mourning fans watched from behind ropes as a mahogany casket draped with a blanket of gardenias and a single red rose was carried out of the church by Jack Lemmon, Billy Wilder, Dean Martin, Joe Mikolas, Frank Sinatra, and Mervyn LeRoy. At Forest Lawn Memorial Park, just over the hill from Hollywood, a private burial was held for a handful of close friends and family (and an equal number of reporters). Kippie and Bette did not attend; Kippie says it was because "Edie didn't want us to go," probably to protect the girls from the pain; Elisabeth says she simply "couldn't bear it." (Richard Quine did not attend either; he told Elisabeth, "I cannot see my best friend buried.") The spot chosen for Ernie's grave was a gentle green slope named "Remembrance." The grave is marked by a bronze plaque bearing a facsimile of his flamboyant signature, setting it apart from the other names with their square cut letters. Underneath the signature are the years of his life, and across the bottom is the inscription

"NOTHING IN MODERATION"
WE ALL LOVED HIM.

After Ernie Kovacs' death a tangle of unresolved business emerged. Suddenly Bette Wilcox Kovacs showed up to lay claim to her daughters. Having obtained custody of them in a Florida court back in 1955, she now went through legal channels to compel Edie Adams to give them up. She also filed a claim against the Kovacs estate for $500,000 in damages, citing her late ex-husband's "wrongful and unlawful abduction [and] detaining" of Kippie and Bette from Florida.

Bette had obtained a $420-a-month job at a record store in Los Angeles and rented a furnished apartment big enough for three. She was attempting to show that she could support her daughters, but she was probably at a disadvantage fighting Edie, who had the public sympathy accorded a grieving celebrity widow as well as the services of a powerful lawyer, Murray Chotiner, a former campaign manager for Richard Nixon. In response to Bette's claims, Edie petitioned to have herself appointed the girls' guardian. The matter would have to be slugged out in court.

First, however, "the judge wanted us to see her for enough time for us to get to know her better," says Kippie Kovacs of her mother, who was granted twice-weekly visits through the summer. The encounters were often chilly and awkward. "We put up an impenetrable wall," admits Kippie. "No matter how hard she tried, she couldn't get through." In July, said Edie, the girls told her, "We don't belong to anyone." But Kippie and the younger Bette signed papers expressing a preference for Adams as their legal guardian. Mary Kovacs, their grandmother, also signed a form consenting to their choice, and she took Edie's side during the trial.

At the end of summer the girls had to endure a painful drama played out in a public courtroom, with reporters and photographers there every day. On September 13, Superior Court Judge Clarence Kincaid ruled that, while both Edie and Bette were "fit and proper" guardians, the teenage girls were "of sufficient age to form an intelligent preference." He turned down Bette's petition and granted custody to Edie. Bette Wilcox Kovacs stared straight ahead for several minutes, then broke into tears.

Edie later declared to a reporter, "I can never desert them. The bond that holds us together is the love we had for Ernie." The bond, however, appears to have been Ernie himself. Elisabeth left home at seventeen, Kippie at sixteen. Without Ernie's presence at the center of the family, the ties between Edie and his daughters eventually came undone.

The custody matter was straightforward compared to Ernie's estate. No will was found. Two weeks after his death, the gross value of Ernie's estate was reported to be $2.1 million, but a large portion of this represented mortgaged holdings, and the figure did not take into account the Kovacses' massive debts. Edie issued a statement saying that her husband "was deeply in debt and had been working with the government for a long time trying to untangle his affairs"; indeed, the government was still going over the Kovacses' books for 1958 to 1960. Before the end of January the IRS had put a lien on the estate for $176,000 in back taxes; the state of California had filed for $7,500 it was owed in back taxes; New York was claiming back taxes of $15,900; ABC had obtained a court order to attach $124,000 from E. & E. K. Enterprises, the Kovacses' production company, for below-the-line expenses on Ernie's last four specials; and still other creditors were standing in line.

Edie was advised by some to declare bankruptcy and to sell the Bowmont Drive house. It is unclear why she did not sell the huge house, but in 1962 bankruptcy was charged with stigma. The other alternative—to earn enough money to pay off the estate's debts—would force her to push her career out of the doldrums. She told her advisors she would take the latter course. "They didn't believe I could make it," she said. "It just never occurred to them that I could earn any money at all."

At the time Edie was given to telling reporters things like, "It's very tough for me to be a man. I like being a girl. I like belonging to somebody." But her actions indicate that she was more shrewd and capable than such an image suggests. First she enrolled in an advanced federal tax accounting course at UCLA—the only woman in a class full of lawyers and CPAs—to try to make some sense of the estate's problems. When Jack Lemmon, Richard Quine, Barry Shear, and Billy Wilder came up with a plan to produce four celebrity-studded benefit TV specials, which would have yielded an estimated $750,000 profit specifically for the Kovacs estate, Edie made a public announcement turning down the offer. Her stated reason was that it "would have embarrassed" Ernie, and this was true. But the announcement, which was reported in newspapers nationally, also signaled to the entertainment community that she was in the market for work.

Consolidated Cigar offered Edie $66,000 for ten TV commercials and sponsored her in her own special, *Here's Edie*, that spring. The show, which was directed by Barry Shear and nominated for two Emmys, was so well received that the cigar company signed her for eight more specials, paying $450,000 directly to her new production company, Ediad Productions. By the end of 1963 Edie had also cut a record album, appeared in four movies (though never in more than secondary roles), and obtained a $25,000-a-week contract to perform at the Riviera in Las Vegas.

In December 1962, however, Mary Kovacs brought legal action to have Edie removed as administratrix of her late son's estate, accusing her of having "wrongfully mismanaged, wasted, and neglected" it "for the purpose of promoting her own selfish interests." Mary claimed that Edie's alleged mismanagement threatened to render the estate insolvent and therefore jeopardized the portions that might eventually go to the minor heirs, Kippie, Bette, and Mia, and she petitioned to have herself appointed guardian for her grandchildren's estate. She accused Edie and her press agents, "for the purpose of furthering her own career," of having created "the fiction of an Edith Adams Kovacs who was left nothing by [Ernie] and is now penniless." Mary was the only one to point out publicly that Ernie and Edie had been having marital problems; according to Mary, they had decided on a divorce.

As for Edie's guardianship of Kippie and Bette, Mary claimed that Edie "has never held any genuine interest in [them] except during the recent court hearings when, for the sake of publicity, she fought for their custody to promote her career" and that the girls were "now being cared for by servants." Later she filed additional petitions: one to restrain Edie from interfering in her visits with her grandchildren, another to restrain Edie from misrepresenting to the public that she was the mother of Kippie and Bette or, alternatively, to require her to adopt Kippie and Bette. She said that Edie had "attempted to poison the minds of the children" against their grandmother and that she had been reduced to visiting the girls at school.

"It will be constant with her," Edie told one reporter who asked about Mary's legal actions. "She has a lot of problems, and she's very lonely. And I just can't call her every day and talk to her for a couple of hours, as Ernie did. If I did she'd be fine." It is true that some of Mary's accusations were purely personal and seemed to bear only a thin, if any, relation to the legal issues in question: her allegation that Edie used to "impersonate and insult" Ernie's friends at social gatherings, for instance, causing him to tell Mary "that he was ashamed of the way his wife behaved." But the bulk of Mary's charges were more substantial and precise than just the rantings of a lonely old woman.

The only personal concerns she ever brought up in her extensive court filings were that Edie had allegedly withheld life insurance proceeds that Mary claimed were due her and that her daughter-in-law had allegedly deprived her of her home, furniture, and personal property in New City. (The New City house had been put in Andrew Kovacs' name in 1960, but within three weeks of Ernie's death, the deed was transferred to Edie; nearly thirty years later, it remains in Edie's name.) These two issues aside, the general tenor of her accusations is one of protectiveness toward her grandchildren's interests.

For example, shortly after Ernie's death Edie had paid $62,000 of his estate's money to trust deeds on the Motor Avenue health club, but then a few months later she had purchased the property from the estate at a private sale in which she was the only bidder. (Half of the money she paid went to the estate, half to her personally, in accordance with California community-property law.) The health club had produced a $13,000 monthly income, which Edie was now receiving "for her own personal use to the injury of the estate," according to Mary, who also charged that Edie's having reduced the property's indebtedness with estate money prior to purchasing it for herself was injurious to the estate.

Another of Mary's numerous charges involved the fact that in September 1962, in another private sale, Edie had bought the personal property of Ernie's estate for $20,000. Mary alleged that Edie had concealed such assets as $50,000 worth of art; that she had "wrongfully asserted" the entire estate was community property, thereby seeking to deprive Ernie's children of their interest in Ernie's separate property; and that she had purchase most of the estate's assets "for inadequate payment." Some of the assessments of the personal property Edie purchased do seem low: Ernie's collection of arms and armor was valued at $2,500, for example, although three years earlier Ernie had told *TV Guide* it was worth $40,000.

In response, Edie counterfiled her own petitions, mainly seeking to discredit Mary. Since Ernie's death, Edie alleged, Mary had acted "in an irrational and abnormal manner to such an extent that a serious question has been raised in my mind as to her mental capacity and sanity." She accused Mary of shouting and using vulgar language "for no apparent reason," of being prone to sudden hysterical outbursts, of frequently and repeatedly telephoning Edie and the children "despite my requests that she refrain from calling," and of making "untrue and derogatory statements" about Edie to her TV sponsors, jeopardizing Edie's ability to earn a living. Edie denied Mary's accusations concerning her attitude toward Kippie and Bette. Answering Mary's other charges, Edie claimed that tax liens on the insurance policies prevented insurance money from being released; that the New City property had been transferred to Andrew Kovacs before Ernie's death; and that she had put $62,000 into the Motor Avenue property to prevent foreclosure and had sold it because it required payments higher than the income it produced. Regarding whatever might be left of Ernie's estate for the minor heirs, Edie claimed that "virtually all the assets in said estate have been sold and reduced to cash, and most of the cash in the estate has been paid to the United States Government in partial payment of income taxes due from decedent. . . . Said estate is and has always been hopelessly insolvent and there will be no assets to distribute to the heir or heirs of said decedent, whomever they may be."

Mary fought these cases for years, petitioning and appealing until 1967, when finally all the petitions—both hers and Edie's—were legally dismissed. Even apart from the legal struggles between Mary and Edie, the settling of the estate was a slow, trickling process. In 1965, for instance, the government foreclosed its lien on the insurance proceeds and applied them toward payment of the taxes. As of 1966, the IRS debt had been reduced to $135,200, the California state tax debt to $1,400. The debts were all settled and administration of the estate was finally brought to a close in November 1967.

When Edie turned down her friends' offer to produce the benefit special in 1962, Barry Shear explained to an interviewer, "Edie didn't want to be known as Young Widow Brown." Adams married twice again: she wed music publisher Martin Mills in 1964, had a son by him, and divorced him in 1972; she was married to musician Pete Candoli from 1972 to 1979 and helped raise his children. Many are surprised to learn of her other marriages, however. Her strongest public identity is that of Ernie Kovacs' widow, and it is an identity that seems only to intensify with the passage of time. In the public eye, at least, Edie Adams appears to have found a way to reconcile with her first husband.

Ernie was a pack rat, and after his death Edie gathered together a great quantity of material he had left behind. In the 1970s she donated scripts, production notebooks, and other materials pertaining to his TV, radio, and movie work to UCLA's Department of Special Collections, where it is now available to scholars. There was enough print material to fill thirty-five boxes, as well as TV-show sound tracks, popular records he used on his programs, and radio transcription disks (including a ringside account of a Trenton wrestling match that may be the audition record Ernie sent to WPTZ for his first TV job). Over the years Edie also collected all of the Kovacs-related tape and film she could find; most notably, with the help of Ernie's old ABC crew members, she rescued the videotapes of his ABC shows when it was discovered that the network was taping other programs over them. By the early 1980s she had some 200 hours of tapes and kinescopes, not only whole shows but also outtakes and experiments that documented Ernie's working methods. She made a substantial gift of these materials to the Museum of Broadcasting in New York, and the museum obtained a grant to begin preserving them. For herself she has kept many mementos of Ernie's work, ranging from Percy Dovetonsils' lace-covered poetry book and the little Kapusta puppets to the DuMont viewers' original "snepshots."

In other ways Ernie left a legacy that has extended far beyond his short lifetime. Mainstream broadcast TV, the medium in which he labored most deeply, has certainly felt his influence. He pioneered teaser openings and blackouts, forms subsequently used by Benny Hill, Monty Python, and *Laugh-In*, among others. His sketches parodying the familiar programming genres of his day anticipated those of *Second City TV* and *Saturday Night Live*. David Letterman's off-the-wall late-night antics and Garry Shandling's behind-the-scenes revelations to his audience seem descended from Kovacs' unrestricted live shows (in fact, Letterman screened some of Kovacs' early Philadelphia shows for inspiration in developing his program). In matching images to music, Ernie created some of the precursors to music videos, and subsequent videos for such groups as the Cars and the Talking Heads are infused by the Kovacsian spirit. (The video for the Cars' "You Might Think," filled with such surreal images as the love-stricken singer turning into a fly and buzzing toward his beloved's nose, is practically a minihomage to Ernie's 1950s camera tricks.) Chevy Chase has acknowledged Ernie as a major influence; Billy Crystal is a reported Kovacsphile. Ernie's Mr. Question Man lives on in Johnny Carson's Carnac the Magnificent; his old trick of matting himself into vintage movies was used in Woody Allen's *Zelig* and Carl Reiner's *Dead Men Don't Wear Plaid;* and the Muppets' "Pigs in Space" sketches are the descendants of Ernie's own puppet space spoof, "The Kapusta Kid in Outer Space."

Ernie's legacy is unusual, however, in that it crosses over from the mainstream media into the world of the artistic avant-garde. Articles discussing Kovacs have appeared in such art journals as *Artforum, High*

Performance, and *C*, and his work has been screened at such places as the University of Pennsylvania's Institute of Contemporary Art, New York's Museum of Modern Art, and Minneapolis' Walker Art Center. With the intuition of a true visionary, Ernie gravitated toward many of the issues that would later fascinate cutting-edge video artists, a type of creator that was only beginning to emerge at the time of his death. Ernie's attempts to break down the traditional barriers between TV viewers and practitioners anticipated Wolf Vostell's exhibitions of pie-splattered, barbed-wire-covered, and otherwise "treated" TV sets and Nam June Paik's interactive TVs, which were outfitted with special controls so that viewers could manipulate ordinary broadcasts. Direct audience address, a relaxed delivery style, and improvisations with everyday objects and with isolated parts of the body, all integral to Ernie's Philadelphia and New York shows, are also integral to the video work of such artists as Mitchell Kriegman and William Wegman. Teddy Dibble's humorous, unexpected takes on the TV medium's conventions pick up where Kovacs left off, and the matting of two or more images to create surreal video pictures, as Ernie often did, has been used by choreographer Merce Cunningham and many others.

Kovacs fans are an extraordinarily dedicated lot, but the mass media showed little interest in him in the decade after his death; virtually the only exposure his work received was in *The Comedy of Ernie Kovacs*, a 1968 ABC special sponsored by Consolidated Cigar, and in the 1971 documentary *Kovacs!*, a Stone-Galanoy Production distributed to colleges. In 1977, however, PBS aired *The Best of Ernie Kovacs*, a series made up mostly of the late ABC material; it received wide press and introduced a new generation of viewers to Kovacs' work. The following year twenty episodes of *Take a Good Look* were syndicated nationally.

In the 1980s, as suddenly as it had waned, media interest in Kovacs began to swell. Two documentaries, WNJT's *Cards and Cigars: The Trenton in Ernie Kovacs* (1980) and Showtime Cable's *Ernie Kovacs: Television's Original Genius* (1982), have aired numerous times, as has the ABC Television movie *Ernie Kovacs: Between the Laughter* (1984), which starred Jeff Goldblum as Ernie and dramatized the kidnapping and recovery of Kippie and Elisabeth Kovacs. His TV work was the subject of special tributes at the American Film Institute's National Video Festival in 1983 and at the Museum of Broadcasting/Los Angeles County Museum of Art's annual television festivals in 1986 and 1987. The most important tribute has been "The Vision of Ernie Kovacs," a four-month-long series mounted by New York's Museum of Broadcasting in 1986.

"The Vision of Ernie Kovacs" showcased Ernie's work in such diverse areas as late-night television, talk shows, TV and movie spoofs, blackout skits, improvisation, character comedy, music video, and TV dramatic anthologies. (With the exception of this and a four-film series at the New Jersey State Museum in 1985, however, Ernie's acting work in movies and TV anthologies has remained woefully ignored.) The series received national media coverage and became the most popular program ever mounted by the museum. When a shortened version, "The Ernie Kovacs Exhibit," was shown at Temple University in Philadelphia the following year, it was again extremely well attended. The museum published an excellent catalogue as a companion to the series, a book that continues to sell today.

Popular recognition has continued. In 1987 Ernie Kovacs was inducted into the Academy of Television Arts & Sciences' Hall of Fame. In 1988 his work was included in "On the Air: Pioneers of American Broadcasting," an exhibition cosponsored by the National Portrait Gallery and the Museum of Broadcasting. In 1989, on the occasion of television's fiftieth anniversary, he was named one of the medium's top twenty-five stars of all time in a special issue of *People* magazine.

The recognition is well earned and long overdue. In his lifetime, despite a loyal contingency of fans and a supportive critical establishment, Ernie's insistence on swimming against the mainstream tide prevented him from achieving the high prime-time ratings that are regarded as the badge of success in network TV. But the same qualities that kept him from reaching the high numbers were what made him such a special talent—the endlessly curious intellect, the love of experimentation, the boundless imagination, the subversive and surreal wit. Ernie Kovacs loved nothing more than to create his bizarre visions for the world to enjoy. We are fortunate that for a dozen years at the beginning of the most important medium of our time, he was able to do just that.

NOTES

15 *"we had to work"*:   Ann Beierfield, "Ernie Was No Stranger to Failure," *Trenton Sunday Times Advertiser*, Mar. 31, 1968.

15 *"You'd have to know"*:   Interview with Helen Wilson, Dec. 10, 1988.

CHAPTER 2

16 *"You could tell"*:   Interview with Warren Ermeling, Dec. 9, 1988.

16 *"They made the second"*:   August P. Ciell, taped letter to DR, Dec. 1988.

16 *"was just a little"*:   Interview with Helen Wilson, Dec. 10, 1988.

16 *"As you entered"*:   August P. Ciell, taped letter to DR, Dec. 1988.

18 *"It was very soon"*:   Interview with Helen Wilson, Dec. 10, 1988.

18 *"I was thoroughly"*:   CBS Television, *Person to Person*, June 24, 1955.

19 *"You couldn't help"*:   Interview with Sarah Christie, Oct. 5, 1988.

19 *"He was always in"*:   Ann Beierfield, "Ernie was No Stranger to Failure," *Trenton Sunday Times Advertiser*, Mar. 31, 1968.

19 *"October 10, 11, 12"*:   *The Bobashela* (Trenton: Trenton Central High School, 1936), p. 149.

19 *"He said that this"*:   WNJT, *Cards and Cigars: The Trenton in Ernie Kovacs*, prod. Calvin Iszard and Laurel Spira, 1980 (hereinafter cited as *Cards and Cigars*).

19 *"Any student who"*:   Interview with Sarah Christie, Oct. 5, 1988.

20 *"very masculine"*:   Interview with Nathaniel Doughty, Oct. 4, 1988.

20 *"We did the necessary"*:   *Cards and Cigars.*

21 *"Ernie, do you sing?"*:   ibid.

21 *"He was in costume"*:   Interview with Tom Durand, May 12, 1987.

22 *"a professional company"*:   Interview with Martin Manulis, Oct. 23, 1987.

22 *"a very educated man"*:   Interview with Jane Hess, Oct. 6, 1988.

23 *"In the summer"*:   Interview with Martin Manulis, Oct. 23, 1987.

23 *"The theater was beautiful"*:   Interview with Jane Hess, Oct. 6, 1988.

00 *"with standees outside"*:   "Studio Group Gives Pleasing 'Stunt Night,' " n.p., Aug. 5, 1937 (in Guild Hall scrapbook, vol. III, p. 79).

24 *"One can never"*:   Interview with Martin Manulis, Oct. 23, 1987.

24 *"horsing around"*:   Interview with Jane Hess, Oct. 6, 1988.

25 *"Ernie Kovacs [is] now ready"*:   The Observer, "Studio Group Opens with 'Warrior's Husband,' " n.p., July 1938 (in Guild Hall scrapbook, vol. IV, p. 32).

25 *"Obviously, the director"*:   "Studio Players in Bulgaria, 1885–1938," n.p., July 1938 (in Guild Hall scrapbook, vol. V).

25 *"The Observer issues"*:   The Observer, "Rollins Players in 'Stage Door,' " n.p., Aug. 1938 (in Guild Hall scrapbook, vol. V, p. 36).

25 *"That review would"*:   Interview with Jane Hess, Oct. 6, 1988.

26 *"Among the 'character actors' "*:   "The Observer, "Molnar's 'Liliom' Given by Rollins Studio Group," n.p., Sept. 1938 (in Guild Hall scrapbook, vol. V, p. 40).

26 *"Van Kirk was"*:   Interview with Martin Manulis, Oct. 23, 1987.

27 *"shy and tended"*:   Interviews with Jane Hess, Oct. 6 and Nov. 6, 1988.

27 *"There was so"*:   Interview with Jim Miller, Jan. 16, 1989.

27   *"He'd come onstage":*   Cards and Cigars.

27   *"I'm supposed to say":*   Interview with Jane Hess, Oct. 6, 1988.

28   *"Something revolutionary":*   in Guild Hall scrapbook, vol. V, p. 3B.

CHAPTER 3

30   *"It was so dark":*   Interview with Helen Wilson, Dec. 10, 1988.

30   *"He had one narrow":*   Interview with Dwight Dickinson, Feb. 11, 1989.

31   *"He was caught":*   Interview with Helen Wilson, Dec. 10, 1988.

31   *"I think Frances Pole":*   Interviews with Jane Hess, Oct. 6 and Nov. 6, 1988.

32   *"He was very much":*   ibid.

32   *"It had been":*   Interview with Dwight Dickinson, Feb. 11, 1989.

33   *"I used to sit":*   "Hedda Hopper's Hollywood," Chicago Tribune – New York News Syndicate, Aug. 27, 1961.

33   *"We need to have":*   Interview with Jane Hess, Oct. 6, 1988.

33   *"in hospital pajamas":*   Interview with Dwight Dickinson, Feb. 11, 1989.

34   *"we were all":*   Interview with Martin Manulis, Oct. 23, 1987.

34   *"these badly afflicted":*   Cards and Cigars.

34   *"his mother smuggled in":*   ibid.

35   *"I knew he was frustrated":*   Interview with Helen Wilson, Dec. 10, 1988.

35   *"with home cooking":*   Charles Roland, "Kovacs Hit Top on Nerve and Verve," n.p., Jan. 14, 1962.

35   *"they would have one":*   Interview with Kippie Kovacs, Jan. 28, 1989.

35   *"there was an outer":*   Interview with Edna Vine, Oct. 7, 1988.

     "my uncle, who was":   Cards and Cigars.

35   *"a man came":*   Interview with Edna Vine, Oct. 7, 1988.

36   *"Four days before":*   Robert H. Prall, "Who Said He's Mad?," *New York World-Telegram and Sun*, Mar. 19, 1955.

36   *"a con artist":*   Interview with Edna Vine, Oct. 7, 1988.

36   *"He thought it was":*   ibid.

37   *"very long store":*   Richard Schickel, "The Real Ernie Kovacs IS Standing Up," *Show*, Dec. 1961, p. 82.

37   *"he always tried":*   Interview with Marion Shapiro, Oct. 3, 1988.

38   *"He had her picture":*   Interview with Edna Vine, Oct. 7, 1988.

38   *"one time":*   Interview with Marion Shapiro, Oct. 3, 1988.

39   *"because my grandmother":*   Interview with Kippie Kovacs, Jan. 28, 1989.

39   *"He took an awful":*   Interview with Marion Shapiro, Oct. 3, 1988.

PART TWO: RADIO WAVES (1941 – 1950)

CHAPTER 4

43   *"In people's homes":*   Interview with Steve Allen, Feb. 17, 1988.

43   *"the same entertainment":*   Irving Settel, *A Pictorial History of Radio* (New York: Citadel Press, 1960), p. 73.

45 *"At the station"*:   Michael Fonde, letter to DR, July 10, 1987.
45 *"He looked like"*:   Interview with Edna Vine, Oct. 7, 1988.
45 *"I'll never forget"*:   Eddie Hatrak to Mary Lou Cassidy, interview, Jan. 1969.
46 *"wherever you saw"*:   Interview with George Quinty, Sr., Nov. 20, 1986.
46 *"Ernie was always playing"*:   Eddie Hatrak to Mary Lou Cassidy, interview, Jan. 1969.
46 *"One was a puzzle"*:   Interview with Edna Vine, Oct. 7, 1988.
46 *"He wanted a script"*:   Interview with Minerva Davenport, Nov. 2, 1987.
47 *"He never knew how"*:   Interview with Michael Fonde, May 11, 1987.
47 *"He wanted to be"*:   Interview with Joe Butera, Oct. 4, 1988.
47 *"him jumping into"*:   Interview with Helen Wilson, Dec. 10, 1988.
47 *"viewed him as"*:   Interview with Edna Vine, Oct. 7, 1988.
48 *"If Ernie had it"*:   Interview with Marion Shapiro, Oct. 3, 1988.
48 *"Will you go in"*:   *Cards and Cigars.*
48 *"but he would never"*:   Interview with Michael Fonde, May 11, 1987.
48 *"When I came back"*:   Interview with Donald Mattern, Oct. 4, 1988.
48 *"Anytime there was"*:   Interview with Joe Butera, Oct. 4, 1988.
48 *"They didn't know"*:   Interview with Donald Mattern, Oct. 4, 1988.
49 *"WTNJ had bigger"*:   Interview with Joe Butera, Oct. 4, 1988.
49 *"The network affiliation"*:   Interview with Donald Mattern, Oct. 4, 1988.
49 *"would get knotted"*:   Interview with Tom Durand, May 12, 1987.
49 *"What gripped radio's"*:   Norman Corwin, "Those Radio Days: When Listening Was the Rule," *Los Angeles Times*, April 9, 1987.
50 *"We were always out"*:   Interview with Michael Fonde, May 11, 1987.
50 *"He'd ask people"*:   "Ernie's Mother Refuses to Believe He's Dead," *Trenton Sunday Times Advertiser*, Mar. 31, 1968.
50 *"and they used to"*:   Interview with Elaine Vulgaris, Oct. 4, 1988.
50 *"Ernie followed him"*:   Interview with Francis J. Lucas, Dec. 9, 1988.
51 *"He was like"*:   Eddie Hatrak to Mary Lou Cassidy, interview, Jan. 1969.
51 *"cooked up a deal"*:   Interview with Tom Durand, May 12, 1987.
51 *"His daily round"*:   "Radio Marathon in 75th Hour in Jersey," *New York Herald Tribune*, Sept. 29, 1949.
52 *"At times . . . I recorded"*:   Interview with Michael Fonde, May 11, 1987.
52 *"I could never"*:   Eddie Hatrak to Mary Lou Cassidy, interview, Jan. 1969.
52 *"too dangerous even"*:   Interview with Michael Fonde, May 11, 1987.
53 *"He used to wear"*:   Interview with Donald Mattern, Oct. 4, 1988.
53 *"She started screaming"*:   Interview with Michael Fonde, May 11, 1987.
53 *"an extremely jumpy"*:   Interview with Tom Durand, May 12, 1987.
53 *"There was one announcer"*:   Interview with Billie Durand, May 12, 1987.
53 *"Breaking them up"*:   Interview with Donald Mattern, Nov. 6, 1988.
54 *"would be directed"*:   Interview with Tom Durand, May 12, 1987.
54 *"He would sell"*:   Interview with Donald Mattern, Nov. 6, 1988.

CHAPTER 5

55 *"like the back"*: Cards and Cigars.
55 *"We were walking"*: Interview with Helen Wilson, Dec. 10, 1988.
56 *"before we recorded"*: Interview with Michael Fonde, May 11, 1987.
56 *"a frightened gallant"*: Interview with Deke Heyward, Feb. 12, 1987.
56 *"would do these"*: Interview with George Kudra, Nov. 6, 1988.
56 *"very pretty"*: Interview with Billie Durand, May 12, 1987.
57 *"it seemed as though"*: Interview with Elisabeth Kovacs, Feb. 13, 1989.
57 *"He fell in love"*: Interview with Edna Vine, Oct. 7, 1988.
57 *"They were very much"*: Interview with Marion Shapiro, Oct. 3, 1988.
57 *"Every time we went"*: Interview with Michael Fonde, May 11, 1987.
58 *"She was a volatile"*: Interview with Marion Shapiro, Oct. 3, 1988.
58 *"Mary did not travel"*: Interview with Donald Mattern, Nov. 6, 1988.
58 *"was afraid of her"*: Interview with Michael Fonde, May 11, 1987.
58 *"Ernie got along"*: Interview with Edna Vine, Oct. 7, 1988.
58 *"It was a one-man"*: Interview with Eunice Jacobs, Oct. 4, 1988.
60 *"personal juke box"*: Ernie Kovacs, "Kovacs," *Trentonian*, Sept. 13, 1947.
60 *"Dear Commissioner"*: ibid., Oct. 2, 1947.
61 *"The restaurants skirting"*: ibid., Sept. 16, 1947.
61 *"How come the five-chunker"*: ibid., Sept. 17, 1947.
61 *"Please help us"*: ibid., April 1, 1947.
61 *"Erratum: The Creston"*: ibid., May 20, 1947.
61 *"We'll be broadcasting"*: ibid., Nov. 4, 1947.
62 *"One of Ernie's pet"*: Interview with Joe Butera, Oct. 4, 1988.
62 *"put four miles"*: Ernie Kovacs, "Kovacs," *Trentonian*, Sept. 13, 1947.
62 *"We have never seen"*: ibid., Sept. 17, 1947.
62 *"Rich people are only"*: ibid., Oct. 4, 1947.
62 *"Mr. Bingeleh Crosby"*: ibid., Sept. 13, 1947.
62 *"Somewhere outside Camden"*: ibid., Sept. 16, 1947.
63 *"This is WA to Z"*: quoted in David Walley, *The Ernie Kovacs Phile* (New York: Bolder Books, 1975), pp. 47–48 (hereinafter cited as *Kovacs Phile*).
63 *"Open letter to F.W."*: ibid., p. 46.
64 *"if you lived"*: ibid., p. 48.
64 *"We were all newlyweds"*: Interview with Billie Durand, May 12, 1987.
64 *"a boxes-without-topses"*: Interview with Tom Durand, May 12, 1987.
64 *"It was a very simple"*: Interview with Billie Durand, May 12, 1987.
64 *"our ivy-covered"*: Walley, *Kovacs Phile*, p. 53.
64 *"was always joking"*: Interview with Michael Fonde, May 11, 1987.
65 *"she made it miserable"*: Interview with Marion Shapiro, Oct. 3, 1988.
65 *"and we'd have a beer"*: Interview with Helen Wilson, Dec. 10, 1988.
65 *"after the conventional"*: Interview with Tom Durand, May 12, 1987.
65 *"Rizzolved! Never again"*: Ernie Kovacs, "Kovacs," *Trentonian*, May 19, 1947.
67 *"He was a wonderful"*: Interview with Helen Wilson, Dec. 10, 1988.
67 *"He was really great"*: Interview with Billie Durand, May 12, 1987.
67 *"This is very much"*: Walley, *Kovacs Phile*, p. 127.

67   *"She was very young"*:   Interview with Marion Shapiro, Oct. 3, 1988.

67   *"We always had the feeling"*:   Interview with Elisabeth Kovacs, Feb. 13, 1989.

67   *"finding little Bette"*:   Interview with Marion Shapiro, Oct. 3, 1988.

68   *"Wouldn't you be"*:   Interview with Helen Wilson, Dec. 10, 1988.

68   *"they were having"*:   Interview with Dean Wilson, Dec. 9, 1988.

68   *"and she had every"*:   Interview with Marion Shapiro, Oct. 3, 1988.

68   *"Take over, Mike"*:   Interview with Michael Fonde, May 11, 1987.

68   *"As we'd be sitting"*:   Eddie Hatrak to Mary Lou Cassidy, interview, Jan. 1969.

68   *"in a very tiny"*:   Interview with Donald Mattern, Oct. 4, 1988.

69   *"Some weeks ago"*:   Ernie Kovacs, "Kovacs," *Trentonian*, Nov. 4, 1947.

69   *"I think Ernie liked"*:   Interview with Dean Wilson, Dec. 9, 1988.

69   *"Ernie was stubborn"*:   *Cards and Cigars*.

CHAPTER 6

71   *"the first person"*:   Interview with Bill Freeland, Nov. 11, 1987.

71   *"Appliance stores were"*:   Interview with Tom Durand, May 12, 1987.

72   *"I said to him"*:   Interview with Michael Fonde, May 11, 1987.

72   *"At that time"*:   Interview with Preston Stover, Nov. 12, 1987.

73   *"He just sat in"*:   ibid.

73   *"The host had not"*:   Interview with Andy McKay, Sept. 27, 1988.

73   *"I don't think"*:   Ronald Simon, "An Interview with Joe Behar," *The Vision of Ernie Kovacs* (New York: Museum of Broadcasting, 1986), p. 66 (hereinafter cited as *Vision*).

74   *"There would be two"*:   Interview with Bill Freeland, Nov. 11, 1987.

74   *"show their most famous"*:   Ronald Simon, "An Interview with Joe Behar," *Vision*, p. 66.

74   *"Whatever you like"*:   Richard Schickel, "The Real Ernie Kovacs IS Standing Up," *Show*, Dec. 1961, p. 82.

74   *"he was serious"*:   Interview with Bill Freeland, Nov. 11, 1987.

74   *"worked well together"*:   Interview with Preston Stover, Nov. 12, 1987.

75   *"Bink thought he"*:   Interview with Barney Kramer, Jan. 16, 1989.

75   *"Network shows aren't"*:   "You May Be the Lucky Lady," *TV Digest*, Aug. 25, 1951, p. 8.

75   *"In the total"*:   Ernie Kovacs, "Kovacs," *Trentonian*, June 2, 1950.

76   *"Yesterday we started"*:   ibid., Aug. 25, 1950.

76   *"We've had several"*:   ibid., June 2, 1950.

76   *"The F.W. was on"*:   ibid., April 6, 1950.

76   *"I remember arguing"*:   Interview with Elisabeth Kovacs, Feb. 13, 1989.

76   *"He picked up"*:   Interview with Michael Fonde, May 11, 1987.

77   *"When we stopped"*:   Interview with Billie Durand, May 12, 1987.

77   *"Eddie, . . . Bette and I"*:   Eddie Hatrak to Mary Lou Cassidy, interview, Jan. 1969.

77   *"I'd never seen him"*:   Interview with Michael Fonde, May 11, 1987.

77   *"It was heartbreaking"*:   Interview with Billie Durand, May 12, 1987.

PART THREE: **ERNIE IN TELEVISIONLAND (1950–1952)**

CHAPTER 7

81   *"I believe he loved"*:   Interview with Kippie Kovacs, Jan. 28, 1989.

81   *"kind of a nuisance"*:   Robert Metz, *The Today Show* (Chicago: Playboy Press, 1977), pp. 13–14 (hereinafter cited as *Today*).

82   *"He told me that"*:   Interview with Jane Hess, Nov. 6, 1988.

82   *"Morning television was"*:   Metz, *Today*, pp. 33–34.

82   *"At one point"*:   Interview with Preston Stover, Nov. 12, 1987.

83   *"They wanted a very"*:   Ronald Simon, "An Interview with Joe Behar," *Vision*, p. 66.

85   *"we'd be shooting"*:   Interview with Bill Freeland, Nov. 11, 1987.

85   *"I remember him"*:   Interview with Barney Kramer, Jan. 16, 1989.

86   *"We never had"*:   Interview with Andy McKay, Sept. 27, 1988.

86   *"When he made"*:   Andy McKay, "A First-Hand Remembrance," *Vision*, pp. 58–59.

88   *"Ernie couldn't remember"*:   Interview with Barney Kramer, Jan. 16, 1989.

89   *"Benny was a free"*:   Interview with Preston Stover, Nov. 12, 1987.

90   *"When NBC picked him"*:   Interview with Ron Hower, Oct. 5, 1988.

90   *"It was just quietly"*:   Interview with Bill Freeland, Nov. 11, 1987.

91   *"Oh, a beautiful"*:   Interview with Joe Earley, Nov. 2, 1987.

91   *"Of course, you have"*:   Pete Martin, "I Call on Edie Adams and Ernie Kovacs," *Saturday Evening Post*, Dec. 28, 1957, p. 42.

92   *"odd-ball summer jobs"*:   ibid.

92   *"They were singing"*:   Susan King, "Click," *Los Angeles Herald Examiner*, Feb. 28, 1986.

92   *"When [mother and daddy] found out"*:   Pete Martin, "I Call on Edie Adams and Ernie Kovacs," *Saturday Evening Post*, Dec. 28, 1957, p. 42.

93   *"My mother was"*:   Susan King, "Click," *Los Angeles Herald Examiner*, Feb. 28, 1986.

93   93 *You gotta swim"*:   Pete Martin, "I Call on Edie Adams and Ernie Kovacs," *Saturday Evening Post*, Dec. 28, 1957, p. 42.

93   *"Of course, they didn't"*:   Hyman Goldberg, "Edie Is a Lady," *Cosmopolitan*, Dec. 1955, p. 28.

94   *"This poor little"*:   Eleanor Blau, "Ernie Kovacs: Zany Influence on TV Comedy," *New York Times*, May 30, 1986.

94   *"I'm going out"*:   Edie Adams Kovacs and John M. Ross, "Ernie Kovacs—What a Husband!," *American Weekly*, July 20, 1958, p. 12.

94   *"I tried to ignore"*:   Walley, *Kovacs Phile*, p. 123.

95   *"I couldn't believe"*:   ibid.

95   *"She wasn't inhibited"*:   Interview with Preston Stover, Nov. 12, 1987.

96   *"Technically I was"*:   Diana Rico and Ben Herndon, "Great Shows: Ernie Kovacs," *Emmy*, Summer 1981, p. 50.

CHAPTER 8

97   *"The cast was just":*   Interview with Joe Earley, Nov. 2, 1987.
97   *"Most of the people":*   Interview with Karl Weger Jr., Nov. 2, 1987.
98   *"theater of poverty:"*   John Minkowsky, "An Intimate Vacuum: Ernie Kovacs in the Aura of Video Art," *Vision,* p. 39.
98   *"we only had $15":*   Interview with Andy McKay, Sept. 27, 1988.
102   *"Ernie Kovacs—the most":*   Merrill Panitt, "TV Pats and Pans," *Philadelphia Inquirer,* Nov. 22, 1951.
102   *"He made use of":*   Interview with Merrill Panitt, Sept. 29, 1988.
102   *"When he started":*   Interview with Harry Harris, Oct. 4, 1988.
102   *"wild and casual":*   Harriet Van Horne, "Importance of Kovacs Being Ernie," *New York World-Telegram and Sun,* July 24, 1951.
103   *"Ernie really saw":*   Interview with Mike Marmer, April 22, 1981.
103   *"direct standing up":*   Interview with Karl Weger, Jr., Nov. 2, 1987.
104   *"The whole crew":*   Interview with Rene Heckman, Oct. 4, 1988.
104   *"If something didn't":*   Interview with Bill Hofmann, Nov. 9, 1987.
104   *"I was a great":*   Interview with Karl Weger, Jr., Nov. 2, 1987.
105   *"He'd be sitting":*   Interview with Bill Freeland, Nov. 11, 1987.
106   *"We used a little":*   Interview with Karl Weger, Jr., Nov. 2, 1987.
106   *"Bill would just":*   Interview with Rene Heckman, Oct. 4, 1988.
106   *"I always thought":*   Interview with Bill Hofmann, Nov. 9, 1987.
107   *"Ernie would walk":*   ibid.
108   *"I had a sense":*   Interview with Andy McKay, Sept. 27, 1988.
108   *"He would jump":*   Interview with Bill Hofmann, Nov. 9, 1987.
110   *"We'd take anything":*   Diana Rico and Ben Herndon, "Great Shows: Ernie Kovacs," *Emmy,* Summer 1981, p. 50.

CHAPTER 9

112   *"There was a rundown":*   Ronald Simon, "An Interview with Joe Behar," *Vision,* p. 66.
112   *"There is still":*   "3 to Get Ready," *Variety,* Dec. 5, 1951.
112   *"having someone who":*   Andy Rooney, "CBS' Morning Show Needs More Than a Pretty Face," *Los Angeles Herald Examiner,* Oct. 10, 1987.
113   *"I had sold":*   Interview with Robert Jawer, Nov. 11, 1987.
113   *"The clients, having seen":*   Interview with Harold J. Pannepacker, Nov. 11, 1987.
115   *"We always used to":*   Interview with Bill Hofmann, Nov. 9, 1987.
115   *"When he came into":*   Interview with Rene Heckman, Oct. 4, 1988.
116   *"Ernie did not like":*   Interview with Donald Mattern, Nov. 6, 1988.
116   *"Ernie's problem was":*   Interview with B. Calvin Jones, Jan. 16, 1989.
116   *"I think he had":*   Interview with Karl Weger, Jr., Nov. 2, 1987.
117   *"Sometimes I used to":*   Pete Martin, "I Call on Edie Adams and Ernie Kovacs," *Saturday Evening Post,* Dec. 28, 1957, p. 39.
117   *"With nervous energy":*   Robert Rosen, "A Tribute to Ernie Kovacs, Video Artist," *1983 National Video Festival* (Washington, D.C.: American Film Institute, 1983), p. 57.

117 *"As things progressed"*: Interview with Karl Weger, Jr., Nov. 2, 1987.
118 *"This smells like money"*: Interview with Jane Hess, Nov. 6, 1988.
118 *"I believe that"*: Interview with Kippie Kovacs, Jan. 28, 1989.
118 *"But once you do"*: Interview with George Kudra, Nov. 6, 1988.
118 *"He didn't want to be"*: Interview with Joe Earley, Nov. 2, 1987.
118 *"those writs that were"*: Interview with Bill Freeland, Nov. 11, 1987.
118 *"After a while"*: Interview with Bill Hofmann, Nov. 9, 1987.
119 *"He never was too"*: Interview with Elisabeth Kovacs, Feb. 13, 1989.
119 *"The court clerk"*: Interview with Helen Wilson, Dec. 10, 1988.
119 *"he was very emotional"*: Interviews with Jane Hess, Oct. 6 and Nov. 6, 1988.
120 *"We didn't know Bette"*: Interview with Helen Wilson, Dec. 10, 1988.
120 *"most of his friends"*: Interview with Marion Shapiro, Oct. 3, 1988.
120 *"When my mother"*: Interview with Elisabeth Kovacs, Feb. 13, 1989.
120 *"were terrified"*: Interview with Elisabeth Kovacs, Dec. 20, 1988.
120 *"sitting on the judge's"*: Interview with Kippie Kovacs, Jan. 28, 1989.
120 *"I remember begging"*: Interview with Elisabeth Kovacs, Feb. 13, 1989.

CHAPTER 10

122 *"Radio not only"*: Les Brown, *The New York Times Encyclopedia of Television* (New York: Times Books, 1977), p. 298 (hereinafter cited as *Times Encyclopedia*).
122 *"could (and would)"*: Alex McNeil, *Total Television: A Comprehensive Guide to Programming from 1948 to the Present*, 2nd ed. (New York: Penguin Books, 1984), pp. 429–430.
122 *"Then began the wholesale"*: Brown, *Times Encyclopedia*, p. 298.
124 *"The listener will become"*: Metz, *Today*, p. 30.
124 *"the nerve center"*: Harry Castleman and Walter J. Podrazik, *Watching TV* (New York: McGraw-Hill, 1982), p. 70.
124 *"an important market"*: Merrill Panitt, "Garroway Will Replace Kovacs' '3 to Get Ready,' " *Philadelphia Inquirer*, Mar. 14, 1952.
125 *"The network was definitely"*: Interview with Karl Weger, Jr., Nov. 2, 1987.
125 *"they just wanted"*: Interview with Andy McKay, Sept. 27, 1988.
125 *"It is just"*: Mitchell Swartz, "TV Chatter," *Philadelphia Daily News*, Mar. 20, 1952.
125 *"He did retain"*: Interview with Karl Weger, Jr., Nov. 2, 1987.
125 *"A very bright guy"*: Interview with Robert Jawer, Nov. 11, 1987.
126 *"He used to have"*: Interview with Donald Mattern, Nov. 6, 1988.
126 *"They canceled us"*: Ronald Simon, "An Interview with Joe Behar," *Vision*, p. 67.
126 *"definite sadness"*: Interview with Karl Weger, Jr., Nov. 2, 1987.
127 *"We have had a lot"*: Merrill Panitt, "Ernie Kovacs' Fans Deliver Protests as Show Bows Out for Dave Garroway," *Philadelphia Inquirer*, Mar. 23, 1952.

127 *"The light has gone":*   Merrill Panitt, "Fans Rally 'Round Dagmar; Mourn Kovacs' Absence," *Philadelphia Inquirer*, April 1952.

PART FOUR: **NETWORK ROULETTE (1952–1957)**

CHAPTER 11

131 *"Should Kovacs click":*   "Ernie Kovacs to WCBS-TV," *Billboard*, April 12, 1952.
131 *"I think up three":*   Harold Brown, "Kovacs' Zany Daytime Show," *New York Herald Tribune*, May 4, 1952.
132 *"Channel 2's Ernie Kovacs":*   "Televiewing and Listening in with Rudy Bergman," *New York Daily News*, Nov. 19, 1952.
132 *"Kovacs tries to make":*   " 'Kovacs Unlimited' Is Good Parlor Antics TV," *Tide*, Aug. 8, 1952.
137 *"I was awfully green":*   Hyman Goldberg, "Edie Is a Lady," *Cosmopolitan*, Dec. 1955, p. 27.
137 *"one of the hottest":*   Rosalind Russell and Chris Chase, *Life Is a Banquet* (New York: Random House, 1977), p. 154 (hereinafter cited as *Banquet*).
138 *"I didn't want them":*   Hyman Goldberg, "Edie Is a Lady," *Cosmopolitan*, Dec. 1955, p. 30.
138 *"I didn't want to play":*   Russell and Chase, *Banquet*, p. 156.
138 *"You're not the type":*   Hyman Goldberg, "Edie Is a Lady," *Cosmopolitan*, Dec. 1955, p. 27.
138 *"Apparently there is":*   Pete Martin, "I Call on Edie Adams and Ernie Kovacs," *Saturday Evening Post*, Dec. 28, 1957, p. 42.
138 *"each time I was":*   Philip Minoff, "Edie's Quite a Lady," *Cue*, April 4, 1953.
139 *"If I seem relaxed":*   ibid.
139 *"I didn't know upstage":*   Pete Martin, "I Call on Edie Adams and Ernie Kovacs," *Saturday Evening Post*, Dec. 28, 1957, p. 42.
139 *"I got so I wasn't":*   Russell and Chase, *Banquet*, p. 155.
140 *"We all thought":*   Hyman Goldberg, "Edie Is a Lady," *Cosmopolitan*, Dec. 1955, p. 29.
140 *"Put the tray down":*   Russell and Chase, *Banquet*, p. 156.
140 *"Nerves like mine":*   Pete Martin, "I Call on Edie Adams and Ernie Kovacs," *Saturday Evening Post*, Dec. 28, 1957, p. 42.
140 *"By the time":*   George Abbott, *Mister Abbott* (New York: Random House, 1963), p. 234.
140 *"the best new musical":*   Brooks Atkinson, "Wonderful Town," *New York Times*, Mar. 8, 1953.
140 *"absolutely perfect":*   Brooks Atkinson, "Wonderful Town," *New York Times*, Feb. 26, 1953.
140 *"a trained singer":*   Brooks Atkinson, "Wonderful Town," *New York Times*, Mar. 8, 1953.
141 *"I remember her as":*   Hyman Goldberg, "Edie Is a Lady," *Cosmopolitan*, Dec. 1955, p. 29.

141   *"there seemed many":*   Pete Martin, "I Call on Edie Adams and Ernie Kovacs," *Saturday Evening Post*, Dec. 28, 1957, p. 43.

CHAPTER 12

144   *"about eight bucks":*   " 'Uncle Ernie' Kovacs," *Newsweek*, Jan. 12, 1953, p. 70.
144   *"one of television's":*   ibid.
144   *"Audiences couldn't see":*   Diana Rico and Ben Herndon, "Great Shows: Ernie Kovacs," *Emmy*, Summer 1981, p. 50.
144   *"When you have":*   Eddie Hatrak to Mary Lou Cassidy, interview, Jan. 1969.
145   *"Chalk up an 'E' ":*   "Ernie Kovacs Show," *Variety*, Jan. 7, 1953.
146   *"It is earnestly":*   "Ernie Kovacs," *Billboard*, April 4, 1953.
146   *"Ernie's show was done":*   Interview with John Hess, Nov. 6, 1988.
146   *"would sit in":*   Interview with Shirley Mellner, Feb. 23, 1987.
146   *"We were dropped off":*   Interview with Kippie Kovacs, Jan. 28, 1989.
147   *"I stood out there":*   Interview with Elisabeth Kovacs, Feb. 13, 1989.
147   *"I flew down":*   "Kovacs Daughters Vanish," *New York Daily Mirror*, Oct. 29, 1953.
147   *"Ernie would leave":*   Ann Beierfield, "Epitaph: Nothing in Moderation," *Trenton Sunday Times Advertiser*, Mar. 31, 1968.
147   *"He had this detective":*   Eddie Hatrak to Mary Lou Cassidy, interview, Jan. 1969.
147   *"To tell you":*   "Kovacs Daughters Vanish," *New York Daily Mirror*, Oct. 29, 1953.
147   *"I hope things happen":*   ibid.
148   *"leap for his life":*   ibid.
149   *"He would introduce me":*   Eddie Hatrak to Mary Lou Cassidy, interview, Jan. 1969.
150   *"funnier than Bugs":*   "One of the Funniest Things Under the Sun," NBC Television press release, June 11, 1956, p. 2.
152   *"It can safely":*   "Ernie Kovacs Show," *Variety*, April 14, 1954.
153   *"He had a great":*   Interview with Shirley Mellner, Feb. 23, 1987.
154   *"She was very special":*   Interview with Shirley Mellner, Nov. 4, 1986.
154   *"I thought you'd like":*   Showtime Cable, *Ernie Kovacs: Television's Original Genius*, prod. John Barbour, 1982 (hereinafter cited as *TV's Original Genius*).
155   *"The manner, nuance":*   Frederic Morton, "Ernie Kovacs: The Last Spontaneous Man," *Holiday*, Oct. 1958, pp. 88–89.
155   *"Nairobi Trio Specialist":*   Interview with Wally Stanard, Mar. 4, 1987.
155   *"I told Ernie":*   Edie Adams Kovacs and John M. Ross, "Ernie Kovacs— What a Husband!" *American Weekly*, July 20, 1958, p. 10.
155   *"Go ahead":*   ibid.
156   *"Life with Ernie":*   Sally Friedman, "Edie Adams: Never Settling for Less," *Windsor Heights* (N.J.) *Herald*, Dec. 24, 1982.

156   *"We'd get up":*   Ann Beierfield, "Epitaph: Nothing in Moderation," *Trenton Sunday Times Advertiser*, Mar. 31, 1968.

156   *"I look forward":*   Pete Martin, "I Call on Edie Adams and Ernie Kovacs," *Saturday Evening Post*, Dec. 28, 1957, p. 43.

158   *"a remarkable rapport":*   Sid Shalit, "Is Ernie Kovacs Crazy? Yes—Crazy Like a Fox," *New York Daily News*, Nov. 14, 1954.

CHAPTER 13

160   *"I said to Kippie":*   Interview with Elisabeth Kovacs, Feb. 13, 1989.

160   *"came running":*   Interview with Kippie Kovacs, Jan. 28, 1989.

161   *"that they hated him":*   Florabel Muir, "Who'll Get the Kovacs Children?," *New York Daily News*, Sept. 9, 1962.

161   *"a hardness and harshness":*   ibid.

161   *"squalor":*   Interview with Kippie Kovacs, Jan. 28, 1989.

161   *"You couldn't argue":*   Interview with Elisabeth Kovacs, Feb. 13, 1989.

162   *"I had finally convinced":*   Interview with Elisabeth Kovacs, Feb. 13, 1989.

162   *"a castle":*   Interview with Kippie Kovacs, Jan. 28, 1989.

162   *"She was a pretty":*   Interview with Elisabeth Kovacs, Feb. 13, 1989.

163   *"at first I was":*   David Brian Barker, *Every Moment's a Gift: Ernie Kovacs in Hollywood, 1957–1962* (master's thesis, University of Texas, Austin, 1982), p. 92 (hereinafter cited as *Every Moment*).

163   *"we were traumatized":*   Interview with Elisabeth Kovacs, Feb. 13, 1989.

163   *"The words and":*   Interview with Kippie Kovacs, Jan. 28, 1989.

163   *"I always worried":*   Interview with Elisabeth Kovacs, Mar. 14, 1989.

163   *"and I was very":*   Interview with Kippie Kovacs, Jan. 28, 1989.

164   *"Is there a nice":*   Jack O'Brian, "Flash: Singer Fired and Not by Godfrey," *New York Journal-American*, Mar. 10, 1955.

164   *"This is wild":*   Interview with Tom Loeb, June 23, 1988.

165   *"I had great hopes":*   Interview with Pat Weaver, April 29, 1987.

166   *"We saw every play":*   Interview with Kippie Kovacs, Jan. 28, 1989.

166   *"We would fly":*   Interview with Elisabeth Kovacs, Feb. 13, 1989.

167   *"an expert in sauces":*   "Hedda Hopper's Hollywood," *Chicago Tribune–New York News Syndicate*, Dec. 29, 1959.

167   *"He never took off":*   Interview with Elisabeth Kovacs, Feb. 13, 1989.

167   *"he used to get":*   Interview with Kippie Kovacs, Jan. 28, 1989.

168   *"I had the feeling":*   Hyman Goldberg, "Edie Is a Lady," *Cosmopolitan*, Dec. 1955, p. 32.

168   *"They're trying to grow":*   ibid.

168   *"if I did that":*   Interview with Elisabeth Kovacs, Feb. 13, 1989.

168   *"would do anything":*   Interview with Ken McCormick, May 13, 1987.

169   *"He had made":*   Interview with Elisabeth Kovacs, Mar. 14, 1989.

CHAPTER 14

171   *"but he didn't":*   Interview with Rex Lardner, July 6, 1988.

171   *"There was a cachet":*   Interview with Deke Heyward, Feb. 12, 1987.

172   *"He had deep roots":*   Interview with Rex Lardner, July 6, 1988.

172 *"Shirley was one"*: Interviews with Deke Heyward, Feb. 12 and April 10, 1987.

172 *"At ten thirty"*: Interview with Mike Marmer, Mar. 14, 1987.

173 *"Something different"*: Daniel Richman, "Look Out! Kovacs Is Coming Back," *Philadelphia Inquirer*, Dec. 9, 1955.

173 *"quite big"*: Interview with Mike Marmer, Mar. 14, 1987.

173 *"glorious—total chaos"*: Interview with Deke Heyward, Feb. 12, 1987.

174 *"Sometimes I would"*: Interview with Shirley Mellner, Feb. 23, 1987.

174 *"it was exciting"*: Interview with Mike Marmer, Mar. 14, 1987.

174 *"He would call me"*: Interview with Perry Cross, Dec. 8, 1988.

175 *"We'd come in"*: Interview with Deke Heyward, Feb. 12, 1987.

175 *"Ernie used to love"*: Interview with Shirley Mellner, Nov. 4, 1986.

175 *"Edie would disappear"*: Interview with Rex Lardner, July 6, 1988.

175 *"The only thing"*: Frederic Morton, "Ernie Kovacs: The Last Spontaneous Man," *Holiday*, Oct. 1958, p. 90.

175 *"nickel-dime games"*: Interview with Deke Heyward, Feb. 12, 1987.

175 *"He was a bad"*: Interview with Rex Lardner, July 6, 1988.

176 *"We were all young"*: Interview with Perry Cross, Dec. 8, 1988.

176 *"That . . . was the climate"*: Peter Kerr, "A Network of the Past Could Be a Model for the Future," *New York Times*, June 3, 1984.

177 *"Ernie was the master"*: Interview with Mike Marmer, Mar. 14, 1987.

177 *"You did everything"*: Interview with Deke Heyward, Feb. 12, 1987.

178 *"He took a forlorn"*: ibid.

179 *"He did things"*: Interview with Mike Marmer, April 22, 1981.

180 *"There was nothing"*: Interview with Mike Marmer, Mar. 14, 1987.

180 *"Ernie would come in"*: Interview with Deke Heyward, Feb. 12, 1987.

181 *"Strange materials affected"*: ibid.

182 *"The radio show ate"*: Interview with Rex Lardner, July 6, 1988.

182 *"The Kapustas, strangely"*: Interview with Mike Marmer, Mar. 14, 1987.

182 *"Sometimes we'd announce"*: Interview with Rex Lardner, July 6, 1988.

183 *"I was a fan"*: Interview with Harvey Kurtzman, Jan. 16, 1989.

183 *"at something like"*: Interview with William Gaines, Jan. 16, 1989.

CHAPTER 15

184 *"I've had so many"*: Earl Wilson, "Edie and Ernie," *New York Post*, April 8, 1956.

184 *"That was Ernie's big"*: Interview with Mike Marmer, Mar. 14, 1987.

185 *"While we're not"*: "One of the Funniest Things Under the Sun," NBC Television news release, June 11, 1956, p. 3.

185 *"the guests were treated"*: Interview with Perry Cross, Dec. 8, 1988.

186 *"loved big introductions"*: ibid.

188 *"had a tremendous"*: ibid.

188 *"I'm paying no"*: Interview with Ken McCormick, May 13, 1987.

188 *"was willing to spare"*: Interview with Rex Lardner, July 6, 1988.

189 *"We didn't pay"*: Interview with Perry Cross, Dec. 8, 1988.

189 *"The burden was very"*: Interview with Rex Lardner, July 6, 1988.

189   *"I loved that house"*:   Interview with Kippie Kovacs, Jan. 28, 1989.

190   *"Oh, she could weave"*:   Interview with Elisabeth Kovacs, Feb. 13, 1989.

190   *"was a genius"*:   Interview with Elisabeth Kovacs, Mar. 14, 1989.

190   *"I was embarrassed"*:   Interview with Kippie Kovacs, Jan. 28, 1989.

190   *"She got him"*:   Interview with Elisabeth Kovacs, Feb. 13, 1989.

190   *"I know my mother"*:   Robert H. Prall, "Who Said He's Mad?," *New York World-Telegram and Sun*, Mar. 9, 1955.

190   *"My grandmother wanted"*:   Interview with Kippie Kovacs, Jan. 28, 1989.

190   *"I made furs"*:   Interview with George Kudra, Nov. 6, 1988.

191   *"He used to be"*:   Interview with Rex Lardner, July 6, 1988.

191   *"She could be"*:   Interview with Elisabeth Kovacs, Feb. 13, 1989.

191   *"Ernie totally"*:   Interview with Deke Heyward, Feb. 12, 1987.

191   *"Ed Sullivan came"*:   Pete Martin, "I Call on Edie Adams and Ernie Kovacs," *Saturday Evening Post*, Dec. 28, 1957, p. 43.

192   *"dizzy mock commercials"*:   John Crosby, "Not Quite Unlimited," *New York Herald Tribune*, Jan. 7, 1953.

192   *"She had tremendous"*:   Interview with Rex Lardner, July 6, 1988.

192   *"there was this goofy"*:   Interview with Deke Heyward, Feb. 12, 1987.

192   *"I thought"*:   Pete Martin, "I Call on Edie Adams and Ernie Kovacs," *Saturday Evening Post*, Dec. 28, 1957, p. 43.

193   *"about twenty times"*:   Interview with Kippie Kovacs, Jan. 28, 1989.

194   *"It's become a matter"*:   Marie Torre, "NBC Perplexed by Allen Subs," *New York Herald Tribune*, Aug. 22, 1956.

194   *"Gee, if you click"*:   Philip Minoff, "That Krazy Kovacs," *Cue*, July 14, 1956.

194   *"The summer show"*:   Interview with Perry Cross, Dec. 8, 1988.

195   *"I believe that Ernie"*:   Interview with Deke Heyward, Feb. 12, 1987.

CHAPTER 16

196   *"Suddenly somebody came"*:   Interview with Steve Allen, Feb. 17, 1988.

196   *"They were going to"*:   Interview with Roger Gimbel, Jan. 19, 1989.

197   *"I'm not keen"*:   Marie Torre, "NBC Perplexed by Allen Subs," *New York Herald Tribune*, Aug. 22, 1956.

197   *"I know that Ernie"*:   Interview with Mike Marmer, Mar. 14, 1987.

198   *"Ernie did it all"*:   Interview with Roger Gimbel, Jan. 19, 1989.

198   *"In a way"*:   Marie Torre, "Ernie Kovacs Stars New Blonde 'Wife,' " *New York Herald Tribune*, Oct. 2, 1956.

198   *"intuitive feel"*:   "She Out-Talked 299 Rivals," *TV Guide*, Dec. 22, 1956.

198   *"It was an opportunity"*:   Interview with Roger Gimbel, Jan. 19, 1989.

199   *"His was the easiest"*:   ibid.

200   *"Ernie would be"*:   Robert Metz, *The Tonight Show* (Chicago: Playboy Press, 1980), pp. 98–99 (hereinafter cited as *Tonight*).

200   *"The drama department"*:   Interview with Roger Gimbel, Jan. 19, 1989.

201   *"a great audience house"*:   ibid.

201   *"He, too, is"*:   Interview with Deke Heyward, Feb. 12, 1987.

202   *"It was hard"*:   Interview with Roger Gimbel, Jan. 19, 1989.

203 *"Jacques Tati was one"*:   Interview with Mike Marmer, Mar. 14, 1987.

203 *"Hulot is a situational"*:   Yvonne Gerald, "Mon Oncle," *Films in Review*, Dec. 1958, p. 590.

203 *"He was trying"*:   Interview with Roger Gimbel, Jan. 19, 1989.

204 *"Look, it was"*:   Interview with Steve Allen, Feb. 17, 1988.

204 *"must have been"*:   Metz, *Tonight*, p. 101.

204 *"It seemed to me"*:   Interview with Roger Gimbel, Jan. 19, 1989.

206 *"If you have enough"*:   Interview with Shirley Mellner, Feb. 23, 1987.

206 *"Bob Sarnoff discussed"*:   *Philadelphia Evening Bulletin*, May 21, 1959.

206 *"being put in a spot"*:   Marie Torre, "Coming Up: Kovacs Without Words," *New York Herald Tribune*, Dec. 28, 1956.

206 *"We had talked"*:   Interview with Deke Heyward, Feb. 12, 1987.

206 *"Having once bought"*:   Jack O'Brian, "Lewis: No; Kovacs: Yes," *New York Journal-American*, Jan. 21, 1957.

208 *"these tiny, moving"*:   Harriet Van Horne, "Jerry Lewis Makes Bow as TV Single," *New York World-Telegram and Sun*, Jan. 21, 1957.

208 *"He always had kind"*:   Interview with Shirley Mellner, Feb. 23, 1987.

209 *"from the looks"*:   Jack O'Brian, "Lewis: No; Kovacs: Yes," *New York Journal-American*, Jan. 21, 1957.

209 *"Where Lewis relied"*:   *New York Daily News*, Jan. 21, 1957.

209 *"In technique"*:   Harriet Van Horne, "Jerry Lewis Makes Bow as TV Single," *New York World-Telegram and Sun*, Jan. 21, 1957.

209 *"reasoned nonsense"*:   John Crosby, "Pantomime Nightmare," *New York Herald Tribune*, Jan. 25, 1957.

209 *"If his rating"*:   "Utility Expert," *Time*, Jan. 28, 1957, p. 66.

210 *"His work did not"*:   Interview with Pat Weaver, April 29, 1987.

210 *"We never utilized"*:   Interview with Pat Weaver, Mar. 20, 1987.

CHAPTER 17

211 *"who was crazy about"*:   Interview with Ken McCormick, May 13, 1987.

212 *"I think the contract"*:   ibid.

213 *"The people who earn"*:   Ernie Kovacs, *Zoomar* (Garden City, N.Y.: Doubleday, 1957), pp. 344–347.

214 *"The principal fascination"*:   Martin Levin, "Close-Up Shot," *Saturday Review*, Nov. 30, 1957, p. 27.

214 *"To Edie"*:   Kovacs, *Zoomar*, p. v.

214 *"body held a scintillating"*:   ibid., p. 8.

214 *"Would you understand"*:   ibid., pp. 336–337.

214 *"was absolutely sure"*:   interview with Ken McCormick, May 13, 1987.

214 *"Edie always acted"*:   Bob Williams, "TV Comedy 'Spent,' Kovacs Believes," *Philadelphia Sunday Bulletin*, Sept. 20, 1959.

215 *"one of the things"*:   Interview with Ken McCormick, May 13, 1987.

215 *"appreciating a pretty"*:   Interview with Elisabeth Kovacs, Feb. 13, 1989.

215 *"He was enormously"*:   Interview with Deke Heyward, Feb. 12, 1987.

215 *"I think I've got"*:   Bob Williams, "TV Comedy 'Spent,' Kovacs Believes," *Philadelphia Sunday Bulletin*, Sept. 20, 1959.

215 *"I ad-libbed":*   Frederic Morton, "Ernie Kovacs: The Last Spontaneous Man," *Holiday*, Oct. 1958, p. 155.

216 *"I had my doubts":*   Interview with Rex Lardner, July 6, 1988.

216 *"I kept reading":*   Interview with Ken McCormick, May 13, 1987.

216 *"Now they call it":*   Frederic Morton, "Ernie Kovacs: The Last Spontaneous Man," *Holiday*, Oct. 1958, p. 91.

216 *"The one thing":*   *Cards and Cigars.*

216 *"My greatest pleasure":*   "Hedda Hopper's Hollywood," Chicago Tribune – New York News Syndicate, Aug. 27, 1961.

216 *"This was written":*   Interview with Rex Lardner, July 6, 1988.

216 *"he was very close":*   Interview with Perry Cross, Dec. 8, 1988.

217 *"Ernie was faced":*   Interview with Deke Heyward, Feb. 12, 1987.

217 *"I used to write":*   Richard F. Shepard, "Comedian on the Run: Time, Tide, and Kovacs Wait on No Man," *New York Times*, Aug. 5, 1956.

217 *"Ernie worked from":*   Interview with Roger Gimbel, Jan. 19, 1989.

217 *"it was hard to delineate":*   Interview with Perry Cross, Dec. 8, 1988.

218 *"about this deal":*   Interview with Ken McCormick, May 13, 1987.

218 *"By then, he was":*   Interview with Shirley Mellner, Feb. 23, 1987.

218 *"the undisputed social":*   Dominick Dunne, "Letter from L.A.: Teardown," *Vanity Fair*, April 1989, p. 70.

219 *"If you don't like":*   Barker, *Every Moment*, pp. 28–29.

219 *"with lots of drunken":*   James Bacon, "Zany Kovacs 'Lives It Up' in Zany Hollywood Way," *Philadelphia Sunday Bulletin*, Sept. 4, 1960.

220 *"Then I didn't nail":*   Walley, *Kovacs Phile*, p. 174.

220 *"Television was like":*   *Jack Lemmon Seminars at the Museum of Broadcasting, April 1985* (New York: Museum of Broadcasting, 1985), p. 5 (hereinafter cited as *Lemmon Seminars*).

220 *"Sherman Billingsley":*   ibid., p. 67.

221 *"He knows the camera":*   Joe Baltake, "Jack Lemmon," *Films in Review*, Jan. 1970, p. 5.

221 *"We engulfed Ernie":*   Barker, *Every Moment*, p. 31.

221 *"It was one of those":*   *TV's Original Genius.*

221 *"He's a member":*   Frederic Morton, "Ernie Kovacs: The Last Spontaneous Man," *Holiday*, Oct. 1958, p. 155.

222 *"For a long":*   *Lemmon Seminars*, p. 35.

222 *"gives you time":*   Pete Martin, "I Call on Edie Adams and Ernie Kovacs," *Saturday Evening Post*, Dec. 28, 1957, p. 39.

222 *"he loved . . . except":*   Interview with Elisabeth Kovacs, Feb. 13, 1989.

222 *"I was mesmerized":*   Interview with Kippie Kovacs, Jan. 28, 1989.

223 *"I change my suit":*   Harry Harris, "Ernie Kovacs Enjoys NOT Working, Too," *Philadelphia Inquirer*, Nov. 22, 1959.

223 *"This is like":*   Marie Torre, "Kovacs Will Shun the Frenzy," *New York Herald Tribune*, May 6, 1957.

223 *"noteworthy for":*   "Operation Mad Ball," *Variety*, Sept. 4, 1957.

223 *"It is Ernie Kovacs":*   Archie Winsten, " 'Operation Mad Ball' at Victoria," *New York Post*, Nov. 21, 1957.

224   "*Arthur Carter's*": Hollis Alpert, "Jocularities: Domestic and Imported," *Saturday Review*, Nov. 30, 1957.

224   "*I discovered*": Reg Ovington, "A Workhorse 'Retires' to His Green Pasture," *Pictorial TView*, Sept. 1, 1957.

224   "*When I first*": ibid.

224   *It used to be*": ibid.

225   "*four or five TV*": Joe Hyams, "Kovacs Will Quit TV, 'Live Longer,' " *New York Herald Tribune*, May 9, 1957.

225   "*Look, I'm not*": ibid.

225   "*I did not want*": Margaret McManus, "Kovacses Find Peace, Gold in Hollywood," *New York World-Telegram and Sun*, Mar. 4, 1961.

225   "*Ernie loved California*": Ann Beierfield, "Epitaph: Nothing in Moderation," *Trenton Sunday Times Advertiser*, Mar. 31, 1968.

226   "*overrated . . . there is*": Margaret McManus, "Kovacses Find Peace, Gold in Hollywood," *New York World-Telegram and Sun*, Mar. 4, 1961.

226   "*Before the curtain*": Hyman Goldberg, "Edie Is a Lady," *Cosmopolitan*, Dec. 1955, pp. 30–31.

227   "*warmed over some*": Jack O'Brian, " 'New' Ernie Not So Funny," *New York Journal-American*, July 22, 1957.

227   "*For one guest shot*": Harry Harris, "Fabulous Money Keeps Rolling in for Ernie Kovacs," *Philadelphia Inquirer*, Aug. 28, 1957.

228   "*It requires no*": ibid.

228   "*only if I'm*": Pete Martin, "I Call on Edie Adams and Ernie Kovacs," *Saturday Evening Post*, Dec. 28, 1957, p. 42.

228   "*On paper, I'm in*": Harry Harris, "Fabulous Money Keeps Rolling in for Ernie Kovacs," *Philadelphia Inquirer*, Aug. 28, 1957.

228   "*Don't worry about it*": Barker, *Every Moment*, p. 45.

228   "*He had just gotten*": Interview with Rex Lardner, July 6, 1988.

229   "*I don't believe*": Atra Baer, "There's No Ulcers for Ernie, the Relaxed Man," *New York Journal-American*, Sept. 5, 1957.

229   "*the name was part*": Interview with Martin Manulis, Oct. 23, 1987.

230   "*a wildly infantile*": Jack Gould, " 'Topaze' Assaulted," *New York Times*, Sept. 27, 1957.

230   "*Jack-of-all-trades*": Marie Torre, "Kovacs Plays 'Topaze,' " *New York Herald Tribune*, Sept. 27, 1957.

PART FIVE: **THE RAINBOW'S END (1957–1962)**

CHAPTER 18

233   "*mainly to keep*": Marie Torre, "Marilyn Monroe Fan," *New York Herald Tribune*, n.d.

233   "*We used to gamble*": Interview with Kippie Kovacs, Jan. 28, 1989.

233   "*the biggest of*": "Ernie Kovacs & Edie Adams," *Variety*, Nov. 27, 1957.

234   "*It was a furnished*": Interview with Kippie Kovacs, Jan. 28, 1989.

234   *"It was a horrible"*:   Interview with Elisabeth Kovacs, Feb. 13, 1989.

234   *"As I recall"*:   Interview with Julian Blaustein, Dec. 2, 1988.

234   *"an intuitive actor"*:   Barker, *Every Moment*, pp. 176–177.

235   *"himself, highly"*:   Bosley Crowther, "A Witch in Love," *New York Times*, Dec. 27, 1958.

235   *"John van Druten had"*:   Interview with Julian Blaustein, Dec. 2, 1988.

235   *"This is romance"*:   *Cosmopolitan*, Nov. 1960, p. 54.

236   *"a comedy standout"*:   "Bell, Book and Candle," *Variety*, Oct. 22, 1958.

236   *"there were bats"*:   Interview with Kippie Kovacs, Jan. 28, 1989.

236   *"We had to walk"*:   Barker, *Every Moment*, p. 32.

236   *"It was a terrible"*:   Marie Torre, "His One Business Is Show Business," *New York Herald Tribune*, Sept. 11, 1958.

236   *"I lost a lot"*:   *TV's Original Genius*.

237   *"I think it was"*:   Barker, *Every Moment*, p. 32.

237   *"So . . . I went out"*:   *TV's Original Genius*.

237   *"We watched the act"*:   Interview with Kippie Kovacs, Jan. 28, 1989.

237   *"It was so beautiful"*:   Interview with Elisabeth Kovacs, Feb. 13, 1989.

238   *"My sister instigated"*:   Interview with Kippie Kovacs, Jan. 28, 1989.

238   *"We would need"*:   Helen Dudar, "Nothing but the Best of Ernie Kovacs," *New York Post*, April 6, 1968.

238   *"I'm just one"*:   James Bacon, "Zany Kovacs 'Lives It Up' in Zany Hollywood Way," *Philadelphia Sunday Bulletin*, Sept. 4, 1960.

238   *"She was a schoolteacher"*:   Interview with Kippie Kovacs, Jan. 28, 1989.

238   *"I don't think"*:   Margaret McManus, "Kovacses Find Peace, Gold in Hollywood," *New York World-Telegram and Sun*, Mar. 4, 1961.

239   *"I lost thirty-five"*:   "Hedda Hopper's Hollywood," Chicago Tribune–New York News Syndicate, Dec. 29, 1959.

239   *"was really upsetting"*:   Interview with Kippie Kovacs, Jan. 28, 1989.

240   *"At three o'clock"*:   Michael Freedland, *Jack Lemmon* (New York: St. Martin's, 1985), p. 55.

241   *"skits of considerable"*:   "It Happened to Jane," *Variety*, April 22, 1959.

241   *"As long as somebody"*:   Barker, *Every Moment*, p. 44.

241   *"I never thought"*:   Marie Torre, "Drama Debut Tonight for Edie," *New York Herald Tribune*, Feb. 24, 1958.

242   *"My production"*:   Interview with Ken McCormick, May 13, 1987.

242   *"Every time I go"*:   Marie Torre, "Kovacs Not Nostalgic about TV Circus Role," *New York Herald Tribune*, Mar. 5, 1959.

242   *"Everything about Arthur"*:   Harriet Van Horne, "A Masquerade Touches Heart," *New York World-Telegram and Sun*, Feb. 3, 1959.

243   *"We don't read scripts"*:   Margaret McManus, "Kovacses Find Peace, Gold in Hollywood," *New York World-Telegram and Sun*, Mar. 4, 1961.

CHAPTER 19

244   *"very gilded"*:   Alec Guinness, *Blessings in Disguise* (New York: Warner Books, 1985), p. 203 (hereinafter cited as *Blessings*).

245   *"He was afraid":*   Interview with Elisabeth Kovacs, Feb. 13, 1989.

245   *"The city was full":*   Guinness, *Blessings,* p. 203.

245   *"My father was deeply":*   Interview with Elisabeth Kovacs, Feb. 13, 1989.

245   *"what looked like tumbrils":*   Guinness, *Blessings,* p. 203.

245   *"was every instant":*   Robert Emmett Ginna, "Our Man from New York Observes Carol Reed Directing 'Our Man in Havana,' " *Horizon,* Nov. 1959, p. 124.

245   *"The first day":*   Guinness, *Blessings,* pp. 204–205.

246   *"he loved Alec Guinness":*   Interview with Elisabeth Kovacs, Feb. 13, 1989.

246   *"better than innuendo":*   CBS, *The Lively Arts: Ernie Kovacs,* Oct. 31, 1961.

246   *"One evening, . . . I was":*   Guinness, *Blessings,* p. 205.

246   *"an ante-chamber":*   ibid., p. 203.

246   *"He was sitting":*   ibid., p. 205.

246   *"What he'd done":*   Interview with Jane Hess, Nov. 6, 1988.

246   "Miren a Ernie":   Halsey Raines, "Shooting 'Our Man in Havana' on the Spot," *New York Times,* April 26, 1959.

246   *"Especially crossing":*   Philip K. Scheuer, "Cubans Help 'Make' Film," *Los Angeles Times,* June 7, 1959.

247   *"That was the heavy-duty":*   Interview with Kippie Kovacs, Jan. 25, 1989.

247   *"showed himself":*   Robert Emmett Ginna, "Our Man from New York Observes Carol Reed Directing 'Our Man in Havana,' " *Horizon,* Nov. 1959, pp. 124–125.

248   *"We walked in":*   Barker, *Every Moment,* p. 111.

251   *"Poker players never":*   Joe Hyams, "Ernie Kovacs Discusses Poker," *New York Herald Tribune,* June 16, 1959.

252   *"Mia means 'my own' ":*   Interview with Kippie Kovacs, Jan. 25, 1989.

252   *"I felt I was":*   Interview with Kippie Kovacs, April 15, 1989.

252   *"She totally disengaged":*   Interview with Kippie Kovacs, Jan. 28, 1989.

252   *"a closet about":*   James Bacon, "Zany Kovacs 'Lives It Up' in Zany Hollywood Way," *Philadelphia Sunday Bulletin,* Sept. 4, 1960.

252   *"Every summer":*   Interviews with Kippie Kovacs, Jan. 28 and April 15, 1989.

CHAPTER 20

254   *"I hate panel shows":*   Harry Harris, "Ernie Kovacs Enjoys NOT Working, Too," *Philadelphia Inquirer,* Nov. 22, 1959.

255   *"There was a period":*   Interview with Mike Marmer, Mar. 14, 1987.

255   *"What we did":*   Interview with Rex Lardner, July 6, 1988.

255   *"the same stage":*   Interview with Robert Kemp, Feb. 13, 1987.

255   *"Peggy Connelly wanted":*   Interview with Jolene Brand Schlatter, Mar. 18, 1989.

255   *"He was a hard-liver":*   ibid.

257   *"Ernie had tremendous":*   Interview with Robert Kemp, Feb. 13, 1987.

258   *"Some of the things":*   Interview with Bobby Hughes, Mar. 4, 1987.

259   *"It seemed like":*   ibid.

260 *"These commercials"*: "Edie Adams: Biography," Cleary-Strauss-Irwin & Goodman press release, 1963, p. 6.

260 *"he wanted to smoke"*: Diana Rico and Ben Herndon, "Great Shows: Ernie Kovacs," *Emmy*, Summer 1981, p. 50.

260 *"With sponsors he was"*: Barker, *Every Moment*, pp. 144–145.

261 *"It was a struggle"*: ibid., p. 167.

262 *"once again that"*: A. H. Weiler, "Study of Infidelity," *New York Times*, June 30, 1960.

263 *"The four performers"*: Neil Rau, "Explosion for Scene Baffles Four Actors," *Los Angeles Examiner*, Dec. 27, 1959.

264 *"perhaps the most"*: Bosley Crowther, "Witless Situation," *New York Times*, April 9, 1960.

264 *"comic strength"*: "Wake Me When It's Over," *Variety*, Mar. 30, 1960.

264 *"Ernie Kovacs' sole"*: "Strangers When We Meet," *Variety*, May 25, 1960.

264 *"There was no"*: Walley, *Kovacs Phile*, pp. 151, 155.

264 *"I don't want"*: James Bacon, "Zany Kovacs 'Lives It Up' in Zany Hollywood Way," *Philadelphia Sunday Bulletin*, Sept. 4, 1960.

264 *"He'd say"*: Interview with Kippie Kovacs, Jan. 28, 1989.

264 *"I think what happened"*: Interview with Mike Marmer, Mar. 14, 1987.

265 *"I have wonderful"*: "Hedda Hopper's Hollywood," Chicago Tribune–New York News Syndicate, Dec. 29, 1959.

265 *"I knew he was"*: Interview with Ken McCormick, April 1987.

266 *"every time they"*: Bart Andrews, *Lucy and Ricky and Fred and Ethel: The Story of "I Love Lucy"* (New York: Popular Library, 1976), p. 214.

CHAPTER 21

267 *"It was in a little"*: Interview with Robert Kemp, Feb. 13, 1987.

267 *"He had some"*: Interview with Bobby Hughes, Mar. 4, 1987.

268 *"I finally got"*: Richard Schickel, "The Real Ernie Kovacs IS Standing Up," *Show*, Dec. 1961, p. 81.

268 *"It was kind of"*: Interview with Robert Kemp, Feb. 13, 1987.

268 *"He had everybody"*: Interview with Bobby Hughes, Mar. 4, 1987.

268 *"I'd wake up"*: Interview with Elisabeth Kovacs, Feb. 13, 1989.

268 *"Those poker games"*: Ann Beierfield, "Epitaph: Nothing in Moderation," *Trenton Sunday Times Advertiser*, Mar. 31, 1968.

269 *"The crux of"*: Interview with Richard J. Rosenthal, Mar. 2, 1989.

269 *"relieves all fears"*: Susan Berman, "My Husband Was a Compulsive Gambler," *Family Circle*, Feb. 1, 1979, p. 29.

269 *"suddenly we were"*: Barker, *Every Moment*, p. 93.

270 *"somewhat dissipated"*: Interview with Elisabeth Kovacs, Feb. 13, 1989.

270 *"It's hard to swallow"*: Interview with Kippie Kovacs, Jan. 28, 1989.

270 *"The members of"*: Marie Torre, "Ernie Kovacs Happier on Coast Than in N.Y.," *New York Herald Tribune*, Aug. 7, 1961.

270 *"There were millions"*: Interview with Kippie Kovacs, Jan. 28, 1989.

270 *"helped me to do"*: Interview with Elisabeth Kovacs, Feb. 13, 1989.

270 *"Ernie would call"*: Interview with Jolene Brand Schlatter, Mar. 18, 1989.

271 *"I've sometimes thought"*: Margaret McManus, "Kovacses Find Peace, Gold in Hollywood," *New York World-Telegram and Sun*, Mar. 4, 1961.

271 *"We'd come back"*: Barker, *Every Moment*, p. 94.

271 *"didn't hurt"*: Interview with Kippie Kovacs, Jan. 28, 1989.

271 *"I would still"*: Interview with Elisabeth Kovacs, Feb. 13, 1989.

271 *"I never had to worry"*: KQED, *Take Charge!*, prod. John Norton, Mar. 26, 1988.

272 *"He treated me"*: *TV's Original Genius*.

272 *"This is great"*: Thomas McDonald, "Scriptless in 'Nome,' California," *New York Times*, June 19, 1960.

273 *"I had about five"*: James Bacon, "Zany Kovacs 'Lives It Up' in Zany Hollywood Way," *Philadelphia Sunday Bulletin*, Sept. 4, 1960.

273 *"They made you"*: Interview with Kippie Kovacs, Jan. 18, 1989.

273 *"Wayne and Kovacs"*: "North to Alaska," *Variety*, Nov. 9, 1960.

275 *"too much onus"*: "Five Golden Hours," *Variety*, Mar. 8, 1961.

275 *"a wicked, happy"*: "Five Golden Hours," *Sunday Times* (London), Feb. 26, 1961.

276 *"Why?"* Barker, *Every Moment*, p. 186.

276 *"After you pay"*: Margaret McManus, "Kovacses Find Peace, Gold in Hollywood," *New York World-Telegram and Sun*, Mar. 4, 1961.

276 *"about 1960 Ernie"*: Interview with George Kudra, Nov. 6, 1988.

276 *"It has become"*: Marie Torre, "His One Business Is Show Business," *New York Herald Tribune*, Sept. 11, 1958.

276 *"Ernie had nine"*: Walley, *Kovacs Phile*, p. 184.

276 *"It was the first"*: ibid.

277 *"The IRS didn't hold"*: *TV's Original Genius*.

277 *"really, really bad"*: Barker, *Every Moment*, p. 188.

CHAPTER 22

278 *"There's a complete"*: Joe Hyams, "The Man Behind the Cigar," *New York Herald Tribune*, Mar. 1961.

278 *"Ernie and I"*: Interview with Norm Silvers, Mar. 3, 1987.

279 *"I asked them not"*: Joe Hyams, "The Man Behind the Cigar," *New York Herald Tribune*, Mar. 1961.

280 *"This wasn't just"*: Interview with Maury Orr Demots, April 22, 1987.

280 *"I've spent as many"*: "King Leer," *Newsweek*, Sept. 18, 1961, p. 64.

280 *"All my rehearsals"*: Murray Schumach, "Kovacs Explains Wordless Shows," *New York Times*, Dec. 21, 1961.

281 *"I bought a record"*: Interview with Bobby Hughes, Mar. 4, 1987.

281 *"A lot of them"*: Interview with Bob Haley, Mar. 10, 1987.

283 *"We'd come in"*: Interview with Robert Kemp, Feb. 13, 1987.

283 *"We'd never leave"*: Interview with Norm Silvers, Mar. 3, 1987.

284 *"ABC management would"*: Interview with Robert Kemp, Feb. 13, 1987.

284 *"because the star"*: Interview with Bob Haley, Mar. 10, 1987.

284 *"as long as they"*: Interview with Bobby Hughes, Mar. 4, 1987.

284 *"he seemed to have"*: Interview with Robert Kemp, Feb. 13, 1987.

285 *"Ernie always believed":*   Interview with Maury Orr Demots, April 22, 1987.
285 *"The attitude then":*   Interview with Robert Kemp, Feb. 13, 1987.
285 *"He would be":*   Interview with Wally Stanard, Mar. 4, 1987.
285 *"exciting parties":*   Interview with Robert Kemp, Feb. 13, 1987.
286 *"Bob, go around":*   Interview with Bob Haley, Mar. 10, 1987.
286 *"The shows were getting":*   Interview with Maury Orr Demots, April 22, 1987.
287 *"When you're shooting":*   Interview with Wally Stanard, Mar. 4, 1987.
287 *"He'd have little":*   Diana Rico and Ben Herndon, "Great Shows: Ernie Kovacs," *Emmy*, Summer 1981, p. 51.
287 *"he would immediately":*   Interview with Wally Stanard, Mar. 4, 1987.
287 *"We had no idea":*   Interview with Robert Kemp, Feb. 13, 1987.
288 *"There were a couple":*   Interview with Wally Stanard, Mar. 4, 1987.
288 *"It is eight":*   "Kovacs' Short Course in Kinetics," *Show Business Illustrated*, Oct. 17, 1961, p. 40.
288 *"back in the booth":*   ibid., p. 44.
288 *"which kept him":*   Interview with Maury Orr Demots, April 22, 1987.
289 *"in the smoking jacket":*   Interview with Bob Haley, Mar. 10, 1987.
289 *"He's sitting back":*   Interview with Wally Stanard, Mar. 4, 1987.
289 *"At the time":*   Interview with Bob Haley, Mar. 10, 1987.

CHAPTER 23

290 *"which turned out":*   Interview with Philip Barry, Jr., Dec. 6, 1988.
290 *"They told me":*   Interview with Irving Brecher, Dec. 10, 1988.
291 *"They built enormous":*   Interview with Philip Barry, Jr., Dec. 6, 1988.
292 *"I didn't think he":*   Interview with Irving Brecher, Dec. 10, 1988.
292 *"Edie used to drop":*   Interview with Philip Barry, Jr., Dec. 6, 1988.
292 *"that stunned me":*   Interview with Irving Brecher, Dec. 10, 1988.
293 *"I'd tell him about":*   Interview with Bob Haley, Mar. 10, 1987.
293 *"Ernie likes to live":*   Margaret McManus, "Kovacses Find Peace, Gold in Hollywood," *New York World-Telegram and Sun*, Mar. 4, 1961.
293 *"I sat and held":*   *TV's Original Genius.*
293 *"he was clearly":*   Interview with Ken McCormick, May 13, 1987, and letter to DR, June 24, 1987.
294 *"It was evident":*   Interview with Jolene Brand Schlatter, Mar. 18, 1989.
294 *"So Jack Lemmon":*   Interview with Elisabeth Kovacs, Feb. 13, 1989.
294 *"I had read all":*   Interview with Elisabeth Kovacs, April 22, 1989.
295 *"luxuriously and happily":*   Earl Wilson, "It Happened Last Night," *San Francisco Examiner*, Aug. 4, 1961.
295 *"knock off":*   Tom Mackin, "Kovacs in N.J. Writing Novel," *Newark Evening News*, Sept. 13, 1961.
295 *"They were usually":*   Interview with Ken McCormick, May 13, 1987.
295 *"This is the woman":*   Ernie Kovacs, *How to Talk at Gin* (Garden City, N.Y.: Doubleday, 1962), pp. 104–105.
295 *"He would do ink":*   Interview with Elisabeth Kovacs, Mar. 14, 1989.

296 *"Cleopatra to girl friend"*: Tom Mackin, "Kovacs in N.J. Writing Novel," *Newark Evening News*, Sept. 13, 1961.

296 *"They may well be"*: Dwight Whitney, "10⅝ Years Ahead of His Time," *TV Guide*, Sept. 2, 1961, p. 10.

297 *"After Alec read"*: "Hedda Hopper's Hollywood," Chicago Tribune–New York News Syndicate, Aug. 27, 1961.

297 *Guinness, however:* Alec Guinness, letters to DR, Sept. 11, 1987, and Feb. 15, 1989.

298 *"he tried to get"*: Interview with Bobby Hughes, Mar. 4, 1987.

298 *"all expenses paid"*: Interview with George Kudra, Nov. 6, 1988.

298 *"We had dinner"*: Interview with Helen Wilson, Dec. 10, 1988.

298 *"I dreamed I lost"*: Interview with Elisabeth Kovacs, Feb. 13, 1989.

299 *Right before New Year's:* Barker, *Every Moment*, p. 300.

299 *"I don't think he"*: Interview with John Hess, Nov. 6, 1988.

299 *"I took a look"*: *TV's Original Genius.*

300 *"He wanted to be"*: Interview with Jolene Brand Schlatter, Mar. 18, 1989.

300 *"he did not want"*: Interviews with Kippie Kovacs, Jan. 28 and Feb. 12, 1989.

300 *"He was furious"*: Interview with Elisabeth Kovacs, Feb. 13, 1989.

300 *"Ernie was in great"*: "Yves Montand Refused Ride with Kovacs," *Philadelphia Inquirer*, Jan. 14, 1962.

301 *"All it takes"*: ibid.

301 *"It's Mrs. Kovacs"*: Barker, *Every Moment*, pp. 319–320.

302 *"Are you all right?"*: Interviews with Kippie Kovacs, Jan. 28 and Feb. 12, 1989.

302 *"Your father's been"*: Interview with Elisabeth Kovacs, Feb. 13, 1989.

302 *"Everybody started coming"*: Interview with Kippie Kovacs, Jan. 28, 1989.

302 *"I walked around"*: Interview with Elisabeth Kovacs, Feb. 13, 1989.

302 *"came up to the house"*: Interviews with Kippie Kovacs, Jan. 28 and Feb. 12, 1989.

302 *According to Mary:* Mary Kovacs, "Amended Petition for Removal of Administratrix," Superior Court of State of California, WEP no. 451 691, Dec. 24, 1962, p. 6.

302 *"Edie was terrified"*: Barker, *Every Moment*, p. 321.

302 *"very religious"*: Interview with Kippie Kovacs, Jan. 28, 1989.

303 *"I knew something"*: Joyce Persico, "Brother Tom—Close, but No Cigar," *Trenton Evening Times*, Jan. 28, 1972.

303 *"Edie didn't want"*: Interview with Kippie Kovacs, Jan. 28, 1989.

303 *"couldn't bear it"*: Interview with Elisabeth Kovacs, Feb. 13, 1989.

EPILOGUE

"wrongful and unlawful": Bette Kovacs, "Creditor's Claim," Superior Court of State of California, WEP no. 451 691, July 23, 1962.

305 *"the judge wanted us"*: Interview with Kippie Kovacs, Feb. 12, 1989.

305 *"We don't belong"*: "Edie Adams Pleads for Two Stepdaughters," *Phila-delphia Evening Bulletin*, Sept. 12, 1962.

305 *"fit and proper"*: "Here and There: Edie Gets Custody," *Philadelphia Evening Bulletin*, Sept. 14, 1962.

305 *"I can never desert"*: Florabel Muir, "Who'll Get the Kovacs Children?," *New York Daily News*, Sept. 9, 1962.

306 *"was deeply in debt"*: "Kovacs Estate $2,100,000," *New York Times*, Jan. 26, 1962.

306 *"They didn't believe"*: Richard Warren Lewis, "A Year in the Life of Edie Adams," *Saturday Evening Post*, April 13, 1963, p. 25.

306 *"It's very tough"*: Cindy Adams, "Edie Adams Comes Back Fighting Hard," *Philadelphia Inquirer Magazine*, Dec. 9, 1962.

306 *"would have embarrassed"*: James Bacon, "Edie Adams Rejects Plans of Friends for Benefit," *Philadelphia Evening Bulletin*, Feb. 21, 1962.

307 *"wrongfully mismanaged"*: Mary Kovacs, "Amended Petition for Removal of Administratrix," Superior Court of State of California, WEP no. 451 691, Dec. 24, 1962, p. 3.

307 *"for the purpose"*: Mary Kovacs, "Declaration of Mary Kovacs in Opposition to Motion to Dismiss," Superior Court of State of California, WEP no. 451 691, Jan. 31, 1963, p. 2.

307 *"has never held any"*: ibid., p. 3.

307 *"attempted to poison"*: Mary Kovacs, "Declaration of Mary Kovacs," Superior Court of State of California, WEP no. 1828, Feb. 24, 1963, p. 3.

307 *"It will be constant"*: Richard Warren Lewis, "A Year in the Life of Edie Adams," *Saturday Evening Post*, April 13, 1963, p. 26.

307 *"impersonate and insult"*: Mary Kovacs, "Declaration of Mary Kovacs," Superior Court of State of California, WEP no. 1828, Feb. 24, 1963, p. 1.

308 *"for her own personal"*: Mary Kovacs, "Amended Petition for Removal of Administratrix," Superior Court of State of California, WEP no. 451 691, Dec. 24, 1962, pp. 5–6.

308 *"wrongfully asserted"*: ibid., p. 5.

308 *"for inadequate payment"*: ibid., p. 6.

308 *"in an irrational"*: Edith Adams Kovacs, "Declaration of Edith Adams Kovacs," Superior Court of State of California, WEP no. 1828, Feb. 19, 1963, p. 1.

308 *"despite my requests"*: ibid., p. 2.

309 *"virtually all the assets"*: Edith Adams Kovacs, "Objections to the Appointment of Mary Kovacs," Superior Court of State of California, WEP no. 1828, Jan. 16, 1963.

309 *"Edie didn't want"*: Richard Warren Lewis, "A Year in the Life of Edie Adams," *Saturday Evening Post*, April 13, 1963, p. 25.

311 *"Ernie's attempts to break"*: John Minkowsky, "An Intimate Vacuum: Ernie Kovacs in the Aura of Video Art," *Vision*, pp. 35–47.

Dates, show times, and credits are based on primary sources, such as scripts, production notes, and newspaper television listings of the time. Occasionally, a name or date is followed by * to indicate that it came from a secondary source (such as a book, catalog, or article published after Kovacs' death) and was unconfirmable through primary sources.

PHILADELPHIA (1950–1952)

DEADLINE FOR DINNER, daytime cooking, WPTZ (NBC local affiliate). March 20, 1950, to April 18, 1952. Monday, Tuesday, and/or Friday, various half-hour afternoon time slots. *Directors:* Joe Behar, Elmer Jaspan. *Cast:* Ernie Kovacs, Peter Boyle, Albert Mathis.

PICK YOUR IDEAL, daytime fashion quiz, WPTZ (NBC local affiliate). August 22, 1950, to May 31, 1951, and August 9, 1951, to April 16, 1952. Thursday, 1:30 to 1:45 P.M. (to August 16, 1951); Wednesday, 2:30 to 2:45 P.M. (from August 22, 1951). *Director:* Elmer Jaspan.* *Cast:* Ernie Kovacs, Nancy Ault, Norman Brooks.

3 TO GET READY, wake-up, WPTZ (NBC local affiliate). November 27, 1950, to March 28, 1952. Monday to Friday, 7:30 to 9:00 A.M. (to September 14, 1951), 7:00 to 9:00 A.M. (from September 17, 1951). *Directors:* B. Calvin Jones, Joe Behar. *Cast:* Ernie Kovacs, Edie Adams, Trigger Lund, Andy McKay, Norman Brooks. *Music:* Tony deSimone Trio.

TIME FOR ERNIE, daytime comedy, NBC. March 7* to 9* and May 14 to June 29, 1951. Monday to Friday, 3:15 to 3:30 P.M. *Director:* Joe Behar. *Cast:* Ernie Kovacs. *Music:* Tony deSimone Trio.

NOW YOU'RE COOKING, daytime cooking, WPTZ (NBC local affiliate). May 15 to June 12 and September 18 to October 16, 1951. Tuesday, 2:00 to 2:30 P.M. *Director:* Elmer Jaspan.* *Cast:* Ernie Kovacs.

ERNIE IN KOVACSLAND, prime-time comedy variety, NBC. July 2 to August 24, 1951. Monday to Friday, 7:00 to 7:30 P.M. *Director:* Benny Squires. *Writers:* Ernie Kovacs, Ollie Crawford, Hugh Prince.* *Cast:* Ernie Kovacs, Edie Adams, Joe Earley, Andy McKay. *Music:* Tony deSimone Trio.

KOVACS ON THE CORNER, daytime comedy variety, NBC. January 3 to March 28, 1952. Monday to Friday, 11:00 to 11:30 A.M. *Producer:* B. Calvin Jones. *Director:* Joe Behar. *Writers:* Ernie Kovacs, Marge Greene, Donald Mattern. *Cast:* Ernie Kovacs, Edie Adams, Peter Boyle, Joe Earley, Marge Greene, Ed McDonnell, "Little" Johnny Merkin. *Music:* Dave Appell Trio.

NEW YORK (1952–1957)

KOVACS UNLIMITED, daytime comedy variety, WCBS-TV (CBS local affiliate). April 21, 1952, to January 15, 1954. Monday to Friday, 12:45 to 1:30 P.M. (to December 26, 1952), 8:30 to 9:30 A.M. (December 29, 1952, to March 27, 1953), 8:00 to 9:00 A.M. (from March 30, 1953). *Producers:* Ernie Kovacs, Dan Gallagher. *Directors:* Ned Cramer, Chuck Hinds, Frank Moriarity. *Writer:* Ernie Kovacs. *Cast:* Ernie Kovacs, Edie Adams, Trigger Lund, Andy McKay, Sandy Stewart. *Music:* Eddie Hatrak, Bernie Leighton.

THE ERNIE KOVACS SHOW, prime-time comedy variety, CBS. December 30, 1952, to April 14, 1953. Tuesday, 8:00 to 9:00 P.M. *Producer:* Ernie Kovacs. *Director:* Ned Cramer. *Writer:* Ernie Kovacs. *Cast:* Ernie Kovacs, Edie Adams, Trigger Lund, Andy McKay. *Music:* Eddie Hatrak and orchestra, six-voice chorus.

TAKE A GUESS, prime-time quiz, CBS. June 11 to September 10, 1953. Thursday, 8:00 to 8:30 P.M. *Host:* John K. M. McCaffery. *Panelists:* John Crawford, Dorothy Hart, Ernie Kovacs, Margaret Lindsay, Audrey Meadows.

THE ERNIE KOVACS SHOW, late-night comedy, WABD (DuMont local affiliate). April 12, 1954, to April 7, 1955. Monday to Friday, 11:15 P.M. to 12:15 A.M. (to January 7, 1955); Tuesday and Thursday, 10:30 to 11:00 P.M. (January 11 to February 24, 1955); Tuesday and Thursday, 10:00 to 11:00 P.M. (from March 1, 1955, under title *The Ernie Kovacs Rehearsal**). *Producer:* Ernie Kovacs. *Directors:* Barry Shear, Frank Bunetta. *Writer:* Ernie Kovacs. *Cast:* Ernie Kovacs, Edie Adams, Peter Hanley, Henry Lascoe, Barbara Loden. *Music:* Eddie Hatrak Trio.

ONE MINUTE PLEASE, prime-time quiz, DuMont. July 6, 1954, to February 17, 1955. Tuesday, 8:30 to 9:00 P.M. (to October 1954); Tuesday, 9:00 to 9:30 P.M. (October 1954); Friday, 9:30 to 10:00 P.M. (November 1954 to January 1955); Thursday, 9:30 to 10:00 P.M. (from January 1955). *Hosts:* John K. M. McCaffery, Allyn Edwards. *Panelists:* Cleveland Amory, Marc Connelly, Hermione Gingold, Ernie Kovacs, Alice Pearce.

TIME WILL TELL, prime-time quiz, DuMont. August 20 to October 15, 1954. Friday, 10:30 to 11:00 P.M. *Host:* Ernie Kovacs.

THE ERNIE KOVACS SHOW, daytime comedy variety, NBC. December 12, 1955, to July 27, 1956. Monday to Friday, 10:30 to 11:00 A.M. *Producers:* Jacques Hein, Perry Cross. *Directors:* Jacques Hein, Barry Shear. *Writers:* Ernie Kovacs, Rex Lardner, Louis ("Deke") Heyward, Mike Marmer. *Cast:* Ernie Kovacs, Edie Adams, Matt Dennis, Barbara Loden, Dylan Todd, Bill Wendell. *Music:* Archie Koty and orchestra.

THE ERNIE KOVACS SHOW, prime-time comedy variety, NBC. July 2 to September 10, 1956. Monday, 8:00 to 9:00 P.M. *Producer:* Perry Cross. *Director:* Barry Shear. *Writers:* Ernie Kovacs, Rex Lardner, Louis ("Deke") Heyward, Mike Marmer. *Cast:* Ernie Kovacs, Edie Adams, Peter Hanley, Al Kelly, Henry Lascoe, Barbara Loden, Bill Wendell, Bob Hamilton Trio. *Music:* Harry Sosnik and orchestra.

TONIGHT, late-night comedy variety, NBC. October 1, 1956, to January 22, 1957. Monday and Tuesday, 11:30 P.M. to 1:00 A.M. (to October 22, 1956), 11:30 P.M. to 12:30 A.M. (from October 29, 1956). *Producers:* Ernie Kovacs, Roger Gimbel. *Director:* Barry Shear. *Writers:* Ernie Kovacs, Rex Lardner, Mike Marmer. *Cast:* Ernie Kovacs, Maureen Arthur, Peter Hanley, Barbara Loden, Bill Wendell. *Music:* LeRoy Holmes and orchestra.

SATURDAY COLOR CARNIVAL: THE ERNIE KOVACS SHOW ("NO DIALOGUE"), prime-time special, NBC. January 19, 1957. Saturday, 10:00 to 10:30 P.M. *Producer:* Ernie Kovacs. *Director:* Barry Shear. *Writer:* Ernie Kovacs. *Cast:* Ernie Kovacs, Maureen Arthur, Betty Colby, Peter Hanley, Mary Mayo. *Music:* Harry Sosnik and orchestra.

WHAT'S MY LINE, prime-time quiz, CBS. August 11 to November 3, 1957. Sunday, 10:30 to 11:00 P.M. *Host:* John Daly. *Panelists:* Bennett Cerf, Arlene Francis, Dorothy Kilgallen, Ernie Kovacs.

LOS ANGELES (1958–1962)

KOVACS ON MUSIC, prime-time special, NBC. May 22, 1959. Friday, 8:00 to 9:00 P.M. *Producer:* Ernie Kovacs. *Director:* Barry Shear. *Writer:* Ernie Kovacs. *Cast:* Ernie Kovacs, Edie Adams, James Darren, Al Kelly, Louis Jourdan. *Music:* André Previn and orchestra.

TAKE A GOOD LOOK, prime-time quiz, ABC. October 22, 1959, to July 21, 1960, and October 27, 1960, to March 16, 1961. Thursday, 10:30 to 11:00 P.M. *Producers:* Maury Cohen, Milt Hoffman. *Directors:* Barry Shear, Joe Behar. *Writer:* Ernie Kovacs. *Host:* Ernie Kovacs. *Panelists:* Edie Adams, Ben Alexander, Hans Conried, Carl Reiner, Cesar Romero. *Performers:* Ernie Kovacs, Jolene Brand, Peggy Connelly, Bobby Lauher.

SILENTS PLEASE, silent-film excerpts, ABC. March 23 to October 5, 1961. Thursday, 10:30 to 11:00 P.M. *Host:* Ernie Kovacs.

THE ERNIE KOVACS SHOW, monthly prime-time specials, ABC. May 18, 1961, to June 15, 1961, and September 21, 1961, to January 23, 1962. Thursday, 10:30 to 11:00 P.M. *Producer:* Ernie Kovacs. *Directors:* Ernie Kovacs, Joe Behar, Maury Orr. *Writer:* Ernie Kovacs. *Cast:* Ernie Kovacs, Jolene Brand, Maggi Brown, Bobby Lauher, Joe Mikolas.

APPENDIX 2: TELEVISION GUEST APPEARANCES

Dates, show titles, and other facts are based on primary sources, such as scripts, production notes, and newspaper television listings of the time. Brief descriptions of Kovacs' roles are included whenever possible. Occasionally, a listing is followed by * to indicate that it came from a secondary source (such as a book, catalog, or article published after Kovacs' death) and was unconfirmable through primary sources.

1 9 5 1

September 2. TALENT SEARCH, late-night talent, WNBT (NBC local affiliate). Panelist.*

September 20. QUICK ON THE DRAW, late-night quiz, WNBT (NBC local affiliate). Panelist.*

September 30. TALENT SEARCH, late-night talent, WNBT (NBC local affiliate). Guest judge.*

October 11. QUICK ON THE DRAW, late-night quiz, WNBT (NBC local affiliate). Panelist.*

Between 1952 and 1954, Kovacs did not make any confirmable TV guest appearances.

1 9 5 5

April 27. TONIGHT, late-night talk, NBC. Guest.*

June 24. PERSON TO PERSON, prime-time talk, CBS. Guest; Edward R. Murrow interviews Kovacs and his family at their Central Park West home.

August 25. TONIGHT, late-night talk, NBC. Guest; performs movie preview satire (as Rock Mississippi).

August 29 to September 13. TONIGHT, late-night talk, NBC. Guest host.

October 3 to 7. THE JACK PAAR SHOW, daytime comedy variety, CBS. Guest host.

December 9. TODAY, wake-up, NBC. Guest.*

—————. TONIGHT, late-night talk, NBC. Guest.*

1 9 5 6

January 15. THE NBC COMEDY HOUR, prime-time comedy variety, NBC. Guest; reads "Ode from a Germ's-Eye View" (as Percy Dovetonsils), does routine with Jonathan Winters.

July 1. THE STEVE ALLEN SHOW, prime-time comedy variety, NBC. Guest.*

September 21. IT COULD BE YOU, daytime audience participation, NBC. Guest.*

September 28. TODAY, wake-up, NBC. Guest; performs horticultural skit with Dave Garroway.*

November 22. THE THIRTIETH ANNUAL MACY'S THANKSGIVING DAY PARADE, daytime special, NBC. Guest.

December 22. SATURDAY COLOR CARNIVAL: HOLIDAY ON ICE, prime-time special, NBC. Guest.

1 9 5 7

February 15. TONIGHT! AMERICA AFTER DARK, late-night magazine, NBC. Guest.*

February 16. SATURDAY COLOR CARNIVAL: EMMY AWARDS NOMINATIONS, prime-time special, NBC. Guest.

February 23. THE PERRY COMO SHOW, prime-time musical variety, NBC. Guest; makes himself and Tony Bennett disappear above the waist.

March 16. SATURDAY COLOR CARNIVAL: THE NINTH ANNUAL EMMY AWARDS, prime-time special, NBC. Cowriter,* guest.

March 31. WIDE WIDE WORLD: SPRING JUBILEE, live documentary, NBC. Guest.*

May 20. TRUTH OR CONSEQUENCES, quiz, NBC. Guest.*

May 27. PRODUCERS' SHOWCASE: FESTIVAL OF MAGIC, prime-time special, NBC. Host; does sword-balancing act, performs running "magic" gags in which he shoots, saws, and otherwise tries to destroy some NBC vice-presidents.

July 21. THE ED SULLIVAN SHOW, prime-time variety, CBS. Guest host; performs skits, including "Welcome Transients" and the Nairobi Trio.

July 26. TONIGHT! AMERICA AFTER DARK, late-night magazine, NBC. Guest; Kovacs and Edie Adams are interviewed in their Central Park West home.*

August 20. THE TEX AND JINX SHOW, daytime talk, NBC. Guest.*

September 26. PLAYHOUSE 90: TOPAZE, prime-time drama, CBS. Stars as Topaze, an ethical French schoolteacher who becomes corrupted.

October 5. THE POLLY BERGEN SHOW, prime-time musical variety, NBC. Guest; performs "We're a Couple of Swells" with Bergen.

October 23. TODAY, wake-up, NBC. Guest; discusses his new novel, *Zoomar*, with Dave Garroway.

October 26. THE PERRY COMO SHOW, prime-time musical variety, NBC. Guest; spoofs commercials, sings "Baby, It's Cold Outside" with Edie Adams.

October 29. BRIDE AND GROOM, daytime wedding show, NBC. Guest.*

November 10. WIDE WIDE WORLD: THE FABULOUS INFANT, live documentary, NBC. Guest; performs silent comedy skit, recounts his television career.

November 24. THE DINAH SHORE CHEVY SHOW, prime-time musical variety, NBC. Guest; performs with Edie Adams as part of show about married couples.

December 20. TRUTH OR CONSEQUENCES, quiz, NBC. Guest.*

December 31. THE GEORGE GOBEL SHOW, prime-time comedy variety, NBC. Guest; joins forces with Gobel's TV wife Alice (Jeff Donnell) to spearhead a wild party in a New Year's Eve sketch.

1958

June 18. TODAY, wake-up, NBC. Guest; has his head shaved for role in upcoming movie *It Happened to Jane.**

July 27. THE ED SULLIVAN SHOW, prime-time variety, CBS. Guest; conducts symphony orchestra of Nairobi apes.

September 30. THE EDDIE FISHER SHOW, prime-time musical variety, NBC. Guest.

October 16. THE FORD SHOW, prime-time musical variety, NBC. Guest; salutes 1958 football season with host Tennessee Ernie Ford.

October 19. G.E. THEATER: THE WORLD'S GREATEST QUARTERBACK, prime-time drama, CBS. Stars as Sam Lund, a former football hero who returns broke to his hometown.

1959

January 25. THE JACK BENNY SHOW, prime-time comedy, CBS. Guest; shows off his mustache collection, joins Benny for skit set in jail of the future.

February 2. WESTINGHOUSE DESILU PLAYHOUSE: SYMBOL OF AUTHORITY, prime-time drama, CBS. Stars as Arthur Witten, a Walter Mitty-esque proofreader.

February 15. G.E. THEATER: I WAS A BLOODHOUND, prime-time comedy, CBS. Stars as Barney Colby, a private detective with an exceptional sense of smell.

February 17. THE EDDIE FISHER SHOW, prime-time musical variety, NBC. Guest.

March 9. HIGH SPOTS OF "THE GREATEST SHOW ON EARTH," prime-time special, ABC. Circus ringmaster.

March 27. SCHLITZ PLAYHOUSE: THE SALTED MINE, prime-time Western, CBS. Guest stars as Hack, a grizzled old miner, in pilot episode for proposed Western series *Shotgun.*

April 6. THE THIRTY-FIRST ANNUAL ACADEMY AWARDS, prime-time special, NBC. Guest.

October 6. FORD STARTIME: THE WONDERFUL WORLD OF ENTERTAINMENT, prime-time musical comedy, NBC. Guest; spoofs 1940s movies with Rosalind Russell, explains the history of television.

December 11. THE BOB HOPE SHOW, prime-time special, NBC. Guest.

1 9 6 0

April 1. WESTINGHOUSE DESILU PLAYHOUSE: THE LUCILLE BALL–DESI ARNAZ SHOW, prime-time situation comedy, CBS. Guest stars with Edie Adams as neighbors of Lucy and Ricky Ricardo in an episode titled "Lucy Meets the Moustache."

April 11. ALCOA/GOODYEAR THEATER: AUTHOR AT WORK, prime-time drama, NBC. Stars as Maximilian Krob, a mystery writer who is unveiled as a murderer.

1 9 6 1

March 8. THE U.S. STEEL HOUR: PRIVATE EYE, PRIVATE EYE, prime-time musical comedy, CBS. Cowriter, guest; performs in several sketches satirizing detectives, including "The Case of the Nairobi Safe Robbery," "The Private Eye Circa 1901" (as Percy Dovetonsils), and "The Cavendish Pilferage."

October 31. THE LIVELY ARTS, prime-time talk, CBS. A half-hour Canadian interview with Kovacs in his Beverly Hills backyard.

1 9 6 2

n.d. A PONY FOR CHRIS, prime-time Western, ABC. Stars as Doc, a con man of the old West, in an unaired pilot episode for proposed Western series *Medicine Man.*

APPENDIX 3:
FEATURE FILMS

OPERATION MAD BALL, 1957.   A Jed Harris production for Columbia. Screenplay by Arthur Carter, Jed Harris, and Blake Edwards, from a play by Carter. Directed by Richard Quine. Produced by Jed Harris.

Private Hogan	Jack Lemmon
Lieutenant Betty Bixby	Kathryn Grant
Captain Paul Lock	Ernie Kovacs
Colonel Rousch	Arthur O'Connell
Yancey Skeebo	Mickey Rooney
Corporal Bohun	Dick York

BELL, BOOK AND CANDLE, 1958.   A Phoenix production for Columbia. Screenplay by Daniel Taradash, from a play by John van Druten. Directed by Richard Quine. Produced by Julian Blaustein.

Sheperd Henderson	James Stewart
Gillian Holroyd	Kim Novak
Nicky Holroyd	Jack Lemmon
Sidney Redlitch	Ernie Kovacs
Mrs. De Pass	Hermione Gingold
Queenie	Elsa Lanchester
Merle Kittridge	Janice Rule

IT HAPPENED TO JANE, 1959.   An Arwin production for Columbia. Screenplay by Norman Katkov, from a story by Max Wilk and Norman Katkov. Produced and directed by Richard Quine.

Jane Osgood	Doris Day
George Denham	Jack Lemmon
Harry Foster Malone	Ernie Kovacs
Larry Hall	Steve Forrest
Billy Osgood	Teddy Rooney

OUR MAN IN HAVANA, 1960.   A Carol Reed production for Columbia release. Screenplay by Graham Greene, from a novel by Greene. Produced and directed by Carol Reed.

James Wormold	Alec Guinness
Dr. Hasselbacher	Burl Ives
Beatrice	Maureen O'Hara
Captain Segura	Ernie Kovacs
Hawthorne	Noel Coward
"C"	Ralph Richardson
Milly	Jo Morrow

WAKE ME WHEN IT'S OVER, 1960.   A Mervyn LeRoy production for 20th Century–Fox. Screenplay by Richard Breen, from a novel by Howard Singer. Produced and directed by Mervyn LeRoy.

Captain Charlie Stark	Ernie Kovacs
Lieutenant Nora McKay	Margo Moore
Doc Farrington	Jack Warden
Ume	Nobu McCarthy
Gus Brubaker	Dick Shawn
Sergeant Warren	Don Knotts

STRANGERS WHEN WE MEET, 1960.   A Bryna-Quine production for Columbia. Screenplay by Evan Hunter, from a novel by Hunter. Produced and directed by Richard Quine.

Larry Coe	Kirk Douglas
Maggie Gault	Kim Novak
Roger Altar	Ernie Kovacs
Eve Coe	Barbara Rush
Felix Anders	Walter Matthau

NORTH TO ALASKA, 1960.   A Henry Hathaway production for 20th Century–Fox. Screenplay by John Lee Mahin, Martin Rackin, and Claude Binyon, from a play by Laszlo Fodor. Produced and directed by Henry Hathaway.

Sam McCord	John Wayne
George Pratt	Stewart Granger
Frankie Canon	Ernie Kovacs
Billy Pratt	Fabian
Michelle	Capucine

PEPE, 1960.   A George Sidney production for Columbia. Screenplay by Dorothy Kingsley and Claude Binyon, screen story by Leonard Spigelgass and Sonya Levien, from a play by L. Bush-Fekete. Produced and directed by George Sidney.

Pepe	Cantinflas
Ted Holt	Dan Dailey
Suzie Murphy	Shirley Jones

Guest stars: Joey Bishop, Michael Callan, Maurice Chevalier, Richard Conte, Bing Crosby, Bobby Darin, Sammy Davis, Jr., Jimmy Durante, Zsa Zsa Gabor, Judy Garland (voice), Greer Garson, Hedda Hopper, Ernie Kovacs, Peter Lawford, Janet Leigh, Jack Lemmon, Jay North, Kim Novak, André Previn, Donna Reed, Debbie Reynolds, Edward G. Robinson, Cesar Romero, Frank Sinatra

FIVE GOLDEN HOURS, 1961.   A Mario Zampi production for Fabio Jenner and Columbia. Screenplay by Hans Wilhelm. Produced and directed by Mario Zampi.

Aldo Bondi	Ernie Kovacs
Baronessa Sandra	Cyd Charisse
Mr. Bing	George Sanders
Martha	Kay Hammond
Raphael	Dennis Price

SAIL A CROOKED SHIP, 1962.   A Philip Barry production for Columbia. Screenplay by Ruth Brooks Flippen and Bruce Geller, from a novel by Nathaniel Benchley. Directed by Irving Brecher. Produced by Philip Barry, Jr.

Gilbert Barrows	Robert Wagner
Elinor Harrison	Dolores Hart
Virginia	Carolyn Jones
Rodney	Frankie Avalon
The Captain	Ernie Kovacs
George Wilson	Frank Gorshin